HOW AUTOCRATS ARE HELD ACCOUNTABLE

Chronicling and analyzing resistance to the threat that autocracy poses to American liberal democracy, this book provides the definitive account of the roles that courts and elections played in holding Trump accountable for his actions.

This book describes the many lawsuits brought against Trump and his supporters for their autocratic actions. Trump was found liable in two civil lawsuits: for nearly $100 million for sexually abusing and defaming E. Jean Carroll and for nearly $500 million for fraudulently valuing his real estate properties. Trump supporters and associates suffered even greater liabilities for defamation. And many of his lawyers were disciplined by professional associations. New York successfully prosecuted Trump for falsifying business records in connection with hush money payments to Stormy Daniels. Georgia obtained guilty pleas from four Trump associates implicated in efforts to change that state's electoral votes, although the case against Trump was derailed by prosecutorial misconduct. Special Counsel Jack Smith initiated two prosecutions against Trump: for concealing classified papers and for seeking to overturn the 2020 election. But the Supreme Court created a novel doctrine of presidential immunity; and those cases were dismissed before Trump's second inauguration. The book also analyzes the 2024 election, which Trump won with a bare 1.5 percent majority. It exposes his intensifying vilification of immigrants and transgender people and the numerous falsehoods he and his supporters disseminated. The book concludes by evaluating all the varied forms of resistance to autocracy described in the five volumes of the *Defending American Democracy* mini-series.

This definitive account and analysis of Trumpism and the resistance to it will appeal to scholars, students, and others with interests in politics, populism, and the rule of law and, more specifically, to those concerned with resisting the threat that autocracy poses to liberal democracy.

Richard L. Abel is Michael J. Connell Distinguished Professor of Law Emeritus and Distinguished Research Professor, UCLA, USA.

Defending American Democracy

Other books included in the series:

How Autocrats Seek Power
How Autocrats Abuse Power
How Autocrats Attack Expertise
How Autocrats Subvert Elections
How Autocrats Are Held Accountable

A GlassHouse book

HOW AUTOCRATS ARE HELD ACCOUNTABLE

Resistance to Trump and Trumpism

Richard L. Abel

Routledge
Taylor & Francis Group
a GlassHouse Book

First published 2025
by Routledge
4 Park Square, Milton Park, Abingdon, Oxon OX14 4RN

and by Routledge
605 Third Avenue, New York, NY 10158

Routledge is an imprint of the Taylor & Francis Group, an informa business

A GlassHouse book

British Library Cataloguing-in-Publication Data
A catalogue record for this book is available from the British Library

Library of Congress Cataloging-in-Publication Data
Names: Abel, Richard L. author
Title: How autocrats are held accountable : resistance to Trump and Trumpism / Richard L. Abel.
Description: Abingdon, Oxon [UK] ; New York, NY : Routledge, 2025. | Series: Defending American democracy | Includes bibliographical references and index.
Identifiers: LCCN 2025007382 (print) | LCCN 2025007383 (ebook) | ISBN 9781032629179 hardback | ISBN 9781032629162 paperback | ISBN 9781032629186 ebook
Subjects: LCSH: Government liability—United States | Government, Resistance to—United States | Torts—United States | Despotism—United States | Trump, Donald, 1946–
Classification: LCC KF1250 .A71 2025 (print) | LCC KF1250 (ebook) | DDC 342.7308/8—dc23/eng/20250305
LC record available at https://lccn.loc.gov/2025007382
LC ebook record available at https://lccn.loc.gov/2025007383

ISBN: 978-1-032-62917-9 (hbk)
ISBN: 978-1-03262916-2 (pbk)
ISBN: 978-1-032-62918-6 (ebk)

DOI: 10.4324/9781032629186

Typeset in Sabon
by Apex CoVantage, LLC

CONTENTS

FIGURE 0.1 Fulton County Sheriff's Office Photo of Donald J. Trump when booked for 13 felonies on August 24, 2023

Source: Reproduced with permission from the Fulton County Sheriff's Office

PREFACE

This is the fifth and final book in my mini-series "Defending American Democracy." All share the unifying theme embodied by the common subtitle "Resistance to Trump and Trumpism," because I firmly believe Trump represents the greatest domestic threat to American liberal democracy since the Civil War. The first three books dealt with the ways in which Trump sought to gain power in 2016 and retain it in 2020 by undermining the ultimate foundation of democracy—elections (*How Autocrats Seek Power*, Abel 2024b), the multiple illegalities in his campaign against immigrants and his politicization of criminal justice to protect cronies convicted in connection with Russia's efforts to influence the 2016 election (*How Autocrats Abuse Power*, Abel 2024a), and his disastrous response to the COVID-19 pandemic (*How Autocrats Attack Expertise*, Abel 2024c). The fourth book (*How Autocrats Subvert Elections,* Abel 2025) examined efforts since the January 6, 2021, insurrection to redress the actions of Trump and his collaborators: impeachment, Congressional investigation, the responses of civil society, prosecutions of the January 6 rioters, and resistance to attempts to overturn the 2020 election and skew the 2024 election. The present volume, *How Autocrats Are Held Accountable*, analyzes state and federal civil and criminal cases against Trump and his supporters and that most basic check on autocracy—the campaign for the 2024 election. Trump's defiance of the rule of law, the judiciary, and democratic elections is epitomized by his scowl in the photograph taken when he was booked on 13 felony charges by the Fulton County Sheriff's Office.

I have benefited from numerous opportunities to present material in this book to colleagues studying autocratic legalism in other countries; students and faculty at many law schools; and radio, television, and internet audiences

I reached through the invaluable assistance of JRB Communications. My wife Emily, always my best audience, sympathetically listened to nightly narratives of Trumpian autocracy through nearly 3,000 dinners over eight years.

Contemporary history is not breaking news. I write this last sentence shortly after Trump's first day in office, hoping my books will encourage others to keep documenting the ways in which his second administration violates the basic tenets of liberal democracy and evaluating the forms of resistance this provokes.

ACRONYMS

ABA	American Bar Association
ABC	American Broadcasting Company
ACLU	American Civil Liberties Union
AFL-CIO	American Federation of Labor-Congress of Industrial Organizations
AI	artificial intelligence
AP	Associated Press
ATF	DoJ Bureau of Alcohol, Tobacco, Firearms and Explosives
AUSA	Assistant United States Attorney
BLM	Black Lives Matter
CBP	Customs and Border Patrol
CBS	Columbia Broadcasting System
CDCP	Centers for Disease Control and Prevention
CEO	chief executive officer
CFO	chief financial officer
CIA	Central Intelligence Agency
CIPA	Classified Information Procedures Act
CNBC	NBC's Television News Channel
CNN	Cable News Network
COO	chief operating officer
CPA	certified public accountant
CPAC	Conservative Political Action Committee
CREW	Citizens for Responsibility and Ethics in Washington
DA	district attorney
DC	District of Columbia
DDC	US District Court for the District of Columbia

DEI	diversity, equity, and inclusion
DHHS	Department of Health and Human Services
DHS	Department of Homeland Security
DNC	Democratic National Committee
DNI	Director of National Intelligence
DoD	Department of Defense
DoJ	Department of Justice
DoS	Department of State
EO	executive order
FARA	Foreign Agents Registration Act
FBI	Federal Bureau of Investigation
FCC	Federal Communications Commission
FDA	Food and Drug Administration
FEC	Federal Election Commission
G	Guardian
GOP	Grand Old Party (Republican Party)
GWB	George W. Bush
HJC	House Judiciary Committee
IBEW	International Brotherhood of Electrical Workers
ICE	Immigration and Customs Enforcement
ID	identification
JCS	Joint Chiefs of Staff
LDAD	Lawyers Defending American Democracy
LGBTQ+	Lesbian, Gay, Bisexual, Transgender, Queer
LULAC	League of United Latin American Citizens
MAGA	Make America Great Again
MSNBC	NBC Universal Cable News Channel
NARA	National Archives and Records Administration
NATO	North Atlantic Treaty Organization
NBC	National Broadcasting Company
NDA	nondisclosure agreement
NDNY	US District Court for the Northern District of New York
NFT	non-fungible token
NGO	nongovernmental organization
NIAID	National Institute of Allergy and Infectious Diseases
NIH	National Institutes of Health
NLJ	National Law Journal
NPR	National Public Radio
NYT	New York Times
OAN	One America News
OANN	One America News Network
ODC	Office of Disciplinary Counsel (District of Columbia)
OLC	DoJ Office of Legal Counsel

ORR	DHHS Office of Refugee Resettlement
PAC	political action committee
PBS	Public Broadcasting Service
PRRI	Public Religion Research Institute
RICO	Racketeer Influenced and Corrupt Organizations Act
RINO	Republicans in Name Only
RNC	Republican National Committee; Republican National Convention
SCIF	sensitive compartmented information facility
SEIU	Service Employees International Union
SDNY	US District Court for the Southern District of New York
SJC	Senate Judiciary Committee
SLAPP	strategic lawsuit against public participation
TO	Trump Organization
TPS	Temporary Protected Status
UAW	United Auto Workers
UFW	United Farm Workers
USPS	United States Postal Service
WP	Washington Post
WSJ	Wall Street Journal
X	Elon Musk's social media outlet; formerly Twitter

DRAMATIS PERSONAE

Greg Abbott: Republican Texas Governor
Pete Aguilar: Democratic California Representative
American Thinker: right-wing online daily magazine
Ashli Babbitt: January 6 rioter killed by police while she was trying to break window in Capitol
Bret Baier: Fox News host
Stephen Bannon: Trump adviser and right-wing social media commentator
William Barr: Trump Attorney General
Maria Bartiromo: Fox News host
Eli Bartov: NYU Stern Business School accounting professor
Sheena Bellows: Democratic Maine Secretary of State
Hunter Biden: Joe's son
Joe Biden: Democratic President
Andy Biggs: Republican Arizona Representative
Todd Blanche: Trump lawyer
Richard Blumenthal: Democratic Connecticut Senator
Christina Bobb: Trump lawyer and OAN host
Lauren Boebert: Republican Colorado Representative
Terrence Bradley: friend and associate of Nathan Wade
Alvin Bragg: Manhattan DA
Jay Bratt: Trump lawyer
Breitbart News Network: right-wing media organization
Taylor Budowich: Trump spokesperson
Patrick Byrne: Overstock founder and Trump supporter and election denier
Tucker Carlson: Fox News commentator

E. Jean Carroll: successfully sued Trump for defamation and emotional distress
Jimmy Carter: Democratic President
Bill Cassidy: Republican Louisiana Senator
Dick Cheney: George W. Bush vice president
Liz Cheney: Republican Wyoming Representative and chair of House Republican Conference
Kenneth Chesebro: lawyer advising Trump on 2020 election
Steven Cheung: Trump campaign spokesperson
Chris Christie: former Republican NJ governor, sometime presidential aspirant
Pat Cipollone: Trump White House Counsel
Jeffrey B. Clark: Trump Assistant Attorney General for the Environment and Natural Resources Division and for the Civil Division
Stephanie Clifford: witness in "hush money" prosecution (acted in pornographic films under the name Stormy Daniels)
Andrew Clyde: Republican Georgia Representative
Michael Cohen: Trump personal lawyer
Susan Collins: Republican Maine Senator
James Comer: Republican Kentucky Representative and House Oversight and Accountability Committee chair
Eric Coomer: Dominion Voting Systems director of product strategy and security
Evan Corcoran: Trump lawyer
Jake Corman: Republican Pennsylvania state Senate President Pro Tem
John Cornyn: Republican Texas Senator
Ted Cruz: Republican Texas Senator
Dinesh D'Souza: conservative media figure
Stormy Daniels: film name of Stephanie Clifford, witness in "hush money" prosecution
Carlos De Oliveira: Mar-a-Lago property manager
Ron DeSantis: Republican Florida Governor and Trump rival for presidential nomination
Viet Dinh: Fox Corp. chief legal and policy officer
Lou Dobbs: Fox News host
Dominion Voting Systems: manufacturer of machines that tabulated votes in the 2020 election
Leslie Dubeck: Manhattan DA's general counsel
Rodrigo Duterte: Philippine President 2016–22
John Eastman: Trump lawyer
John Eisenberg: Trump lawyer
Jenna Ellis: Trump personal lawyer

Douglas Emhoff: husband of Kamala Harris
Tom Emmer: Republican House majority whip
Arthur F. Engoron: NY Supreme Court Justice who heard civil fraud cases
Epoch Times: right-wing newspaper associated with Falun Gong
Boris Epshteyn: Trump lawyer
Mark Esper: Trump Defense Secretary
Michael Fanone: Capitol Police officer severely injured on Jan. 6
Anthony Fauci: director National Institute of Allergy and Infectious Diseases and Trump's chief medical adviser
Mark Finchem: Republican Arizona state representative and election denier
Michael Flynn: Trump National Security Adviser and right-wing commentator
Ruby Freeman: Fulton County (Georgia) election worker
Matt Gaetz: Republican Florida Representative
Merrick Garland: Biden Attorney General
Alan Garten: TO general counsel
Gateway Pundit: far-right fake news site
Rudy Giuliani: Trump lawyer
Louie Gohmert: Republican Texas Representative
Paul Gosar: Republican Arizona Representative
Lindsey Graham: Republican South Carolina Senator
Charles "Chuck" Grassley: Republican Iowa Senator and senior SJC member
Mark Green: House Homeland Security Committee chair
Marjorie Taylor Greene: Republican Georgia Representative
Allison Greenfield: Justice Engoron's clerk
Kimberly Guilfoyle: Donald Trump Jr. fiancée
Alina Habba: Trump lawyer
Avril Haines: Director of National Intelligence
Nikki Haley: Republican presidential candidate
Misty Hampton: Coffee County (Georgia) elections supervisor
Sean Hannity: Fox News host
Roberta Kaplan: E. Jean Carroll's lawyer
Kamala Harris: Vice President and Democratic presidential candidate
Josh Hawley: Republican Missouri Senator
Robert Hur: special counsel investigating Biden's handling of classified papers
Asa Hutchinson: Republican Arkansas Governor
Cassidy Hutchinson: assistant to Trump chief of staff Meadows
Laura Ingraham: Fox News commentator
Ronny Jackson: Republican Texas Representative
Letitia James: New York Attorney General
Hakeem Jeffries: Democratic New York Representative and House Speaker
Mike Johnson: Republican Louisiana Representative and House Speaker
Alex Jones: right-wing conspiracy theorist
Jim Jordan: Republican Ohio Representative and HJC chair

Lewis Kaplan: SDNY Judge who heard E. Jean Carroll cases
John F. Kelly: Trump White House chief of staff
Brian Kemp: Republican Georgia Governor
Robert J. Kennedy Jr.: anti-vax activist and briefly third-party presidential candidate in 2024
Bernard Kerik: Giuliani aide
Brian Kilmeade: Fox News host
Adam Kinzinger: Republican Illinois Representative
Charlie Kirk: Turning Point USA founder
Christopher Kise: Trump lawyer
Emily Kohrs: Forewoman of Georgia special purpose grand jury on election interference
Chris LaCivita: Trump 2024 campaign strategist
Kari Lake: Republican Arizona election denier and losing gubernatorial candidate
Stephanie Lambert: lawyer for Powell and Byrne
Cathy Latham: Coffee County (Georgia) GOP chair, fake elector, and defendant in Georgia election prosecution
John Lauro: Trump lawyer
Mike Lindell: MyPillow founder and Trump supporter
Kelly Loeffler: unsuccessful Republican candidate for Senate from Georgia in 1.5.21 runoff
Anna Paulina Luna: Republican Florida Representative
J. Michael Luttig: former Fourth Circuit judge
Joseph Manchin: West Virginia Senator (Democrat who declared as Independent in 2024)
Thomas Massie: Republican Kentucky Representative
Alejandro Mayorkas: Biden Homeland Security Secretary
John McCain: Republican Arizona Senator and presidential candidate
Kevin McCarthy: Republican California Representative, sometime House Speaker
Mitch McConnell: Kentucky Republican Senator, sometime Majority Leader
Jeffrey McConney: TO controller
Ronna Romney McDaniel: RNC Chair
Johnny McEntee: Trump White House personnel office director
Mike Meadows: Trump chief of staff
Ashleigh Merchant: lawyer for Michael Roman
Jason Miller: senior Trump campaign adviser
Mark Milley: JCS Chair
Cleta Mitchell: Trump lawyer and Election Integrity Network leader
Wandrea "Shaye" Moss: Fulton County (Georgia) election worker
Robert Mueller: special counsel investigating Russian influence in 2016 election
Mick Mulvaney: White House chief of staff

Lachlan Murdoch: son of Rupert and Fox News CEO
Rupert Murdoch: Fox Corporation CEO
Jerrold Nadler: Democratic New York Representative
Waltine "Walt" Nauta: Trump White House valet and then body man
Alexei Navalny: opposition leader who died in prison in Russia after government assassination attempt
Peter Navarro: White House Assistant to Trump
Susan R. Necheles: Trump lawyer
Newsmax: right-wing online media
Alexandria Ocasio-Cortez: Democratic New York Representative
Joseph Oltmann: right-wing podcaster
Stefan Passantino: White House Counsel's Office and Cassidy Hutchinson lawyer.
Kashyap "Kash" Patel: Acting chief of staff to Acting Defense Secretary Christopher Miller
Kenneth Paxton: Republican Texas AG
Nancy Pelosi: California Democratic Representative and House Speaker
Paul Pelosi: Nancy's husband
Michael Pence: Trump Vice President
Scott Perry: Republican Pennsylvania Representative
Patrick Philbin: Deputy White House counsel, later Trump lawyer
Jeanine Pirro: Fox News host
Mark Pomerantz: Manhattan DA's Office lawyer
Michael Pompeo: Republican Secretary of State
Jack Posobiec: alt-right conspiracy theorist
Sidney Powell: lawyer and conservative activist
Brad Raffensperger: Republican Georgia Secretary of State
Vivek Ramaswamy: Republican presidential candidate
Jamie Raskin: Democratic Maryland Representative
Kevin Roberts: Heritage Foundation president
Michael A. Roman: Trump campaign 2020 director of election day operations
Mitt Romney: Republican Utah Senator
Mike Rounds: Republican South Dakota Senator
Chip Roy: Republican Texas Representative
Marco Rubio: Republican Florida Senator
Steven Sadow: Trump lawyer in Georgia case
Pete Sandalakis: Prosecuting Attorneys Council of Georgia head
Ben Sasse: Republican Nebraska Senator
Stephen Scalise: Republican Louisiana Representative
Dan Scavino: Trump White House deputy chief of staff
Adam Schiff: Democratic California Representative and House Intelligence Committee chair
Chuck Schumer: Democratic New York Senator, sometime Majority Leader

Rick Scott: Republican South Carolina Senator
Suzanne Scott: Fox News CEO
Raj Shah: Fox News vice-president
Marc Short: Pence chief of staff
Smartmatic: Manufacturer of software used in tabulating votes in the 2020 election
Alexander Smirnov: FBI informant charged with lying to the FBI
Jack Smith: Special Counsel for the classified papers and 2020 election cases
Jason Smith: Republican House Ways and Means Committee chair
George Soros: philanthropist
Bryan Steil: Republican Wisconsin Representative and House Administration Committee chair
Elise Stefanik: Republican New York Representative and #3 in House
Gary Stern: NARA chief counsel
Roger Stone: adviser to Trump's 2016 campaign, convicted in Mueller investigation
Joe Tacopina: Trump lawyer
Yuscil Taveras: Mar-a-Lago IT manager
John Thune: Republican South Dakota Senator and minority whip
Thom Tillis: Republican North Carolina Senator
Rashida Tlaib: Democratic Michigan Representative
Laurence Tribe: Harvard law professor
James Troupis: Wisconsin lawyer involved in election denial
Donald Trump Jr.: Trump's older adult son
Eric Trump: Trump's younger adult son
Ivanka Trump: Trump's daughter
Tommy Tuberville: Republican Alabama Senator
Cyrus Vance: Manhattan DA
JD Vance: Republican Ohio senator and 2024 Trump running mate
Stephen Vladeck: University of Texas law professor
Russell T. Vought: Center for Renewing America president
Nathan Wade: prosecutor in Georgia case
Phil Waldron: election conspiracy theorist
Herschel Walker: unsuccessful Trump-backed candidate for Georgia Senator
Scott Walker: Republican Wisconsin Governor
Debra Steidel Wall: NARA Acting Archivist
Tim Walz: Minnesota Governor and Harris running mate
Kelli Ward: Arizona GOP state chair
Frances Watson: Georgia's top elections investigator
Jesse Watters: Fox News host
David Weiss: special counsel prosecuting Hunter Biden
Allen Weisselberg: TO CFO
Gretchen Whitmer: Democratic Michigan Governor

Susie Wiles: Trump 2024 campaign senior advisor
Fani Willis: Fulton County (Georgia) DA
L. Lin Wood: Georgia lawyer involved in Trump's election challenges
Christopher Wray: FBI Director
Robert Zeidman: computer forensics expert who "proved Mike [Lindell] wrong"

1

HOLDING AUTOCRATS ACCOUNTABLE

This is the last of five volumes in my mini-series *Defending American Democracy*. The first three volumes documented and analyzed resistance to autocracy during Trump's first term. *How Autocrats Seek Power* (Abel 2024b) addressed the two elections at the beginning and end of that term. It examined Special Counsel Mueller's inconclusive investigation of Russian interference and Trump's anticipatory delegitimation of what he (and most contemporary observers) expected would be Hillary Clinton's victory (a strategy he repeated in his 2024 contest, see Chapter 6). Most of that book, however, was devoted to the 2020 election. Before the vote, Trump railed against mail ballots and drop boxes, appointed an unqualified Postmaster General who hindered delivery of those ballots, and disseminated numerous lies about nonexistent fraud. After his dismal performance (losing the popular vote by over 7 million), Trump and his supporters challenged the results in more than 60 lawsuits (but won just one, which did not alter the outcome of that contest). He and his supporters pressured electors in several states to defy the voters' mandate, most notoriously in his phone call to Georgia Secretary of State Raffensperger. Trump and his supporters also urged states to choose "alternate" slates of electors (illegal acts for which some have been prosecuted). He contemplated declaring a state of emergency and ordering the military to seize voting machines (on the advice of lawyers later disciplined for unethical conduct). After Attorney General Barr resigned at the eleventh hour, and Acting Attorney General Rosen refused to do Trump's bidding, he appointed the compliant (but unqualified) Assistant Attorney General Clark. Trump was convinced by John Eastman (also disciplined by his bar association) that state legislatures could change their electoral votes and that, if there were disputed slates, the president would be chosen by a vote of those

DOI: 10.4324/9781032629186-1

legislatures (of which Republicans enjoyed a majority). When all else failed, Trump summoned his supporters (including Oath Keepers and Proud Boys) to a January 6 demonstration in Washington, promising it would be "wild," and exhorted the tens of thousands who assembled to march on the Capitol, where they trashed the building and battled outnumbered police, injuring 140 and leading to five deaths. Nevertheless, Joe Biden was inaugurated on January 20, 2021, demonstrating the resilience of democratic institutions and processes.

How Autocrats Abuse Power (Abel 2024a) focused on two of the many abuses during Trump's first term—immigration and criminal justice—because they threatened essential elements of liberal democracy: equal respect and the rule of law. Trump made his attacks on immigrants (first Muslims and then Latinos) the centerpiece of his 2016 and 2020 campaigns. Lacking control of Congress, Trump relied on executive orders: the Muslim bans, punishment of sanctuary cities, family separation, obstruction of asylum applications, the border wall, a citizenship question on the census, the public charge rule, visa denials, deferred action for childhood arrivals, and temporary protected status. All these were struck down by federal courts except for the third Muslim ban, upheld by a Supreme Court that divided along partisan lines (6–3), like federal judges in immigration cases generally. In his 2024 campaign Trump promised even harsher treatment of immigrants: mass detention and deportation of the estimated 11 million undocumented people, revival of family separation, and an end to birthright citizenship. His post-election nomination of the men who had conceived and implemented his 2016–20 immigration policies (e.g., Stephen Miller as White House deputy chief of staff, Tom Homan as White House border czar) demonstrates his determination.

Trump also undermined the rule of law by intervening in the successful prosecution of cronies implicated in Russia's efforts to influence the 2016 election—Roger Stone, Michael Flynn, Paul Manafort, and Rick Gates—and then pardoning all of them (as he pardoned military personnel convicted of war crimes in Afghanistan and Iraq). Here, too, Trump has vowed to repeat his actions by pardoning some or all of the more than 1,500 convicted of crimes committed during the January 6, 2021 riot. And he nominated loyalists who would do his bidding as Attorney General: Matt Gaetz (forced to withdraw because of alleged sexual crimes) and Pam Bondi.

How Autocrats Attack Expertise (Abel 2024c) scrutinized Trump's disastrous response to the greatest domestic challenge of his first term: the COVID-19 pandemic. He had boasted about relying on his gut rather than the expertise of others in a range of domains as varied as hurricane predictions and foreign and economic policy. But it was his subordination of science to political expedience that had the most tragic consequences. He sought to distract attention from his own blunders by blaming China for what he labelled "Kung-flu." He suppressed embarrassing information, thereby endangering the public. He blithely assured Americans that COVID-19 was no more serious than the seasonal flu and would disappear with warm weather. He recklessly disseminated the misinformation retailed by his favorite media source, Fox News. He opposed testing (blaming it for the rising number of cases), masks (which he refused to wear when greeting "dictators, kings, queens"), and social distancing (convening superspreader events like the nomination of Justice Barrett and exposing Secret Service personnel to his own COVID). He touted hydroxychloroquine and ivermectin and suggested ingesting bleach, with harmful, even fatal, results for those who credulously followed his advice. He openly repudiated highly respected experts like Anthony Fauci and elevated unqualified scientists to highly visible positions, where they advocated "herd immunity," increasing the risks of the most vulnerable populations (the elderly, those with compromised immune systems). He pressured the FDA, NIH, and the pharmaceutical companies to release the vaccine before the 2020 election, even if clinical trials were incomplete. And he laid the groundwork for continued opposition to preventive measures (school and business closures, vaccine mandates) after the end of his term. In the numerous lawsuits challenging public health practices, federal judges again divided along partisan lines, as they had in cases involving the 2020 election and immigration. Following his 2024 election, Trump doubled down on his contempt for science by nominating people with even more dubious credentials: leading anti-vaxxer Robert F. Kennedy Jr. for Secretary of Health and Human Services, and David Weldon, who still falsely blames vaccines for autism, to direct the Center for Disease Control and Prevention.[1]

How Autocrats Subvert Elections (Abel 2025), the fourth volume and a companion to this one, begins my analysis of efforts to hold Trump accountable after his term ended. Widespread outrage at the January 6, 2021 attack on the Capitol, which interrupted certification of Biden's Electoral College victory, prompted failed efforts to invoke the Fourteenth and Twenty-fifth Amendments (to find Trump disqualified to hold office or incapable of performing his duties), the impeachment of Trump (whose conviction was defeated by Senate Republicans), Republican obstruction of a bipartisan Congressional investigation, and the House Select Committee's gripping televised hearings and comprehensive report, which documented the complicity of Trump and his supporters in the insurrection. Republicans quickly constructed and disseminated a revisionist counternarrative: misrepresenting January 6 as an exercise in free speech; minimizing the violence, which they blamed on antifa, BLM, and FBI informants, as well as security rendered inadequate by Democrats; and sanctifying the January 6 defendants as patriots and political prisoners, unfairly prosecuted and held in unacceptably harsh prisons. Nevertheless, the prosecution of more than 1,500 people led to the conviction of all but two; DDC judges appointed by presidents of both parties harshly condemned the defendants and displayed no partisanship in the sentences they imposed. By contrast, Republican state and local officials continued to contest the outcomes of the 2020 election and sought to skew future elections by gerrymandering districts and obstructing the votes of those they believed favored Democratic candidates, and federal judges again evinced political partisanship in deciding challenges.

The present volume completes my analysis of resistance to autocracy. It analyzes the full range of legal efforts to hold Trump accountable: civil actions by E. Jean Carroll for defamation and sexual abuse and by the New York State Attorney General for fraudulent misstatement of property values; other defamation cases and Trump's retaliatory litigation; professional discipline of lawyers involved in baseless election challenges; state prosecutions in New York (for misrepresenting the hush money payment to Stormy Daniels) and Georgia (for interfering in vote counting); and the two federal prosecutions: for wrongly retaining official documents and seeking to overturn the 2020 election. I then turn to documenting the ways in which Trump manipulated hatred in his 2024 campaign—behavior I analyzed in my introductory chapter on "The Origins of Autocracy" in *How Autocrats Seek Power* and analogized to the rise of Hitler in my introductory chapter on "Prelude to Autocracy" in *How Autocrats Subvert Elections*. This volume concludes by comparing forms of resistance to autocracy examined in all five books, in order to inform the essential struggle to preserve liberal democracy during the next four years and thereafter.

Note

1 Weinberger, "Incoming!" *London Review of Books* 17 (12.26.24).

2

CIVIL JUSTICE AS A SITE OF RESISTANCE TO AUTOCRACY

Civil justice has been an important site of resistance to Trump and his supporters. This chapter describes and analyzes four such contestations: E. Jean Carroll's lawsuits against Trump for defamation, battery, and emotional distress; other defamation actions against Trump associates and the right-wing media; the New York Attorney General's civil fraud case against Trump and his children and business associates for misstating the value of his properties; and professional discipline of Trump lawyers.

2.1 E. Jean Carroll v. Trump

E. Jean Carroll is a successful author and journalist, whose "Ask E. Jean" advice column ran in *Elle* magazine from 1993 to 2020.[1] In a *New York* magazine article and a book, *What Do We Need Men For? A Modest Proposal* (both published in 2019), she accused Trump of sexually assaulting her in the mid-1990s when she worked at Bergdorf Goodman. (She and other women also made sexual assault allegations against CBS CEO Les Moonves, who resigned.) Trump claimed he had never met Carroll, despite a 1987 photo showing them together. In November 2019, she sued him in the New York Supreme Court for defamation and emotional distress. (The New York Adult Survivors Act had just extended the statute of limitations from three years to 20.) Asserting that Trump had acted in an official capacity when denying the accusation, the DoJ sought to remove the case to federal court. SDNY Judge Lewis Kaplan allowed the removal but held that Trump had not been acting in an official capacity. Trump appealed, but both the DC and Second Circuit Courts of Appeal returned the issue to Kaplan. On October 12, 2022, Trump

DOI: 10.4324/9781032629186-2

said on Truth Social: "This 'Ms. Bergdorf Goodman' case is a complete con job. . . . I don't know this woman. . . . It is a Hoax and lie . . . it never happened." In a deposition, he accused Carroll's lawyer, Roberta Kaplan (no relation to the judge) of being a Democratic political operative. He added, insultingly, that Carroll was "not my type," and he gratuitously told Roberta Kaplan: "You would not be a choice of mine either." He called Carroll "sick," "a wack job" and "nut job."

In November 2022, Carroll filed a second lawsuit against Trump in SDNY, adding battery to her defamation claim.[2] Judge Kaplan denied a motion by Joe Tacopina, Trump's lead lawyer, to offer a DNA sample (to compare with semen on Carroll's dress), finding it exemplified a pattern of tactics "the effect and probably purpose of which" was to delay the trial. This was notable "in view of the fact that Ms. Carroll now is 79 years old." Judge Kaplan rejected the defense's "rebuttal damage expert," finding he was not an expert. Kaplan ordered that the jury remain anonymous, even to the lawyers, because Trump had attacked "courts judges, various law enforcement officials and other public officials, and even individual jurors in other matters" and urged supporters to "protest" against this case and "take our nation back."

Kaplan denied Trump's claim of "absolute privilege" and ruled that his October 2022 comments about the first lawsuit were not privileged as a "fair and true report" of a "judicial proceeding" but rather "an amalgamation of Mr. Trump's personal views and comments on a wide range of subjects." The judge denied a defense motion to delay the trial because of media coverage of the hush money case (see Chapter 3.1): "It does not sit well for Mr. Trump to promote pretrial publicity and then to claim that coverage that he promoted was prejudicial to him." Kaplan refused Tacopina's request to instruct the jury that Trump wished to appear but would not for "logistical" reasons. Noting that the defendant planned to attend a New Hampshire campaign event on the third day of the trial, Kaplan told Tacopina: "If the Secret Service can protect him at that event, certainly the Secret Service, the Marshals Service and the City of New York can see to his security in this very secure federal courthouse." Kaplan denied another request to delay the trial while defense lawyers sought to discover who was paying for Carroll's lawsuit, and he sealed the results of discovery.

Kaplan directed both sets of lawyers to caution clients and witnesses against making "statements that are likely to incite violence or civil unrest."[3] But on the first day of trial, Trump said on Truth Social that the case was "a made up SCAM" and a "fraudulent & false story." The judge told Tacopina those statements were "entirely inappropriate." "Your client is basically endeavoring to speak to his 'public,' but, more troublesome, to the jury in this case about stuff that has no business being spoken about." Tacopina promised to talk to Trump, but later that day Eric Trump posted on Twitter that a prominent backer of Carroll's case (Democratic billionaire donor

Reid Hoffman) was motivated by "pure hatred, spite or fear of a formidable candidate." Kaplan then warned Tacopina that the "remedies that might be available from this court may not be the only relevant remedies. If I were in your shoes, I'd be having a conversation with the client." Later in the trial Trump discussed on Truth Social the DNA found on Carroll's dress, evidence the judge had excluded. Kaplan urged Tacopina to warn his client about further liability. The judge denied a motion for a mistrial based on the claim that he had unfairly explained to the jury Carroll's reference to Jonathan Swift's ironic "A Modest Proposal" (that the Irish should sell their children to be eaten during the potato famine). While playing golf in Ireland during the trial, Trump complained: "I have to go back for a woman that made a false accusation about me, and I have a judge who is extremely hostile."

Before the verdict, Trump said on Truth Social:[4]

> Waiting for a jury decision on a False Accusation where I, despite being a current political candidate and leading all others in both parties, am not allowed to speak or defend myself, even as hard nosed reporters scream questions about this case at me. In the meantime, the other side has a book falsely accusing me of Rape & is working with the press.

After deliberating just three hours (following eight days of trial), the jury found Trump had sexually abused and defamed Carroll, awarding her \$2 million compensatory and \$20,000 punitive damages for sexual abuse, \$1.7 million for defamation, and \$1 million compensatory and \$280,000 punitive damages for emotional distress. The next day Trump reiterated he had never met Carroll and called her a "whack job," her story "fake" and "made up," and the trial a "rigged deal." He also bragged that his poll numbers had improved (although there had been no new polls). Kaplan denied motions for a new trial and reduction of damages, dismissed Trump's counterclaim, and held that the jury had found that Trump had raped Carroll in the ordinary meaning of that word.

Tacopina said Kaplan displayed "highly prejudicial" bias. "There were things that happened in this case that were beyond the pale. In New York you can't get a fair trial." "We should have been able to tell something about the background" of the jurors. Trump said on Truth Social: "I HAVE ABSOLUTELY NO IDEA WHO THIS WOMAN IS. THIS VERDICT IS A DISGRACE—A CONTINUATION OF THE GREATEST WITCH HUNT OF ALL TIME!" Judge Kaplan was a "terrible person" who was "completely biased and should have recused himself." Carroll's lawsuit was just "another scam" financed "by Democrat operatives," and "she totally lied about it." Republican Senators echoed Trump. Hagerty called it "yet another act in the ongoing legal circus in Manhattan to take down Donald Trump." Rubio said: "the jury is a joke. The whole case is a joke." Graham pronounced: "I think you could convict Donald Trump of kidnapping Lindbergh's baby" (which happened in 1932 before Trump was born). But Cornyn warned: "I don't think [Trump] can get elected." Thune worried: "it has a cumulative effect." And Cassidy called Trump's behavior "reprehensible." Former Gov. Hutchinson said the verdict "should be treated with seriousness and is another example of the indefensible behavior of Donald Trump." *The Washington Post* asserted: "Mr. Trump received a fair trial."

The DoJ, which had sought to intervene in the case under both Trump and Biden (on the ground Judge Kaplan had rejected: that Trump had been engaged in official behavior), decided not to do so in Carroll's pending defamation case (the original one, which would be tried second).[5] Kaplan denied Trump's motion to delay the second case while he appealed Kaplan's rejection of absolute immunity, finding the grounds "frivolous." Trump had waived his claim of irreparable injury by waiting more than 3.5 years to raise the immunity defense to justify the delay. The judge held that because Trump's 2019 statements were "substantially the same" as those adjudicated in the earlier case, this second trial would be limited to damages. "Mr. Trump is precluded from offering any testimony, evidence or argument suggesting or implying that he did not sexually assault Ms. Carroll, that she fabricated her account of the assault or that she had any motive to do so." The judge again ordered that jurors remain anonymous, noting that Trump had been fined twice for violating Justice Engoron's orders in the civil fraud case (see Chapter 2.3). The same day, Engoron disclosed that he had received hundreds of "harassing and threatening phone calls, voicemails, emails, letters and packages" following public criticism by Trump and his lawyers. Judge Kaplan denied a motion to postpone the trial for the funeral of Amalija Knavs, Melania's mother. Roberta Kaplan sought limits on Trump's testimony in light of his performance before Justice Engoron: "It takes little imagination to think that Mr. Trump is gearing up for a similar performance here—only this time, in front of a jury." Tacopina withdrew from representing Trump in both this case and the Stormy Daniels case (see Chapter 3.1). Trump wanted to testify, and Tacopina advised against it, as he had done in the first case.

In anticipation of the second trial, Trump reiterated that Carroll had faked her story. "I'm going to explain I don't know who the hell she is."[6] Roberta Kaplan asked the judge to require Trump to take an oath that he understood what was off limits. Alina Habba (now his principal lawyer) said this "proposed [sic] unprecedented hurdles." "We presume that this is not a kangaroo court of a third-world country where a party to a lawsuit is involuntarily made to say what a court and an opposing party wants them to say." When the judge denied a delay, Trump called him a "crazed Trump hating judge," who presided over an "Election Interference Witch Hunt, disguised as a trial of a woman I have never met before."

In his opening statement, Carroll's lawyer Shawn Crowley said that "even while sitting in the courtroom" Trump had posted more than a dozen "defamatory statements, more lies about Ms. Carroll and this case," claiming she was "seeking fame, fortune, and publicity."[7] He had called Judge Kaplan a "bully" and a "disgrace," who "should put this whole corrupt, Crooked Joe Biden-directed Election Interference attack on me immediately to rest." A Trump supporter had texted Carroll right after the earlier verdict: "I hope someone really does attack, rape and murder you." When Boris Epshteyn (sitting with defense counsel) tried to address the judge outside the hearing of the jury, Kaplan told him to sit down because he was not admitted to practice in SDNY. Habba said in her opening that Carroll "is someone who craves fame and seeks fame wherever she could get it." "Regardless of a few mean tweets, Ms. Carroll is now more famous than she has ever been in her life."

While Carroll was testifying on the second day, Trump repeatedly shook his head, exhaled loudly, whispered to his lawyers, and muttered "con job" and "witch hunt."[8] Her lawyers complained to the judge, who had been clashing with Habba over defense objections to Carroll's testimony. Judge Kaplan declared: "Let's just get this clear for both sides right now. The first lawyer who says anything when a witness is on the stand says everything there is to be said for that side. This is not tag-team lawyering." He criticized Habba for not knowing how to question a witness or refer to exhibits. He reprimanded defense lawyers: "no, we are not going to read out loud a document not yet in evidence. We are going to take a break here, and you're going to refresh your memory about how you get a document into evidence." When he stopped Habba's questions about tweets, she objected: "I can't ask about them? With all due respect," Kaplan interrupted: "all due respect means that when I issue a ruling, you say next question." He acknowledged that "Mr. Trump has a right to be here" but warned: "that right can be forfeited . . . if he is disruptive." Outside the jury's presence, Kaplan addressed Trump directly: "I hope I don't have to consider excluding you from the trial. I understand you're probably very eager for me to do that." Trump threw up his hands: "I would love it. I would love it!" Kaplan replied: "I know you would. You just can't control yourself in these circumstances, apparently." Trump retorted: "You can't either!"

Carroll testified that, as the author of five previous books, she had regularly appeared on "Good Morning America" and the "Today" show before her 2019 book was published; but those invitations dried up after Trump accused her of lying, and she was threatened. "Previously, I was known simply as a journalist, and now I'm known as the liar, the fraud and the wack job" and targeted with messages like: "stick a gun in your mouth and pull the trigger." Trump's lawyer moved to recuse Kaplan, citing his "general hostility toward the defense throughout this case." The judge refused.

After that hearing Trump called him "a nasty man," a "nasty judge," and "a Trump-hating guy." "I, frankly, am the one that suffered damages."

When Judge Kaplan said the jury would be instructed that the previous trial found Carroll had been sexually assaulted by Trump, he muttered "unbelievable" and shook his head.[9] When Habba asked if Trump had ever told people to hurt Carroll, he said: "no." "I just wanted to defend myself, my family and, frankly, the presidency." Kaplan struck everything after "no." As Trump left the courtroom, he muttered: "this is not America." He testified that he stood "100%" behind his 2022 deposition denying the assault—"She said something: I consider it a false accusation"—and again called Carroll a "whack job." (In that deposition Trump had declared that those who made false rape accusations should "pay dearly" and so should their lawyers. He told Roberta Kaplan: "I think the attorneys like you are a big part of it, because you know it's a phony case.") Carroll's lawyers played Trump's video deposition in the civil fraud case (see Chapter 2.3), in which he claimed his brand alone was worth "maybe $10 billion." Before the jury entered the courtroom, Trump repeated: "I never met the woman. I don't know who the woman is." He stalked out of the court in the middle of closing arguments.

After deliberating less than three hours (following six days of trial), the jury awarded Carroll $18.3 million compensatory and $65 million punitive damages.[10] Before dismissing the jurors, Judge Kaplan told them: "my advice to you is that you never disclose that you were on this jury and I won't say anything more about it either." Carroll called the verdict "a great victory for every woman who stands up when she's been knocked down and a huge defeat for every bully who has tried to keep a woman down." "I'm not going to waste a cent of this" judgment. "We're going to do something good with it." Trump denounced this second trial as another "Biden Directed Witch Hunt" and "absolutely ridiculous." "Our Legal System is out of control, and being used as a Political Weapon. They have taken away all First Amendment Rights. THIS IS NOT AMERICA!" Rep. Greene agreed Trump "was denied a fair trial in NY where judges are now political" activists. Rep. Stefanik denounced the trial as an effort by Democrats to weaponize the justice system and "bankrupt" Trump. Trump boasted on Truth Social: "I AM WORTH MUCH MORE THAN THE NUMBERS SHOWN ON MY FINANCIAL STATEMENTS."

Judge Kaplan denied a motion to set aside the verdict and a request to delay payment of the judgment.[11] "Mr. Trump's current situation is a result of his own dilatory actions. He has had since Jan. 26 to organize his finances." Trump posted a $91 million appeal bond, having posted $5 million cash in Carroll's earlier case. Noting that "the statute of limitations for defamation in most jurisdictions is between one and three years," Roberta Kaplan said: "we continue to monitor every statement that Donald Trump makes about our client."[12] Undeterred, Trump complained about the bond at a March 2024 rally in Rome, Georgia, and repeated that Carroll's accusations were false and she was "not a believable person." On CNBC he mocked her as Miss Bergdorf Goodman and called the judgments against him "ridiculous." "I got charge—I was given a false accusation and had to post a $91 million bond on a false accusation." In September, following a hearing of his appeal from what he called "a ridiculous verdict of a woman I've never met," he repeated: "I've never met this woman. It's a made up fabricated story by someone looking to promote a book." "Never happened." "She has gone around for years saying this story and it's a total lie." At the end of December, Trump reposted images of Carroll and himself with the caption "Should a woman go to jail for falsely accusing a man of rape" and urged others to repost it. But days later, 2024, the Second Circuit affirmed the $5 million judgment.

Carroll's case was a victory for both her and the civil justice system. Judge Kaplan ran a tight ship: rebuffing Trump's efforts at delay, excluding a witness as inexpert, keeping the jury anonymous to protect it from attacks, imposing and enforcing a gag order (even threatening to eject Trump from court), rejecting baseless claims of privilege, and reprimanding Habba for incompetence. Trump could not restrain himself: continuing to defame Carroll before, during, and after the trials; declaring she was not "his type" (a negative pregnant apparently conceding he <u>would</u> rape women who were); gratuitously insulting her lawyer; violating the gag order; and abusing Judge Kaplan as "extremely hostile," a "terrible person," "bully, "disgrace," "nasty man," and "crazed Trump hating judge." Trump flaunted his open contempt for both judge and jury by walking out of court during closing arguments. Both Trump lawyers followed his example, Habba assailing the "kangaroo court of a third-world country." (But Tacopina quit after the first trial, apparently despairing about his ability to control his willful client.) Trump explicitly challenged the legitimacy of the legal system, calling the verdict "absolutely ridiculous," a "rigged deal," "scam," "Joe Biden directed," "Election Interference Witch Hunt" financed by "Democrat operatives," and concluding: "Our Legal System is out of control, and being used as a Political Weapon." His Congressional cheerleaders predictably echoed him. Trump claimed it was <u>he</u>, not Carroll, who had been victimized. And yet he was left with two adverse jury verdicts and judgments totaling nearly $100 million.

2.2 Other Defamation Cases

Other cases demonstrate that defamation claims can be an effective resistance strategy.[13] Alex Jones, the far-right radio show host, made a fortune by promoting lies about fictitious conspiracies, including the 1993 Branch Davidian siege in Waco, the 1995 Oklahoma City bombing, and the 9/11 attacks. One of Jones's most offensive allegations was that the 2012 Sandy Hook Elementary School massacre in Connecticut was a "false flag" operation by gun control advocates, in which no one died. Survivors and relatives of the 26 dead sued.

In August 2022, a Texas jury found Jones liable for $4.1 million compensatory and $45.2 million punitive damages. His company, Free Speech Systems, had anticipated this by filing for bankruptcy in Texas a month earlier. In October, a Connecticut jury awarded $965 million in compensatory damages for slander and emotional distress. (Superior Court Judge Barbara Bellis had found liability by default, based on Jones's "willful noncompliance" with discovery.) A month later, Bellis ordered Jones to pay an additional $473 million in punitive damages. He filed for personal bankruptcy in December 2022. The following November, plaintiffs proposed to settle for a minimum of $85 million, paid over ten years; Jones responded with an offer to pay $5.5 million a year for ten years. US Bankruptcy Judge Christopher Lopez ordered Jones to liquidate his personal assets and sell Infowars. It was bought by *The Onion*, which planned to restart it in January as a parody, mocking "weird internet personalities" like Jones. None of this deterred him: after Elon Musk let him return to X in December 2023 (he had been barred from Twitter in 2018), he posted an average of 40 times a day, repeating falsehoods about election fraud and claiming the first attempt to assassinate Trump was a "coup" by the "big state."

Dinesh D'Souza's film *2,000 Mules*, which was seen by more than a million people in its first two weeks and grossed over $10 million, featured covert surveillance videos of Mark Andrews putting ballots in a drop box near Atlanta, with D'Souza calling it a "crime" and declaring "these are fraudulent votes."[14] Tucker Carlson and Charlie Kirk publicized that scene. Trump called the film "the greatest and most impactful documentary of our time." Andrews sued D'Souza, Salem Media Group (which produced the film), and two people associated with the conservative group True the Vote. Salem settled by apologizing and promising not to promote the film or the book. ND GA Judge Grimberg (Trump) refused to dismiss the case, which is pending against the other defendants. D'Souza also apologized to Andrews but continued to maintain that "the underlying premise of the film holds true."

Defamation also can be an effective weapon against malicious falsehoods in the culture wars, which the far right has revived to fire up Trump supporters. After Eric Posey, a drag performer, danced during a pride event in Coeur d'Alene, Idaho, in 2022, Summer Bushnell falsely said in videos and online that Posey had exposed his genitalia to minors.[15] He sued, winning $926,000 in compensatory and $250,000 in punitive damages. His lawyer said Posey had been "called names and racial slurs. He was harassed."

2.2.1 Dominion and Smartmatic Lawsuits

The outlandish lies Trump lawyers and right-wing media peddled about election machines and software used in the 2020 election provoked the targeted companies to allege defamation.[16] Dominion Voting Systems sued Sidney

Powell, her law firm, and her group Defending the Republic in DDC for $1.3 billion, claiming Dominion employees had been stalked, harassed, and threatened, forcing the company to spend more than $565,000 for security. It had sent demands for retractions and preservation of documents to Powell, L. Lin Wood, Pat Cipollone, Giuliani, Fox News, Newsmax, OAN, and *The Epoch Times*. It told Facebook, Parler, YouTube, Twitter, and other social media sites to preserve posts from Dan Bongino, Maria Bartiromo, Mike Lindell, Powell, Fox News, OAN, Newsmax, and Trump. Dominion filed similar lawsuits against Giuliani, Lindell, Byrne, OANN, and Newsmax. Powell tweeted defiantly: "retracting nothing. We have #evidence. They are #fraud masters!" Wood was contemptuous: "I'd call it nonsense."

After Byrne's law firm McGlinchey Stafford withdrew, he retained Stefanie Lambert, who had been charged with accessing, tampering with, and unlawfully possessing voting machines in Michigan used in the 2020 election. She told DDC Mag. Judge Upadhyaya she had shared over a million pages of Dominion's discovery documents with law enforcement, after swearing to keep them confidential, because they contained "evidence of a crime," for example proof that "Dominion conspired with foreign nationals in Serbia" to undermine the US election. She used them to argue that a Michigan prosecution was illegitimate, giving them to Barry County Sheriff Dar Leaf, who also was being investigated about voting machines. He put over 2,000 pages of the documents on X and distributed them to other sheriffs and Members of Congress; and Byrne gave them to "the U.S. attorney's office," though Lambert did not know which one. She claimed Byrne was "a national intelligence asset" entitled to share "national security information" with law enforcement. (He had had a romantic relationship with Maria Butina, falsely claiming this was at the FBI's behest. She was convicted of acting as an unregistered foreign agent for Russia and deported at the end of her sentence.) Dominion's lawyer asked Upadhyaya to remove Lambert from the case and sanction her. The judge denied Lambert and Byrne access to Dominion records and ordered that she move to seal the Michigan court documents. After Oakland County (Michigan) Circuit Judge Jeffrey Matis issued a bench warrant for Lambert, who failed to appear at a hearing, she was arrested by DDC US Marshals and held as a "fugitive from justice" until DC Superior Court Judge Heide L. Herrmann released her on bond and ordered her to surrender to Michigan police. Upadhyaya ordered Byrne to appear at the next hearing to explain what he did with the papers. He told the *Washington Post*: "I'm just a humble concerned citizen." Dominion learned about the leaks from Byrne's previous attorney, Robert Driscoll, who also represented Butina. Lambert had been involved in Powell's "Kraken" lawsuit to block certification of the election (see Abel 2024b: Chapter 3) and was an unindicted co-conspirator in the Georgia prosecution of Powell (see Chapter 3.2). Michigan charged Lambert with permitting unauthorized access to voter data. Hours after a hearing before Upadhyaya on whether she should be removed from the case for leaking documents to Leaf, Dominion said Byrne had again violated the court's orders by posting up to a million Dominion documents on X. Upadhyaya disqualified Lambert from representing Byrne, in a 62-page opinion listing her violations and "many misrepresentations." Her actions "were intentional and clearly meant to inflict the harm that has resulted," including threats against Dominion CEO John Poulos (see Abel 2025: Chapter 5.1.4).

Giuliani threatened to countersue "for violating these constitutional rights," for example the First Amendment. He had said Dominion "really is a Venezuelan company" that "depends completely on the software of Smartmatic," a company "developed in about 2004, 2005 to help Chavez steal elections." "When you pressed down Biden, you got Trump, and when you pressed down Trump you got Biden." He claimed a "Dominion machine flipped 6,000 votes from Trump to Biden" in Antrim County, Michigan. The machines were "62 percent inaccurate," with a "68 percent error rate" and "81.9 percent rejection rate." None of this was true.

Dominion cautioned Lindell against repeating his false allegations, demanded a retraction, and detailed his lies. The next day he released a two-hour "documentary" entitled *Absolute Proof* and continued to allege fraud, blaming "Dominion where we have all our evidence." Dominion sued him in DDC for $1.3 million in February 2021. Lindell was "very happy to hear" about the lawsuit because "now I can get to the evidence faster." He counterclaimed, asserting that

> direct and circumstantial evidence demonstrates that, during the 2020 General Election, electronic voting machines like those manufactured and sold by Dominion were manipulated and hacked in a manner that caused votes for one candidate to be tallied for the opposing candidate

DDC Judge Nichols (Trump) denied Lindell's motion to dismiss, and the Supreme Court declined to intervene.

Powell evaded service of process and then moved to dismiss, arguing that "reasonable people would not accept [her] statements as fact" because of the "well-recognized principle that political statements are inherently prone to exaggeration and hyperbole." Judge Nichols peremptorily rejected this argument: "it is simply not the law that provably false statements cannot be actionable if made in the context of an election." That "Powell's statements expressed or implied a verifiably false fact about Dominion" was "not a close call." She claimed lack of malice because she relied on sworn affidavits. "But there is no rule that a defendant cannot act in reckless disregard of the truth when relying on sworn affidavits—especially sworn affidavits that the defendant had a role in creating." Nichols was unimpressed by one of Powell's alleged "experts," who "publicly claimed that George Soros, President

George H.W. Bush's father, the Muslim Brotherhood, and 'leftists' helped form the 'Deep State' in Nazi Germany in the 1930s—which would have been a remarkable feat for Soros, who was born in 1930." Nichols rejected motions to change venue: Powell's to move to ND TX and Lindell's to D MN. In October, the Supreme Court declined to review. Lindell said: "It's just another poor ruling." All his evidence was "sitting in Nevada." His lawyers would subpoena "a lot of very big names in the next couple of weeks." Nichols denied motions to dismiss by Powell, Byrne, MyPillow, Giuliani, and OANN.

In October 2021, Eric Coomer (former Dominion director of product strategy and security) sued right-wing podcaster Joe Oltmann, Giuliani, Powell, OANN, and the Trump campaign, among others, in Denver County District Court.[17] Oltmann claimed that on a late September 2020 Zoom among antifa members, he heard Coomer say: "Don't worry about the election, Trump is not gonna win. I made fucking sure of that." Coomer denied having been on any such call. Trump and his son Eric retweeted Oltmann's claims. Powell asserted the story was "true" and "I think we have a copy of the call." Giuliani called Coomer a "vicious man" who intended to "fix the election." Newsmax Media apologized on the air and was dismissed from the lawsuit, as did *American Thinker*. The other defendants moved to dismiss under Colorado's anti-SLAPP law. Oltmann was 40 minutes late to a hearing, at the end of which Coomer's lawyers gave Judge Marie Avery Moses posts on Telegram of Oltmann saying she was "so obviously compromised and colluding with the radical agenda" and Coomer and his lawyers were liars. They sought a gag order. But Oltmann vowed to defy Moses's orders, which he compared to "Nazi Germany." "Now that I know [her decision], I will respect the unconstitutional order and make sure I post it for everyone to see while I sue the judge for violating my rights." Earlier he had defied orders to pay costs and legal fees for failing to appear at a deposition and been barred from disputing some evidence after refusing to disclose who gave him access to Coomer's Facebook posts. Judge Moses denied Oltmann's motion to dismiss, and the Colorado Court of Appeals affirmed. Coomer also sued Clayton Thomas "Clay" Clark and his "Thrivetime Show" podcast in federal court after Oltmann repeated the statements on that show and was seconded by Clark, prompting death threats against Coomer. D CO Judge William Martinez (Obama) denied a motion to dismiss, and the Tenth Circuit denied an interlocutory appeal.

In April 2022, Coomer sued Lindell in D CO.[18] During a March 2023, deposition Lindell yelled and swore, saying of Coomer: "How dare he come and sue MyPillow. He's a scumbag for doing that." He called the lawyers traitors, ambulance chasers, criminals, liars, slime, and disgusting. After this tirade, the court reporter refused to return and had to be replaced. Lindell said the lawsuit had "nothing to do with anything" and attacked D CO

Judge Nina Wang (Biden) for not dismissing it. "I've lost everything I've got so far . . . millions of dollars." Coomer's lawyers sought to compel Lindell to appear at another deposition and pay all costs. Lindell claimed that Newsmax's confidential settlement prohibited it from promoting MyPillow products, causing revenues to drop from $3 million in the four months prior to the ban to $300,000 in the four months after it. In October 2023, Lindell's law firms—Parker Daniels Kibort LLC and Lewin & Lewin LLP—sought to withdraw because he owed them millions of dollars.[19] Lindell admitted this: "I can't pay the lawyers." "MyPillow's been decimated. . . . We've lost hundreds of millions of dollars." He blamed Dominion, Smartmatic, and the news media (including Fox News and Newsmax): "You're all doing it because you want me to shut up about security of our elections." But he would never settle: "not in a million years."

After the 2020 election, Lindell had offered $5 million to anyone who could "Prove Mike Wrong" about his assertion that Chinese interference had thrown the election to Biden.[20] He presented the "evidence" at a "cyber symposium" in South Dakota in August 2021. Robert Zeidman, a computer forensics expert, accepted the challenge even though he had voted for Trump both times. A private arbitration panel unanimously concluded that Zeidman had demonstrated that Lindell's fraud allegations "unequivocally did not reflect Nov. 2020 election data" and ordered him to pay in 30 days. Lindell was defiant: "It's going to end up in court. I'm not going to pay anything. . . . He didn't prove anything." Lindell claimed that the fact the arbitrators ruled the day after Fox News settled with Dominion for nearly $800 million (discussed later) showed that the arbitration award was intended to force him to end his campaign against electronic voting. But he declared: "I'll spend everything I have to save the country I love." Ten months later, however, D MN Judge John Tunheim (Clinton) ordered Lindell to pay the award. Lindell vowed to appeal the "corrupt" case (but would have to post a bond to do so). He protested: "I don't have any money. I have a pickup truck and a house that I live in. That's it." Zeidman did not expect to see the money but, if he did, would donate it to nonprofits.

Dominion also sued Fox News for defamation in Delaware Superior Court, seeking $1.6 billion in damages.[21] Judge Eric M. Davis (appointed by the Democratic Gov. Markell) denied a motion to dismiss. Dominion filed similar suits there against Newsmax, OANN, and Patrick Byrne. In a deposition in another own case, Giuliani had said defensively:

> We had a report that the heads of Dominion and Smartmatic, somewhere in the mid-tweens, you know 2013, 2014, whatever, went down to Venezuela for a get-to-know meeting with Maduro so they could demonstrate to Maduro the kind of vote fixing they did for Chavez. . . . Before the [November 2020] press conference I was told about it. Sometimes I go and

> look myself—when stuff comes up. This time I didn't have the time to do it. It's not my job, in a fast-moving case, to go out and investigate every piece of evidence that was given to me. Otherwise, you're never going to write a story. You'll never come to a conclusion.

Discovery exposed Fox's low opinion of Trump's lawyers. Weeks after the election, Fox Corp. Vice President Raj Shah wrote a deputy that Giuliani's press conference "sounds SO FUCKING CRAZY" (see Abel 2024b: Chapter 3.1). (Shah had been a senior White House aide two years earlier.) The deputy agreed: "Rudy looks awful." "He objectively looks like he was a dead person voting 2 weeks ago." But when a Fox News reporter said Giuliani's speech was "simply not true," Shah cautioned: "This is the kinda shit that will kill us. We cover it wall to wall and then we burn that down with all that skepticism."

Tucker Carlson wrote Laura Ingraham on November 17 that "Sidney Powell is lying." Ingraham concurred: "Sidney is a complete nut." A day later Shah wrote Carlson's producer about Powell's claim that an affidavit linked Dominion to Venezuela: "Might wanna address this, but this stuff is so fucking insane. Vote rigging to the tune of millions? Cmon." The next day Fox Corp. CEO Rupert Murdoch described Trump and Giuliani as "both increasingly mad." "The real danger is what [Trump] might do as pres. Apparently not sleeping and bouncing off the walls!" Murdoch wrote Fox News CEO Suzanne Scott that Giuliani's claims were "really crazy stuff," and it was "very hard to credibly claim foul everywhere." Murdoch wrote in early 2021 that Fox's goal was "to make Trump a non person." He accused Sean Hannity, Jeanine Pirro, Lou Dobbs, and Maria Bartiromo of having "endorsed" Trump's fraud claims. (Dominion said Pirro bragged about being "the source for Powell's claims.") Murdoch added: "I would have liked us to be stronger in denouncing it in hindsight." Paul Ryan (the former Republican House Speaker, now a Fox Corp. board member) told another Fox executive that Rupert and Lachlan Murdoch "agree fully" that there was "a huge inflection point to keep Trump down and move on." On January 4, Carlson texted: "We are very, very close to being able to ignore Trump most nights. I truly can't wait." "I hate him passionately." "We're all pretending we've got a lot to show for [his administration], because admitting what a disaster it's been is too tough to digest. But come on. There really isn't an upside to Trump." Hannity said Giuliani was "acting like an insane person." Ingraham called him "such an idiot." Bret Baier said: "there is NO evidence of fraud." Murdoch outlets gave increasing coverage to Ron DeSantis, Trump's rival. A Murdoch company had published DeSantis's book "The Courage to Be Free" and excerpted it in the *New York Post* and *Wall Street Journal*; he was interviewed by the *Post* and the *Times* of London (another Murdoch outlet). Trump responded by attacking Murdoch and a "group of MAGA hating Globalist RINOS" who were "aiding & abetting the destruction of America." Don Jr. accused Fox News leaders of having an "America Last, war forever, garbage, fold-to-the-Democrats agenda."

In March, Abby Grossberg (who had been Carlson's head of booking) sued Fox in Delaware, claiming it had forced her to give false testimony in Dominion's defamation case. She subsequently amended that testimony and leaked some of the damaging communications cited earlier. She also sued in New York, accusing Fox and Carlson of sexist and anti-Semitic harassment. Four days after she filed the lawsuits Fox fired her, claiming she had disclosed privileged information. (In June, Fox paid $12 million to settle her lawsuits.)

On April 4, Robert Schwartz filed a shareholder derivative action in Delaware Chancery Court against Rupert and Lachlan Murdoch and Fox Corp. board members Chase Carey, Roland Hernandez and Jacques Nasser. After the settlement of Dominion v. Fox (later), New York City's five pension funds filed a shareholder derivative action suit in the same court. NYC Controller Brad Lander said: "we are shareholders at a company that, unfortunately, has a longstanding practice of allowing conspiracy theories that its executives and its board know are false to be repeated over and over and over again, despite the very clear and present risk of defamation lawsuits eroding shareholder value. And there has been no effort to make governance reforms." The Oregon Investment Council and Oregon Public Employees Retirement Fund joined the lawsuit. Another suit was brought by Rhode Island and Swedish pension funds, but Delaware Vice Chancellor J. Travis Laster chose New York and Oregon as lead counsel in the consolidated lawsuit.

As the April 2023 defamation trial approached, Judge Davis ruled that Fox had not engaged in "good-faith, disinterested reporting."[22] "The evidence developed" makes it "CRYSTAL clear that none of the statements relating to Dominion about the 2020 election are true." "It appears oxymoronic to call the statements 'opinions' while also asserting the statements are newsworthy allegations and/or substantially accurate reports of official proceedings." Davis ruled that "newsworthiness is not a defense to defamation," but he also prohibited Dominion from mentioning the January 6 insurrection and limited evidence about death threats to its employees. He rebuked the defendants for not disclosing that Murdoch was an officer of Fox News as well as the Fox Corporation (which could affect both his evidence and the defendants' liability). "Omission is a lie." Because of this, Davis held that Dominion was entitled to additional discovery at Fox's expense and considered appointing a special master to investigate whether Fox had improperly withheld information. Attacks on Dominion were undiminished by the impending trial: there had been nearly 9 million mentions of the company in social media and broadcasts in the two years since the lawsuit was filed. Mike Lindell called the lawsuit "frivolous" and pronounced Dominion "guilty."

After the parties postponed the trial for a day, they announced a settlement for $787.5 million on April 17. Although Fox did not apologize, it "acknowledge[d] the Court's rulings finding certain claims against Dominion to be false." A subsequent poll found that half of respondents and almost a third of Republicans believed that Fox hosts had said things about Dominion they knew were untrue. Fox fired Carlson, but Lachlan Murdoch insisted "there's no change to our programming strategy," which was "obviously a successful strategy" (Raj Shah left Fox the following month.)

Six months after the settlement, Fox's former Chief Legal and Policy Officer Viet Dinh said Judge Davis had issued "illogical" rulings" which "hamstrung" Fox. At least half the materials Fox was forced to disclose were "completely irrelevant to the case." Private emails were "exposed to the world" and scrutinized by "navel-gazing" journalists who wanted to "feed the gossip beast." "The court lost control of the media circus, to our detriment." The trial would have inflicted "three to four months of utter pain." "We knew we were right in the law, [but] the trial judge put us in a situation increasingly where it was very obvious that we were not able to win the trial, but we were very confident we would prevail on appeal."

> As the judge compounded error upon error, we would get more and more confident in our ultimate chances of prevailing on appeal—because at some point it became not just a matter of reversible error, it called into [question] the fundamental fairness and integrity of the Delaware civil justice system.

Dinh was said to have strongly opposed settlement. Fox had announced his departure two months earlier, with a golden handshake of $23 million and annual payments of $2.5 million for two years as "special adviser."

Smartmatic also filed a $2.7 billion defamation action in New York Supreme Court against Fox News and three of its reporters (including Dobbs and Bartiromo), as well as Powell and Giuliani.[23] Fox called the lawsuit "meritless," but the next day it dropped "Lou Dobbs Tonight," the highest rated program on Fox Business (though he retained a contract with Fox News media). Dobbs responded by retweeting a tweet urging viewers to "ditch Fox for @OANN." In January 2022, Justice David B. Cohen denied a motion to dismiss by Bartiromo, Dobbs and Fox: "there is a substantial basis for plaintiffs' claim that, at a minimum, Fox News turned a blind eye to a litany of outrageous claims about plaintiffs, unprecedented in the history of American elections, so inherently improbable that it evinced a reckless disregard for the truth." But he dismissed some claims against Giuliani and all those against Pirro (who had not accused Smartmatic of illegality) and Powell (for lack of jurisdiction). (Smartmatic has a pending suit against her in federal court.) And he denied Smartmatic's motion to dismiss Fox's counterclaim under New York's Anti-SLAPP Law. Fox called Smartmatic's claims "baseless" and appealed the denial of the motion to dismiss. But in February 2023, the Appellate Division reinstated the claims against Giuliani, revived those against Pirro, and affirmed the denial of her motion to dismiss. In October, Justice Cohen rejected defense requests to subpoena George Soros and his son to support Powell's claims of their involvement in election fraud. In January 2024, Cohen denied the Fox Corporation's motion to dismiss (finding sufficient involvement in Fox News decisions). In January 2025 the Appellate Division affirmed.

In January 2022, Smartmatic separately sued Mike Lindell and MyPillow in DDC.[24] In May 2022, DDC Judge Kelly (Trump) said he would sanction Lindell for unfounded counterclaims and "third-party claims" against Dominion and Smartmatic, granting motions to dismiss those claims. Smartmatic also sued Lindell for defamation and deceptive trade practices in D MN in January 2022. Judge Wilhelmina M. Wright (Obama) denied Lindell's motion to dismiss on September 19, 2022.

In November 2021, Smartmatic sued Newsmax in Delaware Superior Court and OANN in DDC.[25] Newsmax denounced the lawsuit as "a clear attempt to squelch the rights of a free press." But in August 2023, Delaware Superior Court Judge Davis let Smartmatic amend its complaint to add 26 other allegedly defamatory statements, rejecting Newsmax's invocation of the statute of limitations. In May 2024 Smartmatic alleged that Newsmax had destroyed evidence. Davis denied a motion to dismiss and scheduled trial for Sept. 30. Just before that, Newsmax settled for an undisclosed amount. DDC Judge Nichols denied OANN's motion to dismiss, based on the fact that its headquarters was in California. A DDC Magistrate Judge rejected a recusal motion based on the fact that she had briefly represented Venezuela and Maduro as a Venable LLP attorney in 2019. On April 15, 2024, the parties reached a confidential settlement.

2.2.2 Fulton County (Georgia) Election Workers Freeman and Moss

In December 2021, Fulton County, Georgia, election board employees Ruby Freeman and Wandrea "Shaye" Moss (mother and daughter), represented by Protect Democracy, sued *The Gateway Pundit* in St. Louis, Missouri, Circuit Court for defamation for accusing them of manipulating ballots.[26] On January 6, 2021, a crowd had surrounded Freeman's home, shouting at her through a bullhorn. She fled and did not return for two months. ED MO Judge Henry Edward Autrey (GWB) denied a motion to remove to federal court. In October 2023, plaintiffs' lawyers accused the defendants of delaying discovery; Circuit Court Judge Michael Stelzer had dismissed their counterclaim earlier that year. In April 2024, *The Gateway Pundit* declared bankruptcy, which founder Jim Hoft blamed on "progressive liberal lawfare attacks" intended to "silence" his company, explaining that he was just using "a common tool for reorganization and to consolidate litigation when attacks are coming from all sides" and would continue to publish during bankruptcy. But after a federal judge in Florida dismissed the bankruptcy petition, finding it had been brought in "bad faith to avoid defamation damages," the defendant admitted that an inquiry had cleared the plaintiffs of voting fraud, and the parties settled without disclosing their terms.

The two election workers also sued OAN and Giuliani in DDC. OAN settled in May 2022, tweeting a broadcast stating that Georgia officials "have concluded that there was no widespread voter fraud by election workers" and the plaintiffs "did not engage in ballot fraud or criminal misconduct." In July 2023, Giuliani admitted in court papers that his statements "carry meaning that is defamatory per se" and were "actionable" and "false," and he no longer disputed the "factual elements of liability." He made those concessions "to avoid unnecessary expenses in litigating what he believes to be unnecessary disputes" and so he could move to dismiss. But he still maintained his statements were "constitutionally protected" and plaintiffs had suffered no damage. DDC Judge Howell (Obama) entered summary judgment, finding Giuliani liable for defamation, intentional infliction of emotional distress, civil conspiracy, and punitive damages and declaring that his reasoning had "more holes than Swiss cheese." She rebuked him for suddenly requesting a bench trial, calling the switch "simply nonsense." She accused him of paying mere "lip service" to discovery "by failing to take reasonable steps to preserve or produce information." His claim of victimhood "thwarted" the plaintiffs' procedural rights to obtain any meaningful discovery. "Donning a cloak of victimization may play well on a public stage to certain audiences, but in a court of law this performance has served only to subvert the normal process of discovery in a straightforward defamation case." She ordered him to pay the plaintiffs $90,000 in legal fees. When he missed a final hearing in defiance of her order, Howell rebuked his lawyer: "it sets the tone, doesn't it, for the whole case." Ted Goodman, a representative for Giuliani, denounced the trial as the "weaponization of our justice system."

During the damages phase, Moss testified that the day after Giuliani's tweet she cried as she read messages calling her a "dirty fucking nigger bitch." She cut and dyed her hair to avoid recognition. She had to quit the job she loved after being diagnosed with acute stress disorder and major depressive disorder. Her 14-year-old son was subjected to racist texts and phone calls and failed all his finals that semester. Her grandmother, with whom she lived, was gaslighted with unsolicited pizza deliveries for which she had to pay. Texts, voicemails, and emails accused Moss of treason. "They kept telling me it was punishable by death and they could hang me and they could hang my mom." After the trial's first day, Giuliani told reporters: "Everything I said about them is true. Of course I don't regret it. . . . They were engaged in changing votes." The next day Howell warned that such comments could support another defamation claim. Giuliani's lawyer explained that the case had taken "a toll" on his client, who was almost 80, and the $47 million claimed "will be the end of Mr. Giuliani—a civil death penalty." Howell dismissed that as "hyperbolic."

After deliberating just eight hours, the jury awarded $148 million in damages, giving each plaintiff about $16 million for damage to reputation and $10 million for emotional distress and the two collectively $75 million in punitive damages. Giuliani expostulated: "the absurdity of the number underscores the absurdity of the entire proceeding." "I don't regret a damn thing." Moss said: "our greatest wish is that no election worker or voter or school board member or anyone else ever experiences anything like what we went through."

After the verdict, Giuliani complained he had been unable to present evidence of "all the videos at the time" showing "what happened at that arena." The plaintiffs responded by suing him again, seeking a "targeted injunction" to stop such repetitions. They also asked the judge to let them enforce the judgment immediately rather than grant Giuliani the automatic 30-day stay because he had not paid the penalties she imposed. Howell agreed. "Giuliani has never denied that he has taken steps to hide his assets from judgment creditors, and has offered no affirmative pledge that he will take no steps to do so." Claims of penury "are difficult to square with the fact that Giuliani affords a spokesperson, who accompanied him daily to trial." He "simply ignored" her orders to produce information "without . . . making any excuse." There was an "ample record in this case of Giuliani's efforts to conceal or hide his assets." Given what jurors had heard about his "past and continuing—including up to and during trial—defamation" of the plaintiffs, the judgment was "conservative." Giuliani filed for Chapter 11 bankruptcy, listing debts of nearly $500 million and assets of just $10 million. (Damages for intentional torts and most punitive damages are not dischargeable in bankruptcy.) He called Howell "hopelessly biased." "The amount, $148 million, is so irrational it tells you the trial was irrational because the result is the result of a completely unfair trial." Robert J. Costello's law firm sued Giuliani, claiming he owed it more than $1.3 million in legal fees. In June, creditors asked the judge overseeing his bankruptcy to appoint an independent trustee because of Giuliani's failure to comply with routine filings. SDNY Bankruptcy Court Judge Sean H. Lane agreed "there are reasons to be very concerned here." The US Trustee representative said the government was prepared to move to dismiss the case, which would terminate bankruptcy protection. In July, Giuliani sought to convert his Chapter 11 bankruptcy to Chapter 7, putting an independent trustee in charge of his assets but letting him keep all future income. After Giuliani moved to dismiss his bankruptcy, Judge Lane did so on July 12, 2023: "The record in this case reflects Mr. Giuliani's continued failure to meet his reporting obligations and provide the financial transparency required of a debtor in possession." In May 2024, Giuliani agreed in bankruptcy court to stop repeating that the plaintiffs "engaged in wrongdoing" in the 2020 election. Their lawyer said: "today ends [Giuliani's] efforts to profit off lies about these two heroes of American democracy." If the order were made permanent, his clients would drop their second lawsuit. He settled the bankruptcy case by giving his lawyers $100,000 to help pay the creditors' financial adviser and paying the rest of the $350,000 by selling his New York apartment or Florida condominium. Freeman and Moss could seek to enforce the $148 million judgment in DDC, and the other lawsuits against Giuliani could proceed (Dominion and Smartmatic for defamation, and Noelle Dunphy for sexual harassment and wage theft). In August Freeman and Moss sued him in SDNY for trying to exclude his Florida condominium from their debt collection efforts. Judge Lewis Liman (Trump) ordered Giuliani to surrender his New York apartment, cash, and jewelry, including a watch given by his grandfather: it "may be distinctive to defendant as an item of sentimental value, but it is not distinctive to the law." The plaintiffs also could seek $2 million in legal fees Giuliani was owed by the Trump campaign and RNC. But when they finally got access to his New York apartment on October 31 they found he had moved art, furniture, expensive watches, and his vintage Mercedes Benz convertible to Florida. At a hearing two days after the election, Judge Liman demanded to know "what can be delivered now." The defense lawyer's claim that including the watch was "vindictive" was "ridiculous." "Bodega owners have family heirlooms, and if they have a debt, they have to pay the debt." "The notion that your client doesn't have any knowledge of where his assets are located is farcical." He ordered Giuliani to comply fully within a week or face civil contempt. Afterwards, Giuliani called the case "obviously a political vendetta." His lawyers quit, citing "fundamental disagreements" with their client. The plaintiffs finally got the car, watches, and a ring. When Giuliani repeated his defamatory falsehoods in podcasts, the plaintiffs sought additional damages. On January 6, Liman found Giuliani in contempt for not cooperating in discovery about his condo. "The defendant has been attempting to run out the clock." On January 10, 2025, Judge Howell found Giuliani in contempt for repeating the defamatory falsehoods. His claim that he was being treated unfairly was "outrageous and shameful." He could only avoid punishment if he reaffirmed within ten days that they were contradicted by sworn evidence and agreed to pay the plaintiffs' attorneys fees. On the day of the contempt trial the parties settled.

Two weeks before the 2024 election, the Central Park Five, who had been accused of rape and assault in 1989 and jailed but exonerated in 2002, sued Trump in ED PA for saying falsely during his debate with Harris that they had "pled guilty" and "badly hurt a person, killed a person."[27] New York City had settled their lawsuit in 2014.

2.2.3 Trump's Retaliatory Lawsuits

Trump repeatedly sued the media for defamation, following the adage that the best defense is a good offense (perhaps recalling the advice of his mentor, Roy Cohn).[28] After Timothy L. O'Brien published *TrumpNation: The Art of Being the Donald*, Trump sued for an alleged understatement of his wealth, choosing to do so in family court in Camden, NJ. The case was dismissed, and an appellate court affirmed. Many of Trump's recent lawsuits arose out of media coverage of the Mueller investigation and Trump's first impeachment for conditioning military aid to Ukraine on an investigation of the Bidens (see Abel 2024a: Chapter 3). Trump sued CNN for an op ed by Larry Noble (former FEC general counsel) about Trump's phone call to President Zelensky. Noble had written that the Trump campaign "assessed the potential risks and benefits of again seeking Russia's help in 2020 and has decided to leave that option on the table." ND GA Judge Michael L. Brown (Trump) dismissed the lawsuit for lack of evidence of actual malice. The Trump campaign sued *The New York Times* for a March 2019 opinion piece by former executive editor Max Frankel, entitled "The Real Trump-Russia Quid Pro Quo." NY Supreme Court Justice James E. d'Auguste dismissed the case because it was "nonactionable opinion" and the campaign lacked standing and failed to show actual malice. The campaign also sued *The Washington Post* for two opinion columns. Greg Sargent's was entitled: "Trump just invited another Russian attack, Mitch McConnell is making one more likely." Paul Waldman wrote: "Who knows what sort of aid Russia and North Korea will give to the Trump campaign, now that he has invited them to offer their assistance?" In February 2023, DDC Judge Contreras (Obama) dismissed the case. The same month, Trump sued the Pulitzer Prize board in the Nineteenth Judicial Circuit Court in Okeechobee County, Florida, seeking recission of its award of the 2018 National Reporting prize jointly to *The New York Times* and *The Washington Post* for articles on alleged Russian collusion in the 2016 election. The board announced it had commissioned "two independent reviews" of the reporting, both of which concluded that the stories were not "discredited by facts that emerged subsequent to the conferral of the prizes." Trump lawyers sought to depose board members to reveal the reviewers' identity. Senior Circuit Court Judge Robert Pegg denied a motion to dismiss. Trump sued Christopher Steele and Orbis Business Intelligence in the London High Court for "personal and reputational damage and distress" from the Russia dossier. Judge Karen Steyn dismissed the case, finding it was "bound to fail," and ordered Trump to pay legal fees of £300,000 (less than half of what the lawyers claimed).

(On his last day in office, Trump declassified Steele's testimony to Mueller and gave a copy to a journalist. Steele said: "two of the named Russian sources have not been seen or heard of since.") Trump sued CNN for $475 million for accusing him of "the Big Lie," which associated him with the Nazis. SD FL Judge Raag Singhal (Trump) dismissed, finding this was not defamatory. Trump Media & Technology Group sued *The Washington Post* in Florida's Twelfth Judicial Circuit for a critical article about Truth Social. After the case was removed to federal court, MD FL Judge Tom Barber (Trump) dismissed it for failure to allege actual malice. Trump sued ABC News and George Stephanopoulos in March 2024 for saying he had been found liable for raping Carroll. (Judge Kaplan had explicitly made this finding, see Chapter 2.1.) SD FL Chief Judge Cecilia Altonaga (GWB) denied a motion to dismiss. (She had urged Cannon to decline the classified papers case, see Chapter 4.1.) Trump called it "BIG WIN" against "ABC FAKE NEWS." Trump sued CBS for "election interference," seeking $10 billion for its editing of the transcript of a Harris interview; he chose ND TX to ensure he would get Judge Kacsmaryk, whom he had appointed and who ruled against the FDA in the mifepristone case.[29]

Trump's sometime supporters adopted a similar strategy. Lachlan Murdoch sued Crikey (an Australian news source) for an opinion column accusing him and his father of falsely claiming election fraud, under the headline: "Trump is a confirmed unhinged traitor. And Murdoch is his unindicted co-conspirator."[30] Lachlan dropped the lawsuit two days after Fox News settled with Dominion, agreeing to pay $840,000 for legal fees; Crikey said it would donate the $378,000 it had raised for those costs to the Alliance for Journalists' Freedom.

Trump filed other retaliatory lawsuits. He sued his niece Mary L. Trump, *The New York Times*, and three of its reporters for the *Times* 2018 investigation of his finances and taxes (which won a Pulitzer Prize), claiming an "insidious plot."[31] NY Supreme Court Justice Robert Reed dismissed the case and ordered Trump to pay legal fees of nearly $400,000. "Courts have long recognized that reporters are entitled to engage in legal and ordinary news-gathering activities without fear of tort liability—as these actions are at the very core of protected first amendment activity."

In March 2022, Trump filed a mammoth RICO lawsuit in SD FL, seeking $70 million from 31 defendants—including Hillary Clinton, the DNC, former DNC chair Debbie Wasserman Schultz, Clinton campaign head John Podesta, Fusion GPS, Christopher Steele, and former FBI officials Andrew McCabe, Peter Strzok, and Lisa Page—for allegedly conspiring to "weave a false narrative" about his collusion with Russia during the 2016 election.[32] Alina Habba, Trump's lawyer, said: "this lawsuit seeks to hold all parties accountable for their heinous acts and uphold the principles of our sacred democracy." Judge Middlebrooks (Clinton) denied a motion to recuse: "something more must be involved than solely my appointment to the bench twenty-five years ago by the spouse of a litigant now before me. And the conclusory assertions in Plaintiff's Motion do not supply any conceivable, additional grounds. I have never met or spoken with Bill or Hillary Clinton."

Less than six months later, he dismissed the case, imposing sanctions of $50,000 on each of Trump's lawyers: Habba, her partner Michael T. Madaio (whose New Jersey firm had just one other lawyer, an associate), and Peter Ticktin and Jamie Alan Sasson (members of a seven-lawyer Florida firm that advertised it was "known for taking cases that don't fall squarely within conventional boundaries"). Middlebrooks said Trump was merely "seeking to flaunt a two-hundred-page political manifesto outlining his grievances against those who have opposed him." His claims "are not only unsupported by any legal authority but plainly foreclosed by binding precedent." "Many of the Amended Complaint's characterizations of events are implausible because they lack any specific allegations which might provide factual support for the conclusions reached." "What the Amended Complaint lacks in substance and legal support it seeks to substitute with length, hyperbole, and the settling of scores and grievances." The allegations that Hillary Clinton and James Comey conspired to take down Trump were "implausible" and "categorically absurd," "a hodgepodge of disconnected, often immaterial events, followed by an implausible conclusion." "This is a deliberate attempt to harass; to tell a story without regard to facts." "Most of plaintiff's claims are not only unsupported by any legal authority but plainly foreclosed by binding precedent." Habba said Trump would appeal a judgment "rife with erroneous applications of the law," which ignored "numerous governmental investigations which substantiate" his claims. (He did not.) In January 2023, Judge Middlebrooks imposed sanctions of nearly $1 million on Trump and Habba, finding a "pattern of abuse of the courts." Filing lawsuits for political purposes "amounts to obstruction of justice," "undermines the rule of law, portrays the judge as partisan and diverts resources from those who have suffered actual legal harm." The lawsuit "should never have been brought." It was "completely frivolous, both factually and legally, and . . . brought in bad faith for an improper purpose." "Its inadequacy as a legal claim was evident from the start. No reasonable lawyer would have filed it. Intended for a political purpose, none of the counts of the amended complaint stated a cognizable claim." "Mr Trump is a prolific and sophisticated litigant who is repeatedly using the courts to seek revenge on political adversaries." "He is the mastermind of strategic abuse of the judicial process, and he cannot be seen as a litigant blindly following the advice of a lawyer. He knew full well the impact of his actions." The case had been "brought in bad faith for an improper purpose" and "needlessly harmed" the defendants to "dishonestly advance a political narrative." "Frivolous lawsuits should not be used as a vehicle for fundraising or fodder for rallies or social media. Mr. Trump is using the courts as a stage set for political theater and grievance." Trump appealed the sanctions.

In August 2024, the day before the statute of limitations expired, Trump filed an administrative claim against the DoJ for the Mar-a-Lago search, claiming $15 million compensatory and $100 million punitive damages.[33] He could not sue until the DoJ responded or 180 days expired.

After Trump sued George Stephanopoulos and ABC for saying he had raped E. Jean Carroll, the network issued a statement of "regret" and settled for $15 million, even though Judge Kaplan declared: "the evidence at trial . . . makes clear" that "the jury found that Mr. Trump in fact did exactly that," i.e. raped Carroll.[34] Trump also sued the *Des Moines Register* for publishing a pre-election poll with erroneous numbers.

These cases reveal the complexities of using civil litigation to resist autocracy. Victims won most of their lawsuits (Sandy Hook families, Dominion, Smartmatic, Coomer, Grossberg, Freeman, Moss); autocrats lost most of theirs (Trump, Alex Jones, Powell, Lindell, Byrne, Giuliani, Oltmann, Newsmax, Fox, OANN, *Gateway Pundit*).[35] Like Carroll's judgment, some of these were huge: nearly $1.5 billion against Jones, nearly three-quarters of a billion against Fox, nearly $150 million against Giuliani. But defendants (Jones, Giuliani, *Gateway Pundit*) tried to use strategic bankruptcies to evade paying. And Trump and some of his supporters simply doubled down on their false claims (Giuliani, Lindell, Powell) and attacked the legal system (Oltmann, Giuliani, Viet Dinh), undeterred by fear of further liability. Media companies settled and distanced themselves from the journalists responsible (Carlson and Dobbs—who just moved to other outlets). Settlements (and the defamation cases themselves) prompted shareholder derivative actions. Judges (including those appointed by Trump, like Nichols, Kelly, Brown, and Barber) treated defendants harshly and dismissed Trump's retaliatory actions. Many of the lawyers who were themselves defendants or represented Trump and his supporters seemed incompetent. Stefanie Lambert had been charged with criminal conduct in Michigan and believed in conspiracy theories. Giuliani admitted not verifying facts alleged in his complaints. Powell said her hyperbole should not have been believed. Habba (practicing with just one partner and an associate) was repeatedly hit with sanctions. Trump kept filing defamation actions in which his lawyers offered no evidence of actual malice. (Trump has declared the Supreme Court should overturn *New York Times v. Sullivan*, which held that the First Amendment required such a finding in lawsuits by public figures.[36] Justices Thomas and Gorsuch have supported this.) He was ordered to pay nearly $1 million in sanctions in Florida and £300,000 in England. Reputable firms withdrew because they had not been paid or were unwilling to file frivolous lawsuits. The legal system performed the way it should, undistorted by politics.

2.3 James v. Trump

In a February 2019 hearing of the House Oversight and Government Reform Committee, Rep. Ocasio-Cortez asked Michael Cohen if Trump, his client, had ever inflated the value of his properties in obtaining insurance.[37] Cohen replied: "Trump inflated his total assets when it served his purposes . . . and deflated his assets to reduce his real estate taxes." In July 2020, Allen Weisselberg (TO CFO) lied in a deposition about the size of Trump's triplex. (He pleaded guilty four years later.) A month later, New York Attorney General Letitia James sued TO, Eric Trump, and others in NY Supreme Court and asked Justice Arthur Engoron to compel the defendants to comply with subpoenas. But when Eric was deposed, he invoked the Fifth Amendment more than 500 times.

In May 2021, James joined Manhattan DA Alvin Bragg in investigating Trump, TO, and its officers. Jeffrey McConney (TO controller) told a grand jury (implausibly) he did not know that fringe benefits should be reported as income.[38] In June, Jennifer Weisselberg (the estranged ex-wife of Barry Weisselberg, Allen's son) told investigators she saw Trump discuss fringe benefits with both men. On July 1, the Attorney General's office charged TO and Weisselberg with grand larceny and offering a false instrument for filing. A week later TO removed Weisselberg as director of many of its subsidiaries. On December 1, James subpoenaed Trump, Ivanka, and Don Jr. On December 20, Trump's lawyer Alina Habba sued James in NDNY, seeking to block her investigation by alleging a violation of Trump's civil rights. In May 2022, NDNY Judge Brenda K. Sannes (Obama) dismissed the challenge. Habba sought review in the Second Circuit but withdrew the appeal in January 2023 "for strategic purposes." (She had just been ordered to pay sanctions of nearly $1 million for a frivolous lawsuit in Florida and had withdrawn another lawsuit there, see 5.2.3.)

At a political rally on January 15, 2022, Trump screened clips of James calling him an "illegitimate president" and attacked her as an "unhinged liberal." He made an ominous threat: "Keep our prosecutors out of politics because this could work very much in the other direction."[39] Two weeks later he said about James and Fani Willis (another Black woman, who was prosecuting him, in Georgia, see Chapter 3.2): "If these radical, vicious, racist prosecutors do anything wrong or illegal, I hope we are going to have in this country the biggest protest we have ever had." On February 1, Trump lawyers moved to quash the subpoenas, alleging political animus. Habba accused James of engaging in "prosecutorial misconduct that this nation has never seen." But Justice Engoron replied that

Trump might be "just a bad guy [James] should go after as the chief law enforcement officer of the state." Once Michael Cohen had testified that TO was "cooking the books," it would have been a "dereliction of duty" not to investigate. "There's no viewpoint discrimination." When Habba claimed Trump was a member of a "protected class" the judge asked sarcastically: "what protected class is he a member of?" and ordered the defendants to comply with the subpoenas. The Trumps appealed, but the Appellate Division affirmed. The Trumps appealed again, but the Court of Appeals dismissed. In April, Engoron held Trump in contempt for failing to comply with an order to produce documents, fining him $10,000 for each day he persisted—$110,000 before he complied. Trump appealed, but the Appellate Division affirmed.

In August 2022, Weisselberg pleaded to 15 felonies and agreed to testify against TO in exchange for five months in prison, five years of probation, and nearly $2 million in back taxes, interest, and penalties.[40] TO refused to plead. McConney testified that he had deducted fringe benefits from gross salaries to lower tax payments. Weisselberg admitted that "I committed [the tax-fraud] crimes with Jeffrey McConney [whom] I dealt with directly [as well as the] Trump corporation and Trump Payroll Corporation." In December, Justice Merchan held TO in contempt for failure to comply with grand jury subpoenas and court orders, fining it $4,000. (Merchan presided in the Stormy Daniels prosecution, see Chapter 3.1.) On December 6, the jury convicted TO of all 17 charges. On January 13, 2023, Merchan imposed the maximum fine of $1.6 million ($1 million plus interest) and permanently banned Weisselberg from any financial position in a New York company.

In September 2022, James filed a lawsuit in NY Supreme Court against Trump, his three adult children, and TO for civil fraud.[41] The next month Trump sued in Florida's Fifteenth Judicial Circuit Court, invoking state constitutional privacy rights to bar James from obtaining his financial records and accusing her of waging a "war of intimation and harassment" to "steal, destroy or control all things Trump." He blustered: "Crooked and highly partisan James now thinks it is the business of the State of New York to go after my revocable trust and pry into my private estate plan." TO General Counsel Alan Garten criticized Trump lawyer Boris Epshteyn and the three Florida lawyers who filed the suit. Another Trump lawyer, Christopher Kise (a former Florida solicitor general), also objected. After the case was removed to federal court, James moved to dismiss. SD FL Judge Middlebrooks (Clinton) denied Trump's motion for a preliminary injunction, warning that "this litigation has all the telltale signs of being both vexatious and frivolous." Trump withdrew the action less than a month later—a day after Middlebrooks fined Trump and Habba almost $1 million for his frivolous suit against Hillary Clinton and others (see Chapter 2.2.3).

In November, Engoron scheduled trial for October 2, 2023.[42] He expressed skepticism about a motion to dismiss filed that day, which repeated arguments he had rejected when imposing a financial monitor: "the facts are the same. The law is the same. The parties are the same." Habba objected that "we're in a predetermined situation where you're going to rule against us" and accused the judge of displaying a "clear bias against our client. You have for a year and a half, it is unfair." Engoron denied the motion in January, finding that some of the arguments were "frivolous" and had been "borderline frivolous even the first time defendants made them." "This court (and at least two others) has soundly rejected the 'witch hunt' argument." "Reading these arguments was, to quote the baseball sage Lawrence Peter ('Yogi') Berra, 'Déjà vu all over again.'" "Sophisticated defense counsel should have known better. In its discretion, this Court will not impose sanctions, which the Court believes are unnecessary, having made its point." Engoron rejected a defense request to delay the trial by six months, having vowed earlier the date would not change "come hell or high water."

In his April 2023 deposition, Trump invoked the Fifth Amendment in response to every question—more than 400 times.[43] He said flippantly: "appraisers are right and wrong. Everybody knows that." "You use common sense. You use some other things. You know, people come up with numbers." He had claimed a net worth "in excess of TEN BILLION DOLLARS" in a 2015 campaign disclosure form, even though his financial statement showed less than $4 billion. That year he bragged to a *Forbes* journalist that he had inflated his wealth because "it was good for financing." In this trial, McConney said Weisselberg and he steeply inflated values for the company using fake methods. TO valued Trump Park Avenue condos at $50 million in 2011 and 2012 and then nearly $136 million in 2020, even though they were rent-stabilized and could not be sold as regular condos. Mazars USA accountant Donald Bender testified that he compiled Trump's annual statements of net worth without verifying the figures, simply accepting those provided by McConney and Weisselberg. Bender's cover letter declared that the values had not been verified. Trump triumphantly invoked this: "I have a clause in there that says, don't believe the statement, go out and do your own work." After a *Forbes* 2017 article said: "Donald Trump has been lying about the size of his penthouse," he dropped its value from $327 million in 2016 to $116.8 million in 2017.

The Appellate Division unanimously dismissed the claim against Ivanka because she was not part of TO after 2016 (when she joined the Trump administration) but denied the other defendants' motions to dismiss.[44] Trump brought an Article 78 proceeding, challenging James and Engoron, and asked the Appellate Division to pause the civil fraud trial while it considered this request. First Department Justice David Friedman granted the stay; but a full panel of five judges rejected it, as did the Court of Appeals. Trump later withdrew the proceeding.

On September 26, Engoron rendered a partial summary judgment on liability, finding Trump had committed fraud. The judge ordered cancellation of Trump's business certificates and told the parties to propose receivers for properties within the state.[45] (Appellate Division Justice Peter H. Moulton preserved Trump's business certificates pending a final judgment. James's office did not object.) Engoron also sanctioned Trump's five lawyers for repeating arguments that were "borderline frivolous," ordering each to pay $7,500. "Defendants' conduct in repeating these frivolous arguments is egregious. The defenses Donald Trump attempts to articulate in his sworn deposition are wholly without basis in law or fact." "In Donald Trump's world, rent-regulated apartments are worth the same as unregulated apartments, restricted land is worth the same as unrestricted land; restrictions can evaporate into thin air. That is a fantasy world, not the real world." The defendant had claimed his Trump Tower triplex was 30,000 square feet rather than the actual 11,000: "a discrepancy of this order of magnitude, by a real estate developer sizing up his own living space of decades, can only be considered fraud." James commented: "for years, Donald Trump falsely inflated his net worth to enrich himself and cheat the system. No matter how rich or powerful you are, there are not two sets of laws for people in this country." Trump's lawyer Christopher Kise denounced the decision as "outrageous" and "completely disconnected from the facts and governing law." "Without even conducting a trial, the Court substituted its own judgment for that of nationally recognized experts from the NYU Stern School of Business and beyond." "Everyone has a different opinion as to valuation." "Trump made many billions of dollars being right about real estate investments. His is one of the most successful brands in the world." Trump called Engoron a "deranged" Democrat and protested: "there is no crime. The crime is against me."

During the penalty phase, Engoron criticized Trump's sons as "obstreperous" and dismissed their arguments as "bogus."[46] He told a Trump lawyer: "you cannot make false statements and use them in business." During a lunch break Trump denounced "a disgraceful trial put forward by an Attorney General who is corrupt," "a total crook, a terrible person." It was "a pure witch hunt with the purpose of interfering with the elections of the United States of America. It is totally illegal." Murders in New York City were "an epidemic, and they waste their time on this." He denounced Engoron as "a Democratic judge from the clubhouses," a "disgrace to people that call themselves judges." He "should be disbarred" and dismissed as a "rogue" justice." Trump did not "think the people of this country are going to stand for it." Engoron's clerk, Allison Greenfield, should not be participating in the case because she "hates Trump" more than the judge did. Trump objected that the judge had valued a property worth more than $1 billion at just $18 million. "The banks . . . were very happy, they got all their money back, they weren't defrauded. I've been defrauded." In a fundraiser before the trial, he had said: "after four sham arrests, indictments, and even a mug shot failed to break me, a Democratic judge is now trying to destroy my Family Business." Don Jr. said on The *Charlie Kirk Show*: "This is sort of like the start of the Bolshevik Revolution—we don't like you, so we're going to confiscate property." "Hey, our last name is Trump, so we have to be punished." Habba asserted: "Ms. James said she was going to come into the Attorney General's office and she was going to get Trump."

Engoron issued a gag order a day after Trump attacked Greenfield by name and posted a photo of her with Sen. Schumer (a New York Democrat), calling her "Schumer's girlfriend."[47] Trump complained she was "running this case against me." The Trump campaign had called Engoron a "far-left Democrat judge." He responded: "Personal attacks on members of my court staff are unacceptable, inappropriate and I will not tolerate them under any circumstances." Trump had sent the social media post to millions. Schumer called it "ridiculous, absurd, and false." His spokesman added: "Senator Schumer does not know Ms. Greenfield." Having warned against such posts a day earlier, Engoron now said violations would lead to "serious sanctions." Trump retorted: "We are being railroaded. And I have other trials where we're being railroaded" (referring to DDC Judge Chutkan's gag order, see Chapter 4.2). "My speech has been taken away from me. I'm a candidate that's running for office and I'm not allowed to speak." Engoron fined Trump $5,000 for failing to delete his post, a "blatant violation" of the gag order. Kise claimed this had been "inadvertent" and apologized. But Engoron warned: "future violations, whether intentional or unintentional, will subject the violator to far more severe sanctions," including steeper fines, contempt and "possibly imprisoning him." "In the current overheated climate, incendiary untruths can, and in some cases already have, led to serious physical harm, and worse."

Trump denounced James as a "radical lunatic" and the Stormy Daniels trial (see Chapter 3.1) as a "railroad" "set up by Bragg and his thugs."[48] He assailed Engoron: "We have a judge that's totally out of control and he's totally afraid of Peekaboo James." (The adjective was intended to evoke the racist slur "jigaboo.") "I don't mind being Nelson Mandela because I'm doing it for a reason." (This was an outrageous misappropriation of Mandela's famous speech from the dock before being sentenced in 1964: "I have cherished the ideal of a democratic and free society in which all persons live together in harmony and with equal opportunities. It is an ideal which I hope to live for and to achieve. But if needs be, it is an ideal for which I am prepared to die." He was sentenced to life.)

Days before Michael Cohen was scheduled to testify and Trump was to be questioned under oath, the ex-president dropped a lawsuit against his former lawyer and fixer for providing evidence to Bragg in the Stormy Daniels case (see Chapter 3.1).[49] Cohen then testified before Engoron: "I was tasked by

Mr. Trump to increase the total assets based upon a number that he arbitrarily selected." Weisselberg had the responsibility to "reverse engineer the various different asset classes . . . to achieve the number that Mr. Trump had tasked us." "He would look at the total assets, say, 'I'm actually not worth [$4.5 billion], I'm really worth more like [$6 billion],'" and "then direct [Weisselberg] and I to go back to Allen's office and return after we achieved the desired goal." Cohen admitted on cross-examination that Trump had not directly told him to lie but explained how Trump made his wishes known.

During a break in the trial, Trump again attacked Engoron as partisan, "with a person who's very partisan sitting alongside him, perhaps even much more partisan than he is."[50] Afterwards, Engoron said: "I am very protective of my staff. I don't want anyone to get killed." Kise claimed Trump had been referring to Cohen (who was testifying), but Engoron replied that Trump's target clearly was Greenfield. Required to testify under oath, Trump insisted he had been talking only about Cohen. When pressed, however, he reasserted that Greenfield was "very biased against us. I think we made that clear." Engoron observed: "as the trier of fact I find that the witness is not credible" in claiming he was referring to Cohen. There was a barrier between the witness stand and the judge. Trump actually was "referring to my . . . principal law clerk, who is sitting much closer to me." Trump's testimony "rings hollow and untrue." Engoron fined him $10,000, warning: "don't do it next time, or it'll be worse." "Anyone can run for president, but I am going to protect my staff. I don't think it is impinging on someone's First Amendment rights to protect my staff." Trump's lawyer John Lauro objected: "no court in American history has imposed a gag order on a criminal defendant who is campaigning for public office—least of all, on the leading candidate for President of the United States." (This was not a criminal case, and no other presidential candidate had been a defendant in a civil fraud case.) Engoron denied a defense motion to dismiss: "No way, no how this case is going to be dismissed. There is enough evidence in this case to fill this courtroom." Trump stormed out of court and, while the trial was underway, appealed this denial.

Don Jr. testified he had no significant knowledge of generally accepted accounting principles.[51] "That's what we have CPAs for." Trump fulminated on social media: "Leave my children alone, Engoron. You are a disgrace to the legal profession!" and a "political hack."

Kise complained that communications between Engoron and his clerk created a "perception of bias."[52] He accused Greenfield of improper political contributions to Democrats (based on a story in the right-wing *Breitbart News*), laying a foundation to move for a mistrial or appeal. At the end of the day, Engoron issued a written order prohibiting lawyers from making public statements in or out of court about his private communications with Greenfield and warned that violations would result in "serious sanctions."

After Trump criticized the Attorney General's lawyers, Engoron reprimanded him: "Please just answer the questions, no speeches."[53] Trump then accused the judge of "ruling against me because he always rules against me." Engoron responded: "Mr. Trump, please just answer the question. You can attack me. Do whatever you want. Just answer the question." He directed Kise to "have a talk" with Trump, asking: "can you control your client? This is not a political rally. This is a courtroom." Kise replied that the "former and again soon-to-be commander in chief" understood the rules and needed no instruction. Engoron retorted: "He doesn't abide by them." He reprimanded Trump numerous times and declared "stricken" when Trump went off point. When Engoron refused to let Trump read from a piece of paper, the defendant feigned horror: "I'm shocked."

Before the hearing, James had predicted: "Trump will engage in name-calling and taunts and race-baiting and call this a witch hunt." The defendant followed that script, calling the case politically motivated and James a "racist Attorney General." Trump's campaign claimed he had not realized the gag order had been reimposed when he assailed former Attorney General Barr as "dumb," "weak," and "gutless," but that post remained up 2.5 days later. Trump complained that Engoron "ruled against me and said I was a fraud before he knew anything about me. The fraud is on the court, not on me." When Kise asked that Trump have more leeway in speaking, Engoron ordered defense lawyers to sit down. He threatened to excuse Trump as a witness and "draw every negative inference that I can" from his testimony. Soon thereafter Trump said: "This is a very unfair trial. Very, very. And I hope the public is watching." When he objected to Engoron's earlier ruling, the judge advised him to "read my opinion again" or "for the first time, perhaps." Trump retorted contemptuously: "You're wrong in the opinion." Afterwards, Trump dismissed the case as a "scam." "Everything we did was absolutely right." "You believe this political hack back there?" It was a "very unfair" and "crazy trial." "The fraud is on the court, not me."

Rep. Stefanik filed a complaint with the Judicial Conduct Committee, accusing Engoron of "inappropriate bias and judicial intemperance in New York's disgraceful lawsuit."[54] Kise had also alleged bias after the judge said: "I object now and I continue to object, to your constant insinuations that I have some sort of double standard here. That is just not true. I just make the rulings as I see them." Trump's lawyers moved for a mistrial. "The evidence of apparent and actual bias is tangible and overwhelming. Such evidence, coupled with an unprecedented departure from standard judicial procedure has tainted these proceedings." The evidence included articles Engoron wrote about the case in his high school alumni newsletter and political donations by Greenfield (lawful because she was campaigning for a judgeship). A spokesman for the New York court system said Engoron's "actions and rulings in this matter are all part of the public record and speak for themselves."

Appellate Division Justice David Friedman temporarily suspended Engoron's gag order.[55] Trump immediately posted on Truth Social:

> His Ridiculous and Unconstitutional Gag Order, not allowing me to defend myself against him and his politically biased and out of control Trump Hating Clerk, who is sinking him and his Court to new levels of LOW, is a disgrace.

Jason Miller (a former senior Trump adviser) called Greenfield a "Democrat operative." Habba complained that she "is in the judge's ear time and time again. If she had a real threat, she should get off the bench." A five-judge Appellate Division panel reinstated the gag order, and the Court of Appeals dismissed Trump's appeal, finding "no substantial constitutional question." Trump had just called Greenfield "disturbed and angry." Engoron told Trump's lawyers: "I intend to enforce the gag orders rigorously and vigorously." The court security officers reported that Greenfield was getting 20–30 angry phone calls a day, some anti-Semitic. Kise called the gag order a "tragic day for the rule of law . . . president Trump may not even comment on why he thinks he cannot get a fair trial." Reposting a far-right activist's claim that Engoron's wife had written negative stories about him on X, Trump said on Truth Social: "Another from Judge Engorons Wife, who is almost out of control as he is [sic]. How low can you get?" "This is the Judge's Wife saying this, and many things much worse. At what point do High Court Officials step in, and end this Witch Hunt? Judge Engoron is making fools of the New York State Judicial System!" But Engoron's wife did not have an account on X and could not have posted there. Trump also reposted: "NASTY racist Letitia James is a DESPICABLE HUMAN BEING and Judge Engoron is an absolutely PATHETIC CIRCUS CLOWN! These two moronic idiots are the very reason the courts in New York are a joke and a national disgrace! ELECTION INTEFERENCE!!!"

Engoron denied the mistrial motion.[56] The defense arguments were "utterly without merit." References to Greenfield's political donations were a "red herring." "My rulings are mine and mine alone. There is absolutely no 'co-judging' at play. That I may consult on the trial record, the law, and the facts before issuing any respective ruling is within my absolute discretion." "My principal law clerk does not make rulings or issue orders. I do."

TO Controller McConney testified he thought Eric should review his father's 2021 statement of financial condition.[57] McConney had overestimated the value of Trump's penthouse by more than $100 million because he relied on the TO broker, who reported it was 30,000 square feet. "I figured he knew the property a lot better than I did." Mar-a-Lago was valued at over $500 million because it was declared saleable as a private residence; but Trump had signed a 2002 deed with the National Trust for Historic

Preservation limiting it to a club so the Palm Beach county assessor would value it at less than $28 million, greatly reducing Trump's tax burden. McConney had written on a draft of Trump's 2014 net worth statement: "DJT TO GET FINAL REVIEW." Asked about this, the controller confirmed: "That was my understanding, yes," adding that would have been true for every financial statement until Trump entered the White House in 2017. Mc-Conney's handwriting was all over the drafts, showing he had revised them before giving them to Trump.

Eli Bartov, an NYU Stern Business School accounting professor, testified "there is no evidence whatsoever for any accounting fraud."[58] He dismissed the gross over-estimate of Trump's triplex: "errors like that are not unusual." Engoron expressed skepticism: "Bartov is a tenured professor, but all that his testimony proves is that for a million or so dollars, some experts will say whatever you want them to say." The judge denied the defense motion for a directed verdict, whose "most glaring flaw" was the assumption that expert testimony "is true and accurate, or at least that the Court, as the trier of fact, will accept it as true and accurate." Bartov's "overarching point" was the claim that the financial statements "were accurate in every respect." But Engoron already had found "numerous obvious errors." "By doggedly attempting to justify every misstatement, Professor Bartov lost all credibility." Engoron had already denied five such motions. Trump complained on Truth Social: "Judge Engoron challenges the highly respected Expert Witness for receiving fees, which is standard and accepted practice for Expert witnesses. The ignorant Judge did not even try to listen to the Expert Witness. This is a great insult to a man of impeccable character and qualifications." Bartov was paid $1,350/hour for 650 hours, a total of $877,500, but said he charged the same rate in other cases, claimed to be "very efficient" with his time, and insisted "the fee played no role" in his testimony.

At the end of the defense case Trump changed his mind and chose not to testify: "this is a complete & total election interference (Biden campaign!) witch hunt."[59] He had testified in the guilt phase "very successful and conclusively [sic]." "The judge, Arthur Engoron, put a GAG ORDER on me, even when I testify, totally taking away my constitutional right to defend myself. We are appealing, but how would you like to be a witness and not be allowed free snd [sic] honest speech." (The gag order did not apply to testimony.) Kise sneered: "there is really nothing more to say to a judge who has imposed an unconstitutional gag order and thus far appears to have ignored President Trump's testimony and that of everyone else involved in the complex financial transactions at issue in the case."

Trump ranted on Truth Social:

> Remember, the corrupt and radical Judge Engoron is a political hack who wouldn't give us a Jury, wouldn't let this "case" go to the Commercial

> Division, where it belongs (would have been TERMINATED), incredibly ignored the Appellate Court decision that struck down almost 90% of this fake lawsuit based on Statute of Limitations, etc., and, illegally and Unconstitutionally Gagged me and my lawyers, in a brazen and blatant attempt to prevent us from bringing vital information to the Public and the Courts. The Racist Attorney General, and the Runaway Judge, are causing grave damage to our Justice System, to New York State, and to the United States of America! They attempted to use a disgusting and unfair Statute, which has never been used for this purpose. I am not allowed a jury, and they have, essentially, taken away my Rights. It is a Rigged Court in a Rigged New York State System, with Fraud committed by the Attorney General and Judge in purposefully undervaluing.

(Trump's lawyers never requested a jury; the statute of limitations applied only to Ivanka.)

On the day of closing arguments (right after the aforementioned screed) there was a bomb threat at the judge's home.[60] Trump accused Engoron of trying to "screw me" after the judge directed him to follow the rules and refrain from a "campaign speech." Kise denounced those conditions as unacceptable. When Trump took the stand shortly before the lunch break, Engoron asked if he would stick to the legal issues. The defendant replied defiantly: "What's happened here sir, is a fraud on me. If I'm not allowed to talk about [political motivation]—it really is a disservice. I would say that's a big part of the case. I would say it's 100 percent." Engoron instructed Kise: "please control your client." But the lawyer remained mute. Trump attacked James and reasserted he had been denied a jury trial. When Engoron gave him a minute to sum up, Trump retorted: "I know this is boring to you. You have your own agenda. You can't listen for more than one minute." After Trump maintained he had never been in trouble with banks, Engoron asked sarcastically: "haven't you been sued before?" Trump said: "I should have won it every time." "Your honor, look. I did nothing wrong. They should pay me for what we've had to go through."

Former SDNY Judge Barbara Jones (Clinton), whom Engoron had appointed monitor with the agreement of both parties, found many errors in the TO financial statements, which "may reflect a lack of adequate internal controls."[61] Trump's lawyer Clifford S. Roberts said to Engoron: "the monitor now twists immaterial accounting items into a narrative favoring her continued appointment . . . and thereby the continued receipt of millions of dollars in excessive fees." She had already been paid more than $2.6 million.

Rendering judgment, Engoron ordered that Trump pay $354 million and not serve as an officer or director of a New York company for three years.[62] The New York County Clerk added $99 million in interest (which would continue to accumulate until the judgment was paid or an appeal filed).

Engoron ordered Donald Jr. and Eric each to pay $4 million and imposed a similar ban for two years. He barred some TO units from seeking loans from New York financial institutions for three years. But he vacated an earlier order (stayed on appeal) canceling all Trump business "certificates" in the state. He ordered Weisselberg, whom he called "intentionally evasive," to pay $1 million. He asked Jones to appoint an independent director of compliance to report to her. Engoron was scathing about all three Trumps: "their complete lack of contrition and remorse border [sic] on the pathological." "Defendants are incapable of admitting the error of their ways. Instead, they adopt a 'See no evil, hear no evil, speak no evil' posture that the evidence belies." "Donald Trump rarely responded to the questions asked, and he frequently interjected long, irrelevant speeches on issues far beyond the scope of the trial. His refusal to answer the questions directly, or in some cases, at all, severely compromised his credibility."

> Another great red herring in this case has been that different appraisers can legitimately and in good faith appraise the same property at different amounts. True enough, as appraising is an art as well as a science. However, the science part cannot be fraudulent. When two appraisals rely on starkly different assumptions, that is not evidence of a difference of opinion, that is evidence of deceit.

Trump denounced the "outrageous" penalty, which was "based on nothing other than having built a GREAT COMPANY." He accused James of having "campaigned on the fact that 'I will get Trump, I will get Trump.'" Habba called the judgment

> manifest injustice—plain and simple. It is the culmination of a multiyear, politically fueled witch hunt that was designed to "take down Donald Trump" before Letitia James ever stepped [sic] foot into the Attorney Generals [sic] office. Countless hours of testimony proved that there was no wrongdoing, no crime, and no victim.

Kise condemned the "draconian and unconstitutional" penalty, warning it "will cause irreparable damage to both the business community and the rule of law in our country." James replied: "there cannot be different rules for different people in this country, and former presidents are no exception."

Trump declared the judgment "all comes out of Biden" and accused Engoron of corruption.[63] A GoFundMe appeal for legal fees raised $415,462. He ranted at a Michigan rally: "the judge is a lunatic" and "our court system is a mess. What's happening in our country, they have to straighten it out. All you see is bitterness and revenge and hatred. Judge Engoron just fined me $355 million for doing everything right." "These repulsive abuses of power are not just an attack on me, they're really an attack on you and all Americans. We're all in this mess together." The decision was a "lawless and unconstitutional atrocity that sets fire to our laws like no one has ever seen in this country before." He assailed "CROOKED, Radical Left Politicians, Prosecutors and Judges leading us down a path to destruction." "Open Borders, Rigged Elections, and Grossly Unfair Courtroom Decisions" had made us a "nation in decline, a failing nation." Trump said: "The sudden death of Alexei Navalny has made me more and more aware of what is happening in our Country." (Trump never criticized Putin during the years he persecuted, poisoned, and jailed Navalny.) He told Laura Ingraham on Fox News Town Hall that the judgment was "a form of Navalny. It's happening in our country too. We are turning into a communist country in many ways. I got indicted four times, I have eight or nine trials. All because of the fact that I'm in . . . politics." Newt Gingrich echoed this on X: "Watch the Biden administration speak out against Putin and his jailing of his leading political opponent while Democrats in four different jurisdictions try to turn President Trump into an American Navalny." James and Engoron received letters containing white powder (which turned out to be harmless).

Trump's lawyers sought to propose a counter-judgment, but Engoron declined to schedule a conference because the Attorney General's proposal was identical to his own.[64] The judge also refused to delay enforcement: "you have failed to explain, much less justify, any basis for a stay." Appellate Division Justice Anil C. Singh denied Trump's request to post $100 million or delay payment, but he let Trump's sons remain at TO and stayed the ban on it seeking loans in New York. The judgment would be reviewed by a panel of five judges, but James felt Trump was "exceedingly unlikely to succeed on the merits."

Weisselberg pleaded guilty to felony perjury for lying in the earlier case against him and TO.[65] When he left the company in 2023, he got a $2 million severance package barring cooperation with law enforcement except under judicial order. He had already spent 100 days in Rikers Island prison. Prosecutors now sought another five months. Engoron had found in his judgment that Weisselberg's "testimony in this trial was intentionally evasive, with large gaps of 'I don't remember.'" The severance agreement "renders his testimony highly unreliable." "The Trump Organization keeps Weisselberg on a short leash. And it shows." Engoron asked Trump's lawyers "whether Mr. Weisselberg is now changing his tune, and whether he is admitting he lied under oath in my courtroom at this trial." "I do not want to ignore anything in a case of this magnitude." He suggested the plea negotiations might lead him to eliminate Weisselberg's testimony in Trump's case. Justice Merchan sentenced him to five months, but he was released after 100 days with credit for good behavior.

On Valentine's Day (immediately after the verdict), James posted on X: "roses are red and violets are blue. No one is above the law, even when you think the rules don't apply to you."[66] A week after the judgment she posted: "$464,576,230.62" and said she looked "at 40 Wall Street [one of Trump's premier properties] each and every day" as she walked to her office. During her 2018 victory speech in the Attorney General's race, she had called Trump "an affront to all that I believe in" and "someone who we must keep in check by the long arm of the law." "I will be shining a bright light into every dark corner of his real estate dealings, and every dealing demanding truthfulness at every turn." Rep. Stefanik complained to the N.Y. Appellate Division that James engaged in a "personal vendetta" against Trump. During the trial, and in defiance of the gag order, Trump had said of James on Truth Social: "Bats . . . crazy (AND Racist!)" "Evil, and Corrupt." "WORST ATTORNEY GENERAL IN THE UNITED STATES."

Trump boasted on Truth Social: "I CURRENTLY HAVE ALMOST FIVE HUNDRED MILLION DOLLARS IN CASH, A SUBSTANTIAL AMOUNT OF WHICH I INTENDED TO USE IN MY CAMPAIGN FOR PRESIDENT."[67] (The Bloomberg billionaires index estimated his net worth at $3.1 billion, including $600 million in cash. But Trump did not spend his own money on campaigning.) He claimed Engoron knew this fact, which prompted the high appeal bond (but the law required the bond to cover the judgment). Trump's lawyers reported he could not obtain an appeal bond. They used four brokers to approach 30 surety companies, but none accepted real estate as collateral. They introduced evidence from Gary Glulietti, a Trump insurance broker, who had been "scouring the market" for a bond for several weeks. "Simply put, a bond of this size is rarely if ever, seen." Glulietti sometimes dined and golfed with Trump. When he testified in the trial, Engoron observed critically that he had never encountered an expert witness who "not only was a close personal friend of a party, but also had a personal financial interest in the outcome of the case." Trump's lawyers petitioned to seek review in the Court of Appeals if a full Appellate Division panel declined to stay the judgment. Trump spokesman Steven Cheung assailed

> the unjust, unconstitutional, un-American judgment from New York Judge Arthur Engoron in a political Witch Hunt brought by a corrupt Attorney General. A bond of this size would be an abuse of the law, contradict bedrock principals [sic] of our Republic, and fundamentally undermine the rule of law in New York.

A five-judge Appellate Division panel reduced the appeal bond to $175 million.[68] But Trump had to obtain it in ten days, or the requirement would return to the full amount. Trump said he would "abide by the decision . . . and post either a bond, equivalent securities, or cash . . . very quickly, within the 10 days." He thanked the panel for a decision that had "shattered" the credibility of James and Engoron and again called the judge "a disgrace." The panel also eliminated the ban on Trump's sons working for a New York corporation and on Trump borrowing from a New York lender but did not block the appointment of a director of compliance. In a campaign fund-raising pitch, Trump said James "wants to SEIZE my properties in New York. THIS INCLUDES THE ICONIC TRUMP TOWER." "***KEEP YOUR FILTHY HANDS OFF TRUMP TOWER.***" "Our movement started on the golden escalator in Trump Tower! Now Democrats want to seize it." "Trump Tower is mine!" "I greatly respect the [Appellate Division] decision." "I have a lot of cash" but would "like to be able to use some of my cash to get elected."

On the day of the deadline, Trump posted the $175 million bond (but interest on the judgment would keep accruing by about $100,000 a day).[69] He obtained it from a subsidiary of Knight Insurance, a company associated with California billionaire and Trump supporter Donald Hankey. Trump complained on Truth Social: "I had to pay New York State in order to appeal a corrupt decision by a biased, crooked and highly overturned judge." The next day he lied at a Wisconsin rally: "I won the case because it's called statute of limitations. The Appellate Division ruled in my favor . . . the judge refused to honor it. . . . He's a rogue judge; he's a fake judge." Noting that Knight was not registered to issue appeal bonds in New York, James asked Engoron to compel Trump's lawyers to justify the bond within ten days. Before the scheduled hearing, however, the parties agreed to a slightly modified version.

Four months after the judgment Trump's lawyers asked Engoron to recuse himself because of a state judicial conduct investigation into whether he had talked to an expert real estate lawyer, Adam Leitman Bailey, three weeks before the judgment.[70] Bailey had told NBC New York in February: "I wanted him to know what I think and why . . . I really want him to get it right." He claimed he had advised Engoron about the law and why harsh penalties would hurt business and the judge asked "a lot of questions." "I gave him everything I knew . . . we went over it." Although the two "never mentioned the word Donald Trump . . . obviously we weren't talking about the Mets." A month later Engoron denied the recusal motion without a hearing. Bailey, "a professional acquaintance and a distant friend," had "accosted and started haranguing" Engoron as he left the courthouse. Bailey's "sudden appearance and vehement speech took me aback, and I simply told him that he was wrong. He railed after me, still droning on. . . . I entered my vehicle without saying another word and departed." "I would have forgotten all about it by now had Bailey not attempted to burnish his reputation as someone who could easily influence judges." "The entire 90-second incident, after three and a half years of studying and being immersed [in the case] . . . was, to use the vernacular, 'a nothingburger.'" On July 22, Trump appealed on the ground that the judgment was excessive, among other reasons.

This trial reprised Trump's determined efforts to undermine the civil justice system. He repeatedly assailed the Attorney General (as he had two other Black women lawyers: Fulton County DA Willis and DDC Judge Chutkan, see Chapters 3.2 and 4.2), claiming they were racist when his own attacks were openly sexist and racist. He constantly insulted Justice Engoron, his wife, and his clerk (who was targeted with hate mail and threats), moving the judge to issue a gag order. Trump's lawyers joined in these attacks. Trump defied judicial orders, incurring $110,000 in fines for not complying with subpoenas and $15,000 for violating the gag order, falsely complaining the latter violated his First Amendment rights. He displayed open contempt for the judge by having his lawyers make pointless recusal motions and himself storming out of court. (This was bizarre behavior, given that the judge would decide both the facts and the penalty.) A lavish golden handshake and NDA secured the silence of Weisselberger, who refused to testify against him, paying a huge fine and going to prison twice. Trump's lawyers filed three frivolous lawsuits seeking to block this case, picking inappropriate venues, NDNY and a Florida state court, where they presumably hoped to secure a judge who would favor Trump, like his appointee Cannon in SD FL (see Chapter 4.1). Trump sought to delay the trial and then perversely complained that its timing interfered with his campaign. He maligned the case as election interference, when it was he who had sought to overturn the 2020 election and persisted in denying Biden had won. Trump insisted he had done everything right in valuing his properties (as he claimed about his notorious phone calls with Zelensky and Raffensperger, see Abel 2024b: Chapters 2.1 and 4.4). He claimed to be the victim of fraud, not its perpetrator, shamelessly equating himself with Nelson Mandela and Alexei Navalny, real martyrs in the struggle against autocracy. He warned Americans that the lawsuit showed they all were vulnerable to prosecution, though none had committed fraud of this magnitude. And he exploited his own culpability to rake in money, as he did in the classified papers search (see Chapter 4.1), Georgia prosecution (see Chapter 3.2), and hush money case (see Chapter 3.1). At the end of the day, however, Trump was on the hook for almost half a billion dollars.

2.4 Lawyer Discipline

The legal profession deals with lawyer misconduct almost exclusively by responding to client complaints about matters like misappropriation of funds, conflict of interest, overcharging, neglect and delay, and egregious malpractice.[71] It rarely addresses the problem of excessive zeal (about which clients never complain).[72] But Trump's lawyers were so overzealous, so contemptuous of their responsibilities to the court and the justice system, that many have been or are being disciplined.[73]

2.4.1 *Sidney Powell*

ED MI Judge Linda Parker (Obama) held a five-hour hearing on complaints against Sidney Powell, L. Lin Wood, and seven other lawyers for the lawsuit they filed challenging voting in Wayne County (Detroit).[74] After twice asking if they had spoken to a witness claiming to have seen election workers switching votes, Judge Parker said: "let the record reflect that no one made that inquiry, which was central to [the] allegation." The assertion that people had loaded a mail truck with clear plastic bags, which "could be ballots" intended for the Detroit counting facility, was "really fantastical" and "speculative." "I don't think I've really ever seen an affidavit that has made so many leaps." The lawyers had sought testimony in a sealed hearing from Joshua Merritt—Powell's "expert," who claimed to be a former military intelligence officer but actually had been a wheeled-vehicle mechanic. Powell took "full responsibility" for the pleadings, defiantly declaring she would file them again because she "had a legal obligation to the country" to challenge the election. Wood had signed the complaint (whose contents he could not remember) but maintained he had played no role in the litigation, though "I had generally indicated to Sidney Powell that if she needed a quote-unquote trial lawyer, I would certainly be willing to help her." Finding that the complaint's 960 pages of affidavits did not demonstrate due diligence, Parker sanctioned the nine lawyers for a "historic and profound abuse of the judicial process." "Plaintiffs' attorneys have scorned their oath, flouted the rules, and attempted to undermine the integrity of the judiciary along the way . . . deceiving a federal court and the American people into believing that rights were infringed without regard to whether any laws or rights were in fact violated." "[A]ttorneys cannot exploit their privilege and access to the judicial process" in order "to disseminate allegations of fraud unsupported by law or fact in the public sphere." She ordered them to pay their adversaries' $175,000 attorneys' fees, required them to attend continuing legal education classes, and referred them to the Michigan Attorney Grievance Commission and the disciplinary bodies of the states where they were admitted, finding that their claims were full of "speculation, conjecture and unwarranted suspicion" and unsupported by law and evidence.

The Sixth Circuit (Boggs (Reagan), Kethledge (GWB) and White (GWB)) largely upheld the order.[75] "Plaintiffs' inquiry as to these allegations [about the voting system] were patently inadequate." The affidavit by Merritt was "utterly baseless." The claim of specialized knowledge by Russell Ramsland, another alleged expert, was "questionable on its face," and he assumed "a ballot-marking system nowhere used in Michigan." The alleged expert opinion of Matt Braynard "said nothing about his qualifications or the data he supposedly employed" and "was unreliable on its face." Dr. William Briggs, another "expert," made "statistical extrapolations" from a survey, which "were facially unreliable as well." The complaint misrepresented Dr. Stanley Young's finding of "unexpected" results in nine counties as "likely fraudulent votes." The complaint's claim that Melissa Carone had "witnessed" an "illegal vote dump" actually "illustrates the complaint's pattern of embellishment to the point of misrepresentation," since all she had witnessed was the arrival of "two vans." "Considered both individually and collectively, the affidavits cited in the complaint did not afford counsel a credible basis to allege that 'tens of thousands' of fraudulent votes were counted at TCF [the convention center]." With respect to other alleged violations of Michigan election law, "counsel apparently did not read the statute they said was violated." The Supreme Court declined to review. Following Judge Parker's referral, the Michigan Attorney Grievance Commission filed a complaint to the Attorney Discipline Board against Powell and three other lawyers.

In response to complaints from Michigan state officials and an Arizona lawyer, the Texas Commission for Lawyer Discipline submitted a petition asserting that Powell "had no reasonable basis to believe the lawsuits she filed [in Arizona, Georgia, Michigan and Wisconsin] were not frivolous."[76] Texas's 471st District Court Judge Andrea Bouressa (appointed by Republican Gov. Abbott) dismissed the petition and criticized the Commission for not properly labeling exhibits, leading the judge to examine only two of them. After Powell pleaded guilty in the Georgia case (see Chapter 3.2), 17 lawyers, including two past presidents of the Texas State Bar and two former Texas Supreme Court Grievance Oversight Committee members, asked the Office of Chief Disciplinary Counsel to impose compulsory discipline. But it declined. And the Fifth Court of Appeals (three Democratic judges) upheld Bouressa's dismissal, denouncing the state bar's " 'scattershot' approach to the case." "[D]ishonesty involves some conscious perversion of truth."

2.4.2 Lawrence Joseph, Juli Haller, and Brandon Johnson

The DC Office of Disciplinary Counsel (ODC) filed a complaint against Lawrence Joseph, who was defending Powell in the defamation cases brought by Dominion and Smartmatic (see Chapter 2.2.1).[77] The complaint alleged that Joseph made false claims about fake electors in Arizona, Georgia, Michigan, Pennsylvania and Wisconsin in *Gohmert v. Pence*.[78] ED TX Judge Jeremy Kernodle (Trump) had dismissed that case just five days after it was filed, and the Fifth Circuit denied the appeal a day later. ODC also filed complaints against Juli Haller and Brandon Johnson. Haller was involved in Powell's "Kraken" lawsuit in Georgia. Haller and Johnson allegedly made false claims about voting fraud, which had been rejected by courts in Arizona, Wisconsin, Michigan, and elsewhere.

2.4.3 L. Lin Wood

Delaware Superior Court Judge Craig A. Karsnitz (appointed by Democratic Gov. Carney) revoked Wood's pro hac vice admission to represent Carter Page against Yahoo News and Oath (parent of HuffPost) because Wood did not demonstrate the "appropriate level of integrity and competence."[79] A lawsuit he brought to challenge the election in Georgia was "textbook frivolous litigation," with "no basis in law or fact" (see Abel 2024b: Chapter 3.2.1); and the complaint in a Wisconsin lawsuit (see Abel 2025: Chapter 5.1.6) was "riddled with errors" and "would not survive a law school civil procedure class." The Georgia State Bar began an investigation in 2021 and held a trial in early 2023. Wood sued the Bar after it sought to obtain a health examination but lost in the Circuit Court. He retired, mooting the two pending disciplinary charges. "I wish I had been able to do it two years ago. I was tired of practicing law." In August 2024, after a lengthy lawsuit, a federal court found that he owed his former partners $3.75 million in attorneys' fees and costs.

2.4.4 Rudy Giuliani

After more than 7,500 lawyers signed a New York City Bar statement calling for a "full" and "serious" investigation of Giuliani, the Appellate Division suspended him, finding "uncontroverted evidence that the respondent communicated demonstrably false and misleading statements to courts, lawmakers and the public at large."[80] "The seriousness of respondent's uncontroverted misconduct be overstated." The DC Court of Appeals reciprocated. In July 2024 New York disbarred him for telling lies "designed to create distrust of the elective system of our country in the minds of the citizens and to destroy their confidence in the legitimacy of our government."

Finding that Giuliani lacked a "non-frivolous basis" to bring election fraud claims in Pennsylvania, the DC ODC filed a separate complaint with the DC Court of Appeals Board on Professional Responsibility. Giuliani sought to justify himself: "You don't start a lawsuit being able to prove, but being able to responsibly allege. I was responsibly alleging, based on the things that were told to me by other people." Asked how he knew BLM activists had been bussed into Philadelphia to vote illegally, as alleged in the complaint, he replied: "Of course, I didn't know that at the beginning of the litigation. . . . You find that out when you take discovery. . . . I'm in this case for two days." The Board found he had violated rules against bringing frivolous lawsuits and harming the administration of justice.

After a week of hearings and months of deliberation, the ODC recommended Giuliani be disbarred. "He claimed massive election fraud but had no evidence of it. By prosecuting that destructive case Mr. Giuliani, a sworn officer of the Court, forfeited his right to practice law." He filed the lawsuit challenging the Philadelphia votes "when he had no factual basis, and consequently no legitimate legal grounds, to do so." He had "helped destabilize our democracy" and "done lasting damage" to his oath to support the Constitution. "Mr. Giuliani has not acknowledged or accepted responsibility for his misconduct. To the contrary, he has declared his indignation over being subject to the disciplinary process." "The misconduct here sadly transcends all his past accomplishments." Ted Goodman, a Giuliani adviser, denounced this "great injustice." "The decision-makers at the DC Bar Association are nothing more than an arm of the permanent regime in Washington." "This is also part of an effort to deny President Trump effective counsel" because Giuliani is "objectively one of the most effective prosecutors in American history." The Board held a hearing in November 2023; at the end of May, it recommended disbarment; in July the NY Appellate Division disbarred him for telling lies "designed to create distrust of the elective system of our country in the minds of the citizens and to destroy their confidence in the legitimacy of our government." "[H]e also actively contributed to the national strife that has followed the 2020 presidential election, for which he is entirely unrepentant." The DC Court of Appeals also disbarred him after he failed to respond to it.

2.4.5 Colorado

D CO Mag. Judge N. Reid Neureiter asked lawyers Gary D. Fielder and Ernest John Walker whether they had let themselves be used as Trump's "propaganda tool" in suing Dominion, Facebook, the Center for Technology and Civic Life and elected officials in four states for election fraud, seeking $160 billion in damages.[81] "The lawsuit was filed with a woeful lack of investigation into the law and, under the circumstances, the facts" and repeated "highly inflammatory and damaging allegations that could have put individuals' safety in danger." Finding they had not presented "one iota" of evidence, Neureiter dismissed the Colorado lawsuit and ordered them to pay the defendants' $187,000 attorneys' fees.

> As officers of the Court, these attorneys have a higher duty and calling that requires meaningful investigation before prematurely repeating in court pleadings unverified and uninvestigated defamatory rumors that strike at the heart of our democratic system and were used by others to foment a violent insurrection that threatened our government.

The Tenth Circuit (Holmes and Tymkovich (both GWB) and Rossman (Biden)) affirmed: "an attorney is expected to exercise judgment, and must 'regularly re-evaluate the merits' of claims and 'avoid prolonging meritless claims.'" The Colorado Supreme Court declined to review.

2.4.6 John Eastman

On January 26, 2023 the California State Bar charged Eastman with 11 violations for making "false and misleading statements that constitute acts of 'moral turpitude, dishonesty, and corruption,'" which contributed to "provoking a crowd to assault and breach the Capitol to intimidate then-Vice-President Pence and prevent the electoral count from proceeding."[82] Eastman's strategies "were unsupported by law," "based on false and misleading assertions of fact and designed for the purpose of keeping Trump in office." He "knew or should have known that the factual premise for his proposals—that massive fraud was at play—was false, and that Trump had lost his bid for re-election."

Matthew A. Seligman, the Bar's designated legal expert, submitted a 91-page report finding that "no reasonable attorney exercising appropriate diligence in the circumstances would adopt" the positions Eastman took. "The historical record conclusively demonstrates that the President of the Senate holds no unilateral power to take any substantive action with respect to the elector count." "Dr. Eastman's decision to advance those unfounded legal positions as part of an attempt to reverse the lawful result of a presidential election violates fundamental precepts of American democracy."

State Bar Court Judge Yvette D. Roland made a preliminary finding that Eastman was culpable. Justin Grimmer (Stanford political science professor and senior fellow at the conservative Hoover Institution) testified that Eastman's opinions on rejection rates of Georgia absentee ballots were based on "ridiculous assumptions and errors that ignored legal changes in how absentee ballot envelopes were designed." After 35 days of trial, Judge Roland issued a 128-page opinion finding Eastman guilty of ten of the eleven charges and recommending disbarment.

> Eastman made multiple patently false and misleading statements in court filings, in public remarks heard by countless Americans and to others regarding the conduct of the 2020 presidential election and Vice President Pence's authority to refuse to count or delay counting properly certified slates of electoral votes on January 6, 2021.

Although Eastman challenged his inactive status on April 3, D CO Judge Kato Crews (Biden) ordered him to show cause why he should not be removed as an attorney of record in a pending lawsuit.

2.4.7 Jenna Ellis

Ellis lashed back at a disciplinary complaint by the 65 Project, saying said she was not "intimidated by this dirty political maneuver to undermine the legal profession."[83] "The state bars will see through this thinly veiled tactic to foment a chilling effect upon lawyers from doing our job and zealously representing clients that are political and even controversial." But she soon settled the complaint, admitting ten misrepresentations. On Maria Bartiromo's Fox News program on November 20, 2020, Ellis had said:

> we have affidavits from witnesses, we have voter intimidation, we have the ballots that were manipulated, we have all kinds of statistics that show that this was a coordinated effort in all of the states to transfer votes either from Trump to Biden, to manipulate the ballots, to count them in secret.

Two weeks later she said on Jeannine Piro's show that her legal team had discovered more than 500,000 votes in Arizona "that were cast illegally." Ellis now acknowledged that censure was merited when lawyers "knowingly engaged" in any "conduct that involves dishonesty, fraud, deceit, or misrepresentation" and that her legal work for Trump "caused actual harm by undermining the American public's confidence in the presidential election." Bar officials found aggravating factors: "a selfish motive" and "pattern of misconduct." Immediately after her censure, however, she tweeted that she had not admitted lying, which "requires INTENTIONALLY making a false statement."

After Ellis pleaded in Georgia (see Chapter 3.2), Lawyers Defending American Democracy (LDAD) and Stand United Democracy Center asked the Colorado Office of Attorney Regulation Counsel to take further action. In January 2024, that Office accused her of additional misconduct and asked the Presiding Disciplinary Judge to impose discipline.

2.4.8 Kenneth Chesebro

LDAD organized complaints by prominent private and public sector lawyers to the New York Appellate Division First Department.[84] The 65 Project had filed a similar complaint against Chesebro (as well as more than 50 other lawyers). After Chesebro pleaded in Georgia (see Chapter 3.2), LDAD wrote again. On February 19, 2024, California put him on involuntary inactive status. On March 13, 2024, Massachusetts temporarily suspended him. On October 31, 2024, New York disbarred him.

2.4.9 Stefan Passantino

Prominent lawyers, including past presidents of the ABA and the DC Bar, complained to the DC Court of Appeals Board of Professional Responsibility about Passantino's representation of Cassidy Hutchinson before the January 6 Select Committee, accusing him of subornation of perjury, obstruction of justice, witness tampering, and bribery (see Abel 2025: Chapter 2.3).[85] In February, the 65 Project complained about him in Georgia. LDAD also complained about him in New York and Georgia. DC and Georgia dismissed the complaints for lack of evidence after Hutchinson refused to talk to them. New York seems to have taken no action.

2.4.10 Jeffrey Clark

The DC ODC filed a complaint against Clark, alleging that, in the letter he wanted the DoJ to send to Georgia officials, he "attempted to engage in conduct involving dishonesty" and "conduct that would seriously interfere with the administration of justice" (see Abel 2024b: Chapter 4.4).[86] Clark responded that the Bar could not discipline him "because the President has an absolute right to seek legal and other forms of advice as to the discharge of his responsibilities under the Take Care Clause," and discipline "would intrude on the President's exclusive and unreviewable authority over federal criminal and civil investigations." He asked the DDC to enjoin the ODC investigation. Trump lawyer Todd Blanche wrote Clark that neither he nor other witnesses could discuss confidential conversations covered by Trump's "executive privilege and other related privileges," and Blanche asserted Trump's right to "intervene" in the disciplinary proceedings. On April 4, 2024, after six days of testimony, ODC investigators made a preliminary determination that Clark violated at least one ethics rule and sought disbarment. In August, the three-member ODC panel issued a 216-page report recommending two years' suspension.

2.4.11 Texas[87]

86th District Court Judge Casey Blair denied a motion to dismiss the State Bar's case against Attorney General Kenneth Paxton in May 2022, which claimed he had made "dishonest" statements in the US Supreme Court in *Texas v. Pennsylvania*. The Dallas Court of Appeals (2–1) denied an appeal. In March 2024, state prosecutors dropped fraud charges that had been pending against Paxton for seven years. Another Texas judge had dismissed a related case against Brent Webster, a Paxton aide; an appeal was pending. In April 2024, 18 state Attorneys General filed an amicus brief for Webster.

The 65 Project filed a complaint against Paul Davis, noting that a court had criticized his "fantastic and outright nonsensical" claims about election fraud. He reasserted that "the 2020 election had serious lapses in integrity" and accused Democratic lawyers of seeking to "neutralize anyone who might possibly stand in their way."

2.4.12 Arizona

Arizona state Senator Anthony Kern introduced a bill to prohibit the State Bar and state Supreme Court from "infringing" or "impeding" the "political speech" of a lawyer or client by disciplining them for "bringing a good faith non frivolous claim that is based in law and fact to court"; the bill would penalize both institutions for violations.[88] Kern's Republican colleague, Rep. Alexander Kolodin, was one of nine lawyers against whom complaints had been filed. Kern, Mark Finchem, and Rep. Gosar sued Charlene Fernandez for defamation for a letter she and 43 other Democratic state legislators wrote, seeking an investigation of the plaintiffs' role in the January 6 riot. The plaintiffs lost and were ordered to pay $75 attorneys' fees. Finchem had been sanctioned twice by courts.

2.5 How Effective is Discipline?

Professional discipline presents a mixed picture. Most lawyers against whom complaints were filed were found to have engaged in unethical conduct by falsely alleging facts without adequate investigation or advancing frivolous legal arguments. Some—Giuliani, Powell, Ellis, Wood—displayed stunning levels of incompetence. The weightiest and most difficult cases were those against Eastman, Chesebro, and Clark for making the untenable argument that Pence could refuse to certify the Electoral College votes. Disciplinary bodies and judges did not display the deep partisan divide I found in other federal cases, but Texas openly protected its lawyers. Judges imposed sanctions expeditiously, whereas professional discipline took years (and some cases are unresolved). Sanctions were significant—nearly $200,000 in two cases and $1 million in another, but the lawyers (or their clients) could afford them. Suspension and disbarment were far more powerful deterrents (though two of the lawyers were clearly at the end of their careers: Wood and Giuliani). In earlier research, I found that disciplinary bodies in New York and California demanded clear expressions of remorse before reinstating lawyers.[89] Many of Trump's defenders, however, were ideologues and wholly unrepentant (like many of the January 6 riot defendants, see Abel 2025: Chapter 4.1). Nevertheless, both these lawyers and others may be discouraged in the future from cavalierly disregarding the facts and advancing patently untenable legal arguments.

2.6 Did the Civil Justice System Successfully Resist Autocracy?

Civil justice performed the way it was designed, undistorted by politics. Judges controlled how Trump and his lawyers behaved in court and imposed gag rules to restrict what Trump said outside the courtroom. Judges forestalled efforts to tamper with juries—the legal institution most insulated from politics—by anonymizing their members. Unlike the judges who decided cases involving Trump's immigration policies, response to the COVID-19 pandemic, and efforts to overturn the 2020 election (Abel 2024a, 2024b, 2024c), and those handling the cases involving his retention of classified papers and involvement in the January 6 insurrection (see Chapter 4), the judges handling these civil matters did not divide along political lines (see Table 2.1).

TABLE 2.1 Judicial Decisions Against Trump and Supporters in Civil Actions

Case	*Judge*	*Party (appointing president)*
Carroll v Trump	SDNY Judge Kaplan	D (Clinton)
Jones	Ct Superior Court Judge Bellis	R appointee
Jones	SD Tex Bankruptcy Judge Lopez	R (Trump)
Dominion v Powell	DDC Judge Nichols	R (Trump)
Andrews v Salem	ND Ga Judge Grimberg	R (Trump)
Stefanie Lambert	Oakland County (Mi) Circuit Judge Matis	R appointee
Coomer v Oltmann	Denver County Dist. Ct Judge Moses	D appointee
Coomer v Clark	D Colo Judge Martinez	D (Obama)
Coomer v Lindell	D Colo Judge Wang	D (Biden)
Zeidman v Lindell	D Mn Judge Tunheim	D (Clinton)
Dominion v Fox	Del. Superior Ct Judge Davis	D appointee
Smartmatic v Newsmax	Del. Superior Ct Judge Davis	D appointee
Fox shareholder derivative suit	Del. Vice Chancellor Laster	D appointee
Smartmatic v Fox	NY Supreme Court Justice Cohen	D
Smartmatic v Lindell	DDC Judge Kelly	R (Trump)
Smartmatic v OANN	DDC Judge Kelly	R (Trump)
Smartmatic v Lindell	D Mn Judge Wright	D (Obama)
Freeman and Moss v Gateway Pundit	ED Mo Judge Autrey	R (GWB)
Freeman and Moss v Gateway Pundit	St. Louis Circuit Ct Judge Stelzer	D appointee
Freeman and Moss v OANN	DDC Judge Howell	D (Obama)
Freeman and Moss v OANN	SDNY Bankruptcy Judge Lane	D (Obama)
Trump v CNN	ND Ga Judge Brown	R (Trump)
Trump v New York Times	NY Supreme Court Justice d'Auguste	D

(*Continued*)

TABLE 2.1 (Continued)

Case	*Judge*	*Party (appointing president)*
Trump v Washington Post	DDC Judge Contreras	D (Obama)
Trump v CNN	SD Fla Judge Singhal	R (Trump)
Trump Media v Washington Post	MD Fla Judge Barber	R (Trump)
Trump v Mary Trump, NYT	NY Supreme Court Justice Reed	D
Trump v Hillary Clinton et al.	SD Fla Judge Middlebrooks	D (Clinton)
Trump v James	NDNY Judge Sannes	D (Obama)
James v Trump	NY Supreme Court Justice Engoron	D
James v Trump Organization	NY Supreme Court Justice Merchan	D
Trump v James	SD Fla Judge Middlebrooks	D (Clinton)
James v Trump	SDNY Judge Jones	D (Clinton)
James v Trump	NY App Div Justice Singh	D
Discipline of Powell, Wood, et al.	ED Mich Judge Parker	D (Ob)
Same	Sixth Circuit Judges Boggs, Kethledge and White	All R (Reagan, GWB, GWB)
Wood pro hac vice	Del. Superior Court Judge Karsnitz	D
Fielder and Walker sanctions	Tenth Circuit Judges Holmes, Tymkovich and Rossman	2 R (both GWB), 1 D (Biden)
Eastman discipline	D Colo Judge Crews	D (Biden)
Texas State Bar v Paxton	86th Texas Dist Ct Judge Blair	R

Almost all ruled against Trump: 29 Democrats (elected or appointed) and 17 Republicans—seven of them appointed by Trump. The few who favored him reveal no pattern (retired Florida Circuit Court Judge Pegg and SD FL Judge Altonaga, both of whom I expect to be reversed, and NY App. Div. Justice Friedman, who was reversed twice). In that respect, they resemble the DDC judges who dealt with the January 6 prosecutions (see Abel 2025: Chapter 4). Judges, regardless of their political leanings, deeply believe in the integrity of the legal system and resent challenges to their authority. Trump aggressively sought to undermine the legal system through his constant, explicit, vituperative attacks on prosecutors and judges and his choice of ideologically committed lawyers to represent him. He was incapable of exercising self-control or tolerating any constraint on his power (by courts, lawyers, the administrative state, scientists, even other Republicans), deliberately inflaming his supporters by indulging in outrageous behavior that would guarantee muzzling or punishment and then claiming to be a victim.

That strategy succeeded all too well. Trump was found liable to Carroll for nearly $100 million and New York State for nearly $500 million. He was held in contempt and ordered to pay $125,000. He and his lawyers were sanctioned, compelled to pay large sums (almost $2 million in the US, £300,000 in the UK). His retaliatory lawsuits failed. Trump supporters and right-wing media who embraced his false election fraud allegations by publishing defamation suffered similar judgments: Fox ($800 million to Dominion, $12 million to Grossberg); Lindell ($5 million to Zeidman); Giuliani (nearly $150 million to Freeman and Moss). These liabilities (and the threat of more) prompted shareholder derivative actions. A major media company like Fox wisely settled and distanced itself from some of the worst defamers—but the latter simply found other outlets. Smaller companies like Newsmax and American Thinker apologized. But strategic bankruptcies (Alex Jones, *Gateway Pundit*, Rudy Giuliani) will delay and perhaps defeat recovery, as they have done in mass tort cases against manufacturers (Johns Manville for asbestos, Mallinckrodt, Rite Aid, and Purdue Pharma for opioids). Reputable lawyers withdrew from representing Trump and his collaborators, unwilling to risk their reputations or being stiffed by their clients, leaving Trump with lawyers who demonstrated their ignorance and incompetence by suing for defamation without alleging or seeking evidence of actual malice and filing pointless collateral attacks only to withdraw them. That exposed Trump's lawyers to sanctions and discipline, but the former might not deter, and the latter often took years. The civil justice system successfully resisted politicization; but its ability to curb Trump's actions was limited.

Trump's election in November will not reverse these victories. He appealed the judgments for Carroll and New York State but is unlikely to overturn them, though New York appellate courts could order new trials or reduce damages. Since the underlying conduct in both cases falls outside any official act of his presidency (see Chapter 4.2), the US Supreme Court should not, and probably will not, hear an appeal.

Notes

1 Fabian & Enjeti, "Trump vehemently denies E. Jean Carroll allegation, says 'she's not my type,'" *The Hill* (6.24.19); Dwyer, "Columnist who accused Trump of sexual assault is suing him for defamation," *NPR* (11.4.19); Feuer, "Justice Dept. intervenes to help Trump in E. Jean Carroll defamation lawsuit," *NYT* (9.8.20); Katersky, "DOJ files appeal in E. Jean Carroll lawsuit against President Trump," *ABC News* (11.25.20); Katersky, "Appeals court declines to rule if Trump was acting in official capacity when he allegedly defamed E. Jean Carroll," *ABC News* (4.13.23); Pullano, "Trump defamation suit returns to court that first gave it legs," *Courthouse News Service* (4.21.23); Shoaib, "Trump told a female lawyer 'you wouldn't be a choice of mine either' while explaining that his rape accuser is

not his type," *Business Insider* (5.6.23); Weiser, Fadulu & Christobek, "In rape trial deposition, Trump says vulgar tape simply reflects truth," *NYT* (5.5.23); Bump, "Trump tests how insulated his base is from the Carroll verdict reality," *WP* (5.10.23).

2 Weiser, "Writer who accused Trump of rape to file new defamation lawsuit," *NYT* (11.17.22); Meo, "Trump's offer to provide DNA in rape suit is stalling tactic, judge says," *NYT* (2.16.23); Schonfeld, "Judge denies Trump's offer to give DNA in E. Jean Carroll case, calling it delay tactic," *The Hill* (2.15.23); Ackerman, "The other Manhattan case that can topple Trump: the federal defamation lawsuit of E. Jean Carroll may produce a quick guilty verdict," *NY Daily News* (4.4.23); Berman, "Carroll v. Trump jurors will be anonymous, judge says, citing Trump's reaction to hush money investigation," *CNN* (3.23.23); Stempel, "Judge rejects Trump's bid to learn juror names at defamation trial," *Reuters* (4.14.23); Neumeister, "Judge: if news taints rape-trial jurors, Trump shares blame," *AP News* (4.17.23); Wagner, "Trump seeks 'cooling off' delay in case involving rape claim," *WP* (4.12.23); Weiser, "Trump asks that trial of writer's suit accusing him of rape be delayed," *NYT* (4.12.23); Weiser, "Judge refuses to grant Trump delay in trial of suit accusing him of rape," *NYT* (4.18.23); Knutson, "Trump not legally required to attend civil rape trial, judge says," *Axios* (4.20.23); Collman, "Judge denies Trump's latest request to delay the E. Jean Carroll rape case—this time to probe billionaire Reid Hoffman's support for the litigation," *Business Insider* (4.13.23); Shamsian, "Judge seals filings over whether billionaire Democratic donor is bankrolling E. Jean Carroll's rape lawsuit against Trump," *Business Insider* (4.21.23).

3 Weiser, Fadulu & Christobek, "Lawyers for Trump and his accuser clash over her motives in rape case," *NYT* (4.26.23); Weiser, Fadulu, Christobek & Zraick, "In searing detail, Trump's accuser tells her story," *NYT* (4.27.23); Del Valle, "Judge in E. Jean Carroll trial warns Trump about social media comments," *CNN* (4.26.23); Scannell, "Trump asks for mistrial in battery case, saying judge has made 'unfair and prejudicial' rulings," *CNN* (5.1.23); Fadulu, Christobek & Weiser, "Day 4 of the Trump rape case: Carroll's cross-examination is complete," *NYT* (5.2.23); Orden, "E. Jean Carroll concludes testimony as judge denies Trump's mistrial request," *Politico* (5.1.23); Weiser, Fadulu & Christobek, "In rape trial deposition, Trump says vulgar tape simply reflects truth," *NYT* (5.5.23); Bump, "Trump tests how insulated his base is from the Carroll verdict reality," *WP* (5.10.23).

4 Sullivan, Bernstein, Marritz & Lawrence, "A jury finds Trump liable for battery and defamation in E. Jean Carroll trial," *NPR* (5.9.23); Jacobs, Bellware & Berman, "Jury finds that Trump sexually abused E. Jean Carroll, awards $5 million in damages," *WP* (5.9.23); Reiss & Gregorian, "Trump found liable for sexually abusing and defaming E. Jean Carroll in civil trial and is ordered to pay $5 million," *NBC News* (5.9.23); Paybarah, "Jury finds Trump sexually abused E. Jean Carroll, awards $5 million in damages," *WP* (5.9.23); "The E. Jean Carroll suit brought an astonishing moment of accountability," *WP* (5.10.23); Arnsdorf, Dawsey & LeVine, "Sexual abuse verdict renews Republican doubts about Trump's electability," *WP* (5.10.23); Blake, "4 takeaways from the E. Jean Carroll verdict against Trump," *WP* (5.10.23); Schweber, "Trump's lawyer vows to appeal the verdict," *NYT* (5.10.23); Weiser & Fadulu, "After defamation finding, Trump again says Carroll lied," *NYT* (5.11.23); Watson, Rosen & Rinaldi, "Trump CNN town hall highlights include comments on E. Jean Carroll verdict, Jan. 6 and more," *CBS News* (5.11.23); Doak & Kristensen, "Trump uses CNN town hall to air multiple falsehoods," *Logically Facts* (5.12.23); "Donald Trump loses bid for new trial in E. Jean Carroll case," *HuffPost* (7.19.23); Blake, "Judge

clarifies: Yes, Trump was found to have raped E. Jean Carroll," *WP* (7.19.23); Scannell, "Judge dismisses Trump's defamation lawsuit against Carroll for statements she made on CNN," *CNN* (8.7.23); Stemple, "Donald Trump loses bid for new trial in E. Jean Carroll abuse case," *Reuters* (7.19.23); Zraick, "Judge throws out Trump's countersuit against E. Jean Carroll," *NYT* (8.7.23).

5 Weiner, "DOJ will no longer intervene on behalf of Trump in Carroll defamation suit," *WP* (7.20.23); Cramer & Christobeck, "Why Donald Trump is facing E. Jean Carroll in court a second time," *NYT* (1.19.24); Stempel, "Judge finds Donald Trump's appeal in E. Jean Carroll case 'frivolous,'" *Reuters* (8.18.23); Weiser, "Trump's next defamation trial will skip to what damages he should pay," *NYT* (9.7.23); Weiser, Haberman & Cramer, "As Trump continues to insult E. Jean Carroll, 2nd defamation trial opens," *NYT* (1.15.24); Weiser, "Jurors in Trump defamation trial to go unnamed for their own protection," *NYT* (11.4.23); Jacobs, "E. Jean Carroll seeks limits on Trump's testimony after his courtroom tirade," *WP* (1.13.24); Haberman, "Key Trump lawyer withdraws as Manhattan criminal trial nears," *NYT* (1.15.24).

6 Weiser, Haberman & Cramer, "As Trump continues to insult E. Jean Carroll, 2nd defamation trial opens," *NYT* (1.15.24).

7 Jacobs & Rosenzweig-Ziff, "Jury shown examples of hate speech directed toward Carroll," *WP* (1.16.24); Jacobs, "In opening statement, Trump attorney claims Carroll sought fame," *WP* (1.16.24).

8 Weiser, Cramer & Christobek, "Muttered insults, stern warnings: inside Trump's second defamation trial," *NYT* (1.18.24); Jacobs & Barrett, "In Judge Kaplan's court, Trump plays with fire," *WP* (1.22.24).

9 "Trump briefly testifies in E. Jean Carroll defamation trial," *WP* (1.25.24); Livesay & Tawfik, "Defiant Trump takes legal risk on stand in New York defamation trial," *BBC* (1.26.24); Weiser, Cramer & Christobek, "After days of waiting, Trump spends minutes on the witness stand," *NYT* (1.26.24); Cramer & Christobek, "In Trump's bitter, yearslong brawl with Roberta Kaplan, he keeps losing," *NYT* (1.28.24).

10 Jacobs, "Trump ordered to pay E. Jean Carroll $83.3 million in defamation damages trial," *WP* (1.26.24); Weiser, "Carroll promises to do 'something good' with a fortune won from Trump," *NYT* (1.28.24); Protess, Haberman & Craig, "$83 million verdict renews spotlight on Trump's finances," *NYT* (1.29.24).

11 Scannell, "Judge affirms $83.3 million verdict against Donald Trump in E. Jean Carroll defamation case," *CNN* (2.8.24); Weiser & Protess, "Judge denies Trump's request to delay due date of $83.3 million penalty," *NYT* (3.7.24); Jacobs, "Trump posted $91 million bond while appealing E. Jean Carroll defamation judgment," *WP* (3.8.24); Habeshian, "Trump's bid to slash $83m defamation payout to E. Jean Carroll rejected by judge," *Axios* (4.25.24).

12 Weiser, Haberman & Protess, "E. Jean Carroll could sue Trump again over new attacks, lawyer suggests," *NYT* (3.11.24); Haberman, "Trump, trailing among women, lashes out at his female accusers," *NYT* (9.7.24); Drenon, "Trump claims E Jean Carroll 'fabricated' sex assault," *BBC* (9.6.24); Stein & Jacobs, "Trump loses appeal in $5 million E. Jean Carroll defamation, sexual abuse case," *WP* (12.30.24); Fadulu, "Trump loses appeal of Carroll's $5 million award in sex-abuse case," *NYT* (12.30.24).

13 Mistich, "Conspiracy theorist Alex Jones ruled liable in Sandy Hook defamation case," *NPR* (11.15.21); Faulders, Grant & Katersky, "Alex Jones ordered to pay Sandy Hook parents more than $45 million in punitive damages," *ABC News* (8.5.22); Katersky & Deliso, "Alex Jones ordered to pay $965 million in Sandy Hook defamation trial," *ABC News* (10.12.22); Queen, "Alex Jones ordered to pay $473 million in punitive damages in Sandy Hook defamation case," *Reuters* (11.10.22); "Sandy Hook families offer to settle Alex Jones' $1.5 billion legal debt

for a minimum of $85 million," *NBC News* (11.28.23); Rose, "Alex Jones proposes paying Sandy Hook families a minimum of $55 million to settle lawsuit claims," *CNN* (12.16.23); Williamson, "Alex Jones seeks to liquidate his assets to pay damages to Sandy Hook families," *NYT* (6.7.24); Bellware, Rosenzweig-Ziff & Sommer, "Alex Jones ordered to sell personal assets over Sandy Hook judgment," *WP* (6.14.24); Williamson, "Sandy Hook families' fight for Alex Jones's money takes an ugly turn," *NYT* (2.28.24); Williamson, "Alex Jones's Infowars will be auctioned off to pay Sandy Hook families," *NYT* (9.25.24); Conger, Hsu & Krolik, "Twitter barred them. What happened after Elon Musk brought them back," *NYT* (10.25.24); Bellware, "The Onion wins auction to take control of Alex Jones's Infowars," *WP* (11.13.24); Mullin & Williamson, "The Onion wins bid to buy Infowars, Alex Jones's site, out of bankruptcy," *NYT* (11.15.24).

14 Bensinger, "'2,000 Mules' producer apologizes to man depicted committing election fraud," *NYT* (6.1.24); Andrews v. D'Souza, ND Ga 1:22-cv-04259-SDG (9.30.23); Corasaniti & Bensinger, "Director of '2000 Mules' acknowledges the conspiratorial film was flawed," *NYT* (12.2.24).

15 Fortin, "Idaho drag performer wins over $1.1 million in defamation suit against blogger," *NYT* (5.27.24).

16 Brown, "Dominion sues pro-Trump lawyer Sidney Powell, seeking more than $1.3 billion," *WP* (1.8.21); Brown, "Dominion files defamation lawsuit against Giuliani," *WP* (1.25.21); Helderman, "Impeachment is over. But other efforts to reckon with Trump's post-election chaos have just begun," *WP* (2.22.21); Corasaniti, "Four falsehoods Giuliani spread about Dominion," *NYT* (1.26.21); Telford, "Twitter bans MyPillow CEO Mike Lindell," *WP* (1.26.21); Maheshwari & Hsu, "MyPillow CEO's Trump conspiracy theories put company on the spot," *NYT* (1.27.21); Von Drehle, "Sidney Powell does an about-face on her stop the Steal claims," *WP* (3.24.21); Brown, "Dominion files defamation lawsuit against MyPillow CEO for false claim that voting machines rigged election against Trump," *WP* (2.22.21); Bump, "Mike Lindell's 'fraud' allegations are even more ridiculous than you might think," *WP* (6.4.21); Leman, "Dominion Voting tells Facebook, Parler and other social media sites to preserve posts for lawsuits," *WP* (2.5.21); Flood, "Overstock Ex-CEO must face Dominion voting defamation claims," *Bloomberg* (4.21.22); Larson, "Sidney Powell's claims against Dominion voting tossed by judge," *Bloomberg* (9.29.22); US Dominion v. My Pillow, DDC #1:21-cv-00445 (2.22.21); https://www.dominionvoting.com/latest-news-dominion-files-defamation-suit-against-mike-lindell-and-mypillow/; Berman, "Supreme Court allows defamation lawsuit against MyPillow CEO Mike Lindell to proceed," *CNN* (10.3.22); Reilly, "Mike Lindell's lawyers in Dominion lawsuit seek to quit case over millions of dollars in unpaid legal fees," *CNN* (10.5.23); US Dominion v. Powell, DDC 1:21-cv-00040 (CJN); US Dominion v. Giuliani, DDC 1:21-cv-00213 (CJN); US Dominion v. My Pillow, 1:21-cv-00445 (CJN) (8.11.21); Berman, "Supreme Court allows defamation lawsuit against MyPillow CEO Mike Lindell to proceed," *CNN* (10.3.22); Musumeci, Rojas & Teh, "Supreme Court won't let MyPillow CEO Mike Lindell dodge Dominion's $1.3 billion defamation lawsuit," *Business Insider* (10.3.22); Thomas, "Ex-Overstock CEO taps indicted pro-Trump lawyer as defense counsel in Dominion lawsuit," *Reuters* (3.13.24); Naham, "'She did not feign ignorance': Dominion moves to 'promptly' disqualify indicted 'Kraken' lawyer from representing ex-Overstock CEO in defamation case after discovery leak," *Law&Crime* (3.18.24); Sullivan, "Atty for Ex-Overstock CEO admits Dominion discovery leaks," *Law360* (3.19.24); Weiner & Marley, "Michigan lawyer who claimed election fraud arrested after Dominion hearing," *WP* (3.19.24); Michigan Department of Attorney General, "AG Nessell charges attorney Stefanie Lambert and former Adams Township clerk Scott for 2020 election voter data breach" (5.8.24);

Mauger, "Dominion: Patrick Byrne violated court order hours after hearing on violations," *Detroit News* (5.21.24); Hsu & Marley, "Indicted pro-Trump lawyer who leaked emails is removed from Dominion suit," *WP* (8.13.24); Enrich, "Media case splits a law firm," *NYT* (4.14.24).

17 Coomer v. Donald J. Trump for President; Ducassi, "Rudy Giuliani shed light on Trump campaign as part of a Denver-based defamation lawsuit," *Colorado Sun* (9.24.21); Beedle, "'Probably false,' judge writes in denial of Oltmann anti-SLAPP motion," *Colorado Times Recorder* (5.13.22); Hayes, "No exit for Trump campaign, Powell from Dominion worker's suit," *Bloomberglaw* (4.11.24); Karik, "Ex-Dominion executive's defamation claims may proceed against Trump campaign and supporters," *Colorado Politics* (6.5.24); Ashby, "Appeals court rules former Dominion executive case can go forward," *Daily Sentinel* (7.25.24); Karik, "Federal judge refuses to dismiss defamation suit by former exec of Denver-based Dominion," *Colorado Politics* (3.10.23); Coomer v. Make Your Life Epic, LLC.; Karik, "Ex-Dominion exec prevails in another appeal over unproven election-rigging accusations," *Colorado Politics* (4.24.24).

18 "Mike Lindell sued by former Dominion employee Eric Coomer for defamation," *Colorado Newsline* (4.5.22); Winter, "Mike Lindell goes ballistic during depositions, lashing out at lawyers," *Nebraska Examiner* (9.13.23).

19 Sforza, "Mike Lindell lawyers in Dominion case see to cut ties claiming he owes them millions," *The Hill* (10.5.23); "Election denier and 'MyPillow Guy' Mike Lindell confirms he's out of money, can't pay legal bills," *WCCO News* (10.6.23); Reilly, "Mike Lindell's lawyers in election defamation cases seek to quit over millions of dollars in unpaid legal fees," *CNN* (10.6.23).

20 "MyPillow founder Mike Lindell is ordered to pay $5M in election fraud challenge," *NPR* (4.21.23); Winter, "The cyber expert who took Mike Lindell's $5 million challenge and won," *Minnesota Reformer* (12.12.23); Gregorian, "Judge says Mike Lindell must pay $5 million to man who won his 'Prove Mike Wrong' challenge," *NBC News* (2.22.24); "Federal judge says MyPillow's Mike Lindell must pay $5m in election data dispute," *CBS News* (2.23.24).

21 Izadi, "Fox News sued by Dominion Voting for $1.6 billion over election fraud claims," *WP* (3.26.21); Peters, "Fox Corp. is not spared from defamation lawsuit," *NYT* (6.23.22); Wang, "Newsmax apologizes to Dominion employee for falsely alleging he manipulated votes against Trump," *WP* (5.1.21); Collier, "Newsmax, OANN sued by maker of voting machines," *NBC News* (8.10.21); Cole & Sneed, "Deposition video shows Trump allies under oath discussing debunked election fraud claims," *CNN* (11.4.21); Vakil, "Giuliani says in deposition he 'didn't have the time' to verify election claims: CNN," *The Hill* (11.5.21); Barr & Weiner, "Fox News hosts, executives privately doubted 2020 conspiracy claims shared on air," *WP* (2.17.23); Peters & Robertson, "Fox stars voiced voter fraud doubts," *NYT* (2.17.23); Sherer, Dawsey & Ellison, "Inside the simmering feud between Donald Trump and Fox News," *WP* (3.9.23); Helderman & Dawsey, "Ex-Trump aide at Fox wrestled with election lies, network's interests," *WP* (3.13.23); Blake, "4 takeaways from the new Dominion-Fox lawsuit documents," *WP* (3.7.23); Sherer, Dawsey & Ellison, "Inside the simmering feud between Donald Trump and Fox News," *WP* (3.9.23); Robertson, "Fox News agrees to pay $12 million to settle hostile workplace suit," *NYT* (6.30.23); Godoy & Coster, "Fox shareholder sues Rupert Murdoch, other directors over 2020 election coverage," *Reuters* (4.12.23); Robertson, "Fox sued by NYC pension funds over election falsehoods," *NYT* (9.13.23); Leonard, "Murdochs blamed by NYC pension funds for Fox defamation scandals," *Bloomberglaw* (9.18.23); Ebert, "Fox election lies shareholder suit to be led by NYC pension fund," *Bloomberglaw* (12.29.23); Katz, "NYC, Oregon pension funds named lead plaintiffs in Fox lawsuit," *Chief Investment Officer* (1.9.24).

22 Weisman, "Trump and Fox News, twin titans of politics, hit with back-to-back rebukes," *NYT* (4.1.23); Peters & Robertson, "Fox News suffers major setback in defamation case," *NYT* (4.1.23); Thompson, "Attacks on Dominion voting persist despite high-profile lawsuits," *NYT* (4.6.23); Barr, "Judge bars Dominion from mentioning Jan. 6 riot in Fox defamation trial," *WP* (4.12.23); Bart, "Judge chides Fox News over 'missing' Murdoch documents but refuses 'remedy,'" *WP* (4.12.23); Mulvaney, "Judge in defamation case blasts Fox News on evidence disclosures," *WSJ* (4.13.23); Robertson & Peters, "Judge imposes sanction on Fox for withholding evidence in defamation case," *NYT* (4.13.23); Barr, Izadi & Marley, "Fox News and Dominion agree to settle defamation lawsuit," *WP* (4.18.23); Deghanpoor, Brown & Swaine, "Mike Lindell's firm told to pay $5 million in 'prove Mike wrong' election-fraud challenge," *WP* (4.20.23); Poulos, "Dominion's CEO: we settled the lawsuit against Fox News, but we're not done yet," *NYT* (4.22.23); Barr & Ellison, "Tucker Carlson is out at Fox News after Dominion lawsuit disclosures," *WP* (4.25.23); Blake, "A harsh verdict on Fox News post-Dominion—even from GOP," *WP* (5.4.23); Grynbaum, "Fox's costs from defamation suit lead to a quarterly net loss," *NYT* (5.9.23); Peters, "Fox's Chief Legal Officer will depart," *NYT* (8.11.23); Flint, "Viet Dinh to leave as Fox's Chief Legal Officer," *WSJ* (8.11.23); Cohen, "Fox's top lawyer blasts judge in Dominion case, says trial would've been 'months of utter pain,'" *CNN* (10.16.23).

23 Shamsian, "Election-technology company Smartmatic files $2.7 billion lawsuit against Fox News over election conspiracy theories," *Business Insider* (2.4.21); Barr & Izadi, "Smartmatic files $2.7 billion defamation suit against Fox News over election-fraud claims," *WP* (2.4.21); Izadi, "Fox News has dropped 'Lou Dobbs Tonight,' promoter of Trump's false election fraud claims," *WP* (2.6.21); Grynbaum, "Lou Dobbs's show is canceled by Fox Business," *NYT* (2.6.21); Barr, "Lou Dobbs is lashing out at Fox on Twitter for dropping his show," *WP* (2.9.21); Kristof, "Can we put Fox News on trial with Trump?" *NYT* (2.11.21); Konnath, "Smartmatic defeats Fox News, Giuliani dismissal bids in NY," *Law360.com* (3.8.22); Stempel, "Smartmatic can pursue election-rigging claims against Fox News, Giuliani," *Reuters* (3.8.22); Barnes, "Much of Smartmatic case against Fox News can proceed, judge rules," *NYT* (3.9.22); https://storage.courtlistener.com/recap/gov.uscourts.mnd.198368/gov.uscourts.mnd.198368.52.0_1.pdf; Peltz, "Court nixes Fox News' bid to end voting tech firm's suit," *AP* (2.14.23); Barr, "Smartmatic's lawsuit against Fox News heats up with Murdoch depositions," *WP* (12.1.23); Cohen, "In blow to Fox Corp., judge rules Smartmatic case over 2020 election lies can proceed," *CNN* (1.24.24); Durkee, "Smartmatic settles OANN defamation case," *Forbes* (4.16.24); Adolphus, "Fox News loses last-ditch effort to stop massive $2.7B defamation suit," *Daily Beast* (1.10.25).

24 Villareal, "Smartmatic sues Mike Lindell, accusing him of spreading election lies to sell more pillows," *Newsweek* (1.18.22); Larson, "MyPillow CEO Mike Lindell ordered to face voting-fraud defamation suit," *Bloomberg* (9.19.22); Shuham, "Judge sanctions Mike Lindell for frivolous claims against Smartmatic," *TPM* (5.19.22).

25 Stetter, "Smartmatic is now suing Newsmax and OAN for 'disinformation campaign,'" *CNN* (11.3.21); Hals & Coster, "Judge rejects Newsmax bid to narrow Smartmatic lawsuit over 2020 US election," *Reuters* (8.23.23); Shamsian, "OAN can't dodge Smartmatic's DC lawsuit over election conspiracy theories just because its headquarters is in California, judge rules," *Business Insider* (6.21.22); Foretek, "DC magistrate judge rejects recusal bid in Smartmatic case," *Legal Ethics* (12.12.23); Durkee, "Smartmatic settles OANN defamation case," *Forbes* (4.16.24); Fitzpatrick, "Voting machine firm Smartmatic alleges Newsmax has deleted evidence in lawsuit over false vote-rigging claims," *NBC News* (5.21.24);

Cohen, "In blow to Newsmax, judge rules Smartmatic's case over 2020 election lies will go to trial this month," *CNN* (9.12.24); Hals, "Newsmax settles Smartmatic defamation suit over 2020 false election claims," *Reuters* (9.26.24).

26 Epstein, "Two election workers targeted by pro-Trump media sue for defamation," *NYT* (12.2.21); Jeong, "Rudy Giuliani and One America News sued by Georgia poll workers falsely accused of electoral fraud," *WP* (12.24.21); Brumback, "OAN dismissed from election workers' suit after settlement," *AP* (5.12.22); Keller, "Federal judge sends lawsuit against The Gateway Pundit by 2020 election workers back to state court," *Law&Crime* (6.7.23); "St. Louis judge rules against The Gateway Pundit, clearing way for jury trial," *Gateway Journalism Review* (7.27.23); Hancock, "Gateway Pundit accused of purposely delaying defamation case involving false fraud claims," *Missouri Independent* (10.12.23); Knauth, "Conservative news site Gateway Pundit files for bankruptcy," *Reuters* (4.25.24); Feuer, "Giuliani concedes he made false statements about Georgia election workers," *NYT* (7.26.23); Feuer & Protess, "Giuliani is liable for defaming Georgia election workers, judge says," *NYT* (8.30.23); Feuer, "Giuliani to go on trial for damages in defamation case," *NYT* (12.10.23); Sullivan, "In court with the women he defamed, Giuliani faces millions in damages," *NYT* (12.11.23); Sullivan, "Giuliani may face more than $47 million in damages, jury told," *Legal Ethics* (12.12.23); Hsu & Gardner, "Ga. poll worker describes harrowing threats in Giuliani defamation trial," *WP* (12.12.23); Sullivan, "Election worker tells jury: Giuliani just messed me up," *NYT* (12.14.23); Hsu, Weiner, Jackman, Paybarah & Bailey, "Rudy Giuliani ordered to pay $148 million to Georgia poll workers," *WP* (12.15.23); Sullivan, "Jury orders Giuliani to pay $148 million to election workers he defamed," *NYT* (12.16.23); Feuer, "Judge orders Giuliani to pay $148 million damage award immediately," *NYT* (12.21.23); Hsu & Weiner, "Defamed Georgia poll workers who won $148 million from Giuliani sue him again," *WP* (12.19.23); Sullivan, "Georgia election workers sue Giuliani again," *NYT* (12.19.23); Weiner, "Rudy Giuliani must pay $148 million to two Georgia women immediately, judge says," *WP* (12.21.23); Feuer, "Judge orders Giuliani to pay $148 million damage award immediately," *NYT* (12.21.23); Wang & Weiner, "Rudy Giuliani files for Chapter 11 bankruptcy in New York," *WP* (12.21.23); Protess, "Giuliani sued over legal fees by lawyer who led his defense," *NYT* (9.19.23); Sullivan, "Pressure grows on Giuliani over incomplete bankruptcy filings," *NYT* (6.18.24); Sullivan, "Giuliani seeks to alter bankruptcy to speed asset sale but keep future income," *NYT* (7.2.24); Sullivan, "Judge suggests he is likely to dismiss Giuliani's bankruptcy case," *NYT* (7.11.24); Bailey, "New York judge throws out Rudy Giuliani's bankruptcy case," *WP* (7.12.24); Sullivan, "Giuliani's assets at risk after case is dismissed," *NYT* (7.14.24); Somasundaram, Masih & Javaid, "Giuliani says he will stop accusing Georgia workers of election tampering," *WP* (5.21.24); Collins, "Giuliani agrees to deal to end his bankruptcy case, pay creditors' financial adviser $400k," *AP* (7.31.24); Bailey, "New York judge finalizes dismissal of Rudy Giuliani's bankruptcy case," *WP* (8.2.24); Sullivan, "Giuliani faces new lawsuit from Georgia election workers over luxury condo," *NYT* (8.30.24); Vazquez, "Right-wing site Gateway Pundit acknowledges inquiry cleared two Georgia election workers," *WP* (10.12.24); Sullivan, "Judge orders Giuliani to forfeit millions in assets to election workers he defamed," *NYT* (10.22.24); Shanahan, "Giuliani moved possessions from N.Y. apartment as creditors closed in," *NYT* (11.5.24); Chen & Bensimon, "Giuliani's delay in handing over prized assets makes judge livid," *NYT* (11.7.24); Woodward, "Rudy Giuliani's lawyers abruptly quit defamation case," *Independent* (11.14.24); Sullivan, "Georgia poll workers defamed by Giuliani receive some of his assets," *NYT* (11.15.24); Hsu, "Georgia election workers ask court to punish Giuliani for

more false claims," *WP* (11.20.24); Chen, "Giuliani is held in contempt of court in defamation case," *NYT* (1.6.25); Hsu & Jacobs, "Giuliani found in contempt, again, in $148 million defamation case," *WP* (1.10.25); Chapman, "'Outrageous and shameful': judge admonishes Giuliani as he's held in contempt—again," *Raw Story* (1.10.25); Jacobs, "Giuliani and Georgia election workers reach settlement in defamation case," *WP* (1.16.25).

27 Cole, "'Central Park Five' members sue Trump for defamation after his debate comments on 1989 case," *CNN* (10.21.24).

28 Zirin (2019); Tuttle, "The litigious—and bullying—Mr. Trump," *National Review* (2.19.16); Darcy, "Judge dismisses Trump campaign's lawsuit against CNN," *CNN* (11.12.20); Darcy, "Trump campaign files libel lawsuit against The New York Times over 2019 opinion piece on Russia," *CNN* (2.26.20); Tracy, "Court dismisses Trump campaign's defamation suit against New York Times," *NYT* (3.9.21); Farhi, "Trump campaign sues Washington Post over opinion columns asserting link to Russian election interference," *WP* (3.3.20); Tillman, "Trump 2020 campaign suit against Washington Post dismissed," *Bloomberglaw* (2.3.23); Palmer, "Donald Trump's 'very questionable' lawsuit torn apart by attorney," *Newsweek* (2.9.23); Shamsian, "Trump's lawyers are hunting for the identities of secret consultants who approved Russiagate Pulitzer Prizes," *Business Insider* (3.7.24); Cohen, "Trump wins round in libel suit against Pulitzer Prize Board over Russia stories," *Politico* (7.21.24); Hallam, Holmes & Cohen, "Trump sues former British spy behind controversial Russia dossier," *CNN* (9.29.23); Landler, "'Damage and distress': Trump sues over Russia dossier in London," *NYT* (10.10.23); Specia," U.K. High Court throws out Trump dossier privacy case," *NYT* (2.1.24); Melley, "Trump ordered to pay legal fees after failed lawsuit over Steele dossier," *AP* (3.7.24); Tobin, "Trump committed egregious intelligence breach, ex-UK spy tells court," *Reuters* (10.17.23); Anders, "Judge throws out Trump's 'big lie' defamation lawsuit against CNN," *WP* (7.31.23); Berman, "Judge says CNN's use of 'Big Lie' regarding Trump isn't defamation," *CNN* (7.29.23); Granieri, "Trump media company sues The Washington Post for defamation, requests $3.78B in damages," *First Amendment Watch* (5.22.23); Bolado, "WaPo scores exit in Trump Media's $3.8B defamation suit," *Law360* (3.8.24); Volokh, "Trump Media libel lawsuit against Washington Post dismissed, but might be refiled with more detailed 'actual malice' allegations," *Reason* (3.8.24); Grynbaum, "Trump's lawsuit against ABC and Stephanopoulos can move forward," *NYT* (7.25.24).

29 Raji, "Trump picks one-judge Texas court for lawsuit over CBS Harris interview," *WP* (10.31.24).

30 Robertson, "Lachlan Murdoch pays $840,000 to site he had accused of libel," *NYT* (8.23.23).

31 Mangan, "Trump ordered to pay New York Times, three reporters nearly $400,000 in legal costs over dismissed lawsuit," *CNBC* (1.12.24); Stack, "Judge dismisses Trump's lawsuit against The New York Times," *NYT* (5.3.23).

32 Mangan, "Trump sues Hillary Clinton, DNC for more than $70 million over 2016 election, 'spurious' Russia collusion claims," *CNBC* (3.24.22); Breuninger, "Judge tosses Trump lawsuit against Hillary Clinton, DNC over 2016 Russia collusion claims," *CNBC* (9.9.22); Naham, "Trump lawyer's rant to Turning Point USA crowd about failed and 'frivolous' Hillary Clinton RICO suit isn't the flex she thinks it is," *Law&Crime* (12.18.23); Schmidt, Haberman & Savage, "Judge orders Trump and lawyer to pay nearly $1 million for bogus suit," *NYT* (1.19.23); Colvin, "Judge fines Trump, lawyer for 'frivolous' Clinton lawsuit," *AP* (1.20.23); Scarcella, "Trump lawyers ask US appeals court to throw out Florida judge's sanctions," *Reuters* (2.28.24).

33 Beitsch, "Trump seeks $100 million in damages from DoJ for Mar-a-Lago search," *The Hill* (8.12.24).
34 Grynbaum & Feuer, "ABC to pay $15 million to settle a defamation suit brought by Trump," *NYT* (1215.24); Barnes, "Inside end of ABC suit with Trump," *NYT* (12.20.24); Kanno-Youngs, Haberman, Enrich & Feuer, "Trump sues the Des Moines Register, escalating threats against the media," *NYT* (12.17.24).
35 Lawsuits have also succeeded against far-right violence, Kirkpatrick, "The Infiltrators," *New Yorker* (8.26.24).
36 Liptak & Sullivan, "Trump, angry over Woodward book, renews criticism of libel laws," *NYT* (3.30.17); New York Times v. Sullivan, 376 U.S. 254 (1964); Liptak, "Two Justices say Supreme Court should reconsider landmark libel decision," *NYT* (8.2.21).
37 O'Connell & Fahrenthold, "Trump 'inflated his total assets when it served his purposes,' Cohen alleges in his hearing, citing financial documents," *WP* (2.27.19); Garcia & Feinberg, "How Alexandria Ocasio-Cortez inadvertently sparked the New York attorney general's Trump lawsuit," *The Independent* (9.23.22); Scannell, del Valle & Souza, "Ex-Trump Org. CFO pleads guilty to perjury charges," *CNN* (3.4.24); Webster, "Manhattan judge orders Eric Trump to testify in NY AG's investigation before election," *NYLJ* (9.23.20); Scannell, "Eric Trump sat for deposition as part of investigation by New York attorney general," *CNN* (10.5.20).
38 Pagliery, "He could've taken down Trump Org. Now he's taking the blame," *Daily Beast* (11.18.22); Pagliery, "Explosive interview directly implicates Trump in tax scheme," *Daily Beast* (7.16.21); Protess, Rashbaum & Bromwich, "Trump Organization is charged in 15-year tax scheme," *NYT* (7.1.21); Farenthold & Jacobs, "Trump Organization removes indicted top finance officer Allen Weisselberg from leadership roles at dozens of subsidiaries," *WP* (7.12.21); Dawsey & Fahrenthold, "New York attorney general seeks Trump's deposition as part of civil fraud investigation," *WP* (12.9.21); Katersky, "Eldest Trump children won't comply with subpoenas from New York attorney general," *ABC News* (1.3.22); Gerstein, "Trump sues NY Attorney General James to block fraud probes," *Politico* (12.20.21); Hooper, "Judge dismisses Trump's lawsuit seeking to stop New York civil probe," *Politico* (5.27.22); Larson, "Trump asks appeals court to scrap New York probe of his assets," *Bloomberg* (8.16.22); Sisak, "Trump drops appeal, ending legal fight against New York Attorney General Letitia James," *PBS* (1.24.23).
39 Keith, "At his Arizona rally, Trump played a supercut of NY Attorney General Letitia James, who is investigating his real estate company for fraud, labeling her an 'unhinged liberal,'" *Business Insider* (1.15.22); DeChalus & Shamsian, "Trump is facing criminal investigations into his conduct. Court buildings are bracing for violence and chaos," *Business Insider* (2.3.22); Kyle, "Trump family complaint alleges NY AG Letitia James broke state laws in politically motivated investigation," *Yahoo! News* (2.2.22); Italiano, Sheth & Shamsian, "Trump's lawyers accuse NY AG Tish James of political bias and 'prosecutorial misconduct' in fiery court hearing," *Business Insider* (2.17.22); Bromwich, Protess & Rashbaum, "N.Y. Attorney General can question Trump and 2 children, judge rules," *NYT* (2.17.22); Papenfuss, "'He's just a bad guy': judge slams claim that Trump is unfairly singled out in AG probe," *HuffPost* (2.17.22); Scannell & Reid, "Trumps file appeal to block deposition in NY attorney general investigation," *CNN* (2.28.22); Kates, "Donald Trump, Donald Jr. and Ivanka Trump must testify in New York fraud investigation, appeals court rules," *BS News* (5.26.22); DeGregory, "Trump files to block testimony in NY attorney general investigation," *New York Post* (6.6.22); "New York high court nixes Trump appeal,

clearing way for testimony," *CNBC* (6.14.22); Pagliery, "Judge orders Trump to pay up for missing evidence," *Daily Beast* (5.11.22); Jacobs, "Donald Trump held in contempt for failing to provide business records," *WP* (4.25.22); Italiano, "Donald Trump now owes NY AG Letitia James $80k as appellate court tells him to keep paying," *Business Insider* (5.3.22); Scannell, "Trump must pay $110,000 in sanctions to NY attorney general, court rules," *CNN* (2.14.23).

40 Scannell, "Former CFO of Trump Org pleads guilty for his role in tax fraud scheme," *CNN* (8.18.22); Bromwich, Protess & Rashbaum, "Inside the negotiations that led a top Trump executive to plead guilty," *NYT* (8.19.22); Bernstein, "Updates on three New York cases against former President Trump," *NPR* (11.4.22); Scannell & del Valle, "Trump Org. stopped illegal tax practices when Donald Trump took office, former CFO testifies," *CNN* (11.17.22); Del Valle & Scannell, "Trump Org. entities were held in criminal contempt and fined 4K ahead of tax fraud trial," *CNN* (12.13.22); Jacobs, "Trump Organization convicted in N.Y. criminal tax fraud trial," *WP* (12.6.22); Sisak, "Trump's company fined $1.6 million for tax fraud scheme," *Huffpost* (1.13.23).

41 Gerstein, Durkin & Cheney, "Trump, company and family members sued by New York AG over alleged fraud scheme," *Politico* (9.21.22); Visser, "Donald Trump sues New York attorney general for waging 'crusade' against him," *HuffPost* (11.3.22); Bromwich, Haberman, Protess & Rashbaum, "Trump files a suit against N.Y.'s attorney eneral, and against advice," *NYT* (11.3.22); Katersky, "New York AG asks judge to reject Trump lawsuit seeking emergency protections," *ABC News* (12.7.22); Scannell, "Judge rejects Trump's attempt to block NY attorney general from accessing his trust records," *CNN* (12.21.22); Gerstein, "Judge slams Trump suit aimed at blocking N.Y. attorney general probe," *Politico* (12.21.22); Wagner, "Trump withdraws lawsuit against N.Y. attorney general," *WP* (1.20.23); Gregorian & Reiss, "Trump drops Florida lawsuit against New York attorney general," *NBC News* (1.20.23).

42 Scannell, "Judge sets October 2023 trial for New York attorney general's $250 million lawsuit against Trump," *CNN* (11.22.22); Scannell, "New York judge denies motion from Trump and family to dismiss $250 million lawsuit," *CNN* (1.6.23); Bromwich & Protess, "Judge scolds Trump legal team and lets James's lawsuit proceed," *NYT* (1.6.23); Stemple, "Judge rejects Trump bid to delay New York fraud trial," *Reuters* (9.6.23).

43 Bromwich, Protess & Rashbaum, "Trump invokes Fifth Amendment, attacking legal system as troubles mount," *NYT* (8.10.23); O'Connell & Jacobs, "After years of exaggerating his business assets, Trump confronts them in court," *WP* (10.10.23).

44 Bromwich, Protess & Rashbaum, "Court throws out New York's civil case against Ivanka Trump," *NYT* (6.28.23); Bromwich, Protess & Feuer, "Trump lawsuit against judge could delay N.Y. fraud trial," *NYT* (9.15.23); Bromwich & Protess, "Appeals court rejects Trump's effort to delay trial in fraud case," *NYT* (9.28.23); Jacobs, "N.Y. appeals court refuses to delay Trump fraud trial set to start Monday," *WP* (9.28.23); Pagliery, "Inside Trump's gambit to get rid of a judge by suing him," *Daily Beast* (9.16.23).

45 Jacobs, "N.Y. judge finds Trump committed fraud and sanctions his attorneys," *WP* (9.26.23); Bromwich & Protess, "Judge rules Trump committed fraud, stripping control of key properties," *NYT* (9.27.23); Gershman, "Appeals court preserves Trump's N.Y. business certificates for now," *WSJ* (10.6.23); Bromwich, Protess & Rashbaum, "Here's the latest on Trump's civil fraud trial in New York," *NYT* (10.2.23).

46 Rashbaum, "Jurist presiding at Trump's civil trial will serve as judge and jury," *NYT* (10.2.23); Parnell, "Trump assails case during lunch break," *WP* (10.3.23);

Jacobs, "Trump's attorney Alina Habba contends case is politically motivated," *WP* (10.3.23); Jacobs, Berman, O'Connell & Parnell, "New York's $250 million fraud trial against Donald Trump gets underway," *WP* (10.3.23); Goldmacher & Haberman, "As his fraud trial begins, Trump looks to capitalize on it," *NYT* (10.3.23); Haberman, Nehamas & McFadden, "Trump said shoplifter should be shot, part of a string of violent remarks," *NYT* (10.4.23).

47 Jacobs & Berman, "Judge issues gag order in fraud case after Trump assails staffer on social media," *WP* (10.4.23); Bromwich, "Trump ordered not to comment on judge's staff in fraud case," *NYT* (10.4.23); Bromwich, Protess & Feuer, "How judges restrain Trump: gag orders, fines and possible jail time," *NYT* (10.27.23); Dolan, "Trump appeals gag order in federal 2020 election subversion case," *CNN* (10.17.23); Queen, "Donald Trump turns up at NY fraud trial, complains it distracts from campaign," *Reuters* (10.17.23); Christobek, Bromwich & Protess, "Trump fined $5,000 for breaking gag order by leaving abusive post online," *NYT* (10.21.23).

48 Christobek & Bromwich, "What to know after two weeks of Trump's civil fraud trial," *NYT* (10.20.23); Arnsdorf, Dawsey & Hsu, "Trump seethes at gag order in federal case while his campaign relishes it," *WP* (10.24.23); Mandela, "An ideal for which I am prepared to die," *G* (4.23.07).

49 Protess & Haberman, "Trump drops lawsuit against Michael Cohen, his former fixer," *NYT* (10.6.23); Gershman, "Michael Cohen testifies Trump ordered him to inflate wealth," *WSJ* (10.24.23); Jacobs & Berman, "Michael Cohen and Trump met again during civil fraud trial," *WP* (10.25.23).

50 Bromwich & Christobek, "Judge who set gag order considers more punishment for Trump," *NYT* (10.25.23); Jacobs & Barrett, "Trump fined $10,000 in what judge calls second violation of gag order," *WP* (10.25.23); Bromwich, Protess & Feuer, "How judges restrain Trump: gag orders, fines and possible jail time," *NYT* (10.27.23); Bromwich & Christobek, "3 children of Trump set to testify in civil trial," *NYT* (10.28.23); Bromwich, Protess, Rashbaum & Haberman, "How Cohen's testimony sets the stage for Trump's hush money trial," *NYT* (10.29.23); Stemple, "With trial underway, Trump appeals New York judge's fraud ruling," *Reuters* (10.5.23).

51 Jacobs & Berman, "Trump Jr. testifies, deflects responsibility in N.Y. business fraud case," *WP* (11.2.23); Bromwich & Christobek, "Donald Trump Jr. denies responsibility for company business statements," *NYT* (11.1.23).

52 Bromwich & Christobek, "Trump's lawyers attack judge's clerk, creating a 'sideshow,'" *NYT* (11.4.23).

53 "Donald Trump testifying in New York fraud trial," *WP* (11.6.23); Berman, Vazquez, Jacobs & Parnell, "Trump completes a contentious day of testimony in N.Y. civil fraud trial," *WP* (11.6.23); Blake, "4 things we learned from Trump's testimony in the New York fraud trial," *WP* (11.6.23); LeVine, "Grievance, insults, tangents: Trump brings his 2024 campaign into the courtroom," *WP* (11.7.23).

54 Bromwich & Haberman, "After Trump testifies, Republicans attack judge in civil fraud trial," *NYT* (11.11.23); Bromwich, "Trump lawyers call for mistrial in civil fraud case, attacking judge," *NYT* (11.16.23).

55 Orden, "Appeals court judge puts Trump's New York gag order on hold," *Politico* (11.16.23); Bromwich & Feuer, "Trump and aides immediately attack clerk after gag order is paused," *NYT* (11.17.23); Bromwich & Christobek, "Trump again barred from insulting court staff in civil fraud trial," *NYT* (11.30.23); Basu, "Trump unleashes grievances, warnings in wild 24 hours on Truth Social," *Axios* (11.29.23); Jacobs, "Trump lost chance to challenge N.Y. gag order before trial ends," *WP* (12.4.23); Hartfield & Cole, "NY's top court upholds gag order against Trump in civil fraud trial," *CNN* (1.16.24).

56 Bromwich, "Judge denies Trump's request for a mistrial in fraud case," *NYT* (11.18.23).
57 Charalambous, Katersky, Rubin & Bruggeman, "Trump fraud trial live updates: ex-controller breaks down on witness stand," *ABC News* (11.21.23); Italiano, "Donald Trump has worst day yet in New York civil fraud trial as underling's scribbled note ties him to conspiracy," *Business Insider* (11.21.23).
58 Scannell, Herb & Souza, "Trump attends New York civil fraud trial as accounting expert testifies for defense," *CNN* (12.7.23); Breuninger, "Trump judge slams credibility of paid expert in fraud case, suggests fee influenced testimony," *CNBC* (12.18.23).
59 Gershman, "Trump changes mind, won't testify again as New York fraud trial nears end," *WSJ* (12.10.23); Bromwich, "Trump will not testify as scheduled in civil fraud trial," *NYT* (12.11.23); Kates, "Trump's defense concludes its case in New York fraud trial," *CBS News* (12.12.23).
60 Bromwich, "Judge in Trump's civil fraud trial faces bomb threat at his home," *NYT* (1.11.24); "Closing statements conclude in Trump's N.Y. civil fraud trial," *WP* (1.11.24).
61 Bromwich & Protess, "As Trump awaits fraud penalty, a monitor's report could raise his risk," *NYT* (1.30.24).
62 "Judge orders Trump to pay more than $350 million in N.Y. civil fraud trial," *WP* (2.16.24); O'Connell, "Hefty fines, penalties will rock Trump family's business and fortune," *WP* (2.17.24); Feuer & Haberman, "Trump hit where it hurts most," *NYT* (2.17.24); Bromwich & Protess, "What the civil fraud ruling means for Trump's finances and his empire," *NYT* (2.17.24); Rashbaum, "Highlights from the decision in Trump's fraud case," *NYT* (2.17.24); Protess, Bromwich, Haberman & Lemonides, "A $450 million blow to Trump's finances, and his identity," *NYT* (2.18.24); Christobek, "The civil fraud ruling on Donald Trump, annotated," *NYT* (2.18.24).
63 Poniewozik, "For Donald Trump, recriminations will be televised," *NYT* (2.17.24); Vigdor, "At rally in Michigan, Trump lashes out at judge who fined him $355 million," *NYT* (2.18.24); Scully, "Trump rails against New York judge who slapped him with $355 million fine in fraud case," *The Hill* (2.18.24); Huynh, "Trump breaks silence on Navalny death, but doesn't condemn Putin," *NYT* (2.20.24); Svitek, LeVine & Arnsdorf, "Trump compares death of Navalny to his legal troubles," *WP* (2.21.24); Fahy, "Suspicious powder sent to offices of Trump judge and Attorney General," *NYT* (2.29.24).
64 Jacobs, "Trump lawyers seek delay in enforcement of $350 million fraud judgment," *WP* (2.21.24); Habeshian, "Judge rejects Trump's request for delay in enforcement of civil penalties," *Axios* (2.22.24); Jacobs & Beman, "Judge won't delay Trump financial penalty but lets sons remain atop company for now," *WP* (2.28.24); Protess & Christobek, "Trump rebuffed after asking judge to delay his $454 penalty," *NYT* (2.29.24).
65 Protess, Rashbaum, McKinley & Christobek, "Key figure in Trump's business pleads guilty to felony perjury," *NYT* (3.4.24); Bromwich & Protess, "Judge in Trump's civil fraud case asks whether a key witness lied," *NYT* (2.7.24); Jacobs, "Ex-Trump company executive Weisselberg sentenced to 5 months in jail," *WP* (4.10.24); Christobek, Bromwich & Protess, "Trump's ex-finance chief is sentenced to 5 months in Rikers for perjury," *NYT* (4.10.24); Kates, "Former Trump Organization CFO Allen Weisselberg released from jail," *CBS News* (7.19.24).
66 McKinley, "After Letitia James wins big in courtrooms, she celebrates in public," *NYT* (3.10.24).
67 LeVine, "Trump claims he has $500 million in cash, undercutting his lawyers," *WP* (3.22.24); Jacobs & O'Connell, "Trump unable to finance an appeal bond

for at least $450 million, lawyers say," *WP* (3.18.24); Christobek & Protess, "What we know about Trump's failure to arrange a half-billion-dollar bond," *NYT* (3.19.24).

68 Berman, O'Connell & Jacobs, "Trump wins partial stay of fraud judgment, allowed to post $175 million," *WP* (3.25.24); Gershman, Fanelli & Ramey, "Judge denies Trump request to pause $355 million ruling," *WSJ* (2.28.24); Gold, "In fund-raising blitz, Trump warns Democrats hands off Trump Tower," *NYT* (3.25.24); Arnsdorf, "Trump reels from competing court decisions as trials disrupt campaign," *WP* (3.25.24); Berman, O'Connell & Jacobs, "Trump wins partial stay of fraud judgment, allowed to post $175 million," *WP* (3.25.24).

69 Jacobs, "Trump posts $175 million bond to keep New York authorities from seizing property," *WP* (4.2.24); Kranish & O'Connell, "How a California billionaire known for auto loans provided Trump's bond," *WP* (4.2.24); Dale, "Trump falsely claims that appeals court said 'you won' the civil fraud case he lost," *CNN* (4.4.24); Protess & Haag, "New York attorney general questions Trump's $175 million bond deal," *NYT* (4.4.24); Haag, "Trump and attorney general agree on minor changes to $175 million bond," *NYT* (4.23.24).

70 Russo & Dienst, "Trump legal team calls for Judge Arthur Engoron to recuse himself from civil fraud case," *NBC NewYork* (6.20.24); Schoonover, "NY judge in Trump civil-fraud case declines to step down after recusal motion," *Courthouse News Service* (7.25.24); McKinley & Protess, "Trump appeals $454 million fraud judgment, saying it was excessive," *NYT* (7.22.24).

71 Abel (2008, 2011).

72 But see Abel (2008: Ch. 7; 2011: Ch. 7).

73 Cummings, "Lawyers in Backsliding Democracy," *112 Calif. L. Rev* 513 (2024).

74 Helderman, "Impeachment is over. But other efforts to reckon with Trump's post-election chaos have just begun," *WP* (2.22.21); Rubin, "Rep. Zoe Lofgren embarrassed Republicans with their own words. Now they seek to silence her," *WP* (5.6.21); Helderman, " 'This is really fantastical': federal judge in Michigan presses Trump-allied lawyers on 2020 election fraud claims in sanctions hearing," *WP* (7.13.21); Cottle, "Trump's 'Team Kraken' lands in hot water," *NYT* (7.15.21); Feuer, "Judge orders sanctions against pro-Trump lawyers over election lawsuit," *NYT* (8.2.21); Helderman, "Federal judge in Michigan orders pro-Trump lawyers disciplined over lawsuit seeking to overturn 2020 election," *WP* (8.25.21); Helderman, "Sidney Powell, L. Lin Wood among attorneys ordered to pay $175,000 over Michigan 'Kraken' suit," *WP* (12.3.21); Bowden & Teague (2022: 222–23).

75 Hendrickson, "Michigan commission: discipline 'Kraken' lawyers for lawsuit to overturn 2020 election," *Detroit Free Press* (5.5.23); King v. Whitmer, 6th Circuit (6.23.23); Fritze, "Supreme Court won't review sanctions against pro-Trump lawyers who filed frivolous 2020 election suits," *CNN* (2.20.24).

76 Sneed, "Inside the effort to disbar attorneys who backed bogus election lawsuits," *CNN* (3.10.22); Lee, "Texas judge refuses to dismiss disciplinary case against former Trump attorney Sidney Powell," *Courthouse News Service* (6.22.22); Sneed, "Judge tosses out disciplinary action against Sidney Powell for work on Trump election reversal bid," *CNN* (2.24.23); Pesquera, "17 lawyers want Sidney Powell punished: letter sent to Bar about Trump attorney," *Texas Lawyer* (11.7.23); Thomas, "Trump ally Sidney Powell defeats appeal in Texas attorney ethics case," *Reuters* (4.18.24); Sneed, "Texas appeals court sides with Sidney Powell, rejecting attorney discipline over her Trump election lawsuits," *CNN* (4.22.24).

77 Thomas, "Lawyer for Sidney Powell faces disciplinary charges over 2020 election case," *Reuters* (1.18.24); Cheney, "DC bar authorities file disciplinary charges

against pro-Trump 2020 election lawyers," *Politico* (1.19.24); Gohmert v. Pence, 510 F. Supp. 3d 435 (E.D. Tex. 2021).

78 510 F. Supp. 3d 435 (E.D. Tex. 2021).

79 Durkee, "Lin Wood kicked off Delaware court case over 'toxic' post-election lawsuits," *Forbes* (1.12.21); Hunyh, "L. Lin Wood, lawyer who tried to overturn Trump's 2020 loss, gives up license," *NYT* (7.7.23); Caulder, "Lin Wood must pay ex-partners $3.75m, Ga. Jurors say," *Law360* (8.15.24).

80 Matter of Giuliani (App. Div. First Judicial Department 6.24.21); Hong, Rashbaum & Protess, "Court suspends Giuliani's law license, citing Trump election lies," *NYT* (6.24.21); Weiner, "Rudy Giuliani suspended from practicing law in D.C. Court," *WP* (7.8.21); Goudsward, "Rudy Giuliani charged with ethics violations in DC for baseless election lawsuit," *NLJ* (6.12.22); Lynch, "Giuliani hit with ethics charges by Washington D.C. authorities over false election claims," *Reuters* (6.10.22); Sneed, "Giuliani pressed on role in Trump 2020 election reversal legal gambits during attorney discipline hearing," *CNN* (12.5.22); Goudsward, "Giuliani should be disciplined over 2020 election case, ethics panel says," *Reuter* (12.15.22); Weiser, "Giuliani disbarred from the practice of law in New York," *NYT* (7.2.24); Polantz, "Attorney disciplinary committee recommends Rudy Giuliani be disbarred for 2020 election legal work," *CNN* (7.7.23); Feuer, "Giuliani should lose his law license in D.C., bar panel says," *NYT* (7.8.23); Cheney & Gerstein, "Disciplinary panel calls for Rudy Giuliani's disbarment," *Politico* (7.7.23); Thomas, "Giuliani should be disbarred over election case, DC ethics board says," *Reuters* (5.31.24); Weiser, "Giuliani disbarred from the practice of law in New York," *NYT* (7.2.24); Sullivan, "Giuliani disbarred in D.C. over efforts to overturn 2020 election," *NYT* (9.26.24).

81 Helderman, "'A propaganda tool' for Trump: a second federal judge castigates attorneys who filed a lawsuit challenging the 2020 results," *WP* (7.16.21); Helderman, "'The stuff of which violent insurrections are made': federal judge punishes Colorado lawyers for 2020 election lawsuit," *WP* (8.5.21); Helderman, "Judge orders two lawyers who filed suit challenging 2020 election to pay hefty fees: 'They need to take responsibility,'" *WP* (11.23.21); Scarcella, "Attorney sanctions upheld in 'utterly baseless' lawsuit challenging 2020 election," *Reuters* (12.13.22); O'Rourke v. Dominion Voting Systems.

82 Alfaro, "California seeks to disbar Trump adviser John Eastman over Jan. 6 charges," *WP* (1.27.23); Sneed, "California Bar unveils disciplinary charges against Trump lawyer John Eastman," *CNN* (1.26.23); Rubin, "Eastman's defense is shattered in state bar proceeding," *WP* (8.28.23); Cutler, "Eastman preliminarily found culpable in California bar trial," *Bloomberglaw* (11.2.23); State Bar of California, "State Bar Court Hearing Judge Recommends John Eastman's Disbarment" (3.27.24); Dreisbach, "California judge recommends disbarment of pro-Trump attorney John Eastman," *NPR* (3.27.24); Karlik, "Federal judge orders John Eastman to explain why he should remain attorney on Colorado case," *Colorado Politics* (4.29.24).

83 Sneed, "Inside the effort to disbar attorneys who backed bogus election lawsuits," *CNN* (3.10.22); Feuer, "Trump lawyer admits to falsehoods in 2020 fraud claims," *NYT* (3.9.23); Suter, "Watchdog groups push for disbarment of ex-Trump attorney Jenna Ellis over Georgia charges," *The Hill* (12.16.23); Young, "Former Trump lawyer Jenna Ellis faces second misconduct case in Colorado over conviction," *Colorado Newsline* (1.9.24).

84 Savage, "Lawyers group asks court to punish an author of Trump electors scheme," *NYT* (10.12.22); https://ldad.org/wp-content/uploads/2022/10/Ethics-Complaint-against-Kenneth-Chesebro.pdf; LDAD to Attorney Grievance

Committee (10.30.23); https://apps.calbar.ca.gov/attorney/Licensee/Detail/236022; Skolnik, "Trump lawyer cases show 2020 election punishments come slowly," *Bloomberg Law* (4.15.24); Savage, "New York court suspends lawyer who pushed Trump's fake electors scheme," *NYT* (10.31.24).

85 Savage, "Group seeks disbarment of a Trump-aligned lawyer for a key Jan. 6 witness," *NYT* (3.6.23); Broadwater & Savage, "Ethics panels dismiss complaints against former lawyer for Jan. 6 witness," *NYT* (3.19.24).

86 Benner, "Ethics board moves to penalize Jeffrey Clark, who aided Trump in election plot," *NYT* (7.22.22); Marcus, "The curious case of the strange man who was nearly attorney general," *WP* (9.17.22); Lynch, "Trump ally Clark asks U.S. court to block disciplinary charges against him," *Reuters* (10.17.22); Cheney & Gerstein, "Trump signals intent to block testimony in Jeff Clark disciplinary proceedings," *Politico* (1.6.24); Polantz, Cole & Sneed, "Ex-DOJ official Jeff Clark violated DC attorney ethics rules with 2020 election schemes, bar disciplinary panel says," *CNN* (4.4.24); Cheney, "Key Trump ally in 2020 should lose law license for two years, DC disciplinary panel rules," *Politico* (8.1.24).

87 Scarcella & Thomsen, "Judge says Texas Attorney General Paxton must face ethics lawsuit," *Reuters* (1.31.23); "Denied: Court rejects Ken Paxton's bid to dismiss disciplinary suit," *Texas Layer* (4.19.24); Sneed, "Inside the effort to disbar attorneys who backed bogus election lawsuits," *CNN* (3.10.22); Scherer, "Ken Paxton agrees to community service, paying restitution to avoid trial in securities fraud case," *Texas Tribune* (3.26.24).

88 Macdonald-Evoy, "Sanctions for bogus election lawsuits spur GOP proposal to protect attorneys from punishment," *Arizona Mirror* (2.14.23).

89 Abel (2008, 2011).

3

STATE PROSECUTIONS OF TRUMP

State prosecutors brought two cases against Trump: in Manhattan for falsifying business records about hush money payments to Stormy Daniels and in Fulton County, Georgia, for interfering in its choice of Electoral College votes.

3.1 Stormy Daniels, Hush Money, and Falsifying Business Records

In 2006, Stephanie Clifford (who appeared in pornographic films under the name Stormy Daniels) allegedly had an affair with Trump.[1] In January 2018, the *Wall Street Journal* reported that before the 2016 election, Trump had his lawyer, Michael Cohen, pay Daniels $130,000 not to disclose this. The following month Cohen loyally misrepresented that he had done so out of his own pocket; and two months later Trump denied knowing about the payment. But three weeks after that he admitted Cohen had represented him in "the Stormy Daniels deal," and a month after that Rudy Giuliani, Trump's new lawyer, said his client had reimbursed Cohen. In August, Cohen pleaded to eight criminal charges, admitting he had paid Daniels "in coordination with and at the direction of a candidate for federal office." Daniels won a lawsuit invalidating the NDA Cohen had made her sign but was found liable for defaming Trump and ordered to pay him nearly $300,000 in legal fees and sanctions. When the Ninth Circuit dismissed Daniels's appeal as untimely, Trump gloated that the ruling was "a total and complete victory and vindication for and of me." (Daniels's lawyer, Michael Avenatti, was subsequently convicted of identity theft and wire fraud for stealing from her and sentenced to four years.) The Federal Election Commission (dividing along

DOI: 10.4324/9781032629186-3

party lines) decided not to investigate whether the hush money payment violated federal election laws.

In September 2019, Manhattan DA Cyrus Vance subpoenaed the international accounting firm Mazars USA, seeking eight years of Trump's personal and corporate tax returns.[2] The following month, SDNY Judge Marrero (Clinton) dismissed Trump's action seeking to block the release, finding his claim of immunity from criminal investigation "repugnant to the nation's governmental structure and constitutional values." "Shunning the concept of the inviolability of the person of the King of England and the bounds of the monarch's protective screen, the founders disclaimed any notion that the Constitution generally conferred similarly all-encompassing immunity upon the president." Marrero dismissed three DoJ memos asserting that a sitting president could not be charged with a crime because they relied on "suppositions, practicalities and public policy," not precedent. (Mueller had cited these memos when declining to consider charges against Trump in the Russian collusion investigation, see Abel 2024b: Chapter 2.1.) Trump retorted on Twitter: "The Radical Left Democrats have failed on all fronts, so now they are pushing local New York City and State Democrat prosecutors to go get President Trump. A thing like this has never happened to any president before. Not even close!" A month later the Second Circuit (Katzmann (Clinton), Chin (Obama) and Droney (Obama)) affirmed. In July 2020, the Supreme Court did as well (7–2, Alito and Thomas dissenting). Chief Justice Roberts wrote: "No citizen, not even the president, is categorically above the common duty to produce evidence when called upon in a criminal proceeding." Justice Kavanaugh wrote separately: "In our system of government, as this court has often stated, no one is above the law. That principle applies, of course, to a president." Trump tweeted: "This is all a political prosecution. I won the Mueller Witch Hunt, and others, and now I have to keep fighting in a politically corrupt New York. Not fair to this Presidency or Administration!" DA Vance commented: "This is a tremendous victory for our nation's system of justice and its founding principle that no one—not even a president—is above the law." In February 2021, his office finally got the tax returns.

Although Vance decided not to pursue the matter, Alvin Bragg, who succeeded him in January 2022, revived the investigation the following November.[3] In March 2023, offered the opportunity to testify before the grand jury, Trump responded by accusing Bragg of falling back on an "old and rebuked case which has been rejected by every prosecutor's office that has looked." "The Manhattan District Attorney's threat to indict President Trump is simply insane. It's an embarrassment to the Democratic prosecutors, and it's an embarrassment to New York City." Trump said on Truth Social: "I did absolutely nothing wrong, I never had an affair with Stormy Daniels, nor would I have wanted to have an affair with Stormy Daniels. I relied on counsel in order to resolve this Extortion of me." "Russia, Russia, Russia, Ukraine, Ukraine, Ukraine, the no-collusion Mueller hoax." Trump and his supporters were "victims of this corrupt, depraved, and weaponized justice system." A Trump spokesman declared: "President Donald J. Trump is completely innocent, he did nothing wrong, and even the biggest, most radical left Democrats are making that clear." Trump called the case the "nuclear button," a "political donation by Bragg to Biden," and vowed to condemn a donation by George Soros's foundation to the PAC that helped Bragg. Joe Tacopina, Trump's lawyer, predicted: "If they bring this case, I believe this will catapult him into the White House . . . because this will show how they're weaponizing the justice system." Tacopina explained that Trump had denied knowing about the payments "because it was a confidential settlement so, if he acknowledged that he would be violating the confidential settlement." "So, is it the truth? Of course it's not the truth. Was he supposed to tell the truth?" By lying "he was abiding by not only his rights, but Stormy Daniels's rights."

A week later, Trump proclaimed: "THE FAR & AWAY LEADING REPUBLICAN CANDIDATE AND FORMER PRESIDENT OF THE UNITED STATES OF AMERICA, WILL BE ARRESTED ON TUESDAY OF NEXT WEEK. PROTEST TAKE OUR NATION BACK!"[4] A spokesman explained: "President Trump is rightfully highlighting his innocence and the weaponization of our justice system." His lawyer, Susan R. Necheles, said: "Since this is a political prosecution the DA's office has engaged in a practice of leaking everything to the press, rather than communicating with President Trump's attorneys as would be done in a normal case." Trump exploited the case for fundraising: "MANHATTAN D.A. COULD BE CLOSE TO CHARGING TRUMP. Patriot—With the Deep State gunning for President Trump with phony witch hunts like never before we had to be sure you saw the *private and secure* message he wrote for YOU." House Speaker McCarthy called for a Congressional investigation of Bragg: "I'm directing relevant committees to immediately investigate if federal funds are being used to subvert our democracy by interfering in elections with politically motivated prosecutions." Trump posted on Truth Social: "PROTEST, PROTEST, PROTEST."

At the House GOP retreat, McCarthy denounced what he called the political investigation of Trump as an "abuse of power" and predicted "it will not hold up in court."[5] But he cautioned: "I don't think people should protest this." "We want calmness out there. Nobody, nobody [is] for violence." House Whip Emmer said an indictment would be an "outrageous" use of the criminal justice system against "political adversaries." Rep. Greene declared:

> If Americans want to protest a corrupt, Soros-funded Manhattan DA that's ignoring crime in his own district and spending all of those tax dollars on figuring out how to politically prosecute President Trump, then they have a right to protest. And I completely agree with them.

@TrumpWarRoom admonished supporters: "It has been over 24 hours and some people are still quiet. History will judge their silence." Pence commented: "I think it just tells you everything you need to know about the radical left in this country. It just feels like a politically charged prosecution here." "The American people have a constitutional right to peaceably assemble." New Hampshire Gov. Sununu warned that the potential charges were "building a lot of sympathy for the former president." "There are other issues that really take precedent [sic] in terms of where this country needs to go." Vivek Ramaswamy said: "the ruling party of this country [is] using police power to arrest its political opposition." Rep. Donalds called it "one of the worst uses of the justice system we've ever seen. It's going to descend [sic] all of America into further chaos." Trump posted: "There was no crime, period." "Prosecutorial Misconduct and Interference with an Election." The New York Young Republican Club announced a "peaceful protest" on March 20 against "Alvin Bragg's heinous attack" on Trump.

Florida Gov. DeSantis (Trump's leading rival for the Republican nomination) said: "The Manhattan district attorney is a Soros-funded prosecutor. And so he, like other Soros-funded prosecutors, they weaponize their office to impose a political agenda on society at the expense of the rule of law and public safety." But he added snidely: "I don't know what goes into paying hush money to a porn star to secure silence over some type of alleged affair."[6] This provoked Trump to threaten:

> Ron DeSanctimonious will probably find out about FALSE ACCUSATIONS & FAKE STORIES sometime in the future, as he gets older, wiser, and better known, when he's unfairly and illegally attacked by a woman, even classmates that are 'underage' (or possibly a man!). I'm sure he will want to fight these misfits just like I do!

Trump reposted a photo of DeSantis with three women, insinuating he had been "grooming high school girls with alcohol" as their teacher. DeSantis responded by telling Piers Morgan of the *New York Post*: "You really want to look to people like our Founding Fathers, like what type of character . . . are you bringing?"

Don Jr. advised: "Pay attention to which Republicans spoke out against this corrupt BS immediately and who sat on their hands and waited to see which way the wind was blowing."[7] *The Gateway Pundit* pronounced: "The Silence is Deafening." Ramaswamy "called on my fellow GOP candidates @ RonDeSantisFL and @NikkiHaley to join me in condemning the potential Trump indictment because those of us *running against Trump* can most credibly call on the Manhattan DA to abandon this disastrously politicized prosecution." Rep. Stefanik denounced the indictment as "unAmerican," an example of the "Radical Left" reaching "a dangerous new low of Third

World countries." Rep. Emmer said: "I don't care if you're Republican, Democrat, or other, when your government can literally start turning on its political adversaries because nothing as far as we know has changed with this case." Rep. Scalise warned: "it's more of a concern about how this diminishes law enforcement in America." On Truth Social, Trump called on supporters to protest and "take our nation back." Sen. Vance said the "politically motivated prosecution makes the argument for Trump much stronger." Bernard Kerik (a Giuliani associate) pronounced:

> at some point, local, state and federal law enforcement officers need to stand up and walk out, if they're forced to engage in illegal political persecutions! You cannot break the law to enforce it, and that is exactly what @ManhattanDA is doing.

(Police strikes are illegal, as this former NYPD Commissioner well knew.)

Bragg's office replied: "We will not be intimidated by attempts to undermine the justice process, nor will we let baseless accusations deter us from fairly applying the law."[8] It dismissed the canard that the office was ignoring crime: "New York remains one of the safest big cities in the U.S." Reps. Jordan, Comer, and Steil had threatened: "You are reportedly about to engage in an unprecedented abuse of prosecutorial authority: the indictment of a former president of the United States and current declared candidate for that office." "Your actions will erode confidence in the evenhanded application of justice and unalterably interfere in the course of the 2024 presidential election." "In light of the serious consequences of your actions, we expect that you will testify about what plainly appears to be a politically motivated prosecutorial decision." HJC chair Jordan said: "We want Mr. Bragg to come in and testify . . . and we want the communications that took place between his office and DOJ." "We don't think President Trump broke the law at all." Rep. McCarthy accused Bragg of "trying to create something when he has all the crime happening in New York, and he prides himself on not prosecuting everything else." "There's nothing wrong with [House Committees] asking the question." Rep. Goldman (D-NY) replied: "Defending Trump is not a legitimate legislative purpose for Congress to investigate a state district attorney." "Congress has no jurisdiction to investigate the Manhattan DA, which receives no federal funding nor has any other federal nexus." Rep. Nadler (D-NY) said: "Using a Congressional committee to bully a state DA sounds like . . . the weaponization of the federal government." Republicans "tied themselves in knots protecting" Trump "at the expense of the American people, law enforcement and our legal system." "Quit meddling in ongoing investigations." (Both represented Manhattan.) Rep. Raskin (D-MD) said: "The Representatives' letter to the Manhattan DA represents an astonishing and unprecedented abuse of power as they attempt to use Congressional resources to interfere in an ongoing criminal investigation at another level of government and obstruct a possible criminal indictment." (All three were lawyers; Nadler had served on the HJC and Raskin had been a law professor and Goldman an SDNY AUSA.)

Leslie Dubeck (Bragg's general counsel) criticized the committee request as "an unprecedented inquiry into a pending local prosecution."[9] It "treads into territory very clearly reserved to the states" and was made only after Trump "created a false expectation that he would be arrested . . . and his lawyers reportedly urged you to intervene." "Neither fact is a legitimate basis for Congressional inquiry." Jordan also demanded documents and testimony from Carey R. Dunne and Mark F. Pomerantz, who had resigned from the DA's office to protest Vance's failure to proceed. Bragg offered to talk to Jordan's committee and disclosed that his office had used about $5 million in federal forfeiture money in investigating Trump and the Trump organization. Rep. Comer said: "I fully expect to see Alvin Bragg answering questions in front of Congress as soon as we can make it happen." The HJC subpoenaed the two former prosecutors, but Bragg directed them not to respond, and Pomerantz had already said he would not cooperate with this "attempt to undermine an active investigation and ongoing New York criminal case with an unprecedented campaign of harassment and intimidation."

Rep. Jordan then announced a "field hearing" to examine how Bragg's "pro-crime, anti-victim policies have led to an increase in violent crime and a dangerous community for New York City residents."[10] Bragg retorted: "the House GOP is coming to the safest big city in America for a political stunt. This hearing won't engage in actual efforts to increase public safety, such as supporting national gun legislation and shutting down the iron pipeline," (i.e., arms trafficking). "If Chairman Jordan truly cared about public safety, he could take a short drive to Columbus, Dayton, Cincinnati, Cleveland, Akron or Toledo in his home state, instead of using taxpayer dollars to travel hundreds of miles out of his way." Bragg sued Jordan in SDNY, seeking to enjoin the investigation and quash the Pomerantz subpoena. Jordan "has no power under the Constitution to oversee state and local criminal matters" and was not "free to unconstitutionally deploy Congress's limited subpoena power for raw political retaliation, intimidation, or obstruction." Trump supporters had sent the DA's office more than a thousand calls and emails, many "threatening and racially charged." A poll found that two-thirds of respondents felt Congress should not interfere in Trump's legal cases, but 60 percent of Republicans said it should.

SDNY Judge Vyskocil (Trump) ruled that the HJC had a "valid legislative purpose" in subpoenaing Pomerantz, dismissing the first 35 pages of Bragg's lawsuit as "nothing short of a public relations tirade against former president and current presidential candidate Donald Trump."[11] "In our federalist system, elected state and federal actors sometimes engage in political dogfights. . . . The Court does not endorse either side's agenda." The judge issued her own 25-page opinion just two hours after the hearing (suggesting she wrote it beforehand). But Second Circuit Judge Beth Robinson (Biden) promptly stayed the decision. After the parties settled, Bragg let Pomerantz testify, but he invoked the Fifth Amendment and other privileges, saying he had been threatened with prosecution for violating grand jury secrecy. Rep. Issa (R-CA) complained: "I've never had a more obstructive and less cooperative witness in my over 20 years in Congress."

Trump blustered on Truth Social:[12]

> What kind of a person can charge another person, in this case a former President of the United States, who got more votes than any sitting President in history, and leading candidate (by far!) for the Republican Party nomination, with a Crime, when it is known by all that NO Crime has been committed, & also known that potential death & destruction in such a false charge could be catastrophic for our Country? . . . Why & who would do such a thing? Only a degenerate psychopath that truly hates the USA!

Bragg was a "Soros backed animal," who "IS JUST CARRRYING OUT THE PLANS OF THE RADICAL LEFT LUNATICS. OUR COUNTRY IS BEING DESTROYED, AS THEY TELL US TO BE PEACEFUL!" "Alvin Bragg received in EXCESS OF ONE MILLION DOLLARS from the Radical Left Enemy of 'TRUMP,' George Soros." Other Republicans echoed these anti-Semitic slurs: "Alvin Bragg is bought by George Soros" (Sen. Vance); "Alvin Bragg is bought and paid for by George Soros" (Rep. Luna). (Soros had donated $1 million to Color of Change, a liberal group that endorses progressive prosecutors, which in turn gave $500,000 to Bragg; the two men had never met.)

A fake AI image of Trump's arrest was seen nearly 5 million times. Hours after Trump predicted "death and destruction" if he were charged, the Manhattan DA's office received a letter addressed to Bragg, containing white powder (which turned out to be innocuous) and threatening: "ALVIN: I AM GOING TO KILL YOU!!!!!!!!!"[13] Trump posted a picture of himself holding a baseball bat next to an image of Bragg. Civil rights leaders including Rev. Al Sharpton and former NY Gov. David Paterson said: "This disgraceful attack is not a dog whistle but a bullhorn of incendiary racist and antisemitic bile, spewed out for the sole purpose of intimidating and sabotaging a lawful, legitimate, fact-based investigation." House Minority Leader Hakeem Jeffries said Trump's "reckless, reprehensible and irresponsible" rhetoric could "get someone killed." (Like Bragg, all three were Black.)

Dubeck (Bragg's counsel) rebuked the Republican House chairs.[14]

> Former President Trump has directed harsh invective against District Attorney Bragg and threatened on social media that his arrest or indictment in

> New York may unleash "death & destruction." As Committee Chairmen, you could use the stature of your office to denounce these attacks and urge respect for the fairness of our justice system. . . . Instead, you and many of your colleagues have chosen to collaborate with Mr. Trump's efforts to vilify and denigrate the integrity of elected state prosecutors and trial judges and made unfounded allegations that the Office's investigation . . . is politically motivated. . . . We urge you to refrain from these inflammatory accusations, withdraw your demand for information, and let the criminal justice process proceed without unlawful political interference.

But Trump just doubled down:[15]

> District Attorney Bragg is a danger to our Country, and should be removed immediately, along with Radical Lunatic Bombthrower Jack Smith, who is harassing and intimidating innocent people at levels not seen before, "Get Trump" Letitia James, the worst Attorney General in the United States, and Atlanta D.A. Fani Willis, who is trying to make PERFECT phone calls into a plot to destroy America but reigns over the most violent Crime Scene in America, and does nothing about it.

At his first big presidential campaign rally in 2024, strategically staged in Waco, Texas (scene of the 1992 violent clash between the ATF and David Koresh and the Branch Davidians), Trump said: "The abuses of power that we're currently witnessing at all levels of government will go down as among the most shameful, corrupt and depraved chapters in all of American history."[16] "Prosecutorial misconduct is their new tool and they're willing to use it at levels never seen before in our country." The investigations were "bullshit." Bragg and Willis were "henchmen" of the Democrats. "The Biden regime's weaponization of our system of justice," the "central issue of our time," came "straight out of the Stalinist Russia horror show." Trump was "the most innocent man in the history of our country." "They're not coming after me, they're coming after you." He attacked one of Bragg's senior counsel by name, asserting he had been hired from DC (i.e., the DoJ) as part of a national conspiracy. "They couldn't get it done in Washington, so they said, 'Let's use local offices.'" The rally played "Justice for All" sung by the J6 Prison Choir, which topped some iTunes download charts. The choir also sang "The Star-Spangled Banner," and Trump read the Pledge of Allegiance. Tacopina acknowledged that his client's comments on Bragg were "ill-advised" but refused to "defend or condemn" them: "I'm not his social media consultant."

Two days after the Waco rally, Trump repeated that prosecution was the Democrats' "new form of trying to beat people at the polls. This is worse than stuffing the ballot boxes, which they did."[17] "The new weapon being used by out of control, unhinged Democrats to cheat on election is criminally investigating a candidate. It's a rigged system. Like we had a rigged election." "Prosecutorial misconduct is their new tool and they are willing to use it at levels never seen before in our country. We must stop them and we must not allow them to go through another election where they have yet another tool in their tool kit." An NPR/PBS NewsHour/Marist poll found that 80 percent of Republicans viewed the investigation as a "witch hunt," compared with only 41 percent of all respondents. A Reuters/Ipsos poll found that 80 percent of Republicans but only 32 percent of Democrats said politics was driving the case; nevertheless, 70 percent believed Trump had paid off Stormy Daniels.

During the House Republican retreat in late March, Rep. Jordan observed that former DA Vance had not proceeded against Trump, "and then what happened? President Trump announces he's running for re-election and—shazam!—now we're going to pursue it."[18] "As a leader, as the speaker of the House [to which he was aspiring], if this shoe was on the other foot, I hope I would do the exact same thing—stand up and say it's wrong." Rep. Luna accused Bragg of "trying to cook up charges outside of the statute of limitation [sic] against Trump." "This is unheard-of, and Americans should see it for what it is: an abuse of power and fascist overreach of the justice system." The Trump campaign called Bragg a "woke tyrant," "rogue prosecutor," and "progressive activist." Campaign fundraising appeals collected signatures for a "NO ARREST" petition. Sen. Cruz predicted the indictment "will backfire spectacularly."

The New York Times gave Trump's March 30 indictment a front-page banner headline.[19] He fulminated: "Democrats had done the unthinkable—indicting a completely innocent person in an act of blatant Election Interference." "Weaponizing our justice system to punish a political opponent, who just so happens to be a President of the United States and by far the leading candidate for President, has never happened before." RNC Chair McDaniel denounced the "blatant abuse of power from a DA focused on political vengeance instead of keeping people safe." Rep. Greene promised to attend the arraignment: "We MUST protest the unconstitutional WITCH HUNT." A website that had hosted planning for the January 6 riot now called for civil war and "1776 round 2," envisioning a "real insurrection" this time and exhorting readers to "form organized militias." It displayed a photo of Bragg, observing: "there once was a time when he would have been lynched for much less" and declaring: "This cannot go unpunished. The DA needs to pay dearly." DeSantis accused Bragg of pursuing a "political agenda," adding defiantly: "Florida will not assist in an extradition request given the questionable circumstances at issue." (The Uniform Criminal Extradition Act does not give states that option, as DeSantis—a Harvard Law School graduate—must have known.) "The weaponization of the legal system to advance a political agenda turns the rule of law on its head" and "is unAmerican." Nikki Haley said: "this is more about revenge than it is justice." Michael Pompeo accused Bragg of "playing politics." Sen. Scott said: "this pro-criminal New York DA has failed to uphold the law for violent criminals, yet weaponized the law against political enemies. This is a travesty." Rep. McCarthy accused Bragg of having "irreparably damaged our country." "The American people will not tolerate this injustice, and the House of Representatives will hold Alvin Bragg and his unprecedented abuse of power to account." "As he routinely frees violent criminals to terrorize the public, he weaponized our sacred system of justice against President Donald Trump." Rep. Jordan called it "outrageous." Sen. Graham hyperbolically denounced the indictment as "one of the most irresponsible decisions in American history by any prosecutor," predicting that "it's going to solidify Trump's standing in the Republican Party." Sen. Barrasso said: "if it was anyone other than President Trump, a case like this never would be brought." Pence pronounced: "the unprecedented indictment of a former president of the United States on a campaign finance issue is an outrage." Rep. Stefanik called for people to "peacefully organize." Gov. Youngkin said: "arresting a presidential candidate on a manufactured basis should not happen in America." Former Rep. Rooney said: "I was one of the early people to break with Trump . . . but I think this is kind of outrageous." Even former Arkansas Gov. Hutchinson, a Trump critic, called it a "dark day for America" but also said Trump should "step aside." A Quinnipiac poll found that 98 percent of Republicans and 63 percent of Americans thought the case against Trump was politically motivated.

The right-wing media indulged in even more incendiary rhetoric. Tucker Carlson advised viewers it was "probably not the best time to give up your AR-15s." "The rule of law appears to be suspended tonight, not just for Trump, but for anyone who would consider voting for him." "It's an effort to take him out of the political race. That's not allowed." "If you believe in our system and you want it to continue, you have to raise your hand and say 'stop' because this is too great an assault on our system." Jason Whitlock said on his show: "They are agitating for unrest. . . . If that's what they want, let's get to it." His guest, Glenn Beck, predicted the country would be "at war" by 2025. The indictment was intended "to inflame this country" so someone "could close the cage" on protesters. Fox News pulled out all the stops. Jesse Watters said: "This day will go down as a dark day for America" and predicted: "the country is not going to stand for it." Jeanine Pirro condemned "hate like I have never seen in my lifetime. This is as political as it gets." Dan Bongino declared the US was now a "police state." Sean Hannity called the indictment "repulsive" and "disgusting." Mollie Hemingway (editor-in-chief of the *Federalist*) said: "this ushers in what will probably be a very dark era of political persecution and prosecution, the type we normally associated with the Soviet Union or banana republics." "People who care about the country need to stand up and make sure they let it be known that they don't support this type of political prosecution." On Bannon's "War Room," Sebastian Gorka urged supporters to "peacefully protest." Even David McIntosh, president of the anti-Trump Club for Growth, compared the case to "the old Soviet show trials." "We're crossing the Rubicon here by mixing politics and law enforcement. It's a huge, huge mistake and a threat to our democratic process."

Trump said on Truth Social: "Thugs and Radical Left Monsters" had "INDICATED" [sic] him. "INDICTING A TOTALLY INNOCENT MAN IS AN ACT OF OBSTRUCTION AND BLATANT ELECTION INTERFERENCE. WHILE OUR COUNTRY IS GOING TO HELL!" NY Supreme Court Justice Juan Merchan, who would hear the case, "HATES ME." He "is the same person who 'railroaded' my 75 year old former CFO, Allen Weisselberg, to take a 'plea deal.' He strong armed Allen, which a judge is not allowed to do, & treated my companies, which didn't 'plead,' VICIOUSLY. APPEALING." (See Chapter 2.3.) On Truth Social Trump demanded to know "WHERE'S HUNTER?" Rep. Jordan echoed him: "Is Alvin Bragg looking into Hunter Biden's art sales and business records in New York City?" Trump's fundraising pitch said: "BREAKING: PRESIDENT TRUMP INDICTED" and asked for at least $24 to "defend our movement from the never-ending witch hunts." It promised that contributions would be matched up to 1,500 percent (but failed to reveal who would do so). It quickly raised more than $2 million. Don Jr. said: "stuff like that would make Mao, Stalin, Pol Pot, it would make them blush." Eric Trump called it "third world prosecutorial misconduct."

Other Republicans chimed in. Pence said: "It appears to millions of Americans to be nothing more than a political prosecution driven by a prosecutor who literally ran for office on a pledge to indict the former president." It "should be offensive to every American left, right and center." Sen. Cruz called it a "catastrophic escalation in the weaponization of the justice system." Rep. Womack said: "this is unprecedented and opens a new era in political warfare that has no place in our country. Congress will investigate the conduct of the Manhattan D.A.'s office to determine if the indictment was justified and not partisan weaponization." Rep. Malliotakis said: "Instead of locking up dangerous career criminals wreaking havoc on our city Alvin Bragg has chosen to abuse our tax dollars and his prosecutorial power to politically target a political foe. Shameful." About 10 percent of criticisms by right-wing officeholders and influencers mentioned Soros.

The Trump campaign disseminated statements from six governors, 26 senators, Speaker McCarthy and 63 other House Republicans, and ten state Attorneys General declaring "united support." Trump said on Truth Social: "our justice system has utterly COLLAPSED." He asked for a $1 contribution "to cement your place in history and accept YOUR membership as a FOUNDING DEFENDER OF DONALD J TRUMP AGAINST THIS WITCH HUNT." He claimed to have raised over $4 million in the first 24 hours, more than a quarter from first-time donors. His lawyer, Christopher Kise, said: "this is the lowest point in history for our criminal justice system. What was once the most respected and revered District Attorney's office in the nation has been fully bastardized by an opportunistic politician seeking, like many others, to cash in on the Trump brand." (Of course, it was Trump who was cashing in.) Trump called it a "Case that has NEVER BEEN CHARGED BEFORE." He said of Bragg: "only a degenerate psychopath that truely [sic] hates the USA! . . . would do such a thing." Former Attorney General Barr, who had harshly criticized Trump after January 6, now warned: "I don't think it's going to end up good for the country." "The real danger" is that "we now have thousands" of DAs, and "now that the Rubicon has been crossed, any one of them can find federal candidates or federal officeholders . . . [and] some state law they want to pursue the person on and get themselves into the national arena."

Trump raised another $1.1 million the day before his arraignment (over $7 million since it was announced).[20] Sen. Graham solicited money for Trump, accusing Bragg and other prosecutors of "trying to bleed him dry." On April 6, the campaign claimed $12 million, a third from new contributors. Murdoch's newspapers reembraced Trump. The *New York Post* put his face on the front page with the headline "Trumped Up." The *Wall Street Journal* said: "the question that keeps smacking us upon the head is whether this case would have been brought against any defendant not named Donald Trump. It's hard to avoid answering no." Sen. Romney (a Trump critic) said: "the New York prosecution has stretched to reach felony criminal charges in order to fit a political agenda." Rep. Greene indulged in her typical hyperbole: "Trump is joining some of the most incredible people in history being arrested today. Nelson Mandela was arrested, served time in prison. Jesus—Jesus was arrested and murdered by the Roman government." Trump was another victim of "radical, corrupt governments."

Trump boasted: "my Poll Numbers have never been better, almost $10 Million was raised for the Campaign."[21] CNN found that 60 percent of Americans approved the indictment, but this obscured the profound partisan divide: 94 percent of Democrats approved, while 79 percent of Republicans disapproved. 76 percent of Americans believed politics played a role (52 percent that it played a major role). An ABC News/Ipsos poll found that only 45 percent believed Trump should be charged, while 32 percent were opposed; 47 percent believed the charges were politically motivated (again sharply divided by party: 76 percent of Republicans but just 16 percent of Democrats). A Quinnipiac poll found that 62 percent said the case was mainly motivated by politics, again with a partisan split: 83 percent of Republicans agreed; 66 percent of Democrats said it was motivated by law.

Rep. Gaetz tweeted a photo of Trump raising his fist before surrendering, with the caption: "Witch Hunt."[22] Rep. Jordan tweeted: "Equal justice under the law, unless you're a Republican running for president." Rep. Greene called the indictment "a stain on our Republic." Justice Merchan instructed Trump: "Please refrain from making statements that are likely to incite violence or civil unrest . . . that have potential to incite violence, create civil unrest [or] jeopardize the state or well-being of any individuals," and do not use rhetoric that will "jeopardize the rule of law." Don Jr. and Eric said on social media that Merchan's daughter had worked for the Biden-Harris campaign, which Don Jr. called "yet another connection in this hand-picked democrat [sic] show trial." Eric agreed: "they are all hand picked. It is all pre-arranged. This is corruption on a different level." Defying Merchan, Trump complained: "I have a Trump-hating judge with a Trump-hating wife and family whose daughter worked for Kamala Harris and now receives money from the Biden-Harris campaign. And a lot of it."

He said on Truth Social:[23]

> VERY UNFAIR VENUE, WITH SOME AREAS THAT VOTED 1% REPUBLICAN. THIS CASE SHOULD BE MOVED TO NEARBY STATEN ISLAND—WOULD BE A VERY FAIR AND SECURE LOCATION FOR THE TRIAL. . . . ADDITIONALLY, THE HIGHLY PARTISAN JUDGE & HIS FAMILY ARE WELL KNOWN TRUMP HATERS. HE WAS AN UNFAIR DISASTER ON A PREVIOUS TRUMP RELATED CASE WOULDN'T RECUSE, GAVE HORRIBLE JURY INSTRUCTIONS, & IMPOSSIBLE TO DEAL WITH DURING THE WITCH HUNT TRIAL. . . . Alvin Bragg shut down New York City, brought in 38,000 NYPD officers, and will spend an estimated $200,000,000 of NYC funds, for a totally legal $130,000 NDA. On top of all that, the 9th Circuit Court awarded me $122,000—over the $500,000 already awarded, from Stormy "Horseface" Daniels!

He added:

> From the beginning, the Democrats spied on my campaign, remember that? They attacked me with an onslaught of fraudulent investigations. Russia, Russia, Russia, Ukraine, Ukraine, Ukraine, impeachment hoax No. 1, impeachment hoax No. 2, the illegal and unconstitutional raid on Mar-a-Lago right here. And now this massive election interference at a scale never seen before in our country, beginning with the radical left George Soros-backed prosecutor Alvin Bragg in New York.

"REPUBLICANS IN CONGRESS SHOULD DEFUND THE DOJ AND FBI UNTIL THEY COME TO THEIR SENSES." But a Pew poll found that

52 percent of Americans (even 40 percent of Republicans) thought the FBI was doing a good job, while only 36 percent had a negative opinion.

During arraignment the DA's office criticized Trump's posts, expressing "significant concern about the potential danger this kind of rhetoric poses to our city, to potential jurors and witnesses, and to the judicial process"[24] Trump's lawyer, Todd Blanche, was unapologetic: "President Trump has responded, and responded forcefully . . . he's absolutely frustrated, upset, and believes that there is a grave injustice happening with him being in this courtroom today." He "has rights, he's allowed to speak publicly." Justice Merchan was conciliatory:

> the court would not impose a gag order at this time even if it were requested. Such restraints are the most serious and least tolerable on First Amendment rights. That does apply doubly to Mr. Trump because he is a candidate for the presidency of the United States.

The judge's earlier statement had been "a request." "I'm not making an order." But the DA's office was drafting a protective order prohibiting Trump from posting case material on social media or disseminating it. When Merchan said: "I expect all other defendants to appear in court, even high-profile defendants," Blanche suggested his client might not appear at the next hearing because of "the incredible expense and effort and security issues." The judge rejected this "in the interest of transparency and assuring the rules of law [are applied] evenhandedly."

After his arraignment, Trump repeated that Bragg was a "criminal" and Merchan "a Trump-hating judge with a Trump-hating wife and family."[25] A month later the judge granted the prosecution request to restrict Trump's public comments about the case and prohibit him from posting on social media "any materials and information provided by the People to the Defense." Trump could review those materials only with his lawyers and could not copy them or see "forensic images of witness cell phones."

SDNY Judge Hellerstein (Clinton) denied Trump's motion to remove the case to federal court.[26] "Hush money paid to an adult film star is not related to a president's official acts. It does not reflect in any way the color of the president's official duties" but was just "a cover-up of an embarrassing event." Blanche's argument that the Constitution required Trump to hire Cohen to handle his private affairs was "far-fetched." Alan Garten, TO chief legal officer, said there had been no retainer and no stated purpose for the payments in Trump's official ledger. Most of the $420,000 paid to Cohen was reimbursement for the hush money payment. Trump moved to recuse Merchan because of his actions in the case against Trump's companies (see Chapter 2.3) and that fact that the judge's daughter was a partner and COO of Authentic Campaigns, a Democratic consulting firm that worked for Biden in 2020. After the New York Advisory Committee on Judicial Ethics held that Merchan's impartiality "cannot reasonably be questioned" because of his daughter's activities or his own "modest" political contributions two years earlier, the judge denied the motion.

Tacopina proclaimed to Kimberly Guilfoyle (Don Jr.'s fiancée): "this is an all-out war." Trump will "be there loud and proud, and there's nobody that's gonna make him cower."[27] But he was more professional on ABC News's "This Week": "Do I think the judge is biased? Of course not. How could I subscribe to that when I've had no interactions with the judge that would lead me to believe he's biased?" "I have no issue with this judge whatsoever. He has a very good reputation." Nevertheless, Trump is "entitled to his own opinion and, what he's been through, quite frankly I don't blame him for feeling the way he does."

Trump declared defiantly: "I'd never drop out" of the presidential race because of a conviction. "It's not my thing."[28] He sued Michael Cohen (who was expected to testify against him) for $500 million in SD Florida (perhaps hoping to get Judge Cannon again, see Chapter 4.1), claiming Cohen had breached confidentiality and an NDA. Trump's lawyer was Alejandro Brito (a specialist in franchise disputes who practiced with two associates), perhaps because other Trump lawyers had discouraged the lawsuit. Less than six months later, and just days before Trump was to be deposed in that action, he withdrew it. Cohen celebrated "the end of this latest attempt to deter me from providing truthful testimony against him."

Trump moved to dismiss the case, claiming presidential and absolute immunity.[29] Merchan said the trial would start on March 25 and take an estimated six weeks. Blanche protested: "President Trump is going to now spend the next two months working on this trial instead of out on the campaign trail . . . something that should not happen in this country." Merchan responded: "What is your legal argument?" Blanche said: "that is my legal argument." Merchan was dismissive: "that is not a legal argument." "Tell me something you haven't already said today." Asked if he was done, Blanche said no, but Merchan cut him off: "please have a seat." Blanche called the trial "completely election interference," complaining: "We have been faced with extremely compressed and expedited schedules in each and every one of those trials. It's truly an impossible position for any person to be in." Merchan replied that judges could not wait to see what other courts would do.

Trump objected: "They want to keep me nice and busy so I can't campaign so hard. . . . I'm going to have to sit here for months on a trial I think it's ridiculous, it's unfair." "This is their way of cheating this time. Last time, they had a different way." "This is all from the D.O.J., this all comes out of Washington." "It's all a rigged—it's a rigged state, it's a rigged city, it's a shame." Trump asked Merchan to wait for the Supreme Court decision on immunity (in his election case in DDC, see Chapter 4.2) before starting the trial; but Merchan had said earlier: "the issue of the state proceedings I don't believe is for the Supreme Court." In April, Merchan denied the motion to dismiss as untimely. Filing it shortly before the trial was scheduled to start raised "real questions about the sincerity and actual purpose of the motion." Merchan had also denied another motion to dismiss, holding that the other crimes Trump allegedly intended to commit by concealing the payment (exceeding federal campaign contribution limits, violating state election laws by seeking to influence the 2016 election through unlawful means, and violating state tax laws by paying Cohen $420,000, of which he paid Daniels only $130,000) were "legally sufficient" to support the felony charges. In the decade 2014–23, New York prosecutors filed first-degree falsifying business records charges 11,663 times, 437 times in Manhattan.

Bragg sought an order prohibiting Trump and anyone he directed from speaking about witnesses, jurors, court staff, and Bragg's legal team (but not himself).[30] Trump "has a long history of making public and inflammatory remarks about the participants in various judicial proceedings against him." Shielding the names and addresses of jurors would help "ensure the integrity of these proceedings, minimize obstacles to jury selection, and protect juror safety." Merchan granted the request to conceal the names of jurors and ordered that their addresses be revealed only to the lawyers.

Trump said he "would have no problem testifying . . . it could also make me more popular because the people know it's a scam."[31] He complained that "they decided to wait until now, just before the election, so that I won't be able to campaign." "It's criminal what they're doing, and it's never been done before in this country. I don't know how you can have a trial that's going on right in the middle of an election. . . . It's not fair at all." Merchan was a "Democrat judge" who "cannot go fast enough. He wants to get it started so badly." "This is a case that could have been brought three and a half years ago. And now they're fighting over days because they want to try and do it during the election." "This is . . . election interference and a disgrace." Trump's Truth Social platform reproduced a supporter's note thanking him for taking the "arrows" (like St. Sebastian?) and noting that this coincided with Easter week, when "Christ walked through His greatest persecution." The writer quoted Psalm 109: 3–8: "They have also surrounded me with words of hatred, And fought against me without a cause. In return for my love they are my accusers." On March 30, Trump shared on Truth Social a *Washington Times* article headlined "The Crucifixion of Donald Trump" and commented: "As Easter Sunday approaches, much of the world will commemorate the arrest, death and resurrection of Jesus Christ-the holiest days of the Christian calendar."

Hours after Trump blasted Merchan, his daughter, Bragg, and Cohen, the judge prohibited the defendant from discussing prosecutors (or their families), members of Merchan's staff or their families, jurors or prospective jurors, witnesses or others involved in the case, because Trump's record of "prior extrajudicial statements establishes a sufficient risk to the administration of justice."[32] Trump had called Cohen a "liar and felon" and Mark Pomerantz a "dirtbag lawyer." Merchan cited "the nature and impact of the statements made against this Court and a family member" and said Trump's commentary had gone "far beyond defending himself against attacks." "His statements were threatening, inflammatory, denigrating." Merchan also ordered defense lawyers to stop trying to delay the trial by filing motions without permission and dismissed their efforts to blame Bragg for the delay as "incredibly serious" but unsupported by any evidence. "The court expects that the line between zealous advocacy and willful disregard of its orders will not be crossed." Yet just days later, Trump accused Merchan's daughter Loren of posting an image of him behind bars on her X account, making it "completely impossible for me to get a fair trial." "If the Biased and Conflicted Judge is allowed to stay on this Sham 'Case,' it will be another sad example of our Country becoming a Banana Republic." Merchan "should be immediately sanctioned and recused." However, the New York State Court System said the account on X was fake; Loren had deleted it a year earlier.

Bragg asked Merchan to "make it abundantly clear that the [gag order] protects family members of the Court, the District Attorney, and all other individuals mentioned in the Order" and warn Trump "that his recent conduct is contumacious and direct him to immediately desist" or he would be sanctioned.[33] Necheles and Blanche replied that the gag order did not cover the judge's family and Merchan could not order Trump "to do something that the gag order does not require." They demanded a hearing if Merchan considered expanding it. The New York State Bar Association president condemned "in no uncertain terms the unfounded attack on Supreme Court Justice Juan Merchan and his family." "All judges must be free to decide cases and issue rulings without fear for their safety or that of their family. . . . Our system of justice depends on it."

Federal judges took the highly unusual step of criticizing Trump's actions.[34] DDC Judge Walton (Reagan and GWB) said: "Any reasonable, thinking person" would acknowledge the impact of Trump's rhetoric on his followers. Walton cited a disgruntled litigant who had killed a federal judge in New Jersey and noted that at least half of the DDC judges handling January 6 cases suffered harassment, including death threats at their homes. He was speaking out of concern for the "future of our country and the future of democracy in our country, because if we don't have a viable court system that's able to function efficiently, then we have tyranny." DDC Judge Hogan (another Reagan appointee), who had just retired after 40 years, told Georgetown Law School students that threats against judges had increased, "no question about it, I think encouraged by the prior president, unfortunately."

Trump protested on Truth Social: "The trial should not be allowed to start in the middle of my campaign. They could have filed more than three years ago—THEY WAITED! THIS IS ANOTHER WITCH HUNT FOR PURPOSES OF ELECTION INTERFERENCE!!!"[35] A spokesman said: "Joe Biden and the Democrats' entire strategy to defeat President Trump is to confine him to a courtroom." As Trump continued to attack Merchan's daughter on Truth Social, Bragg asked the judge to confirm that the gag order applied to his family and extend it to them if it did not. The judge quickly did so, explaining: "It is no longer just a mere possibility or a reasonable likelihood that there exists a threat to the integrity of the judicial proceedings. The threat is very real. Admonitions are not enough, nor is reliance on self-restraint." "This pattern of attacking family members of presiding jurists and attorneys assigned to his cases serves no legitimate purpose. It merely injects fear in those assigned or called to participate in the proceedings, that not only they, but their family members as well, are 'fair game' for defendant's vitriol." "Defendant is hereby put on notice that he will forfeit any statutory right he may have to access juror names if he engages in any conduct that threatens the safety and integrity of the jury or the jury selection process." *The Washington Post* reported that Trump had attacked judges or their family members by name 138 times. Reuters found that threats against federal judges had more than doubled since late 2020, when Trump's criticisms increased.

Within hours, Trump said on Truth Social:[36]

> I just was informed that another corrupt New York Judge, Juan Merchan, GAGGED me so that I can not [sic] talk about the corruption and conflicts taking place in his courtroom with respect to a case that everyone, including the DA., felt should never have been brought. They can talk about me, but I can't talk about them??? That sounds fair, doesn't it? This Judge should be recused, and the case should be thrown out. There has virtually never been a more conflicted judge than this one. ELECTION INTERFERENCE at its worst!

A hour later he posted a Fox News video in which host Brian Kilmeade said: "the judge's daughter is a [sic] activist who works for Kamala Harris. That to me is something that, if I'm Donald Trump, I'm clearly concerned about—that the judge has a daughter who feels this way." Kilmeade also repeated the debunked claim that Merchan's daughter had posted a photo of Trump behind bars on her social media account. Trump added:

> If this Partisan Hack wants to put me in the "clink" for speaking the open and obvious TRUTH, I will gladly become a Modern Day Nelson Mandela—It will be my GREAT HONOR. We have to Save our Country

> from these Political Operatives masquerading as Prosecutors and Judges, and I am willing to sacrifice my Freedom for that worthy cause. It would be a "great honor" to be jailed for violating the expanded gag order.

His campaign called the order "unconstitutional and un-American."

Trump again moved that Merchan recuse himself because his daughter's company, Authentic Campaigns, would benefit financially from the outcome of the case.[37] The DA's office responded that Merchan had already denied such a motion, citing the state Advisory Committee on Judicial Ethics, and Trump had offered no new evidence other than "a daisy chain of innuendos," which made "multiple attenuated factual leaps here that undercut any direct connection between Authentic and this case." Appellate Division Justice Lizbeth Gonzalez denied Trump's motions to delay the trial and change the venue. Appellate Division Justice Cynthia Kern denied Trump's motion to delay the trial while he appealed the gag order. In an Article 78 proceeding, Appellate Division Justice Ellen Gesmer denied a third motion to delay the trial on the ground that Merchan should be disqualified, after a hearing in which a witness for the court system said: "there is absolutely no evidence to show that Judge Merchan will stand to benefit from the outcome of this trial."

A week before the trial Trump complained that Merchan has "got me GAGGED because he doesn't want the FACTS behind the Gag to come out."[38] His spokesman called the judge "politically compromised" and said he should "immediately recuse himself in order to show the American people that the Democrats have not destroyed our justice system completely." Five days before the trial, Trump said on Truth Social he would "be forced to sit, GAGGED, before a HIGHLY CONFLICTED & CORRUPT JUDGE." Three days before the start he said: "the truth is that there's no case." In a fundraising email entitled "72 hours until all hell breaks loose!" Trump threatened: "If we fail to have a MASSIVE outpouring of peaceful patriotic support—*right here, right now*—all Hell will break loose. Rabid Democrats are poised to raise MILLIONS while I'm stuck defending myself in court." The New York Young Republicans Club was planning demonstrations. Two days before the trial Trump said at a Pennsylvania rally: "the entire world will witness the commencement of the very first Biden trial." "I will be forced to sit fully gagged. I'm not allowed to talk. Can you believe it? They want to take away my constitutional right to talk." "I'm proud to do it for you. Have a good time watching." He posted on Truth Social: "Has Mark POMERANTZ been prosecuted for his terrible acts in and out of the D.A.'s Office? Has disgraced attorney and felon Michael Cohen been prosecuted for LYING?" Days earlier Trump had called Cohen and Stormy Daniels "two sleaze bags." Prosecutors asked for three $1,000 fines and a warning that "further violations could result in jail time."

Outside court before the start of jury selection, Trump called the trial an "assault on America," a "political prosecution" that "should have never been brought."[39] As the hearing began, Merchan denied Trump's second motion to recuse. "There is no agenda here. We want to follow the law. We want justice to be done." At the end of the first day Trump called the case a "scam" and attacked Merchan for conditioning a recess to let Trump attend his son Barron's high school graduation on whether the trial was on schedule. "He's a very conflicted judge. And he will not allow us to go to that." "We're not going to be given a fair trial." Trump also complained that the judge would not let him attend oral argument in the Supreme Court on the presidential immunity case. When Blanche objected "to having this trial during the campaign season," Merchan replied: "I've already ruled on it." Trump was "required to be here. He's not required to be in the Supreme Court." As Blanche was questioning a juror, Merchan warned that Trump was "audibly uttering something" toward another juror who was about "12 feet" away. "He was audibly gesturing, speaking in the direction of the juror. I won't tolerate that. I will not have any jurors intimidated in this courtroom. I want to make that crystal clear."

The New York Times observed that "the opening days of the trial, devoted to jury selection, have already demonstrated the great care and respect with which everyone involved in the trial, except for Mr. Trump, has treated the process."[40] He promptly confirmed that judgment with a Truth Social post calling Manhattan the "2nd Worst Venue in the Country" (presumably after DC; Biden won Manhattan in 2020 84.5 to 14.5 percent).[41] His spokesman said: "The deck has been stacked against President Trump in a gross abuse of our legal system, wherein his persecutors have deliberately targeted some of the most Democrat-heavy jurisdictions in the country to bring forth their bogus case." Merchan let the defense challenge for cause a potential juror who had written of Trump: "lock him up." One of the seven jurors chosen the first day was allowed to withdraw after reporting that friends, colleagues, and family members had identified her from media accounts of her occupation (nurse) and other details. Merchan then ordered the media not to reveal answers to two questions: "who is your current employer" and "who was your prior employer." "There's a reason why this is an anonymous jury, and we've taken the measures we have taken." Prosecutors told the judge Trump had violated his gag order seven more times, in addition to the earlier violations they had alleged. He posted a quote from Fox News anchor Jesse Watters: "They are catching undercover Liberal Activists lying to the judge in order to get on the Trump jury." Watters also read aloud where jurors lived and worked.

Blanche asked Merchan to direct the prosecution to identify the first three government witnesses.[42] It refused because "Mr. Trump has been tweeting about the witnesses." Blanche offered to promise Trump would not do so, but Merchan was skeptical: "I don't think you can make that representation." He declined to issue the order even when Blanche offered not to share the information with Trump. Merchan refused to disqualify a juror who said she could treat Trump fairly, even though she was not a fan. "I preside over trials all the time involving defendants who are not very likable." He also did not remove a woman whose husband had reviewed a book about Trump. But he struck a woman who had posted on social media in 2016: "We must . . . protect the rights of people at risk from this racist, sexist narcissist." At the end of the third day, a full jury had been selected.

When the trial began on April 22, Trump posted on Truth Social: "ELECTION INTERFERENCE!!!"[43] "This is done for purposes of hurting the opponent of the worst president in the history of our country." At 7am he posted on Truth Social: "America Loving Protesters should be allowed to protest at the front steps of courthouses." "GO OUT AND PEACEFULLY PROTEST. RALLY BEHIND MAGA. SAVE OUR COUNTRY!" At 8:50 am he posted: "Unlike at Columbia University where the Radical Left Palestinian Protesters sat on the Front Lawn, practically took over the School, and screamed, 'Death to the Jews, Death to Israel, Death to America,' and nothing happened to them, Lower Manhattan surrounding the Courthouse, where I am heading now, is completely CLOSED DOWN. SO UNFAIR!!!" Twenty minutes later he compared the courthouse to an armed camp. At noon he said New York should send police to protect Jewish students at Columbia and interfere less at the courthouse. "Republicans want the right to protest in front of the Courthouse, like everyone else!" During a break in argument about whether Trump had violated the gag order, he posted that the judge was denying his "RIGHT TO FREE SPEECH" and he was "NOT ALLOWED TO DEFEND MYSELF." Blanche told Merchan Trump could complain about "two systems of justice." Merchan bristled: "There's two systems of justice in this courtroom? That's what you're saying?" "I'm asking the questions, OK? I'm going to decide whether your client is in contempt or not, so please don't turn it around . . . you're not offering me anything in support of your argument." When Blanche claimed: "We are trying to comply with" the order, Merchan retorted: "You're losing all credibility with the court."

Merchan found Trump in contempt for nine violations of the gag order and fined him $9,000 (the maximum), rejecting the "counterintuitive and indeed absurd" argument that Trump should not be liable for reposting the words of others, since he had "intentionally selected" the posts "to maximize exposure."[44] But the judge found no violation when Trump posted "Thank you to Michael Avenatti—for revealing the truth about two sleaze bags who have, with their lies and misrepresentations, cost our Country dearly!" after the lawyer had criticized Cohen and Daniels for making public statements. (Avenatti was in jail for defrauding Stormy Daniels and may have been hoping for a pardon if Trump were elected.) Just before the contempt finding Trump said: "I've never seen a judge so conflicted, and giving us virtually no rulings. It's the most recusable judge. It's called recusal abuse. . . . But really, more importantly than the recusal, he should terminate the case today." Merchan warned Trump that if these fines did not stop him, the judge would "consider whether in some instances, jail may be a necessary punishment," but he also said if Cohen and Daniels attacked Trump, he might exclude them from the gag order.

After being found in contempt, Trump posted:[45]

> This Judge has taken away my Constitutional Right to FREE SPEECH. I am the only Presidential Candidate in History to be GAGGED. This whole "Trial" is RIGGED, and by taking away my FREEDOM OF SPEECH, THIS HIGHLY CONFLICTED JUDGE IS RIGGING THE PRESIDENTIAL OF 2024 ELECTION. ELECTION INTERFERENCE!!!

At the end of the day's hearing, he posted:

> This is a total Witch Hunt. Hours of sitting down and listening to nothing except EXONERATION AND LIES. The Trial is going like a speeding bullet, because the Judge is working hard to make all of his friends happy. Merchan is Rigged, Crooked, and, above all, and without question, CONFLICTED. It's a disgrace to our Country—They've taken away my Right to Free Speech. ELECTION INTERFERENCE!!!"

On May 2, prosecutors asked Merchan to fine Trump for four more violations: calling Cohen a liar and repeating he was "a convicted liar, and he's got no credibility whatsoever," complimenting David Pecker (another witness) for being "very nice," and saying the jury was "mostly all Democrat."[46] Leaving court that day, Trump said: "This judge is totally conflicted, has me under an unconstitutional gag order. Nobody's ever had that before and we don't like it and it's not fair. Other people are allowed to do whatever they want to us, and I'm not allowed as . . . the Republican Party nominee . . . to talk." (He would not be the nominee until the RNC in August.) "What you're witnessing in New York is not a legal proceeding—it's an unlawful exercise in very stupid and very evil politics."

Before entering the courtroom on May 5, Trump responded to a reporter's query about Cohen: "As you know, they've taken away my constitutional right so I'm not allowed to answer that question." He again called Merchan "conflicted."[47] The judge began the day's hearing by saying:

> I find you in criminal contempt for the 10th time. Going forward, this court will have to consider a jail sentence. Mr. Trump, it's important to

> understand that the last thing I want to do is put you I jail. You are the former president of the United States and possibly the next president as well. To take that step would be disruptive to these proceedings. . . . There are many reasons why incarceration is truly a last resort for you. But at the end of the day, I have a job to do. . . . Your continued violations of this Court's lawful order threaten to interfere with the administration of justice, in constant attacks which constitute a direct attack on the rule of law. I cannot allow that to continue. . . . You not only called into question the integrity, and therefore the legitimacy of these proceedings, but again raised the specter of fear for the safety of the jurors and of their loved ones.

The contempt finding pertained to Trump's April 22 statement to Real America's Voice: "You know he's rushing the trial like crazy. Nobody's ever seen a thing go like this. The jury was picked so fast—95 percent Democrats. The area's mostly all Democrat. You think of it as a—just a purely Democrat area. It's a very unfair situation." Merchan ruled that the other three violations did not constitute contempt. Trump responded outside court at the end of the next day's hearing, calling Merchan a "disaster." "This judge has given me a gag order and said, 'you'll go to jail if you violate it.' Frankly our Constitution is much more important than jail. I'll do that sacrifice any day." "We just found out the government just said they want two to three more weeks. That means they want to keep me off the trail."

Stormy Daniels testified in detail about her sexual encounter with Trump, suggesting it was nonconsensual.[48] Defense lawyers had objected in advance, and Blanche moved for a mistrial afterwards, but Merchan denied the motion. "There are some things that are probably better left unsaid . . . I think the witness was a little difficult to control." However, he had done "everything that I can possibly do to protect both sides." "The defense has to take some responsibility" for not objecting contemporaneously. Merchan also admonished Blanche that, during Daniels's testimony, Trump was "cursing audibly and shaking his head visually and that's contemptuous. It has the potential to intimidate the witness and the jury can see that. I am speaking to you here at the bench because I don't want to embarrass him. You need to speak to him. I won't tolerate that." Merchan denied a defense motion to let Trump speak about Daniels now that she had testified. "The reason why the gag order is in place to begin with is precisely because of the nature of these attacks—the vitriol." After the court rose on May 9, Trump called Merchan "corrupt" and "totally conflicted" and posted on Truth Social that the judge "IS PRESIDING OVER THE DEATH OF THE NEW YORK CITY AND STATE SYSTEM OF JUSTICE." A five-judge Appellate Division panel upheld Merchan's gag order. A spokesman said Trump was asking the Court of Appeals to invalidate

> the unconstitutional and un-American gag order imposed by conflicted Judge Juan Merchan in the lawless Manhattan DA case. The threat to throw the 45th President of the United States and the leading candidate in the 2024 presidential election in jail for exercising his First Amendment rights is a Third World authoritarian tactic typical of Crooked Joe Biden and his comrades.

But on September 12, the Court denied the appeal.

In anticipation of Michael Cohen's testimony on May 13, Merchan asked prosecutors to tell the witness to stop making statements about the case.[49] Campaigning in New Jersey over the weekend, Trump called the prosecutor "fat Alvin" and Merchan "highly conflicted" and accused both of "doing the bidding" of Biden. Complaining he had been indicted on "bullshit," Trump asked the crowd: "Everything [the administration] touch turns to what?" When they obediently roared: "shit" Trump said: "you can't use the word shit." Instead, they chanted: "Let's go Brandon" (a euphemism for "Fuck Joe Biden").

Cohen testified that Trump had instructed him: "Just take care of" Stormy Daniels's story.[50] "I was doing everything and more to protect my boss." "Everything required Mr. Trump's sign-off." After the "Access Hollywood" tape was published on October 7, 2016, Trump worried that Daniels's story could aggravate the situation: "Total disaster. Women are going to hate me. This is going to be a disaster to the campaign." Cohen testified: "I advocated for Trump in the best way possible. I received regular talking points from the campaign." Trump "wasn't thinking about Melania. This was all about the campaign." When Cohen asked how this was affecting Trump's marriage, he was dismissive: "Don't worry." "How long am I going to be on the market" if his marriage failed? "Not long." He wanted Cohen to delay paying Daniels until after the election so he could stiff her without political damage.

After Cohen's testimony, three Members of Congress who had accompanied Trump to court told the press what he could not say.[51] Sen. Vance called Cohen "a convicted felon, who admitted in his testimony that he secretly recorded his former employer. Does any reasonable, sensible person really believe anything that Michael Cohen says?" "The judge inside—his daughter is . . . raising money for Donald Trump's political opponents." "Every single person involved in this prosecution is practically a Democratic operative." Sen. Tuberville said: "I'm sitting here listening to a guy on the stand that they had to get out of house arrest because he lied in another court to testify in this court." (Cohen had lied to Congress, not a court, and been released from home confinement in 2021.) Appearing to question the citizenship of the jurors, Tuberville added: "I am disappointed in looking at the . . . supposedly American citizens—in that courtroom." Rep. Malliotakis disparaged Cohen as a "convicted disbarred perjurer." Iowa Attorney General Brenna Bird said:

"I have never seen in my career a greater perversion of the criminal justice system." House Speaker Johnson called the trial a "sham" and Cohen "a man who is clearly on a mission for personal revenge." As Cohen testified, Eric Trump posted on social media: "I have never seen anything more rehearsed." Rudy Giuliani posted that Cohen was a "serial liar." Four days earlier Sen. Scott (who also had been in court) said: "The judge's daughter is a political operative and raises money for Democrats. You've got the lead prosecutor's wife that is a significant donor to Democrats and I think to Biden." While attending trial on May 16, Rep. Gaetz wrote on social media: "Standing back, and standing by, Mr President" (echoing Trump's encouragement of Proud Boys to commit violence).

While Robert Costello (a lawyer and former Cohen associate) was testifying for the defense, Merchan halted the trial, ordered: "Clear the courtroom," and dressed down the witness, who had spoken back and kept talking after Merchan sustained objections: "you don't give me side-eye and you don't roll your eyes." "Are you staring me down right now?"[52] After Costello had muttered "Jeez" and thrown up his hands, Merchan interrupted:

> What did you say? . . . I would like to discuss proper decorum in my courtroom. So when there's a witness on the stand if you don't like my ruling, you don't say "Jeez," okay? And then don't say "strike it," because I am the only one who can strike testimony in the courtroom. . . . I'm putting you on notice that your conduct is contemptuous. If you try to stare me down one more time, I will remove you from the stand.

He warned Trump's lawyers that further misbehavior would lead him to strike all of Costello's testimony. When Costello asked: "Can I say something, please?" Merchan replied: "No, no. This is not a conversation." Trump later complained: "I've never seen anything like it in my life." Merchan was "a tyrant" and the trial "a disaster for our country . . . for New York state, New York City." "The judge hates Donald Trump. . . . Take a look at him. Take a look at where he comes from." (Merchan's family had emigrated from Colombia when he was six.)

Outside court on the day of closing arguments, Robert De Niro said: "Under Trump, this kind of government will perish from the earth. If Trump returns to the White House, you can kiss these freedoms goodbye that we all take for granted. And elections? Forget about it."[53] Michael Fanone warned Trump would govern like an "authoritarian who answers to and serves only himself." Harry Dunn noted that Trump supporters were heckling Fanone and him as "traitors." (The two former Capitol Police officers had been seriously injured in the January 6 riot.) Trump's senior campaign adviser Jason Miller complained: "after months of saying politics had nothing to do with this trial, they showed up and made it a campaign event."

In closing arguments, Blanche accused prosecutors of being "perfectly happy" to have Cohen lie to jurors, drawling the word "per-jur-y."[54] When Blanche pleaded with the jury not to imprison Trump based on Cohen's word, Merchan said: "Making a comment like that is highly inappropriate. It is simply not allowed." As a former prosecutor, Blanche should have known better. "It's hard for me to imagine how that was accidental." (Juries decide guilt or innocence; judges sentence.) After Fox News anchor John Roberts falsely posted on X that Merchan had instructed the jury "they do not need unanimity to convict," which was reposted on right-wing social media, the judge received numerous death threats.

After deliberating about 11 hours over two days, the jury convicted Trump on all 34 counts.[55] He immediately denounced the verdict as "a disgrace," the product of "a rigged trial by a conflicted judge who was corrupt." "I'm a very innocent man. . . . I'm fighting for our country. I'm fighting for our Constitution. We'll fight till the end and we'll win." "Our whole country is being rigged right now. This is being done by the Biden administration in order to wound or hurt a political opponent." The country "has gone to hell." "We're a nation in decline, serious decline, millions and millions of people, pouring into our country right now, from prisons and from mental institutions, terrorists. And they're taking over our country." In a fundraising solicitation Trump declared: "I'M A POLITICAL PRISONER!" "JUSTICE IS DEAD IN AMERICA! Our country has fallen!"

> I was just convicted in a RIGGED TRIAL meant to interfere in our elections. Their sick & twisted goal is simple: Pervert the justice system against me so much, that proud supporters like You will SPIT when you hear my name. BUT THAT WILL NEVER HAPPEN! NOW IT'S TIME FOR ME & YOU TO SHOVE IT BACK IN THEIR CORRUPT FACES.

"Only with your support can we STOP these people from DESTROYING our country." The campaign boasted: "So many Americans were moved to donate to President Trump's campaign that the WinRed pages went down." Blanche said: "I don't accept that this was a fair place to try President Trump." "Every single person" on the jury knew about Trump. (That would be true of any jury in the US) "The timing of this most recent grand jury . . . kicked into action less than two months after President Trump announced he's running for reelection. And there are coincidences and then there's coincidences and I don't think that's something that just happened."

Republicans chimed in. Sen. Vance said: "we need to be subpoenaing Judge Merchan and his daughter." (This Yale law graduate and *Yale Law Journal* editor must have known better.) "Did George Soros ever talk to Alvin Bragg about using his power to go after Donald Trump?" (The two had never talked.) "This was never about justice—this is about plastering 'convicted felon' all over the airwaves. The only thing that Donald Trump is guilty of is being in the courtroom of a political sham trial." Vance, Rubio, and six other Senators signed a letter announcing they would no longer confirm appointees, approve "non-security related" funding, or allow expedited passage of Democratic bills that were not "directly relevant to the safety of the American people." Sen. Scott called the verdict "un-friggin'-believable." "This lawfare should scare every American." Sen. Graham predicted: "It will be seen as politically motivated and unfair, and it will backfire tremendously on the political Left." Speaker Johnson denounced this "shameful day in American history." The trial was a "purely political exercise, not a legal one." Trump was "a symbol of fighting back against this government corruption, the deep state, the bureaucracy and all the rest." "I do believe the Supreme Court should step in." It "will do the right thing, because they see the abuse of the system right now." (Johnson, another lawyer, knew the Court could not do this.) Rep. Scalise said the verdict had reduced America to a "banana republic." HJC chair Jordon condemned the "travesty of justice" by a "kangaroo court." There would be no money for the new FBI headquarters and none for Jack Smith. "We have rogue prosecutors around the country that have drug [sic] President Trump through this process because of who he is." Jordan's subcommittee on the weaponization of the federal government asked Bragg and Matthew Colangelo (one of his prosecutors) to testify on "the unprecedented political prosecution." (As a lawyer, Jordan knew the House had no jurisdiction over state prosecutions.) Sen. McConnell said: "These charges never should have been brought in the first place. I expect the conviction to be overturned on appeal." Kari Lake (seeking the Republican nomination for the Senate in Arizona, which she later won) called it "the most egregious example of election interference and an outright mockery of the rule of law in the 246-year history of our Republic." Trump supporters displayed the upside-down American flag (also flaunted by the January 6 rioters and flown by Justice Alito's wife). Rep. Greene posted one and grandstanded on X: "NO Federal funding to New York! I'm calling for it!!! New York needs to drop their conviction of Pres Trump! The whole thing was illegal! Republicans should not vote to fund a single penny to that corrupt state." Sen. Lee had 12 co-signers for a vow to close down the Senate because the White House had made "a mockery of the rule of law and fundamentally altered our politics in un-American ways." When Larry Hogan (Maryland's former Republican governor, now running for the Senate) urged "all Americans to respect the verdict and the legal process," RNC co-chair Lara Trump (Eric's wife) responded that Hogan "doesn't deserve the respect of anyone in the Republican Party."

Fox commentators reacted predictably: "a very sad day for all of us . . . we have seen the criminal justice [sic] weaponized to bring down a candidate for president and a former president" (Pirro—a former judge and DA); "a disgraceful day . . . that America may never recover from" (Ingraham—a lawyer and former Justice Thomas clerk); "a conviction without a crime" (Hannity).[56] Ben Shapiro said on the *Daily Wire* (which he founded) it was "a terrible day for the country." *Daily Wire* columnist Matt Walsh wrote on X that Trump "should make and publish a list of 10 high-ranking Democrat criminals who he will have arrested when he takes office." A *National Review* editorial entitled "The Horrendous Trump Verdict" accused Bragg of "selective prosecution" and called Merchan "embarrassingly compliant."

The next day Trump repeated his numerous lies and misstatements: Merchan was "highly conflicted," Trump had been "under a gag order, which nobody's ever been under," "this is all done by Biden and his people," "we weren't allowed to use our election expert under any circumstances," Bragg was "a failed D.A." because "crime is rampant in New York," Trump was not "allowed by the judge to use, in any form the standard RELIANCE ON COUNSEL DEFENSE," the case "was dropped by every agency . . . by the highly respected Southern District," "when I announced I was running for president a long time later, they decided to revive this case," "I'm supposed to go to jail for 187 years."[57] "There's never been a more conflicted judge." "If they can do this to me, they can do this to anyone." "These are bad people . . . sick people." His witnesses had been "literally crucified" by Merchan, who "looks like an angel, but he's really a devil." "We're going to be appealing this scam . . . on many different things." "I'm doing something for our Constitution." He warned ominously that if he were sentenced to prison or house arrest: "at a certain point, there's a breaking point." Trump raised $53 million in the first day after the trial, and the National Republican Senatorial Committee raised about $350,000—both record amounts. They claimed a total of $141 million for May, $70 million in the 48 hours after the conviction. Biden commented:

> It's reckless, it's dangerous and it's irresponsible for anyone to say this was rigged just because they don't like the verdict. Our justice system has endured for nearly 250 years, and it literally is the cornerstone of America. The justice system should be respected, and we should never allow anyone to tear it down.

"The jury was chosen the same way every jury in America has been chosen," "heard five weeks of evidence," and "reached a unanimous verdict."

After the verdict, Trump appeared to violate the gag order by attacking Michael Cohen.[58] Trump and his lawyers asked Merchan to lift the order, while prosecutors asked that it remain at least through sentencing.[59] Republicans vowed revenge. On Fox News Stephen Miller asked provocatively:

> Is every house [sic] committee controlled by Republicans using its subpoena power in every way it needs right now? Is every Republican D.A.

> starting every investigation they need to right now? Every facet of Republican Party politics and power has to be used right now to go toe-to-toe with Marxism and beat these Communists.

Steve Bannon concurred: "There are dozens of ambitious backbencher state attorneys general and district attorneys who need to 'seize the day' and own this moment in history." Sen. Rubio said it was time to "fight fire with fire." Berkeley law professor John Yoo wrote in the *National Review*: "in order to prevent the case against Trump from assuming a permanent place in the American political system, Republicans will have to bring charges against Democratic officers, even presidents. Only retaliation in kind can produce the deterrence necessary to enforce a political version of mutual assured destruction; without the threat of prosecution of their own leaders, Democrats will continue to charge future Republican presidents without restraint." Rep. Ronny Jackson warned that Biden "should just be ready because on Jan. 20 of next year . . . what's good for the goose is good for the gander." Jackson was encouraging "everybody that I have influence over . . . to aggressively go after the president and . . . his entire crime family." Speaker Mike Johnson said on Fox News that the Supreme Court should "step in" and grant Trump immunity. (It did, though probably not affecting this case, see Chapter 4.2.) Mike Davis (a former senior lawyer on the SJC when it was controlled by Republicans) said: "The Republican attorneys general in Georgia and Florida and the county attorney in Maricopa County, Arizona, need to open investigations" into prosecutors and investigators. "Then on Day 1, when he wins, President Trump needs to open a criminal civil rights investigation." (Presidents cannot do that.) Jeffrey Clark (who sought to help Trump overturn the 2020 election and was recommended for suspension in DC, see Chapter 2.4.10) exhorted "brave" DAs to file federal lawsuits seeking damages. (DAs cannot do that.) Three Republican House committee chairs planned to issue criminal referrals of Hunter and James Biden (see Chapter 5.2.3). Trump said: "sometimes revenge can be justified." He told Sean Hannity: "based on what they've done I would have every right to go after them . . . and it's easy, because . . . you see all the criminality, all of the money that's going into the [Biden] family and him."

After the verdict, Daniels offered to settle the defamation judgment Trump had won against her for slightly less than she owed.[60] His lawyer agreed if she signed an NDA promising to say nothing disparaging about his "suitability as a candidate for president." Her lawyer rejected this as "nonsense," and Daniels paid the full amount, having raised it through a GoFundMe page.

Attorney General Garland wrote in *The Washington Post* that attacks on the DoJ were "baseless, personal and dangerous . . . conspiracy theories crafted and spread for the purpose of undermining the public trust in the judicial process itself."[61] He deplored the "false claims that the Department is politicizing its work to somehow influence the outcome of an election," which were "often made by those who are themselves attempting to politicize the Department's work to influence the outcome of an election." He cautioned that "continued unfounded attacks against the Justice Department's employees are dangerous for people's safety" and "dangerous for democracy." A week earlier, a California man had been convicted of threatening to bomb an FBI field office and warning: "I can go on a mass murder spree." On July 26, Spencer Gear was charged in Las Vegas with ten counts of threatening a federal official and 12 of communicating such a threat. On June 3, the day after the verdict, he had left a phone message threatening Bragg and Merchan. Between November 30, 2023, and July 7, 2024 he made dozens of threatening calls and sent an email threatening to assault and kill eight federal officials in DC, Montana, New York, and New Jersey.

A YouGov poll hours after the verdict found that 50 percent agreed with it, 30 percent disagreed, and 19 percent were unsure.[62] Other survey research also found that a majority agreed with it: 50–27 (ABC News/Ipsos), 50–38 (Economist/YouGov), 50–44 (Quinnipiac University poll in Georgia), 46–33 (New York Times/Siena). In April, 58 percent of Republicans were opposed to a felon becoming president and just 17 percent in favor. But after the verdict those proportions reversed: 23–58. In six polls before the conviction, 27–29 percent of Republicans said it was a serious crime to falsify records to conceal hush money payments; after the conviction, just 9 percent said that.

Bragg agreed to testify before the HJC.[63]

> It undermines the rule of law to spread dangerous misinformation, baseless claims and conspiracy theories following the jury's return of a full-count felony conviction in People v. Trump. Nevertheless, we respect our government institutions and plan to appear voluntarily before the subcommittee.

Matthew Colangelo, who led the prosecution, would also testify. But Carlos Felipe Uriarte, a DoJ assistant attorney general, wrote Jordan there were no communications with Bragg's office concerning the prosecution.

After the Supreme Court granted presidents broad immunity in an interlocutory appeal during the 2020 election prosecution in DDC (see Chapter 4.2), Trump moved to dismiss the Daniels judgment.[64] (In May, House Speaker Johnson had boasted on Fox and Friends that he "personally" knew "many" of the Justices and was confident Trump's conviction "will be overturned . . . there's no question about it.") Trump argued that his tweets and testimony by his communications director should have been excluded as official acts. The prosecution response was due September 24. Justice Merchan postponed sentencing from July 11 to September 18 and a ruling on immunity to September 16. Two days after the immunity decision, Missouri sued New York, invoking the Supreme Court's original jurisdiction to claim the hush money case and gag order violated Missouri residents' First Amendment right to "hear from and vote for their preferred candidate." Florida, Iowa, Montana, and Alaska filed an amicus brief. The Court predictably declined to hear the case (Thomas and Alito saying they would hear it but not grant relief).

After Harris replaced Biden as the Democratic nominee, Trump moved for recusal a third time on the ground that Merchan's daughter had worked for Harris in the 2020 campaign. Merchan refused to recuse himself, calling the motion "rife with inaccuracies" and "nothing more than a repetition of stale and unsubstantiated claims." "[I]nnuendo and mischaracterizations do not a conflict create." He also preserved some of the gag order. Trump retorted: "This is the real Fascist 'stuff.'" In a letter to the HJC, Mike Nellis, founder of Authentic Campaigns, for which Merchan's daughter worked, said the company had not had a contract with the Harris campaign since 2019, adding that he and Ms. Merchan had received death threats and harassment. Trump's lawyers asked the judge to postpone sentencing further, until after the election, because he was going to rule on immunity on September 16, giving them only two days to appeal before sentencing. Prosecutors deferred to the judge while criticizing the defense arguments. On August 29, Trump again sought to remove the case to SDNY in order to delay sentencing, but Judge Hellerstein again denied the motion. Only New York courts could consider the allegation of bias. And "nothing in the Supreme Court's opinion affects my previous conclusion that the hush money payments were private, unofficial acts, outside the bounds of executive authority." Trump asked both Hellerstein and the Second Circuit to stay the denial while he appealed. The Second Circuit rejected that request. On September 6, Merchan postponed sentencing to November 26 and his decision on immunity until November 12 (prosecutors did not object). "This matter is one that stands alone, in a unique place in this nation's history." "The integrity of our judicial system" demands that sentencing be "free from distraction or distortion." Despite having won an important round, Trump's campaign said: "there should be no sentencing" in an "election interference witch hunt." Trump welcomed the "big news" that the "witch hunt against me has been postponed because everyone realizes that there was no case."

After Trump won the election, Justice Merchan denied the motion to dismiss based on immunity, finding that "the People's use" of possibly official acts "as evidence of the decidedly personal acts of falsifying business records poses no danger of intrusion on the authority and function of the executive branch," and even if admission of such evidence was "in error, such error was harmless."[65] He also noted the "overwhelming evidence of guilt." When Trump sought to add allegations of juror misconduct to his motion to dismiss, Merchan replied that the "court is prohibited from deciding such claims on the basis of mere hearsay and conjecture." Bragg proposed "abating" the case during Trump's presidency while preserving his conviction record. On January 3, 2025 Merchan denied a second motion to dismiss: "the sanctity of a jury verdict and the deference that must be accorded to it, is a bedrock principle in our Nation's jurisprudence."[66] "Presidential immunity for a sitting president does not extend to a President-elect," and "it would be an abuse of discretion for this Court to create, or recognize" such an immunity "in the absence of legal authority." Because this motion "asks this Court to consider his character," Merchan noted that Trump "has gone to great lengths to broadcast on social media and other forums his lack of respect for judges, juries, grand juries and the justice system as a whole." Despite having been found guilty of 10 counts of contempt, Trump "continues to undermine its legitimacy in posts to his millions of followers." Merchan scheduled sentencing for January 10, when he expected to order an unconditional discharge. Trump responded by again calling the case a "charade" that "should have been dead on arrival." The "corrupt" judge was "just doing the work of the Biden/Harris Injustice Department." "The legal system is broken." Merchan "should be disbarred!" Merchan denied a motion to postpone sentencing, and Appellate Division Judge Gesmer dismissed Trump's appeal; a New York Court of Appeals judge denied a separate application. Trump then sought Supreme Court review and, just before doing so, telephoned Justice Alito, ostensibly about a former clerk applying for a government position. The Court (5–4) denied his request, Roberts and Barrett voting with the three liberals; Alito did not recuse. Merchan imposed a sentence of unconditional discharge because of the imminent inauguration, while asserting that "Donald Trump the ordinary citizen, Donald Trump the criminal defendant" would not be entitled to such leniency. Trump retorted that he was "totally innocent."

Just as Trump sought to delegitimate elections he was afraid of losing (Abel 2024b), undermined scientists whose evidence and expertise opposed his disastrous response to the pandemic (Abel 2024c), and called for the destruction of the "deep state," which was responsible for implementing the law, so he attacked every court that ruled against him: on immigration and prosecutions of his cronies implicated in Russia's efforts to influence the 2016 election (Abel 2024a), the pandemic, elections, the January 6 riot prosecutions (Abel 2025: Chapter 4), his defamation and civil fraud cases (Chapter 2), and now this "hush money" case—his first prosecution. He attacked the criminal justice system from the start of the investigation through the guilty verdict. He sought to block the release of his tax returns to DoJ officials, denouncing this "political prosecution," but his arguments were rejected by the District Judge, the three Circuit Court judges, and seven of the nine Supreme Court Justices. (After obstructing disclosure for 18 months, he turned around and accused the Justice Department of delaying his case in order to interfere with his campaign.) He blamed Biden for this state prosecution. He attacked Bragg in vile language, invoking both racism and anti-Semitism: a "Soros backed animal," "degenerate psychopath," "criminal," "fat Alvin." (He used similarly hateful language to attack James (Chapter 2.3), Willis (Chapter 3.2), and Chutkan (Chapter 4.2)—all of whom were Black women—as well as Smith (Chapter 4).) A Trump appointed federal judge approved the HJC subpoena of Bragg, only to be immediately reversed by the Second Circuit. Trump made equally harsh attacks on Merchan: a "Democrat," "highly partisan," "highly conflicted" judge who "hates me." Trump indulged in a racist slur on Merchan's "looks" and birthplace (Colombia), just as he had maligned a "Mexican" judge (born in the US) for ruling against him (see Abel 2024a: Chapter 2). These ad hominem attacks were followed by predictable threats. Republicans vowed to call both the judge and his daughter before Congress.

Trump launched frivolous collateral attacks on the prosecution—an Article 78 proceeding in New York, a lawsuit against Cohen in Florida—only to lose or withdraw them. He made, and repeated, pointless unsuccessful motions: to recuse (although the Advisory Committee on Judicial Ethics had found no conflict), remove to federal court, change venue, and dismiss. And he engaged in a steady stream of vituperation against the prosecution during the trial: addressing the media and the public before and after hearings, posting on social media during the proceedings, even muttering comments and displaying hostile body language and facial expressions in court.

Justice Merchan maintained a measured response: anonymizing the jury to protect members from tampering and intimidation; doing the same with witnesses before they testified; cautioning Trump; making a limited gag order and extending it (while excluding himself); and finally holding Trump in contempt ten times. But the accused deliberately pushed the boundaries, undeterred by a mere $10,000 fine, perhaps hoping to provoke the judge into an unwise action that could justify a reversal or pay off politically. And Trump exploited the gag order, as well as the entire prosecution, to claim victimhood, drawing an obscene parallel to Nelson Mandela, reposting supporters' comparisons of him to Jesus during a trial that coincided with Easter, and claiming to be a "political prisoner" after the verdict (just as he called convicted January 6 defendants "political prisoners," see Abel 2025: Chapter 3). Trump and the GOP exploited the case to raise campaign funds. Republicans (including some previous critics like Pence, McConnell, Barr, and Romney) eagerly embraced the role of cheerleader, attending court in droves and echoing Trump's criticisms of the case as a "witch hunt" and the criminal justice system as "weaponized" when it was they who were guilty of both. Retired NYPD Commissioner Kerik called on his former employees to "walk out" (which would be illegal). Trump, Republicans, and the right-wing media suggested that violence was inevitable—even necessary (like his summons to "be wild" on January 6). Members of Congress demanded the defunding of the DoJ, FBI, and New York City. Despite all this, prosecutors expertly mobilized the facts and the law, Justice Merchan ensured that Trump received due process while preventing him from hopelessly distorting the trial, and the jury convicted. Law prevailed over politics. Justice was done.

3.2 Trump's Phone Call to Raffensperger and the Georgia Prosecution

On January 3, 2021, *The Washington Post* broke the story of the previous day's phone call in which Trump asked Georgia Secretary of State Brad Raffensperger to "find" the 11,000+ votes that would give him the state's Electoral College votes. The next day Raffensperger described the call (which he had recorded) on ABC News (see Abel 2024b: Chapter 4.4).[67] Hours later, Fani Willis said: "Like many Americans, I have found the news reports . . . disturbing. As I promised Fulton County voters last year [when she won the office], as District Attorney, I will enforce the law without fear or favor." On February 9, she opened an investigation into phone calls by both Trump and Sen. Graham to Raffensperger, Gov. Kemp, Attorney General Chris Carr, and the state's top elections investigator Frances Watson. The next day Willis told MSNBC's Rachel Maddow that she and her staff had received many racist threats.

Willis requested a special purpose grand jury because "a significant number of witnesses and prospective witnesses [including Raffensperger] have refused to cooperate with the investigation absent a subpoena requiring their testimony."[68] The Fulton County Superior Court Judges approved the request. Trump promptly assailed Willis (as well as James and Bragg—all three were Black). "If these radical, vicious, racist prosecutors do anything wrong or illegal, I hope we are going to have in this country the biggest protest we have ever had in Washington, D.C., in New York, in Atlanta and elsewhere because our country and our elections are corrupt." They were "vicious horrible people. They're racist and they're very sick. They're mentally sick." "In reality, they're not after me, they're after you, and I just happen to be the person in the way." Willis was a "young, ambitious, Radical Left Democrat . . . who is presiding over one of the most Crime Ridden and Corrupt places in the USA." (She was 50; Atlanta ranked 38th in crime rates among major American cities.) After two prominent Georgia lawyers (former Gov. Roy Barnes and former AUSA Gabe Banks) declined Willis's request to conduct the prosecution, she hired three lawyers: John Floyd and Anna Cross (both White) and Nathan Wade (who was Black).

The grand jury subpoenaed Graham, five lawyers (Giuliani, Chesebro, Eastman, Ellis, and Mitchell) and Jacki Pick Deason (who had appeared before the Georgia legislature).[69] Graham moved to quash the subpoena, declaring that the Constitution "provides absolute protection against inquiry" and invoked sovereign immunity (which was irrelevant) and a non-existent

"High-Ranking-Official Doctrine." (As a lawyer in both the military and private practice and SJC chair, he must have known these objections were frivolous.) ND GA Judge May (Obama) held that Graham had to testify: the speech or debate clause did not apply because he "was not simply engaged in legislative fact-finding" but also "seeking to influence Secretary Raffensperger's actions" to benefit Trump. Graham's "arguments are entirely unpersuasive, and they do not even demonstrate a 'substantial case on the merits.'" He appealed, claiming he had just been "doing his due diligence before the Electoral Count Act certification vote." The Eleventh Circuit issued a temporary stay and remanded, asking the District Court to determine whether the speech or debate clause applied. Judge May told Graham's lawyers: "you keep saying that it's improper for the court to look at motive, but how can I classify an act as political or legislative without knowing why the act was done?" Graham had said on Fox News on November 9, 2020: "if Republicans don't challenge and change the U.S. election system, there will never be another Republican president elected again." Democrats win "because they cheat." Judge May found that the speech or debate clause was not an absolute bar. Graham "cannot be asked about the portions of the calls that were legislative fact-finding." But Raffensperger

> has stated publicly that he understood Senator Graham to be implying or otherwise suggesting that he (Secretary Raffensperger) should throw out ballots. As the Court has previously stated, any such "cajoling," exhorting, or pressuring of Secretary Raffensperger (or any other Georgia election officials) to throw out ballots or otherwise change Georgia's election processes, including changing processes so as to alter the state's results, is not protected legislative activity under the Speech or Debate Clause.

Graham could be asked about his "communications and coordination with the Trump Campaign and its post-election efforts in Georgia," as well as his "public statements related to Georgia's 2020 elections." The eleventh Circuit (Wilson (Clinton) with Newsom and Grant (both Trump)) affirmed. Graham asked the Supreme Court for a stay (which Justice Thomas granted) while he sought en banc review; but the Supreme Court rejected Graham's arguments (as it did Trump's in a similar case).

Fulton County Superior Court Judge Robert McBurney (appointed by a Republican governor) ordered Giuliani to testify after he failed to appear at a New York hearing.[70] When Giuliani's lawyer said his client's health did not allow him to fly, Judge McBurney suggested Giuliani go "on a train, on a bus, or Uber." Informed that Giuliani was now a target of the investigation, his lawyer invoked lawyer-client privilege. (Graham was not practicing law, and Trump was not his client.) Willis said all 16 fake Trump electors also were targets. McBurney barred Willis from prosecuting Sen. Burt Jones (one of those electors) because she had donated to his opponent. Two years later, Pete Skandalakis, executive director of the Prosecuting Attorneys' Council of Georgia, took over the case against Jones because no other DA was willing to do so. (In September 2024 Skandalakis dropped the charges because Jones had acted in reliance "upon the advice of attorneys and legal scholars" and not "with criminal intent.") Eleven of those electors moved to disqualify Willis for political bias. But Judge McBurney said the inquiry "is inherently 'political' in the simple and unremarkable sense that politicians and leaders of a specific political party are alleged to have undertaken efforts to defeat the will of the Georgia electorate." A prosecutor "is not automatically biased and partisan—and subject to disqualification—because of the common political affiliations of the subjects (and targets) of the investigation." However, McBurney delayed Gov. Kemp's testimony until after the 2022 election, in which he was seeking to retain his office (and did).

Eastman's lawyer, Harvey Silverglate, advised him "to assert attorney-client privilege and the constitutional right to remain silent where appropriate" at the grand jury hearing, which he did.[71] Silverglate thought Eastman probably was a target but confidently declared that "a motion to dismiss will end the case." There had been "no threats, no coercion," just "an attempt to see if they could find a way to change the results of the electoral count." Eastman complained: "We really take issue with the District Attorney's office appearing, apparently, to criminalize contested legal theories." He had told a Georgia Senate committee on December 3, 2020: "the number of underaged individuals who were allowed to register . . . amounts allegedly up to approximately 66,000 people." But Raffensperger said just four had (legally) registered before they were 18 and were 18 when they voted. Eastman also had told the Senate committee: "the election can't be validly certified," and the decision "devolves back to the legislature."

On February 16, 2023, Judge McBurney released the grand jury report.[72] "We find by a unanimous vote that no widespread fraud took place in the Georgia 2020 presidential election that could result in overturning that election." "A majority of the Grand Jury believes that perjury may have been committed by one or more of witnesses testifying before it." They recommended indictments of Trump (21–1); Shafer, Eastman, Chesebro, and Meadows (20–1); Giuliani, Pick, Cheeley, Smith, Hall, Powell, Latham, and Hampton (20–1); Perdue (17–4); Loeffler (14–6); and Graham (13–7–1). Willis decided against seeking indictments of Perdue, Loeffler, Michael Flynn, Boris Epshteyn, L. Lin Wood (because of his uncertain mental competence), Graham, and Mitchell. Flynn's lawyer said the report showed "corruption by a politically motivated prosecutor." Graham asserted: "it should never be a crime for a federally elected official, particularly the chairman of the Senate Judiciary Committee [i.e., himself], who will have to vote to certify a presidential election, to question and ensure the integrity of that election." Burt Jones (now lieutenant-governor) denounced this "political circus."

Trump called the case "ridiculous" and assailed Forewoman Emily Kohrs for "going around and doing a Media Tour revealing, incredibly, the Grand Jury's inner workings & thoughts. This is not JUSTICE, this is an illegal Kangaroo Court."[73] Her comments had "poisoned" the case. However, Judge McBurney had prohibited jurors only from talking about "the discussions they had amongst themselves when it was just the grand jurors in the room." If a witness or prosecutor had been present "they're not prohibited from talking about that, nor are they prohibited from talking about the fruit of their deliberations, which would be the final report." Trump's lawyers moved to quash the report, alleging that McBurney "failed to protect the most basic procedural and substantive constitutional rights of all individuals discussed." The forewoman's statements "violate notions of fundamental fairness and due process and taint any future grand jury pool." A week earlier, five other jurors had discussed their work in the *Atlanta Journal-Constitution*. Trump fulminated: "The Left has turned America into the 'Investigation Capital of the World,' as our country's enemies brilliantly plot their next move to destroy our nation." Democrats "in the wings" had a "local racist Democrat district attorney in Atlanta who is doing everything in their power to indict me." Willis replied that Trump offered insufficient evidence in support of his motion to quash and lacked standing since he had not been summoned before the jury. After the indictments (below), a fringe right-wing website posted the names and addresses of the special grand jury members. A pro-Trump forum then declared: "these jurors have signed their death warrant by falsely indicting President Trump." A Truth Social user urged readers to publicize the "infamous" jurors to "make sure they can't walk down the street." The Fulton County Sheriff's office and the FBI were investigating threats.

Republican members of the Georgia legislature introduced bills that would create a state oversight board with power to punish or remove prosecutors for "willful misconduct" and reduce the number of signatures required for a recall vote from 30 percent of registered voters to just 2 percent.[74] Willis objected: "for the hundreds of years we've had prosecutors, this has been unnecessary. But now all of a sudden this is a priority, and it is racist." Sen. Bill Cowsert, Gov. Kemp's brother-in-law, called that "a racist statement on its own." Sen. Bill Strickland accused Willis of "being emotional." More than 21 of the 50 Georgia DAs supported the bills. Trump praised them on Truth Social: "they want to make it easier to remove and replace local rogue prosecutors who are incompetent, racist or unable to properly do their job." After the indictments (later), Sen. Colton Moore called for a special session of the legislature because Willis was "using taxpayer money, using her government authority, to persecute her political opponent." But Cody Hall, a senior adviser to Kemp, was derisive:

> where have I heard special session, changing decades-old law and overturning constitutional precedent before? Oh, right, prior to Republicans losing two Senate runoffs in January of 2021. What are people hoping to learn in the second kick of the election-losing mule?

Trump asked the Georgia Supreme Court to enjoin Willis's investigation and disqualify her.[75] His lawyers conceded they had found "no case in 40 years" when the court did that. "Then again, never has there been a case like this one." The Supreme Court rejected the petition. (Eight of the nine Justices had been appointed by Republican governors.) There were no "extraordinary circumstances." There was no evidence that constitutional rights were violated, that "the facts or the law" necessary to remove Willis existed, or that other courts had rejected Trump's claims. "A petitioner cannot invoke this Court's original jurisdiction as a way to circumvent the ordinary channels for obtaining the relief he seeks without making some showing that he is being prevented fair access to these ordinary channels." Judge McBurney held that the defendants' "rather overwrought allegations of prosecutorial overreach and prejudicial error do not suffice to show there is a significant risk of wrongful indictment." "The drumbeat from the DA has been neither partisan (in the political sense) nor personal, in marked and refreshing contrast to the stream of personal invective flowing from one of the movants." Trump ultimately dropped his challenge. After he pleaded not guilty, Trump and other defendants demanded the impeachment of Willis. But Gov. Kemp said: "we will not be engaging in political theater that only inflames the emotions of the moment." "We will do what is right, we will uphold our oath as public servants." Republicans would not focus on "distractions," "on the past, or some grifter scam that somebody's doing to help them raise a few dollars into their campaign account." Efforts to remove Willis were "political theater that only inflames the emotions of the moment." But after Kemp signed the law creating a Republican-controlled oversight commission with power to remove elected prosecutors (discussed earlier), eight Republican state senators filed a complaint against Willis. Lawsuits challenged the creation of the commission. Rep. Andrew Clyde (R-GA) introduced amendments to the federal budget bill to prohibit funding state and federal prosecutors who indicted major presidential candidates before the 2024 election. (The amendments never passed.)

HJC Chair Jordan investigated whether Willis collaborated with Biden administration officials and received any federal funding.[76] He wrote her: "it is noteworthy that just four days before this indictment you launched a new campaign fund-raising website that highlighted your investigation of President Trump." Willis replied that Jordan was trying "to obstruct a Georgia criminal proceeding and to advance outrageous partisan misrepresentations." "Your attempt to invoke Congressional authority to intrude upon and interfere with an active criminal case in Georgia is flagrantly at odds with the Constitution." He subpoenaed her office over the use of federal funds.

The Trump campaign aired a video claiming Willis "got caught hiding a relationship with a gang member she was prosecuting."[77] Trump repeated this in a campaign appearance: "They say there's a young woman—a young racist in Atlanta—they say she was after a certain gang member; and she ended up having an affair with the head of the gang or a gang member. And this is a person who wants to indict me . . . for a perfect phone call." There was no evidence for this lie. Willis received an email calling her nigger and "Jim Crow Democrat whore." She was given security.

In August, a regular grand jury indicted Trump and 18 others (including Giuliani, Meadows, Clark, and Phil Waldron), as well as seven connected to the breach of Coffee County electoral records (see Abel 2025: Chapter 5.2.5).[78] It adopted all the charges Willis recommended. Trump's lawyers called this "shocking and absurd," accusing Willis of building the case on "witnesses who harbor their own personal and political interests." A spokesperson at the Center for Renewing America, where Clark now worked, said: "it's clear Willis aspires to higher office and is using this witch hunt to climb the political ladder." Rep. McCarthy called the indictment a "desperate sham" by a "radical DA" who was "using it to fundraise her political career." Rep. Jordan denounced the "WITCH HUNT," declaring that Trump "did nothing wrong." Ron DeSantis called it the "criminalization of politics." "As president," he said presumptuously, "we will lean in against some of these local prosecutors if they are not following the law or if they are abandoning their duty to enforce the law evenly." (He had replaced two for being soft on crime and not prosecuting those seeking or performing abortions. As a Harvard Law School graduate, DeSantis knew the federal government has no power over local prosecutors.) Rep. Stefanik called Willis "another rogue far left radical district attorney" who had targeted "Biden's top political opponent." But *The Washington Post* welcomed the prosecution as "a sound and appropriate step."

The Trump campaign said:[79]

> These activities by Democratic leaders constitute a grave threat to American democracy and are direct attempts to deprive the American people of their rightful choice to cast their vote for president. Call it election interference or election manipulation—it is a dangerous effort by the ruling class to suppress the choice of the people. It is un-American and wrong.

In a fundraising email Trump denounced "the FOURTH ACT of Election Interference on behalf of the Democrats in an attempt to keep the White House under Crooked Joe's control and JAIL his single greatest opponent of the 2024 election." On August 30, he said on Truth Social:

> I understand through illegal leaks to the fake news media that phoney [sic] Fani Willis, the D.A. of Fulton County, Georgia, wants desperately to indict me on the ridiculous grounds of tampering with the 2020 presidential election. No, I didn't tamper with the election! Those who rigged & stole the election were the ones doing the tampering, & they are the slime that should be prosecuted. I made a perfect phone call of protest. Why wasn't this fake case brought 2.5 years ago? Election interference!

Trump called Willis a "rabid partisan" and part of "a dangerous effort by the ruling class to suppress the choice of the people."[80] She was "crooked, incompetent, & highly partisan" and "has allowed Murder and other violent Crime to MASSIVELY ESCALATE." The Trump campaign denounced "Biden's newest lackey: Atlanta DA Fani Willis." "So incompetent, on her watch violent crimes have exploded." "Atlanta violence: Nearly 60% more murders so far this year." (Homicide actually was down 25 percent from the previous year, rape by half, and aggravated assault by 22 percent.) "So tainted Willis was thrown off one case for trying to prosecute a political opponent." (She was disqualified because she had donated to the defendant's opponent.) "So corrupt, Willis got caught hiding a relationship with a gang member she was prosecuting." (That was a lie.) "So dishonest, Willis was accused of creating a fake subpoena." (But the accusation was untrue.) Giuliani said this was "just the next chapter in a book of lies with the purpose of framing President Donald Trump and anyone willing to take on the ruling regime." The case "is an affront to American democracy and does permanent, irrevocable harm to our justice system."

After arraignment, Trump posted his arraignment mug shot on X over the heading: "ELECTION INTERFERENCE NEVER SURRENDER! DONALDJTRUMP.COM."[81] His campaign was selling a $34 t-shirt with the mug shot and "never surrender." In the first two days, it hauled in more than $7 million in online sales of the photo on coffee mugs, bumper stickers and t-shirts. Trump claimed indictments increased his popularity among Black voters. "A lot of people said that's why the Black people liked me, because they had been hurt so badly and discriminated against. And they actually viewed me as I'm being discriminated against. . . . Maybe there's something to it." "When I did the mug shot in Atlanta, that mug shot is number one." Black people "embraced it more than anyone else." "I'm being indicted for you, the Black population."

Meadows promptly sought to remove his case to federal court on the ground that he had been acting under color of law.[82] (He apparently believed the jury venire for ND GA, which included 44 counties, many rural, would be more favorable than Fulton County, which was mostly urban Atlanta and 42 percent Black.) Meadows denied having had "any role" in coordinating bogus electors; but he had written a Trump campaign staffer in December: "we just need to have someone coordinating the electors for the states." He testified he had visited the suburban Atlanta facility where officials were auditing ballot signatures only because he happened to be in Georgia visiting his two children for Christmas. Although he claimed the visit was unconnected to the campaign, he had asked Jordan Fuchs (Deputy Secretary of State and Raffensperger's chief of staff) on December 27 if "there was a way to speed up Fulton County signature verification in order to have results before January 6 if the Trump campaign assist financially." He claimed that though he participated in Trump's January 2 call to Raffensperger, he did not know that Cleta Mitchell, Kurt Hilbert, and Alex Kaufman were involved in a Trump campaign lawsuit against Raffensperger. He admitted attending Trump's Oval Office meeting with Michigan legislators but denied knowing the campaign was contesting results in that state (see Abel 2024b: Chapter 3.2.2). He could not recall events of 2020–21: "My wife will tell you sometimes that I forget to take out the trash." *The Washington Post* opposed removal: "Mark Meadows's job wasn't to help Trump steal the 2020 election."

ND GA Judge Jones (Obama) denied the motion.[83] "There is no federal jurisdiction over the criminal case." Raffensperger had testified that he thought his conversation with Trump and Meadows "was a campaign call." The evidence "establishes that the actions at the heart of the state's charges against Meadows were taken on behalf of the Trump campaign with an ultimate goal of affecting state election activities and procedures." "Meadows's alleged association with post-election activities was not related to his role as White House chief of staff or his executive branch authority." The Eleventh Circuit (Pryor (GWB), with Rosenbaum (Obama) and Abudu (Biden)) denied Meadows's appeal. Removal "does not apply to former federal officers, and even if it did, the events giving rise to this criminal action were not related to Meadows's duties" "Whatever the chief of staff's role with respect to state election administration, that role does not include altering valid election results in favor of a particular candidate." "We are aware of no authority suggesting that the Take Care Clause empowers federal executive interference with state election procedures based solely on the federal executive's own initiative and not in relation to another branch's constitutionally-authorized act." After the Circuit denied en banc review, Meadows sought review in the Supreme Court, which denied it without dissents.

Others also sought removal. David Shafer claimed that, as a "presidential elector," he was "acting under the authority of the Constitution and the Electoral Count Act" and "at the direction of the President and other federal officers."[84] (But he was not an elector.) Clark's lawyer said he "was a high-ranking U.S. Justice Department official at all relevant times." The allegations "relate directly to his work at the Justice Department as well as with the former president." (But his duties were not related to elections.) He had written a letter in the DoJ office and used DoJ email to send it. The request for the letter was "coming from the President of the United States through Mr. Meadows." Judge Jones denied the removal petitions of Clark, Shafer, Shawn, Still, and Latham.

> Even though electors are engaging in a federal function when they meet and cast their ballots, that is insufficient to make someone a federal officer. To find otherwise would convert all citizens who can lawfully vote into federal officers when they cast their ballot for the U.S. House of Representatives.

The case was assigned to Judge Scott McAfee, recently appointed by Kemp.[85] He had been an ND GA AUSA for eight years, Fulton County Assistant DA (under Willis), and state Inspector General. At the University of Georgia Law School, he had been vice-president of the Federalist Society and treasurer of Law Republicans. He ordered Trump not to communicate with witnesses or co-defendants except through lawyers, intimidate them, or make any "direct or indirect threat of any nature against the community or to any property in the community." Prosecutors estimated the trial would take four months after jury selection and hear more than 150 witnesses. Judge McAfee commented: "It just seems a bit unrealistic that we can handle all 19 [defendants] in 40-something days." After Chesebro demanded a speedy trial, Willis proposed October 2023 (she had previously suggested March 4, 2024). Trump's lawyer Steve Sadow moved to sever for this reason (since Trump wanted to delay the trial until after the election). Eastman also moved to sever. Judge McAfee ordered that the trial be televised but jurors' identities kept secret. He granted the early trial motions by Chesebro and Powell. "Severing the remaining 17 co-defendants is simply a procedural and logistical inevitability," "an absolute necessity."

> The Fulton County courthouse simply contains no courtroom adequately large enough to hold all 19 defendants, their multiple attorneys and support staff, the sheriff's deputies, court personnel, and the state's prosecutorial team. Relocating to another larger venue raises security concerns that cannot be rapidly addressed.

But Willis reaffirmed her request for a joint trial of all 19.

Four hundred fifty potential jurors completed a survey.[86] Judge McAfee wanted the jury seated in two weeks, denying the defense more time to question jurors. He was openly skeptical of its request to ask jurors about blanket statements concerning the 2020 election and MAGA, dismissing some questions as like a "Gallup poll" and irrelevant "to the ultimate question of the impartiality of the juror." A defense lawyer complained: "4 minutes and 15 seconds per juror is not enough. That's unconstitutional." McAfee replied: "There are competing values here. I don't think it should be that one can invoke a speedy trial and then run out the clock." Willis did not "expect that we will conclude until the winter or the very early part of 2025." She had been threatened more than 100 times. "In the last three years, I've been called the N-word so many times I couldn't even think to count how many times."

Sadow objected to the prosecution proposal of an August 2024 trial date for the other 17: "This case should not be interfering with an election."[87] Asked by Judge McAfee whether the trial could proceed if Trump won, Sadow asserted it would have to be postponed to the end of his term because it would interfere with his duties under the Supremacy Clause. Defense lawyers asked McAfee to let them file interlocutory appeals, claiming the indictment violated the Supremacy Clause, the First Amendment, and the requirement that it be "perfect in form and substance." Sadow offered to draft subpoenas for information the defense wanted from the DoJ about Trump's other prosecutions; but McAfee doubted he had the authority to demand evidence in a federal case. Sadow said he was not sure Trump would attend all the proceedings.

Scott Hall, a bail bondsman charged with involvement in the breach of Coffee County election equipment (see Abel 2025: 5.1.6), was the first defendant to plead (to misdemeanor charges reduced from a felony because he was a first offender).[88] He accepted five years' probation and a $5,000 fine and agreed to write a letter of apology, have no contact with victims, witnesses, or defendants or speak to the media and testify "truthfully" in the other cases. Powell moved to dismiss, claiming prosecutorial misconduct and failure to disclose evidence. But she pleaded the day before jury selection was to begin, agreeing to turn over documents and testify against the others in exchange for six years' probation, a $6,000 fine, and $2,700 restitution to Georgia. Trump said: "MS. POWELL IS NOT MY ATTORNEY, AND NEVER WAS." (But in January 2021 he had considered naming her a special counsel in the DoJ.) Chesebro moved to dismiss because Wade had not filed an oath of office before joining Willis's team. But McAfee denied what he dismissed as a "parrot of a motion," which had been "blithely" written. Chesebro then pleaded to a single felony, apologizing, writing a letter, promising to testify, and getting 100 hours of community service and 3–5 years' probation, a $10,000 fine, and $5,000 restitution to the state. Ellis also pleaded, wrote a letter of apology, and agreed to cooperate in other cases, receiving 100 hours of community service and 3–5 years' probation. She blamed her failure to perform "due diligence" on her reliance on lawyers "with many more years of experience." "If I knew then what I know now, I would have declined to represent Donald Trump in these post-election challenges." On her Christian broadcasting show the previous month she had said: "I have great love and respect for [Trump] personally," but she could no longer support him politically because he showed a "malignant narcissistic tendency to simply say that he's never done anything wrong."

The guilty pleas included videotaped proffer statements.[89] Ellis said Dan Scavino, Trump's deputy chief of staff, told her in December 2020 that "the boss" did not plan to leave the White House "under any circumstances." When she responded: "it doesn't quite work that way," Scavino was flippant: "we don't care, and we're not going to leave." Powell admitted she would have directed the military to seize election machines if Trump had made her special counsel. She still believed there had been "machine fraud." Chesebro acknowledged playing a role in transporting alternative elector statements from Wisconsin to Washington. Willis complained that the unauthorized disclosure of these statements, which was "clearly intended to intimidate witnesses in this case, subjecting them to harassment and threats prior to trial, constitutes indirect communication about the facts of this case with co-defendants and witnesses, and obstructs the administration of justice." Jonathan R. Miller III, representing defendant Misty Hampton, said he had released them because "this is a very very public trial" and "the public has a right to know" what was in the statements.

Trump moved to dismiss on grounds of immunity, double jeopardy (because of the second impeachment), due process violations, and the First Amendment.[90] McAfee dismissed six counts against Giuliani, Meadows, Cheely, Eastman, and Smith for failure "to allege sufficient detail regarding the nature of their commission, i.e., the underlying felony solicited"—pressure on elected officials. But he gave the prosecution six months to resubmit those counts to a grand jury or appeal (it did the latter). McAfee denied Trump's First Amendment defense. "Free speech—including political speech—is not without restriction." "Even core political speech addressing matters of public concern is not impenetrable from [sic] prosecution if allegedly used to further criminal activity." But he was not "foreclosing the ability [of the defense] to raise" a similar challenge during the trial. Trump sought leave to appeal. McAfee also denied Shafer's motion to strike indictment language referring to "duly elected and qualified presidential electors" and "false Electoral College votes."

In early September (before Chesebro pleaded), his lawyer, Manny Arora, initiated a phone call with other defense counsel to report that Nathan Wade was unqualified and romantically involved with Willis.[91] One lawyer said later: "I thought it was too salacious, and I thought it would irritate the judge." But others picked up the story. Andrew Fleischmann, an Atlanta criminal defense lawyer, posted on X that Willis had "spent almost a million dollars on RICO advice from Nathan Wade, a dude who has never tried a RICO case." The conservative *Washington Examiner* characterized the arrangement as "unorthodox" and quoted an Atlanta lawyer calling it a "cash cow." Contemporaneously, the indictments automatically prompted the Wade law firm computer to contact all the defendants, offering representation. Shafer's lawyer filed a motion objecting to this solicitation. Judge McAfee denied it, ruling that "nothing indicates that Special Prosecutor Wade knowingly sent the mailer or specifically targeted the Defendants."

Michael Roman declined the offer to plead to a single misdemeanor in exchange for cooperating and a $5,000 fine.[92] His lawyer, Ashleigh Merchant, filed open-records requests for Wade's contract and payments and obtained financial records from his ongoing divorce case. And she learned from her long-time friend Terrence Bradley (Wade's former business associate, friend, and lawyer) that Willis and Wade had met in October 2019 and formed a romantic relationship. On September 14, Bradley sent Merchant the first of more than 300 texts and later helped draft her motion to dismiss, alleging a "clandestine" relationship between the two and claiming they had taken vacations together with the more than $650,000 Wade earned from working on this case. The evidence was in Wade's sealed divorce case. Merchant also said the Fulton County Board of Commissioners had not given the required approval to the contract hiring Wade, who had failed to file the requisite sworn oath. But Pete Sandalakis, head of the Prosecuting Attorneys Council of Georgia, said no county authorization was necessary. (And Judge McAfee had rejected similar motions the previous year.) After Sadow congratulated Merchant, Trump declared: "it turns out that that case is totally compromised. In fact, they say [Willis is] in far more criminal liability than any of the people she's looking at." Wade was "a lawyer with absolutely no experience . . . who happens to be her lover or her boyfriend." (He had been admitted to practice in 1999.) Willis "used the phony case against me to hire her 'lover' in a SELF-ENRICHMENT SCHEME of more than half a MILLION dollars!" Willis responded that Wade had "impeccable credentials" and decades of experience. All three lawyers she had hired for the case were her longtime friends and legal "superstars," but only Wade was attacked.

Merchant subpoenaed Willis and planned to call at least ten other witnesses.[93] Willis moved to quash the subpoena on the ground that she "lacks personal knowledge of any matter that is relevant." The Fulton County Board's audit committee chair directed her to provide documents to determine whether funds paid to Wade "were converted to your personal gain in the form of subsidized travel or other gifts." Cobb County Superior Court

Judge Thompson unsealed Wade's divorce records, but after the couple reached a settlement, the judge canceled a hearing.

Republican State Senators established an investigatory committee, which issued subpoenas in its probe of Willis.[94] Georgia GOP chair Josh McKoon circulated a 2020 video of Willis declaring she would fire any employee who slept with a co-worker and promising not to date people "that work under me." Gov. Kemp called the allegations "deeply troubling." State House Speaker Jon Burns agreed: "the allegations . . . are extremely troubling to say the least." Trump referred to Willis and Wade as "the lovebirds" and accused the prosecutors of targeting him "to ENRICH THEMSELVES AND TO LIVE THE Lifestyle of the Rich and Famous."

At a service in the Big Bethel AME Church, Willis said Wade was targeted because he was Black.[95] Trump's lawyers condemned the comment as

> a glaring, flagrant, and calculated effort to foment racial bias into this case [sic] by publicly denouncing the defendants for somehow daring to question her decision to hire a Black man (without also mentioning that she is alleged to have had a workplace affair with the same man) to be a special prosecutor.

Trump's lawyers also said Willis violated the rule that a prosecutor shall "refrain from making extrajudicial comments that have a substantial likelihood of heightening public condemnation of the accused." They asked Judge McAfee to disqualify her office and dismiss the indictment. Rep. Greene filed a complaint with the state ethics commission.

Willis replied in a 176-page filing: "while the allegations raised in the various motions are salacious and garnered the media attention they were designed to obtain, none provide this court with any basis upon which to order the relief they seek."[96] Her relationship with Wade "has never involved direct or indirect financial benefit." "Financial responsibility for personal travel taken is divided roughly evenly." She asked McAfee to dismiss the motions without an evidentiary hearing. Wade said there was "no personal relationship" between them "prior to or at the time" he was appointed. "No funds paid to me in compensation for my role as Special Prosecutor have been shared with or provided to DA Willis." She bought plane tickets for herself and Wade. But Merchant said witnesses had "personal knowledge" that the relationship began before Wade's appointment. Trump declared Willis "was able to get her 'lover'" money by hiring him. The admission "MEANS THAT THIS SCAM IS TOTALLY DISCREDITED & OVER." Judge McAfee excluded testimony about Wade's qualifications because the DA could hire anyone with "a heartbeat and a bar card." But he denied a request by Willis and others to bar all witness testimony. Her lawyer said she would call witnesses to rebut allegations that she and Wade "cohabited" at a rental property. Defendants Trump, Shafer Cheeley, Clark, and Latham joined the motion to disqualify Willis.

At the hearing, Robin Bryant-Yeartie, a longtime friend who used to work in Willis's office, expressed "no doubt" that the relationship began in late 2019.[97] She had seen the two "hugging, kissing" before November 1, 2021, when Wade became special prosecutor. Willis called Merchant "dishonest" and denounced her "highly offensive claims" as "lies, lies, lies." Her "interests are contrary to democracy, your honor, not to mine." Judge McAfee urged Willis to preserve decorum. Willis said: "Mr. Wade is my friend right now. Mr. Wade, I would say, has been my friend since 2020. I think he started out like a mentor and a professional colleague." Wade said the relationship began in March 2022, five months after he was appointed, and ended in summer 2023. Willis repaid him in cash for about half the cost of their trips. (When Shafer chortled at this, McAfee warned: "you'll step out if you do that again.") Merchant said Willis and Wade had lived together in a condo Bryant-Yeartie had rented. Willis denied this and accused Bryant-Yeartie of having "betrayed our friendship." Wade maintained he had never spent the night at Willis's condo, ridden with her security detail, or stayed at her condo without the security detail. He did not deposit the cash she gave him and kept no records of it. His marriage had ended when his wife had an affair in 2015; they agreed to divorce but waited to file until their children were older. Wade did so in November 2021, the day his wife returned to Georgia (allowing him to serve her) and a day after he signed a contract to lead the election interference case. Bradley declined to answer questions about the Willis-Wade relationship, citing attorney-client privilege, and denied talking to Merchant.

Judge McAfee ordered Bradley to testify again, ruling that the parties "did not meet their burden of establishing that the communications are covered" by lawyer-client privilege even though Bradley had briefly been Wade's divorce lawyer.[98] Sadow submitted an affidavit of records documenting "just under 12,000" calls and texts between Willis and Wade in the first 11 months of 2021, before she hired him. After it became clear Bradley was the source of Merchant's allegations, he testified but often suffered memory lapses: "I can't tell you what date that was. It was made in confidence. There was no one else present." He denied "personal" knowledge of when the relationship began. One text said either Andrew Evans (Wade's lawyer), or Evans's wife had seen Willis and Wade having sex. But Bradley disparaged many of his texts to Merchant as mere speculation. Cindi Lee Yeager, Cobb County Deputy DA, said Bradley told her the relationship began before Wade started working for Willis, "during the time that Ms. Willis was running for DA in 2019 through 2020." Yeager also heard Willis warn Bradley in a September 2023 phone call: "they are coming after us." "You don't need to talk to them about anything about us."

Merchant and Sadow argued that the mere "appearance of impropriety" required disqualification.[99] Willis's lawyer replied there had to be an "actual conflict." McAfee found the defendants "failed to meet their burden" to prove a sufficient "conflict of interest" to remove Willis. Bradley's texts did not reveal "the basis for which he claimed such sweeping knowledge" about the relationship. "His inconsistencies, demeanor, and generally non-responsive answers left far too brittle a foundation upon which to build any conclusions." Willis's claim to have repaid Wade in cash was "not so incredible as to be inherently unbelievable"; but an "odor of mendacity" pervaded the affair, and an "appearance of impropriety . . . infects the current structure of the prosecution team."

> [R]easonable members of the public could easily be left to wonder whether the financial exchanges have continued, resulting in some form of benefit to the District Attorney, or even whether the romantic relationship has resumed . . . an outsider could reasonably think that the District Attorney is not exercising her independent professional judgment totally free of any compromising influences.

The judge could not condone "the tremendous lapse in judgment or the unprofessional manner of the District Attorney's testimony during the evidentiary hearing." He ruled that either Willis or Wade had to withdraw. Wade did so within hours.

Trump gloated on Truth Social: "The Fani Willis lover, Mr. Nathan Wade Esq., has just resigned in disgrace. This is the equivalent of Deranged Jack Smith getting 'canned,' BIG STUFF, something which should happen in the not too distant future!!!"[100] McAfee granted Trump and other defendants leave to appeal his ruling but said he would "continue addressing the many other unrelated pending pretrial motions." Trump and eight co-defendants did seek an interlocutory appeal, and Willis moved to block it. McAfee said he would rule on other motions filed by the six defendants who did not appeal.

The Georgia Court of Appeals panel (three Republican-appointed judges) agreed to review McAfee's decision but scheduled argument for October 4, precluding a trial before the election.[101] They stayed all proceedings before McAfee and then canceled the oral argument date. Prosecutors asked the court to dismiss the appeal, arguing that "when a trial court makes determinations concerning matters of credibility or evidentiary weight, reviewing courts will not disturb those determinations unless they are flatly incorrect." McAfee won re-election in a nonpartisan race; Willis won the Democratic primary (tantamount to re-election). The appeals court rescheduled argument for December 5—a month after the election. On September 12, McAfee dismissed charges against Trump, Eastman, Still, Shafer, Latham, Giuliani, Chesebro, Cheeley, Smith, and Roman for filing, attempting to file, and conspiring to file false documents because, under the Supremacy Clause, they fell under federal jurisdiction. But he rejected a motion by Eastman and Still to dismiss the entire state RICO indictment, which he found "facially sound and constitutionally sufficient," and Trump still faced eight charges. On November 18, the Georgia Court of Appeals indefinitely postponed its hearing. But a month later the court (2–1) disqualified Willis, finding this "the rare case in which disqualification is mandated and no other remedy will suffice to restore public confidence in the integrity of these proceedings." She appealed to the Georgia Supreme Court.

Trump sought to politicize this prosecution, as he did the other three. He denounced it as a witch hunt and election interference. He inverted his own racism, vilifying the three Black lawyers bringing cases against him (Willis, Bragg, and James) as "radical, vicious, racist prosecutors," "vicious horrible people," "racist," "mentally sick," "rabid," "partisan," "crooked," and "incompetent." He attacked the grand jury forewoman. He falsely accused Willis of a relationship with a gang member she had prosecuted. He openly sought to delay the trial until after he won the election when (his lawyer claimed) the Supremacy Clause would require its suspension. He warned supporters that prosecutors were "not after me, they're after you." He threatened "the biggest protest we have ever had in Washington, D.C., in New York, in Atlanta and elsewhere." And his words were followed by threats against Willis and the grand jury members (whose identities were publicized by right-wing media). Georgia Republican legislators embraced Trump's cause by seeking the impeachment of Willis. Even Gov. Kemp rejected this as a "grifter scam that somebody's doing to help them raise a few dollars into their campaign account." But then he signed the Republican bill to facilitate replacing Willis as prosecutor.

Despite all these efforts to politicize the case, the legal system did what it is supposed to do. Superior Court Judge McBurney (appointed by a Republican governor) denied a motion to disqualify Willis for political bias, reprimanding Trump for his "stream of political invective." The Fulton County special grand jury recommended indictments of all those Willis brought before it, and the regular grand jury indicted them. The Georgia Supreme Court (eight of whose nine members had been appointed by a Republican governor) unanimously rejected an action seeking to disqualify Willis. The Eleventh Circuit (two of whose three judges were appointed by Trump) rebuffed Sen. Graham's efforts to avoid testifying. Another panel (with one GWB appointee) affirmed the district judge's denial of removal petitions. Prosecutors secured guilty pleas and promises of cooperation from four defendants, including three lawyers whose evidence might implicate Trump (as suggested by their proffer statements). Superior Court Judge McAfee (also appointed by a Republican governor) conducted the trial in an evenhanded manner. He criticized defense lawyers for parroting a motion he had already rejected, which sought to disqualify Wade (on the ground that he had not signed an oath).

And then defense lawyers discovered that Willis had seriously compromised the prosecution through her relationship with Wade, in a momentous case that could have been the capstone of her career. Despite her protestations, Wade clearly was not the best qualified candidate to lead the prosecution. Regardless of when the relationship began (the contradictory evidence suggested the conflicted loyalties of the witnesses), McAfee rightly found that Willis's testimony was "unprofessional" and her behavior demonstrated "a tremendous lapse of judgment." Her combative response to the allegations and attempt to play the race card further weakened her position. Judge McAfee chose a compromise solution, with the inevitable result that Wade promptly resigned. But the Georgia Court of Appeals (with three Republican appointees) halted the trial and scheduled a hearing after the election. A prosecution that appeared to have stronger evidence of Trump's guilt (the phone call with Raffensperger) than Smith's election case (see Chapter 7.2) was needlessly wounded—severely, perhaps fatally.

3.3 Did State Courts Successfully Resist Politicization?

Trump used the same strategies to undermine and politicize both cases. He engaged in personal attacks on prosecutors, judges, and juries, using vile language, much of it racist (while accusing others of racism).[102] Because anonymity prevented him from accusing particular jurors, he maligned entire jurisdictions. He provoked gag orders so he could complain about and defy them (and even court imprisonment for contempt). He discouraged witnesses from testifying against him and sought to recuse judges, change venue, and remove the cases to federal court. He resisted subpoenas and filed frivolous collateral attacks and hopeless appeals. All this was intended to delay the cases until after the election, in the belief they would be suspended during his presidency; and then Trump blamed prosecutors for delaying the trials so they would interfere with his campaign and preparation to assume office. He portrayed himself as victim rather than perpetrator, comparing himself to Mandela while supporters compared him to Jesus. He accused others of what he was doing—politicizing the cases. Republican politicians lavished uncritical support, even threatening to withhold funds from New York and Georgia.

But these strategies failed. Unlike judges dealing with the hot button issues of immigration, the pandemic, and elections (Abel 2024a, 2024b, 2024c), Merchan (a Democrat) and McAfee (a Republican) did not divide along partisan lines, and neither did the state and federal judges handling collateral matters, although the two most consistently conservative Supreme Court justices (Thomas and Alito) and a recent SDNY Trump appointee (Vyskocil) voted against prosecutors (see Table 3.1).

TABLE 3.1 Other Judges' Decisions in Cases Related to State Prosecutions of Trump

Case	*Judge*	*Political orientation*	*For or against prosecution*
Trump's tax returns	SDNY Marrero	R (Clinton)	For
Same	Second Circuit Katzmann, Chin, Droney	D (Clinton), D (Obama), D (Obama)	For
Same	SC Roberts, Kavanaugh, Gorsuch, Ginsberg, Kagan, Sotomayor, Breyer	3 R, 4 D	For
Same	Alito, Thomas	2R	Against
House subpoenas Manhattan DA	SDNY Vyskocil	R (Trump)	Against
	Second Circuit Robinson	D (Biden)	For
Hush money—removal	SDNY Hellerstein	D (Clinton)	For
Hush money—delay, venue	NY AD Gonzalez	D	For
Hush money—delay, appeal gag	NY AD Kern	D	For
Hush money—disqualify Merchan	NY AD Gesmer	D	For
Willis subpoenas Graham	ND Ga May	D (Obama)	For
Same	Eleventh Circuit Wilson, Newsom, Grant	D (Clinton), 2Rs (Trump	For
Giuliani testimony	Fulton County Superior Court McBurney	R	For
Disqualify Willis	Ga SC	8Rs, 1D	For
Remove from Fulton County to fed ct	ND Ga Jones	D (Obama)	For
	Eleventh Circuit Pryor, Rosenbaum, Abudu	R (GWB), D (Obama), D (Biden)	For

Despite repeated provocations by Trump (and other defendants in Georgia), both trial judges scrupulously guaranteed due process and preserved decorum (even if that meant anonymizing the juries and imposing a gag order in response to Trump's repeated outbursts). The New York jury convicted on all counts. Georgia prosecutors obtained guilty pleas from four of the 19 defendants and their agreement to testify in the forthcoming trial. (Yet three out of ten Republicans still refused to believe Trump had phoned

Raffensperger, despite the published transcript.)[103] Nevertheless, there were two important differences. The Republican-dominated Georgia legislature passed a law exposing Willis to removal, which the Republican governor signed. Most critically, Willis's misconduct led to the departure of Ward as lead prosecutor, uncertainty about her own future, and suspension of the proceedings until after the November election.

Trump's victory had immediate consequences.[104] Although Merchan denied repeated motions to dismiss, he gave Trump an unconditional discharge, leaving his conviction intact but imposing no penalty. If the Georgia Supreme Court affirms Willis's removal, the executive director of the Prosecuting Attorneys' Council will appoint a replacement—a process that took years the last time it occurred. The replacement almost certainly will conclude that, as a matter of comity with the OLC ruling, the case cannot proceed during Trump's term. And if it ever does, appellate courts—especially the US Supreme Court—are certain to hold that some, and perhaps all, the conduct charged is immune as official presidential action.

Notes

1 Rothfeld & Palazzolo, "Trump lawyer arranged $130,000 payment for adult-film star's silence," *WSJ* (1.12.18); Haberman, "Trump's longtime lawyer says he paid Stormy Daniels out of his own pocket," *NYT* (2.13.18); Eisen & Canter, "Flashback: Stormy Daniels on '60 Minutes' makes Donald Trump's legal problems even worse," *USA Today* (5.3.18); "Michael Cohen has been disbarred," *NBC News* (2.26.19); "US judge dismisses Stormy Daniels's lawsuit against President Trump to end their NDA," *ABC News* (3.8.19); Whalen, "Court orders Trump to pay Stormy Daniels $44,100 to cover her legal fees," *WP* (8.22.20); Stevens, "Stormy Daniels ordered to pay Trump $293,000 in legal fees," *NYT* (12.11.18); Mangan, "Porn star Stormy Daniels loses appeal in Trump case, vows 'I will go to jail before I pay a penny' of $300,000," *CNBC* (3.23.22); "Stormy Daniels: US election officials drop Trump hush money probe," *BBC News* (5.7.21); Del Valle & Scannell, "Michael Avenatti convicted of wire fraud and aggravated identity theft for stealing from Stormy Daniels," *CNN* (2.4.22); "Avenatti gets 4 years in prison for cheating Stormy Daniels," *AP* (6.6.22).

2 Rashbaum & Protess, "8 years of Trump tax returns are subpoenaed by Manhattan D.A.," *NYT* (9.16.19); Rashbaum & Weiser, "Trump taxes: President ordered to turn over returns to Manhattan D.A.," *NYT* (10.7.19); Weiser & Liptak, "Trump taxes: appeals court rules president must turn over 8 years of tax returns," *NYT* (11.4.19); Liptak, "Supreme Court rules Trump cannot block release of financial records," *NYT* (7.9.20); Scannell, Prokupecz & Cole, "Trump's tax returns and related records turned over to Manhattan district attorney," *CNN* (2.25.21); Biskupic (2023: 166–68, 230–36).

3 Bromwich, Protess & Rashbaum, "Manhattan prosecutors move to jump-start criminal inquiry into Trump," *NYT* (11.21.22); Rashbaum, Protess & Bromwich, "Prosecutors signal criminal charges for Trump are likely," *NYT* (3.9.23); Benen, "Fearing indictment, Trump changes his story in hush money mess," *MSNBC* (3.13.23); Haberman, "As a possible indictment looms, Trump's team plans to attack," *NYT* (3.16.23); Barker, Bromwich & Rothfield, "How a 'nerdy'

prosecutor became the first to try Trump," *NYT* (4.14.24); Cartwright, "Catch and kill," *NYT* (4.7.24).

4 Haberman, Bromwich, Protess, Feuer & Rashbaum, "Trump claims his arrest is imminent and calls for protests, echoing Jan. 6," *NYT* (3.18.23).

5 "Trump looms (again) over House GOP retreat," *WP* (3.20.23); Wagner & Alfaro, "Republicans rally to Trump's defense as he faces possible indictment," *WP* (3.20.23); Paybarah, "Trump's talk of an arrest pushes 2024 rivals to his defense," *WP* (3.20.23).

6 Haberman & Swan, "DeSantis, breaking silence on Trump, criticized Manhattan prosecutor," *NYT* (3.20.23); Swan & Haberman, "Trump allies pressure DeSantis to weigh in on expected indictment," *NYT* (3.20.23); Goldmacher, Haberman, Swan & Karni, "For the G.O.P., a looming Trump indictment takes center stage," *NYT* (3.21.23); Papaycik & Williams, "Donald Trump suggests Ron DeSantis was 'grooming high school girls with alcohol,' causing governor to respond," *WPTV* (2.8.23); Arnsdorf, Dawsey, Sherer & Knowles, "Trump campaign prepares for 'new normal': running under indictment," *WP* (3.22.23).

7 Caldwell, Meyer & Raji, "Some Republicans attack Bragg, but don't defend Trump," *WP* (3.21.23); Haberman, "Out of power, Trump still exerts it," *NYT* (30.20.23).

8 Javaid, "New York prosecutor's office pushes back on GOP demands on Trump investigation," *WP* (3.21.23); Beitsch, "House Republicans seek testimony from Manhattan DA on Trump hush money probe," *The Hill* (3.20.23); Greene, Raju & Zanona, "House GOP requests Manhattan DA's testimony as they seek to discredit investigation into Trump," *CNN* (3.20.23).

9 Broadwater, Bromwich & Protess, "Prosecutor in Trump hush-money case fires back at House Republicans," *NYT* (3.23.23). Wang & Jacobs, "N.Y. prosecutor rebuffs GOP demand for documents related to Trump investigation," *WP* (3.23.23); Broadwater & Swan, "Republicans vowed to grill Bragg about Trump, but it's not so simple," *NYT* (4.6.23); Broadwater, "House G.O.P. subpoenas former Manhattan prosecutor in move to defend Trump," *NYT* (4.7.23); Shanahan, "House panel plans Manhattan hearing. Bragg calls it a 'political stunt,'" *NYT* (4.11.23).

10 Wang, "Manhattan DA assails GOP hearing on N.Y. crime as 'political stunt,'" *WP* (4.10.23); Jacobs & Wang, "Manhattan DA sues Rep. Jim Jordan for 'brazen' attack on Trump probe," *WP* (4.11.23); Bromwich, Haberman, Protess & Rashbaum, "Bragg sues Jim Jordan in move to block interference in Trump case," *NYT* (4.12.23); Oshin, "Two-thirds say Congress shouldn't interfere with Trump's legal probes: poll," *The Hill* (4.17.23).

11 Schonfeld, "Judge denies Bragg's bid to block House GOP's subpoena of Mark Pomerantz in New York Trump case," *The Hill* (4.19.23); Bromwich & Christobek, "Judge rules that lawmakers can ask ex-prosecutor about Trump inquiry," *NYT* (40.20.23); Bromwich & Broadwater, "Appeals court delays ex-prosecutors' deposition on Trump investigation," *NYT* (4.20.23); Bromwich, "Bragg agrees to let ex-prosecutor testify about Trump case in Congress," *NYT* (4.22.23); Broadwater, "In deposition, former prosecutor rebuffs G.O.P. questions about Trump case," *NYT* (5.13.23).

12 Sheth, "Trump says there could be 'death & destruction' if he's indicted in New York," *Business Insider* (3.24.23); Haberman & Bromwich, "Trump, escalating attacks, raises specter of violence if he is charged," *NYT* (3.24.23); Stanley-Becker & Nix, "Fake images of Trump arrest show 'giant step' for AI's disruptive power," *WP* (3.22.23); Qiu, "Explaining the ties between Alvin Bragg and George Soros," *NYT* (3.24.23).

13 Haberman, Bromwich & Rashbaum, "Trump, escalating attacks, raises specter of violence if he is charged," *NYT* (3.25.23); Schmidt, Goldman, Feuer, Haberman &

Thrush, "As Trump prosecutions move forward, threats and concerns increase," *NYT* (9.24.23).

14 Wagner, "Bragg's office accuses House Republicans of 'unlawful political interference,'" *WP* (3.31.23).

15 Beitsch, "Trump calls for removal of every top official investigating him," *The Hill* (3.23.23).

16 Bender & Goldmacher, "Trump puts his legal peril at center of first big rally for 2024," *NYT* (3.26.23); Bradner & Sullivan, "Trump baselessly rails against 'prosecutorial misconduct' at Waco rally as investigations loom," *CNN* (3.26.23); Schmidt & Haberman, "Trump says the justice system has been weaponized. He would know," *NYT* (3.30.23); Garrity, "Trump attorney says he will not 'defend or condemn' Trump's rhetoric toward Manhattan DA," *Politico* (3.26.23).

17 Arnsdorf & Knowles, "Trump extends election-rigging myth to his potential criminal charges," *WP* (3.28.23); Lange, "Americans see Trump investigation as political, but also believable—Reuters/Ipsos," *Reuters* (3.21.23).

18 Karni, "At House Republican retreat, the focus, once again, is on Trump," *NYT* (3.21.23); Arnsdorf, Dawsey, Sherer & Knowles, "Trump campaign prepares for 'new normal': running under indictment," *WP* (3.22.23).

19 "Trump indicted. The first ex-president to face criminal charges," *NYT* (3.31.23); Ramey & Palazzolo, "Trump indicted over hush money," *WSJ* (3.31.23); Jacobs, Dawsey, Barrett & Alemany, "Trump indicted by N.Y. grand jury; first ex-president charged with crime," *WP* (3.31.23); Wagner, "Rep. Greene says she'll be in New York to protest on Tuesday," *WP* (3.31.23); Stanley-Becker, "Calls for violence come from pro-Trump extremist website," *WP* (3.31.23); Alfaro & Knowles, "DeSantis, possible Trump rival, says he won't assist in extradition," *WP* (3.31.23); Scherer & Wagner, "Most Republicans think case against Trump is politically motivated, poll finds," *WP* (3.31.23); Wagner, "House Republicans vocally defend Trump; Senate Republicans more muted," *WP* (3.31.23); Kornfield & Somasundaram, "Trump's potential 2024 rivals attack indictment," *WP* (3.31.23); Bender & Haberman, "Republicans erupt in outrage and rush to defend the defendant," *NYT* (3.31.23); Barr, "Tucker Carlson, other Fox pundits call for protests of Trump charges," *WP* (3.31.23); Bender & Haberman, "Trump's G.O.P. rivals, shielding him, reveal their 2024 predicament," *NYT* (4.1.23).

20 Haberman, "Update," *NYT* (4.4.23); Balla, "Lindsey Graham pleads for people to give Trump money after arraignment," *WP* (4.5.23); Marimow, Helderman & Dawsey, "Trump's criminal case in New York may collide with the 2024 campaign," *WP* (4.5.23); Haberman, Bender & Swan, "For now, Trump and allies focus on political upside of a criminal case," *NYT* (4.6.23); Benen, "Marjorie Taylor Greene likened Trump to Nelson Mandela and Jesus," *MSNBC* (4.5.23); "What's missing in the Trump indictment," *WSJ* (4.5.23).

21 McCormick, "For some Trump voters, legal drama is latest reason to move on," *WSJ* (4.9.23); Doherty, "Polls: most Americans support Trump indictment but say politics played role," *Axios* (4.3.23).

22 Jacobs, Nakamura & Alemany, "Former president Donald Trump pleads not guilty to 34 felony counts," *WP* (4.4.23); Kaur, "Charges are narrow, but prosecutors outline broad scheme to undermine 2016 election," *WP* (4.4.23); Kaur, "Trump gives grievance-filled stump speech on historic night," *WP* (4.5.23).

23 Kessler, "Fact-checking Trump's comments and 'truths' on arraignment day," *WP* (4.5.23); Qiu, "In denouncing charges, Trump repeats familiar grievances," *NYT* (4.5.23); Ayyub, "Trump, newly charged, urges defunding Justice Department and FBI," *Reuters* (4.5.23).

24 Bromwich & Schweber, "What it was like inside the courtroom during Trump's arraignment," *NYT* (4.7.23).

25 Bromwich, Rashbaum & Christobek, "Dilemma for judge in Trump case: whether to muzzle the former president," *NYT* (4.7.23); Bromwich, Protess & Rashbaum, "Legal moves in Trump case reveal challenges of prosecuting a president," *NYT* (5.5.23); Reiss & Gregorian, "Trump prohibited from posting evidence in hush money case to social media, judge rules," *NBC News* (5.8.23).
26 Jacobs, "Judge suggests he's unlikely to move Trump's New York criminal case to federal court," *WP* (6.28.23); Bromwich, "Trump hush money case will remain in New York state court, judge rules," *NYT* (7.19.23); Eisen, Kolb & McQuade, "There is much more at stake in Trump's Manhattan case than just hush money," *NYT* (2.20.24); Rashbaum & Protess, "Trump asks judge in hush money case to step aside," *NYT* (5.30.23); Freifeld, "Judge in Trump hush-money case can stay, New York ethics panel signals," *Reuters* (6.12.23); Bromwich, "Trump case judge in New York declines to step aside," *NYT* (8.15.23).
27 Shapero, "Trump lawyer: if he's indicted 'this is an all-out war,'" *The Hill* (3.21.23); Paybarah, Harwell & Marimow, "Trump claims judge overseeing New York case 'hates' him. His lawyer says it isn't true," *WP* (4.3.23); Haberman & Swan, "A presidential candidate and a city brace for a consequential week," *NYT* (4.2.23).
28 Arnsdorf, "Trump says criminal conviction wouldn't stop him from running for president," *WP* (4.12.23); Bender, "Trump says he won't drop presidential bid if criminally convicted," *NYT* (4.12.23); Del Valle & Cole, "Trump sues Michael Cohen for $500 million, alleging ex-attorney breached his contract," *CNN* (4.12.23); Alfaro, "Trump sues former counsel Michael Cohen for $500 million," *WP* (4.12.23); Haberman, Protess, Rashbaum & Bromwich, "Trump sues Michael Cohen, key witness against him," *NYT* (4.13.23); Colvin & Sisak, "Trump 'temporarily' drops lawsuit against former lawyer-turned-witness Michael Cohen," *AP* (10.5.23).
29 Wendling, "Trump seeks to dismiss election interference charges, saying he had presidential immunity," *BBC* (10.6.23); Bromwich, Rashbaum, Haberman, Christobek & Protess, "As Trump's criminal trial approaches he may be his own worst enemy," *NYT* (3.4.24); Blake, "4 takeaways from Trump's dueling court hearings," *WP* (2.15.24); Jacobs & Barrett, "Trump's first criminal trial set for March in N.Y. on hush money charges," *WP* (2.15.24); Poniewozik, "For Donald Trump, the recriminations will be televised," *NYT* (2.17.24); Haberman & Swan, "Trial will test Trump's limits of reaping political gain from legal woes," *NYT* (2.17.24); Weiser, Protess & Haberman, "For Trump a blizzard of court action is just another Monday," *NYT* (3.12.24); Protess & Rashbaum, "Judge won't delay Trump's criminal trial to wait for immunity ruling," *NYT* (4.3.24); Nakamura, "What to know about Trump's New York charges—and any potential sentence," *WP* (4.8.24).
30 Jacobs, "N.Y. prosecutor seeks Trump gag order, jury protections ahead of 1st criminal trial," *WP* (2.26.24); Protess & Christobek, "Judge's order will prevent Trump from revealing names of jurors," *NYT* (3.8.24).
31 Haberman, Protess & Rashbaum, "How one hour encapsulated the chaos of Trump's coming trial," *NYT* (3.26.24); Isak, Offenhartz & Tucker, "Trump's New York hush money case is set for trial April 15," *AP* (3.26.24); Bender, "The Church of Trump: how he's infusing Christianity into his movement," *NYT* (4.1.24).
32 Jacobs, "Trump placed under limited gag order ahead of N.Y. hush money trial," *WP* (3.26.24); Protess & Rashbaum, "Judge imposes gag order on Trump in Manhattan criminal trial," *NYT* (3.26.24); Gregorian, Winter & Reiss, "Judge in hush money case hits Trump with partial gag order," *NBC News* (3.26.24); McKinley & Protess, "Trump spreads apparent hoax in attacking judge's daughter," *NYT* (3.28.24); Feuer & Haberman, "The judge cracks down," *NYT* (3.28.24);

LeVine, Morse & Jacobs, "Trump ramps up attacks on judges, sparking concerns as criminal trial nears," *WP* (4.2.24).

33 Jacobs, "After Trump attacks hush money judge's daughter, DA seeks broader gag order," *WP* (3.29.24).

34 Hsu, "Republican-appointed judge raises alarm over Trump attacks on law," *WP* (3.29.24).

35 Leary & Ramey, "Trump's split-screen strategy put criminal trial at center of his campaign," *WSJ* (3.30.24); LeVine, Morse & Jacobs, "Trump ramps up attacks on judges, sparking concerns as criminal trial nears," *WP* (4.2.24); McKinley, Protess & Rashbaum, "Gag order against Trump is expanded to bar attacks on judge's family," *NYT* (4.2.24).

36 Blake, "Trump is tempting fate on gag orders—for himself and for the country," *WP* (4.2.24); Vazquez, "Trump says it would be a 'great honor' to be jailed for violating gag order," *WP* (4.6.24).

37 Protess, "Trump asks trial judge to step aside, aiming again at his daughter," *NYT* (4.3.24); Scannell, del Valle & Herb, "Judge denies Trump's request to postpone trial and consider venue change in hush money case," *CNN* (4.8.24); Jacobs, "N.Y. appeals judge rejects Trump's attempt to delay hush money trial," *WP* (4.8.24); Protess, Bromwich & Rashbaum, "Appeals court denies another Trump attempt to delay trial," *NYT* (4.8.24); Jacobs, "N.Y. appeals judge denies Trump's second trial-delay bid in two days," *WP* (4.9.24); Jacobs, "Trump fails to delay N.Y. criminal trial for a third time this week," *WP* (4.10.24); Bromwich, Rashbaum & Protess, "Trump loses his third try in a week to delay Manhattan trial," *NYT* (4.11.24).

38 Protess, McKinley, Christobek & Rashbaum, "Judge in Trump criminal case braces for glare of unprecedented trial," *NYT* (4.8.24); Milbank, "This is why Trump supporters will believe absolutely anything," *WP* (4.12.24); Gold, Bromwich & Protess, "Trump says he intends to testify in his Manhattan criminal case," *NYT* (4.13.24); McKinley & Swan, "Protests, traffic, crowds: court braces for a Trump trial like no other," *NYT* (4.13.24); Gold, "In final rally before New York trial, Trump again casts himself as political victim," *NYT* (4.14.24); Picciotto, "Trump targets two likely witnesses ahead of his criminal trial, despite gag order," *CNBC* (4.13.24); Jacobs & Barrett, "Merchan sounds skeptical that Trump's posts on Cohen don't violate gag," *WP* (4.15.24).

39 Stein, "Trump addresses reporters in courthouse: 'It's an assault on America,'" *WP* (4.15.24); Protess, Bromwich & Rashbaum, "Judge in Trump's criminal trial declines to recuse himself," *NYT* (4.15.24); Stein, "Trump complains judge won't yet approve him to attend son's graduation," *WP* (4.16.24); Blake, "Trump's increasing court outbursts come with increasing risks—for all," *WP* (4.17.24).

40 "Donald Trump and American justice," *NYT* (4.17.24); Barrett, Dawsey & Jacobs, "Trump deploys favorite political tool, social media, as legal cudgel," *WP* (4.18.24); "Day 3 of Trump's hush money trial opens with a juror backing out," *WP* (4.18.24); McKinley & Christobek, "After reports about Trump jurors, judge demands restraint from the press," *NYT* (4.18.24).

41 Geringer-Sameth & Max, "Breaking down final 2020 vote tallies across New York City," *Gotham Gazette* (12.4.20).

42 Barrett, "Judge shoots down request to tell Trump who the first 3 trial witnesses will be," *WP* (4.19.24); Stein, "The jurors and concerns over identifying details circulating online," *WP* (4.19.24); "Full jury selected in Trump hush money trial," *WP* (4.19.24).

43 Blake, "Trump's transparent attempt to play the victim on 'election interference,'" *WP* (2.25.24); Swan, Haberman & Schweber, "The circus Trump wanted outside his trial hasn't arrived," *NYT* (4.23.24).

44 Jacobs, "Trump held in contempt for 9 violations of gag order, fined $9,000," *WP* (4.30.24); Jacobs, "Donald Trump could get locked up if gag order violations continue, judge warns," *WP* (4.30.24); Barrett, "Merchan contempt order against Trump also warns Michael Cohen, Stormy Daniels," *WP* (4.30.24); Jacobs, "Trump response to X post by former lawyer for Stormy Daniels excluded from gag order contempt finding," *WP* (4.30.24); McKinley, "For Trump, a $9,000 rebuke and a stern warning," *NYT* (4.30.24).

45 Arnsdorf, "Trump posts on social media about being unable to speak," *WP* (4.30.24).

46 Feuer, "Prosecutors ask judge to hold Trump in contempt for a second time," *NYT* (5.2.24); Jacobs, "Judge denies bid to allow jurors to learn of Trump's recent gag order contempt findings," *WP* (5.4.24); Barrett, Jacobs & Berman, "Trump defense suggests he was shakedown target, not hush money schemer," *WP* (5.3.24); Gold & Huynh, "Trump praises police crackdowns on campus protests," *NYT* (5.3.24).

47 LeVine & Jacobs, "Trump again found in contempt for violating gag, threatened with jail," *WP* (5.5.24); Feuer, Protess, Bromwich & Rashbaum, "Judge cites Trump for contempt, says he is attacking the rule of law," *NYT* (5.6.24); Jacobs, Jackman, Barrett & LeVine, "Looking Trump in the eye, the N.Y. judge warns he may jail him," *WP* (5.7.24); Jacobs, "Judge again finds Trump in contempt in hush money trial; Trump Org employees testify," *WP* (5.7.24); Stein & Barrett, "The Trump trials: explaining Trump's 10 gag order violations in New York," *WP* (5.6.24).

48 Stein & Barrett, "Why Stormy Daniels's account of sex with Trump may be problematic, and other takeaways," *WP* (5.7.24); Barrett, Jackman, Jacobs & LeVine, "Stormy Daniels testifies, Trump curses in angry day in court," *WP* (5.7.24); Habeshian, "Trump denied second mistrial request, gag order change in hush money case," *Axios* (5.10.24); Feuer, "Appeals court upholds gag order on Trump in Manhattan trial," *NYT* (5.15.24); Sisak & Offenhartz, "Donald Trump asks New York's high court to intervene in fight over gag order in hush money trial," *AP* (5.15.24); Lotz, "Trump's gag order appeal dies at New York's top court," *Axios* (9.12.24).

49 McKinley & Bromwich, "Trump trial week 4: Testy and explicit, then calm before the Cohen storm," *NYT* (5.11.24); LeVine, "Trump insults prosecutor at Jersey Shore rally filled with vulgar jabs," *WP* (5.11.24).

50 Stein & Barrett, "Trump trials: Michael Cohen didn't sound like a 'jerk,' and other takeaways," *WP* (5.14.24); McKinley, "Michael Cohen's riveting day in court," *NYT* (5.14.24); Protess, Bromwich & Haberman, "Michael Cohen, key to Trump case, tells jurors of seedy hush-money plot," *NYT* (5.14.24).

51 Blake, "Trump is gagged. So his surrogates say the forbidden stuff for him," *WP* (5.14.24); Bender, Schweber & Wilson, "J.D. Vance, in the mix to be Trump's running mate, denounces witness," *NYT* (5.14.24); Jacobs, Weiner, Stein & Barrett, "Michael Cohen: 'Yes, I would like to see' Trump convicted," *WP* (5.14.24); Pengelly, "Gaetz invokes Trump's call to far-right Proud Boys at hush-money trial," *G* (5.16.24).

52 Stein & Barrett, "The Trump Trials," *WP* (5.20.24); Jacobs, Barrett & Jackman, "Prosecutors rest in Trump trial, and Judge Merchan erupts at a witness," *WP* (5.20.24); Protess & Haag, "Robert Costello, defense witness in Trump trial, is scolded by judge," *NYT* (5.21.24); LeVine & Usero, "Why Trump keeps reading printouts of news articles at his trial," *WP* (5.22.24); Hillyard & Richards, "'Take a look at where he comes from,' Trump says of Colombian-born judge," *NBC News* (5.21.24).

53 Arnsdorf & Pager, "Biden campaign edges in on Trump trial media frenzy with De Niro outside court," *WP* (5.28.24).

54 Oladipo, "Trump trial judge faces new threats after false reports on jury instructions spread," *G* (5.31.24); Reilly, "False right-wing reports about Trump trial jury instructions fuel threats against judge," *NBC News* (6.1.24).
55 Jacobs, Barrett, Hawkins & Berman, "Donald Trump found guilty on all counts in NY hush money trial," *WP* (5.30.24); Bensinger, "Upside-down flags become symbol for Republicans protesting Trump verdict," *NYT* (5.31.24); McCreesh, "Convicted, Trump blames judge, jury and a country 'gone to Hell,'" *NYT* (5.31.24); Bidgood, "The dark rhetoric after Trump's conviction," *NYT* (5.31.24); Cameron, "Trump's campaign donor website crashes after guilty verdict," *NYT* (5.31.24); Vigdor & Broadwater, "Trump's G.O.P. allies assail his guilty verdict and warn it will backfire," *NYT* (5.31.24); Goldmacher, "Trump announces $34.8 million fund-raising haul after guilty verdict," *NYT* (5.31.24); Vazquez, "Trump fundraising email: 'I am a political prisoner,'" *WP* (6.1.24); Barr, "Fox News hosts trash Trump conviction, vow political redemption," *WP* (5.31.24); Goldmacher & Broadwater, "Trump's conviction binds the G.O.P. even closer to him," *NYT* (6.1.24); Broadwater, "Johnson says Supreme Court should step in to overturn Trump's conviction," *NYT* (6.1.24); Broadwater, "After Trump's conviction, House Republicans vow again to target his foes," *NYT* (6.5.24); Hulse, "Far-right vows to tie up the Senate to avenge Trump are so far mostly empty," *NYT* (6.6.24); Astor, "Lara Trump, R.N.C. leader, denounces Larry Hogan for accept Trump verdict," *NYT* (6.2.24).
56 Nerkar, "How partisan outlets covered the verdict," *NYT* (6.1.24).
57 Kessler, "From the Trump Tower lobby, a gusher of falsehoods about the trial," *WP* (5.31.24); Scherer & Dawsey, "Trump and his allies believe that criminal convictions will work in his favor," *WP* (6.1.24); Vazquez, "Half of Americans agree with jury that Trump is guilty, new poll shows," *WP* (6.1.24); Haberman & Gold, "Trump rails against his guilty verdict, claiming 'sick people' are behind his prosecution," *NYT* (6.1.24); Gold & Haag, "Trump spews false claims and fury in wake of conviction," *NYT* (6.1.24); Epstein & Nehemas, "Democrats push Biden to make Trump's felonies a top 2024 issue," *NYT* (6.1.24); Qiu, "Trump and allies assail conviction with faulty claims," *NYT* (6.1.24); Astor, "Trump gets the friendly treatment from Fox News in his first post-verdict interview," *NYT* (6.3.24); Schleifer, "Trump and R.N.C. announce $141 million haul in May," *NYT* (6.3.24).
58 Jacobs, "Trump asks N.Y. judge to drop gag order after hush money conviction," *WP* (6.5.24); Cohen & Stempel, "Trump loses appeal of gag order in hush money criminal case," *Reuters* (8.1.24).
59 Sisak, "Prosecutors want Donald Trump to remain under a gag order at least until he's sentenced July 11," *WP* (6.5.24); Jacobs, "Trump defense formally asks N.Y. judge to terminate gag order," *WP* (6.12.24); Swan, Haberman & Savage, "The G.O.P push for post-verdict payback: 'fight fire with fire,'" *NYT* (6.5.24); Broadwater, "House Republicans issue criminal referrals of Hunter and James Biden," *NYT* (6.6.24); Cameron, "Trump defends vow to prosecute rivals, saying sometimes revenge can be justified," *NYT* (6.6.24).
60 Protess & Haberman, "After hush-money verdict, Trump tried to silence Stormy Daniels again," *NYT* (10.19.24).
61 Garland, "Unfounded attacks on the Justice Department must end," *WP* (6.11.24); Kwai & Schmall, "Man charged in death threats to Trump trial judge and prosecutor," *NYT* (7.27.24).
62 Blake, "The campaign moment," *WP* (6.6.24); Edsall, "Trump would be long gone if only we could . . .," *NYT* (6.12.24).
63 Broadwater & Protess, "Alvin Bragg will testify to Congress after Trump's sentencing," *NYT* (6.12.24).
64 Jacobs, "Trump seeks dismissal of N.Y. charges, verdict after Supreme Court ruling," *WP* (7.11.24); Protess, Rashbaum & Parnell, "Manhattan prosecutors agree

to delay Trump's sentencing," *NYT* (7.2.24); Jacobs, "Trump's sentencing in N.Y. hush money case postponed until September," *WP* (7.2.24); Protess & McKinley, "Prosecutors say immunity ruling has no bearing on Trump's conviction," *NYT* (7.25.24); "Trump, for 3rd time, asks judge in hush money case to recuse himself," *ABC News* (8.1.24); Kruzel, "US Supreme Court declines to halt Trump's sentencing in hush money case," *Reuters* (8.5.24); Christobek & Protess, "Judge denies Trump's recusal bid, rebuking him for claiming Harris ties," *NYT* (8.14.24); Wilentz, "The 'Dred Scott' of Our Time," *New York Review of Books* (8.15.24); Jacobs, "Trump seeks delay in New York hush money case sentencing until after election," *WP* (8.15.24); Protess, Christobek & Bromwich, "Prosecutors leave decision on delaying Trump's sentencing up to judge," *NYT* (8.19.24); Sorkin, "Comment: troubles, troubles," *New Yorker* (8.26.24); Jacobs, "Trump again asks N.Y. federal court to take over hush money case," *WP* (8.30.24); Lee, "Judge denies Trump bid to move hush money case to federal court," *The Hill* (9.4.24); Schonfeld, "Trump makes new bid to delay hush money sentencing," *The Hill* (9.4.24); Jacobs, "Trump's N.Y. hush money sentencing delayed until after Nov. election," *WP* (9.6.24); Protess, Christobek & Rashbaum, "Judge delays Trump's sentencing until Nov. 26, after Election Day," *NYT* (9.6.24); LeVine, Reston, Dawsey & Knowle, "Trump rants, resurfaces sexual assault allegations for 49 unfocused minutes," *WP* (9.6.24); Sisak, "2nd Circuit rejects Donald Trump's request to halt postconviction proceedings in hush money case," *AP* (9.12.24); Cohen, Trump urges appeals judges to move hush money case to federal court," *Reuters* (10.15.24).

65 Jacobs, "Trump's hush money case could be 'abated' instead of dismissed, DA says," *WP* (12.10.24); Protess & Christobek, "Judge denies Trump's bid to throw out conviction over immunity ruling," *NYT* (12.16.24); Protess, "Trump accuses juror of misconduct in latest move to overturn conviction," *NYT* (12.18.24).

66 People v. Trump, NYS Supreme Court (1.3.25); Jacobs & Nakamura, "Judge upholds Trump's felony conviction, but does not plan to order jail time," *WP* (1.3.25); Aitken, "Donald Trump calls for Judge Juan Merchan to be disbarred," *Newsweek* (1.4.25); Palmer, "Donald Trump blasts 'corrupt' Judge Merchan days before sentencing," *Newsweek* (1.6.25); Reid, Herb & Scannell, "Judge denies Trump's plea to delay Friday's sentencing on his hush money conviction," *CNN* (1.6.25); Kates & Kaufman, "Appeals court refuses to pause Trump sentencing in New York 'hush money' case," *BS News* (1.7.25); Marimow & Jacobs, "Trump asks Supreme Court to halt Friday's hush money sentencing," *WP* (1.8.25); Protess, Christobek & Liptak, "N.Y. prosecutors urge Supreme Court to let Trump's sentencing proceed," *NYT* (1.9.25); Marimow & Jouvenal, "Supreme Court refuses to delay Trump's hush money sentencing," *WP* (1.9.25); "Trump is sentenced in N.Y. criminal case and will avoid jail," *NYT* (110.25).

67 Gardner, "'I just want to find 11,780 votes': In extraordinary hour-long call, Trump pressures Georgia secretary of state to recalculate the vote in his favor," *WP* (1.3.21); Scanlan, "Trump 'just plain wrong' on fraud claims: Georgia Secretary of State Raffensperger," *ABC News* (1.4.21); Isikoff & Klaidman (2024: 201, 223); Fausset & Hakim, "Georgia officials review Trump phone call as scrutiny intensifies," *NYT* (2.9.21); So, "Georgia Secretary of State's office launches probe into Trump's election phone call," *Reuters* (2.9.21); Fausset & Hakim, "Georgia prosecutors open criminal inquiry into Trump's efforts to subvert election," *NYT* (2.11.21); Gardner, Hamburger & Dawsey, "Graham's post-election call with Raffensperger will be scrutinized in Georgia probe, person familiar with inquiry says," *WP* (2.12.21); Hakim & Fausset, "In Georgia, a new DA starts circling Trump and his allies," *NYT* (2.13.21); Wagner, "Georgia prosecutor requests special grand jury in probe of Trump's efforts to overturn state's election results," *WP*

(1.20.22); Wang & Wagner, "Georgia prosecutor granted special grand jury in probe of Trump's efforts to overturn state's election results," *WP* (2.25.22); Pager, "Trump suggests that if he is reelected, he will pardon Jan. 6 Capitol rioters," *WP* (1.30.22); Pager, "Trump's Texas trip illustrates his upsides and downsides for Republicans and their midterm hopes," *WP* (1.31.22); Fausset, "Georgia prosecutors investigating Trump seeks safety assistance from the F.B.I.," *NYT* (1.31.22); Raffensperger (2021).

68 Isikoff & Klaidman (2024: 227); Brown & Hamburger, "Georgia 2020 election inquiry may lead to prison sentences, prosecutor says," *WP* (9.16.22).

69 Brown, "Georgia grand jury subpoenas Sen. Graham, Giuliani and Trump legal team," *WP* (7.5.22); Singh, "Senator Graham ordered to testify in front of grand jury in Trump election probe," *Reuters* (7.11.22); Murray & Barrett, "Lindsey Graham moving to quash subpoena from Georgia grand jury investigating Trump," *CNN* (7.13.22); Brumback, "Sen. Graham challenges 2020 Georgia election probe subpoena," *AP* (8.1.22); Scott, "Graham must testify in Ga. probe of effort to overturn 2020 election, judge rules," *WP* (8.15.22); Wagner & Hamburger, "District Attorney says Graham's testimony is crucial in election probe," *WP* (8.19.22); Wagner & Hamburger, "Sen. Graham gets temporary reprieve in testifying before Ga. grand jury," *WP* (8.22.22); Fausset, "Federal appeals court halts Graham testimony before Atlanta grand jury," *NYT* (8.22.22); Hakim & Fausset, "For Lindsey Graham, a showdown in Georgia," *NYT* (8.24.22); Hamburger & Marimow, "Judge says Graham must testify in 2020 election probe, limits scope of questions," *WP* (9.1.22); Fausset, "Judge says Lindsey Graham can be questioned about election activity," *NYT* (9.1.22); Hakim & Fausset, "In Trump case, Texas creates a headache for Georgia prosecutors," *NYT* (10.8.22); Murray & Morris, "Graham asks appeals court to quash subpoena for his testimony before grand jury in Georgia 2020 election probe," *CNN* (10.11.22); Marimow, "Lindsey Graham must testify in 2020 election investigation, court rules," *WP* (10.20.22); Fausset, "Senator Graham asks Supreme Court to spare him from testifying in Georgia," *NYT* (10.22.22); Barnes, "Supreme Court puts hold on order that Graham testify before grand jury," *WP* (10.24.22); Hurley, "Supreme Court declines to block subpoena of Lindsey Graham in Georgia election probe," *NBC News* (11.1.22); Barnes, "Supreme Court clears way for Trump tax returns to go to Congress," *WP* (11.22.22).

70 Hakim & Fausset, "Giuliani ordered to testify in Georgia criminal investigation," *NYT* (7.20.22); Hakim & Fausset, "By train, bus or Uber, Giuliani is told to come to Georgia," *NYT* (8.10.22); Hamburger & Scott, "Giuliani is target in Ga. criminal probe of 2020 election, lawyer says," *WP* (8.15.22); Fausset & Hakim, "Giuliani is told he is a target in Trump election inquiry in Georgia," *NYT* (8.16.22); Fausset & Hakim, "Georgia Congressman subpoenaed in Trump inquiry," *NYT* (7.18.22); Cohen, Murray & Morris, "Georgia prosecutors say all 16 fake Trump electors are targets in criminal probe," *CNN* (7.20.22); Fausset, Hakim & Keenan, "Prosecutor is barred from pursuing criminal case against Trump ally," *NYT* (7.26.22); Wickert, "State Bar investigates two Georgia Trump electors," *Atlanta Journal-Constitution* (7.26.22); Brown, Hamburger & Marimow, "Georgia judge skeptical of claims of political bias in 2020 election probe," *WP* (8.26.22); Wang & Marimow, "Judge delays Gov. Kemp's testimony in Ga. probe until after November election," *WP* (8.29.22); Fausset, "Georgia's Lt. Gov. will be investigated in Trump case. But by whom?" *NYT* (1.4.24); Fausset & Hakim, "Georgia's Lieutenant Governor to face inquiry for role as fake Trump elector," *NYT* (4.11.24); Bailey, "Georgia lieutenant governor won't face charges connected to 2020 election," *WP* (9.13.24).

71 Fausset & Hakim, "Conservative lawyer a likely target in Atlanta Trump investigation, his lawyer says," *NYT* (9.1.22).

72 Fulton County Superior Court Judge Robert C.I. McBurney, Order (2.16.23) App. A: Special Purpose Grand Jury Report; Fausset & Hakim, "Atlanta D.A. wants grand jury findings kept private in Trump inquiry," *NYT* (1.25.23); Fausset & Hakim, "6 takeaways from the report on the Trump investigation in Georgia," *NYT* (2.18.23); Hakim, "Jury in Georgia Trump inquiry recommended multiple indictments, forewoman says," *NYT* (2.22.23); Gardner & Brown, "Georgia juror unsettles Trump investigation with revealing interviews," *WP* (2.23.23); Fausset & Hakim, "Trump legal team assails Georgia inquiry," *NYT* (2.23.23); Isikoff & Klaidman (2024: 260–62); Bailey, "Georgia grand jury recommended charging Lindsey Graham in Trump case," *WP* (9.8.23); Fausset & Hakim, "Georgia panel recommended charging dozens, including Lindsey Graham, in Trump case," *NYT* (9.9.23).

73 Fausset & Hakim, "6 takeaways from the report on the Trump investigation in Georgia," *NYT* (2.18.23); Fausset, "Trump's Georgia lawyers seek to quash special grand jury report," *NYT* (3.20.23); Alfaro, "Trump gives grievance-filled stump speech on historic night," *WP* (4.5.23); Fausset & Hakim, "Georgia prosecutor rebuts Trump's effort to scuttle elections case," *NYT* (5.16.23); Alexander & Reilly, "Trump supporters post names and addresses of Georgia grand jurors online," *NBC News* (8.16.23); Betts, McKinley & Bogel-Burroughs, "Officials investigate threats against Trump grand jurors in Georgia," *NYT* (8.18.23); "FBI joins investigation of threats to grand jurors in Trump Georgia case," *WP* (8.19.23).

74 Fausset & Hakim, "As Trump inquiry continues, Republicans seek oversight of Georgia prosecutors," *NYT* (3.5.23); Rojas, "Calls for Georgia leaders to stymie Trump prosecution fall flat, so far," *NYT* (8.18.23).

75 Hakim, "Trump seeks order to quash investigation in Georgia," *NYT* (7.15.23); Bailey, "Georgia Supreme Court rejects Trump petition to block election probe," *WP* (7.18.23); Hakim, "Georgia Supreme Court rejects Trump effort to quash investigation," *NYT* (7.18.23); Wolfe & McWhirter, "Judge criticizes Trump for 'overwrought' complaints about Georgia election probe," *WSJ* (7.31.23); Hakim & Fausset, "Trump, waiving arraignment, pleads not guilty in Georgia case," *NYT* (9.1.23); Fausset, "Why Georgia Republicans are protecting the D.A. who indicted Trump," *NYT* (11.16.23); Brandt, "Republicans fight to defund Trump prosecutions," *ABC8 News* (9.1.23).

76 Broadwater, "House Republicans begin investigating Willis as Trump is booked," *NYT* (8.25.23); Fausset & Hakim, "Georgia prosecutor sharply rebukes House Republican investigating her," *NYT* (9.8.23).

77 Bailey, "Georgia prosecutor to begin presenting 2020 election case next week to grand jury," *WP* (8.12.23).

78 Wang, Bailey, Gardner, Brasch, Alfaro, Vazquez & Hennessey-Fiske, "Trump indicted in Georgia over attempts to overturn 2020 election," *WP* (8.14.23); Hsu, "Jeffrey Clark spokeswoman accuses Willis of political 'witch hunt,'" *WP* (8.14.23); Alfaro, "McCarthy calls indictment 'desperate sham,'" *WP* (8.14.23); Olsen, "Republicans defend Trump at their own risk," *WP* (8.16.23); Reston, "As Georgia Republicans rebuke Trump, they are lonely voices in GOP," *WP* (8.16.23); Swaine, "Clues point to identities of 'unindicted co-conspirators' in alleged Coffee County breach," *WP* (8.17.23); "Florida's DeSantis replaces elected Democratic prosecutor," *Reuters* (8.9.23); "The best argument for the Georgia indictment doesn't involve Trump," *WP* (8.16.23).

79 Collinson, "Trump's fourth indictment moves America closer to an election precipice," *CNN* (8.15.23); "Trump blasts Georgia indictment in fundraising email," *CNN* (8.15.23).

80 Haim, Haberman & Fausset, "Bail for Trump set at $200,000 in Georgia election interference case," *NYT* (8.22.23); Kessler, "Trump campaign ad makes false claims against Atlanta DA," *WP* (8.16.23); Fisher, "Trump tested 'counterpuncher' playbook in face of indictments," *WP* (8.17.23); Barry, "From 'America's mayor' to criminal defendant: Giuliani's long tumble," *NYT* (8.17.23).
81 Isikoff & Klaidman (2024: 281); Dawsey, "Trump says Black voters like him more because of his indictments and mug shot," *WP* (2.24.24); Gold, "Trump says his indictments are helping him attract Black voters," *NYT* (2.24.24).
82 Richards & Gile, "Mark Meadows seeks to move Fulton County election interference case to federal court," *NBC News* (8.16.23); Barrett, Vazquez, Stein & Weiner, "Meadows testifies in Atlanta; March trial date for Trump in D.C.," *WP* (8.28.23); Fausset & Hakim, "Meadows testifies in bid to move Georgia Trump case to federal court," *NYT* (8.29.23); Fausset & Hakim, "Mark Meadows's testimony in Georgia case may have done him no favors," *NYT* (9.18.23); "Mark Meadows's job wasn't to help Trump steal the 2020 election," *WP* (8.31.23).
83 Gardner, "Judge denies Mark Meadows effort to move Georgia case to federal court," *WP* (9.8.23); Fausset & Hakim, "Judge denies Meadows's request to move Georgia case to federal court," *NYT* (9.9.23); Sangal, Meyer & Hammond, "Judge rejects Mark Meadows's bid to move 2020 election case," *CNN* (9.8.23); Rubin, "In Georgia, Meadows requests emergency stay as Giuliani seeks to sever his case," *ABC News* (9.11.23); Bailey, "Mark Meadows's bid to move Georgia election case to federal court rejected," *WP* (12.18.23); Hakim & Fausset, "Appeals panel rejects Meadows's request to move Georgia case to federal court," *NYT* (12.19.23); Blake, "How a Trump Supreme Court finalist ruled bigly against his side," *WP* (12.19.23); Bailey, "Mark Meadows takes bid to toss Georgia election charges to Supreme Court," *WP* (7.29.24); Marimow, "Supreme Court rejects Mark Meadows effort to move Georgia 2020 election case," *NYT* (11.13.24).
84 Gardner & Bailey, "Georgia Trump electors argue they acted under federal authority," *WP* (9.21.23); Fausset & Hakim, "Lawyers for fake electors hint at defense strategy in Georgia case," *NYT* (9.21.23); Gardner & Bailey, "Former DoJ attorney acted under Trump's direction, his lawyer says," *WP* (9.19.23).
85 Sanchez, "Newly appointed Judge Scott McAfee gets Trump criminal case in Georgia," *WP* (8.16.23); Bogel-Burroughs, "Judge on Trump case once worked under Fani Willis," *NYT* (8.16.23); Bailey, "Judge approved $200,000 bond for Trump in Georgia election case," *WP* (8.21.23); Bailey, "George prosecutors in Trump election case estimate four-month trial," *WP* (9.6.23); Fausset & Hakim, "Georgia judge says two defendants in Trump case will get early trial together," *NYT* (9.7.23); Knutson, "Fani Willis proposes October 2023 trial date for Trump, co-defendants," *Axios* (8.24.23); Farhi, "Trump's Georgia trial is readied for television, while others are hard to see," *WP* (9.1.23); Richards, "Georgia judge orders jurors' identities to stay secret during Trump election interference trial," *NBC News* (9.25.23); Bailey, "Trump won't have to stand trial in October, Georgia judge says," *WP* (9.14.23).
86 Bailey, "In Georgia, jury selection begins in a Trump case without Trump," *WP* (10.20.23); Bailey & Gardner, "Trump co-defendant Kenneth Chesebro pleads guilty in Georgia election case," *WP* (10.20.23); Fausset & Feuer, "Kenneth Chesebro, a Trump-aligned lawyer, pleads guilty in Georgia," *NYT* (10.21.23); Bailey & Gardner, "Fani Willis: trial involving Trump might not conclude until early 2025," *WP* (11.14.23); Fausset & Hakim, "Georgia's prosecutor sees Trump case stretching into 2025," *NYT* (11.14.23); Isikoff & Klaidman (2024: 2, 6).
87 Bailey & Gardner, "Trump lawyer: Georgia trial would have to wait if Trump wins in 2024," *WP* (12.1.23).

88 Bailey, Gardner & Stanley-Becker, "First Trump co-defendant pleads guilty in Georgia election case," *WP* (9.29.23); Quinn, "Court denies bid by former Justice Dept. official Jeffrey Clark to move 2020 election case to federal court," *CBS News* (9.29.23); Bailey & Gardner, "Trump co-defendant Sidney Powell pleads guilty in Georgia election-interference case," *WP* (10.19.23); Fausset & Hakim, "Sidney Powell pleads guilty in Georgia Trump case," *NYT* (10.19.23); Arnsdorf, Dawsey & Hsu, "Trump seethes at gag order in federal case while his campaign relishes it," *WP* (10.24.23); Rubin, "Georgia election case defendant seeks dismissal of charges due to prosecutor's alleged paperwork error," *ABC News* (10.5.23); Fausset & Hakim, "Jenna Ellis, former Trump lawyer, pleads guilty in Georgia election case," *NYT* (10.24.23); Bailey & Gardner, "Trump co-defendant Jenna Ellis pleads guilty in Georgia election case," *WP* (10.24.23); Feuer & Haberman, "Latest figure to flip in election case had direct ties to Trump and Giuliani," *NYT* (10.24.23); Gardner & Bailey, "Ex-Trump allies detail efforts to overturn election in Georgia plea videos," *WP* (11.13.23); Fausset & Hakim, "Lawyer says Trump aide told her after 2020 election: 'the boss is not going to leave,'" *NYT* (11.14.23).

89 Gardner& Bailey, "Ex-Trump allies detail efforts to overturn election in Georgia plea videos," *WP* (11.13.23); Fausset & Hakim, "Lawyer says Trump aide told her after 2020 election: 'the boss is not going to leave,'" *NYT* (11.14.23); Bailey & Gardner, "After Trump case video leak, Georgia prosecutor seeks emergency seal for evidence," *WP* (11.14.23); Hakim & Fausset, "Prosecutors seek to revoke bond for defendant in Trump election case in Georgia," *NYT* (11.16.23).

90 Bailey, "Trump claims immunity from prosecution in Georgia election case," *WP* (1.8.24); Fausset, "Trump's lawyers say he should be immune from prosecution in Georgia case," *NYT* (1.8.24); Bailey, "Georgia judge dismisses six charges in Trump election interference case," *WP* (3.13.24); Fausset & Hakim, "Georgia judge rejects effort to dismiss Trump case on free speech grounds," *NYT* (4.4.24); Fausset, "Prosecutor in Trump Georgia case to appeal judge's decision to quash six charges," *NYT* (5.24.24).

91 Gardner & Bailey, "How a sleuth defense attorney and a disgruntled law partner damaged the Trump Georgia case," *WP* (3.16.24).

92 Fausset, "Filing in Georgia Trump case claims 'improper relationship' between prosecutors," *NYT* (1.9.24); Timms, Wolfe & McWhirter, "Fani Willis, prosecutor in Trump Georgia case subpoenaed to testify in colleague's divorce," *WSJ* (1.9.24); Bailey & Gardner, "Trump co-defendant accuses prosecutors of misconduct," *WP* (1.10.24); Fausset & Bogel-Burroughs, "Allegations against prosecutors bolster Trump's criticism of Georgia case," *NYT* (1.10.24); Bailey, "Fani Willis, Trump Georgia case prosecutor, ends silence on misconduct accusations," *WP* (1.15.24); Gardner, Bailey & Boburg, "Nathan Wade, embattled prosecutor in Georgia Trump case, has little prosecution experience," *WP* (1.15.24).

93 Bailey, "Fani Willis subpoenaed for hearing on misconduct allegations in Trump Georgia case," *WP* (2.1.24); Fausset, "Trump prosecutor seeks to avoid testifying in colleague's divorce case," *NYT* (1.19.24); Kovaleski & Fausset, "How allegations of an office romance came to complicate the case against Trump," *NYT* (1.20.24); Gardner & Bailey, "Judge in Trump Georgia case orders hearing on Fani Willis misconduct," *WP* (1.18.24); Gardner & Bailey, "Georgia prosecutor in Trump case paid for flights with Fani Willis, filing shows," *WP* (1.19.24); Hakim & Fausset, "Judge unseals records in divorce case that has entangled Trump prosecutors," *NYT* (1.23.24); Gardner & Bailey, "Prosecutor in Trump Georgia case settles divorce, heading off testimony," *WP* (1.31.24).

94 Alexander, Gile & Gregorian, "Georgia Republicans start issuing subpoenas in probe of Fulton County DA Fani Willis," *NBC News* (3.5.24); Gardner & Bailey, "Allegations against Georgia prosecutor likely damaged case against Trump," *WP* (1.21.24).

95 Gardner & Bailey, "Trump attorneys accuse Fani Willis of trying to 'foment racial bias,'" *WP* (1.25.24); Fausset & Hakim, "Trump joins motion to disqualify prosecutor in Georgia election case," *NYT* (1.26.24).
96 Bailey & Gardner, "Fani Willis admits relationship with prosecutor on Trump Georgia case," *WP* (2.2.24); Fausset & Hakim, "Prosecutor in Trump Georgia case admits relationship with colleague," *NYT* (2.3.24); Gardner, Bailey & Jacobs, "Trump plans to attend Georgia hearing on misconduct allegations against prosecutors," *WP* (2.12.24); Fausset & Hakim, "Georgia judge will hear evidence on relationship between Trump prosecutors," *NYT* (2.13.24).
97 "Fani Willis testifying in Georgia after witness contradicted her," *WP* (2.15.24); Bailey & Gardner, "Fani Willis accuses defense of lying in fiery testimony at Georgia hearing," *WP* (2.15.24); Bailey & Gardner, " 'Star witness' mostly silent in hearing to disqualify Fani Willis," *WP* (2.17.24).
98 Fausset & Hakim, "Testimony to resume as Trump and Georgia's co-defendants seek D.A.'s removal," *NYT* (2.26.24); Fausset & Hakim, "Texts show witness readily helped build a case to disqualify Trump prosecutors," *NYT* (2.29.24); Fausset & Hakim, "Lawyers offer new witness in effort to disqualify Trump prosecutors in Georgia," *NYT* (3.5.24).
99 Fausset & Hakim, "Trump lawyer argues 'appearance of impropriety' is enough to disqualify prosecutor," *NYT* (3.1.24); Hailey & Gardner, "Fani Willis can stay on Trump Georgia case, but only if Wade steps aside, judge says," *WP* (3.15.24); Savage, "Highlights of the judge's decision in the Georgia Trump case," *NYT* (3.15.24); Bailey & Gardner, "Fani Willis can stay on Trump Georgia case, judge rules, as Wade resigns," *WP* (3.15.24).
100 Gardner & Bailey, "How a sleuth defense attorney and a disgruntled law partner damaged the Trump Georgia case," *WP* (3.16.24); Fausset & Hakim, "Georgia judge allows Trump and co-defendants to appeal ruling on prosecutor," *NYT* (3.20.24); Bailey, "Trump appeals judge's ruling keeping Fani Willis on Georgia case," *WP* (3.29.24); Fausset & Hakim, "Georgia Trump prosecutor urges appeals court to decline disqualification case," *NYT* (4.8.24); Fausset, "Trump prosecutor in Georgia rebukes critics in speech to Black church group," *NYT* (6.14.24).
101 Fausett, "Georgia court will hear appeal of ruling that kept prosecutor on Trump case," *NYT* (5.8.24); Gardner, "Arguments in Trump's Georgia appeal set for October, likely delaying trial," *WP* (6.3.24); Gardner, "Georgia appeals court pauses lower-court proceedings in Trump election case," *WP* (6.6.24); Fausset, "Georgia appeals court stays most proceedings in Trump election case," *NYT* (6.6.24); Bailey, "Fulton County prosecutors ask Georgia court to dismiss Trump appeal," *WP* (6.12.24); Bailey, "Fani Willis and presiding judge in Trump Georgia case win elections," *WP* (5.21.24); Bailey, "Georgia court sets December argument for Trump appeal to remove Willis," *WP* (7.16.24); Gardner & Bailey, "Georgia judge dismisses two more charges against Trump in election case," *WP* (9.12.24); Hakim & Fausset, "Georgia judge tosses 3 more charges in Trump election interference case," *NYT* (9.12.24); Bailey, "Georgia appeals court cancels arguments on Trump appeal on Willis," *WP* (11.19.24); Bailey, "Fani Willis disqualified from Trump election case by Georgia Appeals Court," *WP* (12.19.24); Hakim, "Atlanta D.A. asks Georgia court to review decision kicking her off Trump case," *WP* (1.9.25).
102 Blake, "A catalogue of Trump's attacks on judges, prosecutors and witnesses," *WP* (10.5.23).
103 Bump, "No amount of evidence will convince Republicans of Trump's 2020 guilt," *WP* (10.3.24).
104 Protess, Christobek & Bromwich, "Emboldened by re-election, Trump renews bid to overturn his conviction," *NYT* (11.12.24).

4

FEDERAL PROSECUTIONS OF TRUMP

Special counsel Jack Smith initiated two prosecutions of Trump: in SD FL for wrongfully retaining classified papers after leaving office; and in DDC for seeking to overturn the 2020 election. This chapter focuses on Trump's efforts to politicize the cases and the success of the courts in resisting such pressure. The final section compares the two prosecutions.

4.1 Trump's Retention of Classified Papers

In January 2021, Trump agreed to return some documents to the National Archives and Records Administration (NARA) but only after an official asked a Trump adviser for help, threatening to refer the matter to Congress or the DoJ.[1] NARA retrieved many boxes from Mar-a-Lago containing papers clearly marked "top secret" and others ripped up and taped back together. Although aides had repeatedly reminded Trump that the Presidential Records Act prohibited such destruction, he regularly did this (as he had in business) and tried to flush them down the toilet, which often clogged up.

In May, NARA chief counsel Gary Stern emailed Trump's lawyers that "roughly two dozen boxes of original presidential records were kept in the Residence of the White House over the course of President Trump's last year in office and have not been returned to NARA, despite a determination by Pat Cipollone in the final days of the administration that they need to be." In September, former White House deputy counsel Patrick Philbin told Stern that chief of staff Mark Meadows had assured him Trump had only 12 boxes of "news clippings" in Mar-a-Lago, none of the material sensitive or classified. On January 17, 2022, Trump returned 15 boxes without

DOI: 10.4324/9781032629186-4

logs or inventories. Despite a DoJ finding that they included 100 classified documents totaling 700 pages, some extraordinarily sensitive, Trump tried to delay an FBI review of them.

On February 9, NARA referred the matter to the DoJ.[2] On April 12, NARA informed Philbin and John Eisenberg (now Trump's personal lawyers) that the FBI would examine the documents, having rejected Trump's claim of executive privilege (which Biden had delegated to NARA). Neither lawyer was willing to review the documents still in Mar-a-Lago. Evan Corcoran (another Trump lawyer) requested a delay. On May 10, a lawyer for Acting Archivist Debra Steidel Wall wrote Corcoran, outlining the weeks of resistance since April 12.

> The executive branch here is seeking access to records belonging to, and in the custody of, the Federal Government itself, not only in order to investigate whether those records were handled in an unlawful manner but also, as the National Security Division explained, to "conduct an assessment of the potential damage resulting from the apparent manner in which these materials were stored and transported and take any necessary remedial steps."

On May 13, Corcoran accepted a grand jury subpoena for classified records remaining at Mar-a-Lago. He and Christina Bobb (another Trump lawyer) led the document review. On June 3, Bobb told Fox News' Laura Ingraham: "We turned over everything that we found" and gave DoJ a written assurance that Trump had returned all the classified material. On June 22, DoJ issued a new subpoena to the TO (which owned Mar-a-Lago) for video surveillance of the storage area.

On August 8, the FBI searched Mar-a-Lago for papers Trump should have given NARA more than 18 months earlier. The furious ex-president ranted: "my beautiful home . . . is currently under siege, raided, and occupied by a large group of FBI agents." (Most of it was closed for the summer, when Trump lived in New Jersey.) The raid was "unannounced" and not "necessary or appropriate." "Biden knew all about this." The search was "a surprise attack, POLITICS, and all the while our Country is going to HELL!" Agents did not want witnesses "to see what they were doing, taking or, hopefully not, 'planting.'" "There was no way of knowing if what they took was legitimate, or was there a 'plant'?" "This was, after all the FBI!" The president of the FBI Agents Association replied that all search warrants were issued by federal judges and "must satisfy detailed and clear procedural rules."

Rep. McCarthy declared that "the Department of Justice has reached an intolerable state of weaponized politicization" and told Attorney General Garland to "preserve your documents and clear your calendar" for a

Congressional investigation. Sen. Scott said Garland, FBI Director Wray, and Biden should disclose "what each of them knew when." "This should scare every American." Rep. Jordan (senior Republican on the HJC) seconded this, declaring it "has never happened in American history" and asking: "What were you really doing?" House Republicans warned: "if they can do it to a former President, imagine what they can do to you." RNC Chair McDaniel said: "President Trump is right when he compared this to Watergate." Anthony Sabatini, running for Congress in Florida, said: "It's time for us in the Florida legislature to call an emergency legislative session & amend our laws regarding federal agencies. Sever all ties with DOJ immediately. An FBI agent conducting law enforcement functions outside the purview of our State should be arrested upon sight." (He lost the primary.) Gov. DeSantis denounced this "un-American" "weaponization" of the criminal justice system. Florida Sen. Scott called the government "the Gestapo." Rep. Greene tweeted: "DEFUND THE FBI." The top trending topics on Truth Social were "#FBIcorruption" and "DefundTheFBI." Stephen Crowder told his 1.9 million Twitter followers: "tomorrow is war." *The Gateway Pundit* agreed: "This. Means. War." Joe Kent, whom Trump had endorsed for a Washington State House seat, said: "We're at war." (He lost.) The white racist Nicholas J. Fuentes asked rhetorically: "Country on the verge of CIVIL WAR??"

Garland said he had approved the search only after "less intrusive" methods failed.[3] SD FL Mag. Judge Bruce Reinhart had signed the search warrant for top secret materials. Trump's possession might have violated the Espionage Act and two other laws making it a crime to destroy or conceal a document to obstruct a government investigation or unlawfully take or destroy government records or documents. Although Trump claimed "it was all declassified" before he left office, that might be irrelevant. Trump complained the FBI "didn't need to 'seize' anything. They could have had it anytime they wanted without playing politics and breaking into Mar-a-Lago." "My attorneys and representatives were cooperating fully, and very good relations had been established." He claimed agents "stole my three Passports (one expired), along with everything else." He warned Garland that "the country is on fire," falsely declaring: "President Barack Hussein Obama kept 33 million pages of documents, much of them classified. How many of them pertained to nuclear? Word is, lots!" NARA replied that it had "exclusive legal and physical custody" of Obama's records, keeping classified records in DC and transferring about 30 million pages of unclassified material to its Chicago facility. Pence was "deeply worried" by the search warrant and asked Garland for more information. But he added: "We can hold the Attorney General accountable for the decision that he made without attacking the rank-and-file law enforcement personnel at the FBI." "Calls to defund the FBI are just as wrong as calls to defund the police." Trump promptly posted on

Truth Social an article headlined "The Fascist Bureau of Investigation," calling it "a government agency weaponized against American citizens it doesn't like." Reps. Schiff and Maloney (chairs of the Committees on Intelligence and on Oversight and Reform) asked DNI Haines for an intelligence assessment of the documents. Trump raised more than $1 million the day after the raid, compared to his daily average of $200–300,000.

The Federal Law Enforcement Officers Association (with 31,000 members) said its agents had received "extreme threats of violence." In the hours after the FBI search, mentions of "civil war" on Twitter increased nearly 3,000 percent.[4] The same happened on Facebook, Reddit, Telegram, Parler, Gab, and Truth Social; threats of civil war more than doubled on radio and podcasts. Ricky Shiffer attacked the FBI's Cincinnati field office in body armor, fled, and fired at officers before they killed him. He had claimed on social media he had been in the January 6 riot and posted a "call to arms" on Truth Social:

> People. This is it. Leave work tomorrow as soon as the gun shop/army-navy-store/pawn shop opens, get whatever you need to be ready for combat. We must not tolerate this one. . . . This time we must respond with force. . . . if you don't hear from me, it is true I tried attacking the F.B.I.

Mag. Judge Reinhart ordered the government to redact the warrant so it could be released.[5] Hours later, two lawyers not admitted in Florida asked SD FL Judge Cannon (Trump) to appoint a special master to review the documents for privilege, citing "two years of noisy 'Russian collusion' investigations" and calling Trump "the clear front-runner" in 2024. Cannon responded that they had bungled the paperwork, noting caustically that "a sample motion can be found on the Court's website." Nevertheless, she issued a notice of "preliminary intent" to appoint a special master. DoJ said its filter team had already "identified a limited set of materials that potentially contain attorney-client privilege information, completed its review of those materials, and is in the process of following the procedures" of the search warrant to handle privilege disputes. Despite this Cannon found that Trump retained some executive privilege, decided to appoint a special master, and ordered the DoJ to stop reviewing documents. Former Attorney General Barr called that decision "deeply flawed in a number of ways" and urged the government to appeal. The ABA had assessed Judge Cannon as merely qualified rather than well-qualified because of her lack of experience. (It had rated ten of Trump's 264 judicial nominees merely qualified compared with none of Biden's 136.)

The affidavit underlying the search warrant application said 184 classified files had been found in the 15 boxes NARA recovered in January, some so sensitive that "even the FBI counterintelligence personnel and Department of Justice attorneys conducting the review required additional clearances before they were permitted to review certain documents."[6] "There is also probable cause to believe that evidence of obstruction will be found." When Trump's lawyers had given the government 38 documents on June 3, "neither counsel nor the custodian asserted that the former President had declassified the documents or asserted any claim of executive privilege." Bobb, the "custodian of records," had furnished a written assurance that, "based upon the information that has been provided to me," there had been a "diligent" search, and all requested documents had been returned. That day Corcoran "explicitly prohibited government personnel from opening or examining any of the boxes that remained in the storage room, giving no opportunity for the government to confirm that no documents with classification markings remained." But Bobb falsely told *The Washington Post* that Trump's lawyers had showed federal officials the remaining boxes and Jay Bratt (DoJ chief of counterintelligence and export control) and others had examined them. The government said the discovery of more than 100 classified papers on August 8 "calls into serious question the representations made in the June 3 certification and casts doubt on the extent of cooperation in this matter."

The government denounced "the wide-ranging meritless accusations leveled against" it.[7] There was no need for a special master because the FBI document review had been completed. It asked Cannon to restore access to the classified material it had seized and threatened to appeal. Instead, she appointed EDNY Judge Dearie (Reagan) as special master to review the documents for attorney-client and executive privilege and prohibited the government from using them. Trump warned that if he was indicted there would be "problems in this country the likes of which perhaps we've never seen before." DoJ appealed, arguing that Trump was not entitled to the records and could not invoke either privilege. Dearie instructed Trump lawyers to state whether their client had declassified "top secret" documents: "you can't have your cake and eat it." DoJ reasserted that only the "current executive branch" could declassify.

Eleven Republican state Attorneys General filed papers supporting Trump's position, decrying the "ransacking" of Biden's "one-time—and possibly future—political rival."[8] When DoJ urged Dearie to consult NARA, Trump lawyers denounced the agency as "political" and "partisan," but Dearie retorted they were painting it with an excessively "broad brush." The Eleventh Circuit (Rosenbaum (Obama) and Grant and Brasher (both Trump)) issued a devastating critique of Judge Cannon's actions, ruling per curiam that the FBI could continue using the documents. The district court had "abused its discretion." "We cannot discern why [Trump] would have an individual interest in or need for any of the one-hundred documents with classification markings." "Plaintiff has not even attempted to show that he has a need to know the information." There was "no evidence that any of these records were declassified." Anyhow, that "argument is a red herring because declassifying an official document would not change its content or render it personal." Trump "suggests that he could be harmed by the disclosure of sensitive information."

> But permitting the United States to retain the documents does not suggest that they will be released; indeed, a purpose of the United States's efforts in investigating the recovered classified documents is to *limit* unauthorized disclosure of the information they contain.

Trump "has not . . . asserted attorney-client privilege over any of the classified documents." Cannon had described Trump's potential injury as "the threat of future prosecution and the serious, often indelible stigma associated therewith." But the Fifth Circuit had held: "if the mere threat of prosecution were allowed to constitute irreparable harm . . . every potential defendant could point to the same harm." Cannon had found that Trump "would have no legal means of seeking the return of his property for the time being." But "Plaintiff has been clear that he is not seeking the return of the classified documents." "And even if he were, he has not identified any reason that he is entitled to them." "No party has offered anything beyond speculation to undermine the United States's representation—supported by sworn testimony—that the findings from the criminal investigation may be critical to its national-security review." "It is self-evident that the public has a strong interest in ensuring that the storage of the classified records did not result in 'exceptionally grave damage to the national security.'" Cannon had limited the special master's review by excluding items marked classified, mooting an issue Trump might have wanted to take to the Supreme Court; and that Court, without noted dissents, declined to intervene. DoJ asked the Eleventh Circuit to remove the special master so it could review the unclassified documents immediately.

Dearie ordered Trump lawyers to state whether they believed the FBI incorrectly described some of the seized items as classified or claimed to have taken items not there (i.e., planted them).[9] Cannon overruled this. Dearie told both parties to complete their reviews by Oct. 21, but Cannon granted Trump an extension to Dec. 16. Dearie directed Trump's team to distinguish between documents whose privilege would shield them from disclosure <u>outside</u> and <u>inside</u> the executive branch, but Cannon overruled that. When Trump claimed that a document was both his personal property and protected by executive privilege, Dearie said: "there's certainly an incongruity there." He wanted the names of every lawyer for whom Trump was claiming attorney-client privilege, adding: "Where third parties are involved in the document, I need some understanding why the presence of the third party doesn't defeat the privilege." Although Trump's lawyers claimed there were about 200,000 pages of documents, there actually were only 21,792.

Trump told Fox News host Sean Hannity that while in office he had "declassified everything" he later took to Mar-a-Lago.[10] "There doesn't have to be a process, as I understand it." "If you're the president of the United States, you can declassify just by saying 'it's declassified,' even by thinking about it." "You're the president—you make that decision." Republican Senators disagreed. GOP Whip Thune said there was a process for declassifying documents, "and I think that should apply to anybody who had access to or dealt with classified information." Tillis concurred: "there is a formal process that . . . needs to be gone through and documented." Rounds warned that "people can get killed if [classified information is] not stored correctly, and if that information gets out." Graham disparaged Trump's claim to have declassified information just by thinking about it: "the process is probably more complicated than that."

Barr escalated his criticism on Fox News: "I can't think of a legitimate reason why [documents] could be taken out of government, away from the government if they are classified."[11] "People say this [search] was unprecedented, but it's also unprecedented for a president to take all this classified information and put them in a country club okay?" "It seems to me [the DoJ] were driven by concern about highly sensitive information being strewn all over a country club, and it was taking them almost two years to get it back."

> If in fact [Trump] sort of stood over scores of boxes, not really knowing what was in them, and said, "I hereby declassify everything in here," that would be such an abuse and show such recklessness that it's almost worse than taking the documents.

"What people are missing" is that, regardless of whether or not the documents were classified, they "still belong to the government and go to the archives." The government "jawboned for a year. They were deceived on the voluntary actions taken." They "went and got a subpoena. They were deceived on that . . . [and] the facts are starting to show that they were being jerked around. And so, how long do they wait?" Asked about the special master, Barr called it "a crock of shit," adding that DoJ was "getting very close" to having enough evidence to indict Trump. Bratt told Trump's lawyers the DoJ believed he had more records. Acting NARA head Wall told Rep. Maloney (chair of the House Oversight Committee): "we . . . know that we do not have custody of everything we should."

Cannon ordered release of the inventory of seized documents, which included 31 confidential and 54 secret documents, 18 of them "top secret"; one described a foreign government's military defenses, even its nuclear capabilities, held on a "need-to-know" basis.[12] Trump spokesperson Taylor

Budowich made the bizarre claim that "the new 'detailed' inventory list only further proves that this unprecedented and unnecessary raid of President Trumps home was not some surgical, confined search and retrieval that the Biden administration claims, it was a SMASH AND GRAB."

At the end of November, the Eleventh Circuit (Pryor (GWB), with Grant and Brasher (both Trump)) terminated the special master.[13] The panel adhered to its usual rule against "block[ing] government investigations after the execution of a warrant." "To create a special exception here would defy our nation's foundational principle that our law applies 'to all, without regard to numbers, wealth or rank.'" Because the special master's review had ended, Cannon dismissed Trump's challenge. He railed against this and the Supreme Court's rejection of his appeal concerning his tax records (see Chapter 3.1), declaring on Truth Social: "Republican judges . . . go ROGUE."

The New York Times urged Garland to consider prosecuting Trump.[14] But Sen. Graham threatened on Fox News: "if there's a prosecution of Donald Trump for mishandling classified information after the Clinton debacle . . . there'll be riots in the street." "Most Republicans, including me, believe when it comes to Trump, there is no law. It's all about getting him." *The Washington Post* warned that this "reads more like a threat." Rep. McCarthy addressed voters in the forthcoming mid-term election: "Joe Biden and a politicized Department of Justice launched a raid on the home of his top political rival, Donald Trump. That is an assault on democracy." Biden said Trump had been "totally irresponsible" in keeping top secret documents at Mar-a-Lago but added: "I don't want to get myself in the middle of whether or not the Justice Department should move or not move on certain actions they could take." In his first political rally since the search, Trump called Biden "an enemy of the state" and the FBI and DoJ "vicious monsters." "It was not just my home that was raided last month. It was the hopes and dreams of every citizen who I've been fighting for." The Senate unanimously passed a resolution condemning violence against the FBI, calls to defund it (which had been made by Reps. Greene, Gosar, Duncan, and Gaetz), and threats of political violence regardless of motivation.

Garland named Jack Smith (a war crimes prosecutor at The Hague and former AUSA in EDNY and head of the DoJ Public Integrity Section) as special counsel to investigate both Trump's retention of classified papers and his efforts to overturn the 2020 election (see 4.2 below).[15] Trump immediately proclaimed his defiance: "I am not going to partake in it. . . . It is not acceptable. It is so unfair. It is so political." He condemned "the appalling announcement today by the egregiously corrupt Biden administration," "the latest in a long series of witch hunts."

DDC Judge Howell (overseeing the DC grand jury) ruled that Evan Corcoran had to testify because of the crime-fraud exception to the lawyer-client privilege.[16] After the DC Circuit issued a stay, the Trump campaign denounced "Fake News ABC for broadcasting ILLEGALLY LEAKED false allegations from a Never Trump, now former judge, against the Trump legal team." (Howell remained a District Judge after her term as Chief Judge expired.) But the DC Circuit (Pillard (Obama) and Childs and Pan (both Biden)) lifted the stay.

In early November 2022, classified documents were found at the Penn Biden Center for Diplomacy and Global Engagement and immediately given to the FBI.[17] Trump asked: "When is the FBI going to raid the many homes of Joe Biden, perhaps even the White House?" Additional documents were found in Biden's Wilmington garage and promptly turned over; then that happened again. Trump demanded that Garland "immediately" end investigations into "anything related to me because I did everything right" and appoint a special counsel to investigate Biden, one who hates "Biden as much as Jack Smith hates me." Garland appointed Robert K. Hur (Principal Associate Deputy Attorney General under Rod Rosenstein and then Trump's appointee as US Attorney in D MD). After Republicans gained control of the House, Rep. Comer, the new Oversight Committee chair, demanded a list of all Biden aides and lawyers involved in the search, all locations searched, and all communications between the White House, DoJ, and NARA. HJC Chair Jordan made a similar demand. Then classified documents were also found at Pence's Indiana home. Days before Pence announced his candidacy in June, DoJ said it would not charge him. During a search ordered by Trump around Thanksgiving 2022, at least two more items with classified markings were found at his Florida storage unit and given to the FBI. In February 2023, Trump's lawyers gave the Justice Department an additional classified folder. That month Hur issued a report harshly criticizing Biden but recommending against prosecution. The Republican-dominated HJC sued Garland to compel release of Hur's interviews with Biden. But after four Republicans joined all the Democrats, the House rejected a Republican effort to fine Garland $10,000 a day for resisting.

In January 2023, Trump denounced Smith as "a Trump Hating THUG . . . who may well turn out to be a criminal."[18] "His conflicts, unfairness, and mental state of derangement make him totally unfit for the job of 'getting Trump.'" "He is a terrorist. He is a Trump hater. His best friends are [Andrew] Weissmann and all of these characters, Lisa Monaco at the Justice Department, one of the top officials." "His wife hates Trump, probably even beyond him. And his wife has a sister who openly hates like a level that you can't even believe."

In April, DoJ applied for a court order to conduct another Mar-a-Lago search because it believed boxes with classified matter had been moved from a storage area after the original subpoena was served.[19] Trump's spokesman said:

> the deranged special counsel and the DoJ have now resorted to prosecutorial misconduct by illegally leaking information to corrupt the legal process and weaponize the justice system in order to manipulate public opinion and conduct election interference, because they are clearly losing all across the board.

After spending two hours with Smith in June, Trump's lawyers said they expected an indictment.[20] He immediately posted on Truth Social: "HOW CAN DOJ POSSIBLY CHARGE ME, WHO DID NOTHING WRONG, WHEN NO OTHER PRESIDENTS WERE CHARGED . . . THE GREATEST WITCH HUNT OF ALL TIME!" The next day he was indicted in SD FL on 38 counts: 31 of willful retention of national defense secrets (under the Espionage Act) and seven of obstruction of justice, conspiracy, and false statements. *The New York Times* ran a front-page banner headline, commenting that "the Justice Department had no choice." *The Washington Post* (dropping earlier reservations) called it "a solid Trump indictment." Trump denounced the "Boxes Hoax." "I never thought it possible that such a thing could happen to a former President of the United States." It was "election interference at the highest level." "I AM AN INNOCENT MAN." He asked supporters to donate at least $24 (signifying the 2024 election) "to peacefully stand with me today and prove that You will NEVER surrender our country to the radical Left—for 1,500% impact." (But he did not explain the source of that impact.)

His Republican rivals promptly pledged fealty. Gov. DeSantis said: "the weaponization of federal law enforcement represents a mortal threat to a free society." Vivek Ramaswamy promised to "pardon Trump promptly on January 20, 2025" if elected. Sen. Scott vowed to "purge all of the injustice and impurities in our system." Sen. Rubio said there "is no limit to what these people will do to protect their power." Nikki Haley declared: "The American people are exhausted by the prosecutorial overreach, double standards, and vendetta politics."

Sen. Barrasso said: "it feels political, and it's rotten." Sen. Hawley accused Biden of using the DoJ to "indict his top political opponent." Rep. Scalise said: "Joe Biden is weaponizing his Department of Justice against his own political rival. This sham indictment is the continuation of the endless political persecution of Donald Trump." Rep. McCarthy vowed to "hold this brazen weaponization of power accountable." "It is unconscionable for a President to indict the leading candidate opposing him. I, and every

American who believes in the rule of law, stand with President Trump against this grave injustice." Rep. Stefanik said: "Joe Biden weaponizes his Department of Justice to indict Donald Trump." Biden retorted that he had "never once, not one single time, suggested to the Justice Department what they should do or not do relative to bringing a charge or not bringing a charge."

Declaring "this is as political as it gets!" Rep. Jordan said the HJC would "get to the bottom" of the fact that "federal agencies have been turned on the American people." He claimed Trump had declassified all the documents and could keep them "wherever he wants." He wrote Garland on June 9, demanding internal communications about the FBI decision to search Mar-a-Lago. The HJC Twitter account denounced the "WITCH HUNT." But Chris Christie said Trump's problems were "completely self-inflicted." "[I]t is bad for anybody in this country to do it, but it's particularly awful for someone who has been president and who aspires to be president again." Trump was "saying, 'I'm more important than the country.'" Barr said: "if even half of it is true he's toast. It is a very detailed indictment and it's very, very damning." "The idea of presenting Trump as a victim here—a victim of a witch hunt—is ridiculous." The argument that he could take any records he wanted under the Presidential Records Act was "facially ridiculous." "They're the government's documents—they're official records. They're not his personal records. Battle plans for an attack on another country or Defense Department documents about our capabilities are in no universe Donald J. Trump's personal documents."

The case was assigned to Judge Cannon. (Although this was random, the three senior judges in the West Palm Beach Division were probably ineligible; one of the seven active judges sat only in Miami; another was not taking cases; and a third got half of his from Miami. Cannon "draws 50 percent of her cases from West Palm Beach, increasing her odds.") She had little criminal experience. In her seven years as SD FL AUSA, she had only four jury trials and was the lead in just two of them. In her 32 months on the bench she had handled 224 criminal cases, but only four routine matters went to trial, for a total of 14 days.

It emerged in June 2024 that SD FL Chief Judge Cecilia M. Altonaga (GWB) had urged Cannon to decline the momentous case for lack of experience and because she had not followed usual practice of letting Mag. Judge Reinhart deal with the dispute over the search.[21] (He had handled criminal matters in the DoJ and Treasury Department for over six years, served as an SD FL AUSA for 11 years, and been a Magistrate Judge for four years.) Another colleague suggested the case be heard in Miami, which had a Sensitive Compartmented Information Facility (SCIF); Fort Pierce, where Cannon sits, does not and is two hours from Miami. Because of Cannon's insistence on retaining the case, a SCIF had to be built in Fort Pierce.

The indictment alleged that when Trump's lawyers told him to comply with the subpoena in May 2022 he retorted: "wouldn't it be better if we just told them we don't have anything here?"[22] He protested to Corcoran: "I don't want anybody looking through my boxes. I really don't." He praised Hillary Clinton's lawyer for having done "a great job" by deleting her 30,000 emails and accused prosecutors of trying to "destroy" the life of Waltine "Walt" Nauta (his former valet, also indicted) so "he will say bad things about 'Trump.'" In July 2021, Trump had ordered that some boxes be brought from Mar-a-Lago to his Bedminster Club in New Jersey. During an interview with two people helping Meadows write his memoir, Trump discussed a classified document mentioning JCS Chair Milley's opposition to attacking Iran and bragged: "I have a big pile of papers, this thing just came up. Secret. This is secret info. . . . See as president I could have declassified it . . . now I can't you know, but this is still a secret . . . isn't that interesting? It's so cool. . . . You probably didn't believe me, but now you believe me. It's incredible." At Bedminster he also met a representative of his PAC and showed someone without security clearance "a classified map" of a foreign country, while admitting "he should not be showing the map" and "warning the other to not get too close." Two weeks after the indictment Trump said: "there was no document" about Iran. Asked if he had shown classified documents to anyone, he said: "not really. I would have the right to," adding disingenuously: "I don't do things wrong. . . . I'm a legitimate person." "What I'm referring to is . . . building plans . . . plans of a golf course."

After Trump was served with the May 11, 2022, subpoena demanding return of the papers, Nauta moved 64 boxes from the Mar-a-Lago storage room to Trump's residence between May 23 and June 2 but denied this to the FBI.[23] During that period, he texted someone (probably Ivanka), explaining: "I think [Trump] wanted to pick from them." "He told me to put them in the room and that he was going to talk to you about them." On June 2, Trump called Nauta, who immediately returned 30 boxes to the storage room. When the FBI searched the next day, Trump's lawyers gave them a folder with more than three dozen classified documents. Neither Nauta nor Trump told the lawyers that nearly three dozen more boxes remained in the residence. Corcoran searched only the storage room, although he later told prosecutors he had made a diligent search and produced every document in response to the subpoena.

Trump ridiculed the indictment, saying: "I got a box."[24] He suggested that a photo showing the spilled contents proved no one could see classified documents, but the DoJ had redacted them.

> This vicious persecution is a travesty of justice. . . . Biden is trying to jail his leading political opponent. As far as the joke of an indictment, it's a

> horrible thing . . . the only good thing about it is it's driven my poll numbers way up.

The FBI and DoJ are "a sick nest of people that needs to be cleaned out immediately." DeSantis said: "the weaponization of these agencies strikes at the heart of what it means to have a free society." He would fire Wray. Kari Lake warned:

> If you want to get to President Trump you're going to have to go through me and you're going to have to go through 75 million Americans just like me. Most of us are card-carrying members of the NRA. That's not a threat, that's a public service announcement.

"We're at war, people—we're at war." Rep. Biggs demanded an "eye for an eye." Kimberly Guilfoyle (Don Jr.'s fiancée) displayed a photo of Trump and declared: "RETRIBUTION IS COMING." Talk show host Pete Santilli said if he commanded the Marine Corps he would order every Marine to grab Biden "throw him in freakin' zip ties in the back of a freakin' pickup truck" and "get him out of the White House." Shortly before this Trump posted on Instagram a video of himself swinging a golf club and an animation of a ball hitting Biden in the head with video footage of Biden falling. In an interview with Roger Stone, Trump repeated his call for protests.

At the arraignment, Mag. Judge Jonathan Goodman said he would order Trump to have no contact with witnesses or co-defendants.[25] When Trump lawyer Todd Blanche objected that his client interacted with many of them daily, Goodman said Trump could not talk about the facts of the case. Cannon refused to seal the list of witnesses, but she granted a prosecution motion requiring Trump to examine classified information in a SCIF, meaning he could not do so at Mar-a-Lago.

In a fundraising email, Trump declared: "They can indict me, they can arrest me, but I know . . . I am an innocent man." In New Jersey, Alina Habba (another Trump lawyer) said: "What we are witnessing today is the blatant and unapologetic weaponization of the criminal justice system." Trump warned:

> If the communists get away with this, it won't stop with me. They will not hesitate to ramp up their persecution of Christians, pro-life activists, parents attending school board meetings, and even future Republican candidates. I am the only one that can save this nation.

He vowed, as president, to appoint a special prosecutor to investigate Biden and his family. Ramaswamy called on the other Republican candidates to join him in promising to pardon Trump. Haley now was "inclined in favor of a pardon" but also called the alleged conduct "incredibly reckless with our national security." Sen. Vance said he would block all DoJ nominations. Fox News pronounced: "wannabe dictator speaks at the White House after having his political rival arrested."

Trump said that "threatening me with 400 years in prison for possessing my own presidential papers, which just about every other president has done, is one of the most outrageous and vicious legal theories ever put forward in an American court of law."[26] "The decision to segregate personal materials from presidential records is made by the president during the president's term and in the president's sole discretion." "I was supposed to negotiate with NARA, which is exactly what I was doing until Mar-a-Lago was raided by gun-toting F.B.I. agents." "Biden sent 1,850 boxes to the University of Delaware, making the search very, very difficult for anybody. And he refuses to give them up and he refuses to let people even look at them." "Unlike me who had absolute declassificatory authority as president, Joe Biden as vice-president had no authority to declassify and no right to possess the documents." (Those boxes were from Biden's senatorial term and not governed by the Presidential Records Act.)

Trump called the indictment "the most evil and heinous abuse of power in the history of our country."[27] He condemned years of an "illegal psychological warfare campaign." "We no longer have a democracy."

> They want to take away my freedom because I will never let them take away your freedom. They want to silence me because I will never let them silence you. And I am the only one that can save this nation because you know they're not coming after me, they're coming after you. And I just happened to be standing in their way. And I will never be moving.

Republican politicians and right-wing commentators had denounced "weaponization" 20 times more often in Spring 2023 than Spring 2022. The Trump campaign had raised $4.5 million online and $2.1 million at an in-person fundraiser since the indictment.

Trump said: "I will appoint a real special prosecutor to go after the most corrupt president in the history of the United States of America, Joe Biden, and the entire Biden crime family. I will totally obliterate the deep state."[28] Jeffrey B. Clark and Russell T. Vought at the Center for Renewing America argued that the president should control the DoJ. Clark (whom Trump had wanted to make acting Attorney General to overturn the 2020 election, see Abel 2024b: Chapter 4) declared: "Biden and the D.O.J. are baying for Trump's blood so they can put fear into America. The Constitution and our Article IV 'Republican Form of Government' cannot survive like this." Vought called the DoJ "ground zero for the weaponization of the government against the American people." DeSantis regretted that "Republican presidents have accepted the canard that the D.O.J. and F.B.I. are—quote—'independent.' They are not independent agencies. They are part of the executive branch. They answer to the elected president of the United States." Heritage Foundation President Kevin D. Robert said: "The F.B.I. has become a political weapon for the ruling elite rather than an impartial, law-enforcement agency" and "must be rebuilt from the ground up."

Trump sought to delay the trial until after the election.[29] Prosecutors wanted to begin in December 2023, noting that "many indicted defendants have demanding jobs that require a considerable amount of their time and energy, or a significant amount of travel." Trump's claim that the Presidential Records Act protected him "borders on frivolous." Cannon scheduled the trial for May 2024. After Trump was indicted in DC in the 2020 election case on August 1 (see 4.2), Cannon ordered prosecutors to "address the legal propriety of using an out-of-district grand jury proceeding [in DC] to continue to investigate and/or seek post-indictment hearings on matters pertinent to the instant indicted matter in this district." In October, Trump again moved to postpone the documents trial until after the election, asking for a three-month delay because prosecutors had not turned over evidence. They accused Trump's lawyers of seeking to "intentionally derail" the timing of the trial by misusing the law on classified material. They had given the defense about 1.28 million pages of unclassified materials and several transcripts of witnesses discussing classified issues. Cannon said disagreements about discoverable information "will require substantial judicial intervention. She was also inclined to make "reasonable adjustments" to the trial date because it could "collide" with the DDC trial, which was scheduled for March 4, 2024.

HJC chair Jordan asked House Appropriations Committee chair Granger to stop funding "politically sensitive" investigations until the DoJ "establishes a policy requiring non-partisan career staff to oversee such investigations."[30] (His Republican colleagues were demanding that the DoJ and FBI be subordinated to the president.) Calling the FBI's work "Orwellian," Jordan recommended "that appropriation bills eliminate any funding for the FBI that is not absolutely essential for the agency to execute its mission" (whatever that would mean). Asked provocatively by Rep. Gaetz "are you protecting the Bidens," FBI Director Wray said: "absolutely not." "The idea that I'm biased against conservatives seems somewhat insane to me, given my own personal background." (A lifelong Republican, he had been nominated by Trump and confirmed by the Senate 92–5.)

Smith added a 32nd count—illegally retaining national defense information (based on the Bedminster conversations)—and others of a cover-up: that Trump, Nauta, and Mar-a-Lago property manager Carlos De Oliveira had asked Mar-a-Lago IT manager Yuscil Taveras to "delete security camera footage at the Mar-a-Lago club to prevent the footage from being provided to a federal grand jury."[31] After Trump received the grand jury subpoena,

Nauta had abruptly changed his plans to travel with his employer to Illinois and instead flew from New Jersey to Florida to discuss the footage with employees, telling them to keep the purpose of his trip secret. De Oliveira was charged with lying to the FBI and "altering, destroying, mutilating or concealing an object." He allegedly told Taveras "the boss" wanted the server with the video footage deleted. Taveras replied that "he would not know how to do that, and that he did not believe that he would have the rights to do that." After the FBI search, Nauta confided in a Trump employee that "someone just wants to make sure Carlos is good" and was reassured that De Oliveira was "loyal" and "would not do anything to affect his relationship with Trump." That day Trump "told De Oliveira that Trump would get De Oliveira an attorney." Taveras subsequently retracted his false grand jury testimony and accused De Oliveira, Nauta and Trump of trying to delete the tape.

The evening of the FBI search Trump had claimed "it was all declassified." He "had a standing order that documents removed from the Oval Office and taken to the residence were deemed to be declassified." In May 2023, he had said "they become automatically declassified when I took them." But in August, Pence (who had presidential aspirations) said: "I was never made aware of any broad-based effort to declassify documents."[32]

> There is a process that the White House goes through to declassify materials. I'm aware of that occurring on several cases over the course of our four years But I don't have any knowledge of any broad-based directive from the president.

And 18 former Trump administration officials, including White House chiefs of staff Meadows, Kelly, and Mulvaney, said they knew of no such order.

On May 6, 2024, Cannon indefinitely postponed the trial (which had been scheduled to start in two weeks) because of "the myriad and interconnected pre-trial and CIPA issues."[33] She extended a CIPA-related deadline because prosecutors acknowledged they might have altered the sequence of documents in a box (while keeping them in the same box). Prosecutors objected that Nauta had failed to raise the issue during the nine months the boxes had been available. Cannon also unsealed two-month-old defense motions (on which she had not ruled) accusing prosecutors of mishandling evidence.[34] They contained a document (from DDC Howell's opinion on the grand jury proceedings) indicating that, when Trump realized Mar-a-Lago security cameras recorded his employees moving boxes of classified information, he directed them to avoid the cameras when doing so. Howell had denied Trump lawyers' claim of attorney-client privilege because prosecutors said they were helping Trump commit a crime. Prosecutors argued that Trump's actions explained why there was no footage of employees returning boxes to the storage room. Noting that Trump's lawyers found four "classified" documents in his personal bedroom four months after the raid, Howell observed: "no excuse is provided as to how the former president could miss the classified-marked documents found in his own bedroom at Mar-a-Lago." She also commented on Nauta's decision to fly to Palm Beach rather than Illinois:

> The government urged that this scramble to Mar-a-Lago in the wake of the June 24, 2022 phone call reflects the former president's realization that the removal of the boxes from the storage room before [redacted] search was captured on camera—and his attempts to ensure that any subsequent movement of the boxes back to the storage room could occur off camera. This theory draws support from the curious absence of any video footage showing the return of the remaining boxes to the storage room, which necessarily occurred at some point between June 3, 2022—when the room had approximately [redacted] boxes, according to FBI agents and [redacted]—and the execution of the search warrant on August 8, 2022—when agents counted 73 boxes.

After a Trump filing noted that FBI agents had been authorized to use "deadly force" in executing the search warrant a year earlier—boilerplate language—Trump sent out a fundraising email: "BREAKING FROM TRUMP: BIDEN'S DOJ WAS AUTHORIZED TO SHOOT ME!"[35] "You know they're just itching to do the unthinkable . . . Joe Biden was locked & loaded ready to take me out & put my family in danger." (The FBI deliberately scheduled the search when Trump and his family were not in Florida.) Trump wrote on Truth Social: "Joe Biden's DOJ, in their Illegal and UnConstitutional Raid of Mar-a-Lago, AUTHORIZED THE FBI TO USE DEADLY (LETHAL) FORCE." Rep. Greene wrote her 3.2 million followers on X: "The Biden DOJ and FBI were planning to assassinate Pres Trump and gave the green light." Was the FBI "going to shoot SS [Secret Service] then Pres Trump, Melania, and Barron too???" "This is grounds for impeachment of Wray and Garland." Right-wing commentator Julie Kelly wrote on social media: "Armed FBI agents were preparing to confront Trump and even engage Secret Service if necessary. They were going door to door to terrorize [Mar-a-Lago] guests and even pick the locks. Gestapo." Fox News went to town. Jesse Watters said: "Biden unleashed armed agents into Trump's house, authorizing them to use deadly force," wearing plain clothes because "maybe they were looking for a little action." Maria Bartiromo said Biden was "authorizing the FBI, if it came to that and he resisted arrest . . . to kill Donald Trump." Kyle Becker, who had nearly 500,000 followers, wrote: "The FBI was basically authorized to assassinate Trump if necessary in Mar-a-Lago raid." Mike Cernovch told his 1.2 million followers: "The FBI raid was designed to provoke a response. This was an assassination attempt on President Trump." Christina Bobb posted: "WTF?!! They were prepared to kill me?!" Bannon declared: "This was an attempted assassination attempt on Donald John Trump or people associated with him." Trump said on Truth Social: "NOW WE KNOW, FOR SURE, THAT JOE BIDEN IS A SERIOUS THREAT TO DEMOCRACY. HE IS MENTALLY UNFIT TO HOLD OFFICE—25TH AMENDMENT!"

Jack Smith asked Cannon to order Trump to stop asserting FBI agents were "complicit in a plot to assassinate him."[36] "[S]everal intentionally false and inflammatory statements recently made by Trump . . . distort the circumstances under which the Federal Bureau of Investigation planned and executed the search warrant at Mar-a-Lago" and "irresponsibly put a target on the backs of the F.B.I. agents involved in this case, as Trump well knows." Trump lawyers lashed back, charging Smith with "pursuing media coverage rather than justice" (talk about a pot calling the kettle black!) and asking Cannon to hold a hearing to ascertain the special prosecutor's "motives and purpose." The prosecutors were "Thought Police," "biased and reckless" and "driven by political animus against President Trump." Defense lawyers accused prosecutors of violating the rule requiring them to "meet and confer" before approaching the judge, calling it part of "a pattern of unprofessional conduct in this case." Judge Cannon refused to issue the gag order because of this failure to consult, which breached "professional courtesy" and relegated important facts to an "editorialized footnote." But she also denied a defense request to strike the motion from the record and sanction prosecutors. Three days later prosecutors renewed their request, confirming they had consulted with the defense, who responded that "the motion is a naked effort to impose totalitarian censorship of core political speech, under threat of incarceration, in a clear attempt to silence President Trump's arguments to the American people about the outrageous nature of this investigation and prosecution." Trump's lawyers denied he had lied about the FBI search; he merely "criticized" it "in a manner that someone in the government disagreed with and does not like."

Cannon cancelled a three-day hearing scheduled for June 24 about whether Trump's lawyers should be able to see communications between prosecutors and national security agencies.[37] She told the parties to be prepared to debate a defense motion to exclude evidence from the Mar-a-Lago search and communications with Corcoran, as well as the gag order. Trump's lawyers filed a motion on June 10, asking Cannon to dismiss the charges or exclude evidence found at Mar-a-Lago, arguing that the government had failed to preserve it properly because the order of documents within a box may have changed. The campaign accused "Deranged Jack Smith" and his "Thugs" of "blatant Evidence Tampering."

Cannon deleted paragraph 36 of the indictment alleging that in September 2021, Trump showed Susie Wiles (a political adviser without security clearance) a classified map of an ongoing military operation, because the paragraph did not specify the crime with which Trump was charged.[38] But the judge said evidence of the incident could be introduced at trial. She did not strike a similar allegation that a few months earlier Trump had shown a classified battle plan to writers helping Meadows with his memoir. Cannon also denied a motion to dismiss for "failure to state an offense," while adding gratuitously that "much of the language in the Superseding Indictment is legally unnecessary."

On June 21, Cannon held a hearing on defense motions to dismiss based on the ground that Smith was improperly appointed and funded, inviting amici, including the conservative Landmark Legal Foundation, to present arguments.[39] Both actions were unusual. She scheduled a June 24 hearing on the gag order and a June 25 hearing on the defense motion to exclude audio notes from Corcoran. Unusually, Cannon did not delegate these motions to Mag. Judge Reinhart. On June 27 she rejected defense claims that the FBI had misrepresented facts to Reinhart in obtaining the search warrant but further delayed the case by scheduling an evidentiary hearing to reconsider DDC Judge Howell's ruling that Corcoran could be compelled to testify under the criminal conduct exception to attorney-client privilege and a separate defense claim that Reinhart's warrant did not adequately specify what the FBI could seize.

After the Supreme Court's July 1 decision on immunity in the 2020 election case (see 4.2), Trump's lawyers asked Cannon to pause her case while they prepared a motion to dismiss.[40] She gave prosecutors two weeks to respond and extended deadlines for other motions. She also denied Nauta's motion to dismiss, which claimed unfair prosecution. On July 12, Smith agreed to submit a brief on immunity but said of Thomas's opinion: "that single-Justice concurrence . . . neither binds this Court nor provides a sound basis to deviate from the uniform conclusion of all courts to have considered the issue that the Attorney General is statutorily authorized to appoint a Special Counsel."

Nevertheless on July 15—just two weeks after the Supreme Court's immunity decision—Cannon issued a 93-page opinion dismissing the classified papers case on the ground Thomas had advocated: that the special counsel was inconsistent with "the role of Congress in the appointment of constitutional officers, and the role of Congress in authorizing expenditures by law."[41] (Thomas may have advanced this superfluous dictum, and Cannon have eagerly embraced it, because both knew Trump could not invoke the immunity the Court's Republican majority had just created since his term had ended before he engaged in the alleged criminal acts.) Rep. Gaetz promptly posted a photo of the judge on X with the caption: "Future Supreme Court Justice Cannon." *The Washington Post* editorialized: "Judge Cannon goes another step too far" by adopting "many conservatives' shared vision for the Justice Department: one that possesses no independence from the person in the Oval Office." Georgetown law professor Neal Katyal, who had drafted the special counsel laws when he served in the OLC, said Cannon's decision "is legally unsupported, ignores decades of precedent and is deeply dangerous." Smith appealed on July 17. On July 30, Garland appeared on NBC News sitting in the DoJ law library. "I picked this room for this interview. . . . For more than 20 years, I was a federal judge. Do I look like somebody who would make that basic mistake about the law? I don't think so." "I think the lessons of Watergate are that there has to be a separation between the Justice Department and the White House . . . to ensure confidence in the rule of law, to ensure confidence that our law enforcement efforts are not political." Retired D MA Judge Nancy Gertner, ethics experts Stephen Gillers and James Sample, and CREW asked the Eleventh Circuit to let them file an amicus brief seeking to remove Cannon from the case. State Democracy Defenders Action, representing former government officials, made a similar request. Trump said criticism of judges should be illegal. "The DoJ should look into the legality of these people taking a brilliant judge [Cannon] and demeaning her . . . it's called playing the ref." On Sept. 17, Trump sought a 30-day extension to respond to the appeal, to Oct. 25, which the Eleventh Circuit granted.

The evidence was clear and uncontested that Trump violated the Presidential Records Act by illegally retaining government documents and probably violated the Espionage Act by his careless handling of classified material. Each time he grudgingly surrendered additional records, over the course of three years, he offered further proof of his offenses. He repeatedly defied government demands to relinquish documents and permit searches. He could not resist showing off classified documents to unauthorized people, even boasting to an Australian billionaire about secret US nuclear submarine capabilities.[42] Trump made the bizarre and patently baseless claim that he could declassify a document simply by thinking about it. He sought to conceal and cover up his misconduct: ordering Nauta to move file boxes between storage rooms and Trump's residence to prevent their discovery, destroy videotapes of those movements, and avoid cameras in the future, and he paid for the lawyers of employees to ensure their "loyalty." (This reprised the seven-hour gap in White House records of Trump's phone calls on January 6, see Abel 2024b: Chapter 4.5, and Trump's efforts to protect cronies prosecuted for alleged collaboration with Russia, see Abel 2024a: Chapter 3, and to influence the testimony of Cassidy Hutchinson before the January 6 Select Committee, see this volume, Chapter 2.3.)

Trump also exploited the investigation and prosecution for political advantage. He insinuated (without any basis) that the FBI had planted evidence and called for its defunding (after condemning BLM protesters for advocating the defunding of police who had killed unarmed Black men). He and his supporters in Congress and the right-wing media threatened violence if he were indicted. (There were numerous threats against FBI agents and one violent attack.) He claimed victimization, warning supporters that they, too, could be investigated and prosecuted. (Did they illegally possess government documents or mishandle classified information?) Trump drew false analogies between his patently illegal conduct and his baseless allegations against Obama, Hillary Clinton, and Biden. He and his supporters tried to politicize the criminal justice process by accusing it of politicization. Republicans in Congress attempted to intimidate and even defund the DoJ. Trump claimed election interference while simultaneously appealing for campaign contributions. Trump exploited the boilerplate instructions governing the August 2022 FBI search to falsely portray it as an assassination attempt.

From the outset, Judge Cannon sought to delay the proceedings, openly favoring the ex-president who had recently nominated her. She quickly confirmed the ABA's unusual rating of her as merely qualified by finding (without a hearing) that Trump retained some executive privilege after leaving office and gratuitously appointing Judge Dearie as special master to review evidence the FBI had already reviewed. She then overruled Dearie, a Reagan appointee with over 30 years more experience, who was critical of defense strategy. The appointment itself was harshly condemned and overturned by two Eleventh Circuit panels (including one Obama appointee, one by GWB, and two by Trump). But it succeeded in delaying proceedings for three months (two of them at the defense's behest). Cannon rebuffed the advice to decline the case proffered by two senior judges (one the Chief Judge and a Republican appointee), perhaps seeing it as an opportunity to repay Trump's favor and gain national prominence and possibly promotion. Her complicity with Trump (by obstructing prosecution efforts to obtain evidence) contrasted sharply with how DDC Judge Howell (Obama) handled the grand jury proceedings, and Howell's decisions, unlike Cannon's, were affirmed by the Court of Appeals. Cannon departed from the practice of having Mag. Judge Reinhart deal with most pre-trial matters, even though he was far more experienced; and she held time-consuming hearings on matters normally decided more quickly on the papers. Cannon ruled against prosecutors on technicalities: changing the sequence of files in a document box; failing to consult with the defense before seeking a gag order; the specificity of a warrant. She offered gratuitous criticism of prosecutorial motions. She denied a motion to seal the list of witnesses, thereby exposing them to possible pressure (contrast Justice Merchan, see Chapter 3.1). She delayed decisions on contested discovery motions. Her conduct of the case was harshly criticized by legal academics and ethicists,[43] government lawyers,[44] a former judge,[45] even a Republican stalwart like Barr.[46] She took the unusual step of inviting conservative amici to submit briefs about the special counsel appointment. She indefinitely postponed the trial. Few if any of these decisions were appealable before a final judgment. And then she defied precedent by invalidating Smith's appointment (following Thomas's suggestion). Regardless of whether she is reversed (as many expect), Cannon achieved her goal: preventing a trial before Election Day in the hope Trump would win and appoint a compliant Attorney General who would terminate the prosecution (as Barr had done for Michael Flynn, see Abel 2024a: Chapter 3.1.b).

4.2 The 2020 Election Case

On November 17, 2022, Garland named Jack Smith special counsel to investigate the efforts of Trump and others to overturn the 2020 election.[47] Pence, one of the first witnesses Smith sought to interview, refused to comply with the subpoena, citing the speech or debate clause.

> I don't know if it is criminal to listen to bad advice from lawyers. The truth is, what the president was repeating is what he was hearing from that gaggle of attorneys around him. Presidents, just like all of us that have served in public life, you have to rely on your team.

J. Michael Luttig, the retired Court of Appeals judge who had called it "the highest honor of my life" to advise Pence he could not disregard the Electoral College vote on January 6 (see Abel 2024b: Chapter 4.5), condemned this decision. "For me, this is a moment where you have to decide where you stand, and I stand on the Constitution of the United States." By characterizing it as a "'Biden D.O.J. subpoena,' Mr. Pence is trying to score points with voters. . . . But Jack Smith's subpoena was neither politically motivated nor designed to strengthen President Biden's political hand in 2024." Trump invoked executive privilege to block testimony by Pence and his former subordinates Greg Jacob and Marc Short. DDC Chief Judge Howell (Obama) compelled the testimony of Trump subordinates Mark Meadows, John McEntee, Nicholas Luna, Robert C. O'Brien, Dan Scavino, John Ratcliffe, Stephen Miller, and Kenneth Cuccinelli. DDC Judge Boasberg (Obama) (who replaced Howell as chief judge, with responsibility for the grand jury) held that Pence was not protected by executive privilege but might have a limited privilege under the speech or debate clause. Trump appealed, but the DC Circuit affirmed (Millett and Wilkins (both Biden) and Katsas (Trump)). The same panel also affirmed Judge Howell's order that Meadows, Scavino, Miller, O'Brien, Ratcliffe, Cuccinelli, and others had to answer questions.

After being informed in July 2023 that he was a target in the investigation, Trump said: "nothing like this has ever happened in our country before or even close."[48] He protested on Truth Social:

> HORRIFYING NEWS for our Country. . . . Deranged Jack Smith. . . . Joe Biden's Attorney General, Merrick Garland, who I turned down for the United States Supreme Court (in retrospect, based on his corrupt and

> unethical actions, a very wise decision!), together with Joe Biden's Department of Injustice, have effectively issued a third indictment and Arrest of Joe Biden's NUMBER ONE POLITICAL OPPONENT. . . . They illegally spied on my Campaigns, attacked me with a totally Fake "Dossier" that was funded by Hillary Clinton's Campaign and the DNC, Impeached me twice (I won!), they failed on the Mueller Witch Hunt (No Collusion!), they failed on the Russia, Russia, Russia Hoax, the 51 "Intelligence" Agents fraud, the FBI/Twitter files, the DOJ/Facebook censorship, and every other scam imaginable. . . . the DOJ staffed and runs the D.A.'s Office in Manhattan . . . Atlanta, where the DOJ are in strict, and possibly illegal, coordination with the DA, whose record on murder and other violent crime is abysmal. . . . THIS WITCH HUNT IS ALL ABOUT ELECTION INTERFERENCE AND A COMPLETE AND TOTAL POLITICAL WEAPONIZATION OF LAW ENFORCEMENT! . . . Under the United States Constitution, I have the right to protest an Election that I am fully convinced was Rigged and Stolen, just as the Democrats have done against me in 2016, and many others have done over the ages. . . . the Democrats have gone much further than has ever happened before—they cheated on the elections. . . . The prosecutor involved in this case, and likewise the Boxes Hoax, the Manhattan and Atlanta DAs, the New York Attorney General, etc., has been overturned unanimously in the Supreme Court and caused the Lois Lerner IRS scandal, and failed miserably in his prosecution of John Edwards, where the case was forced to be dropped along with numerous other catastrophes. He has had a vicious but disastrous career, and is a known biased and obsessed Trump Hater (as is his family) . . . these are all Hoaxes and Scams made up to stop me from fighting for the American People—BUT I WILL NEVER STOP! . . . So interesting that in this case the information was delivered to me on a Sunday night, less than 24 hours after I suggested during a major speech that the Federal Government ASSUME CONTROL of a filthy, unsanitary, neglected, and crime-ridden Washington, D.C., where murder and violent crime are rampant and people no longer want to go to our Nation's Capital . . . and yet, that is where Biden's DOJ actually wants my trial to take place, all because they think especially after my strong words of a Federal takeover at the speech, a D.C. Jury will do whatever they want.

Two Republicans still seeking the presidential nomination responded cautiously.[49] DeSantis characteristically waffled:

> There's a difference between being brought up on criminal charges and doing things. I think it was shown how [Trump] was in the White House and didn't do anything while things were going on. . . . He should have come out more forcefully, of course, but to try to criminalize that, that's a different issue entirely. . . . I hope he doesn't get charged.

Pence repeated he was "not convinced that the president acting on bad advice of a group of crank lawyers that came into the White House in the days before Jan. 6 is actually criminal." Rep. Stefanik denounced this as "another example of Joe Biden's weaponized Department of Justice targeting his top political opponent." Rep. McCarthy said: "President Trump went up in the polls and actually was surpassing President Biden for reelection, so what do they do now? Weaponize government to go after their number-one opponent." Rep. Scalise asked rhetorically: "Is there a double standard? Is justice being administered equally?" Rep. Greene declared: "I STAND WITH PRESIDENT TRUMP!" Rep. Boebert called the indictment "nothing but background noise." Rep. Jordon said it was "as wrong as it gets."

A month later, Smith charged Trump with four counts of conspiring to defraud the US and obstruct an official proceeding and against people's rights.[50] Smith included six unindicted co-conspirators (unnamed but easily identifiable): "an attorney who was willing to spread knowingly false claims and pursue strategies that the defendant's 2020 re-election campaign attorneys would not" (Giuliani); "an attorney who devised and attempted to implement a strategy to leverage the Vice-President's ceremonial role overseeing the certification" (Eastman); "an attorney whose unfounded claims of election fraud the defendant privately acknowledged to others sounded crazy" (Powell); "a Justice Department official who . . . attempted to use the Justice Department to open sham election crime investigations and influence state legislatures with knowingly false claims of election fraud" (Clark); "an attorney who assisted in devising and attempting to implement a plan to submit fraudulent slates of presidential electors to obstruct the certification proceeding" (Chesebro); and "a political consultant who helped implement a plan to submit fraudulent slates of presidential electors" (Epshteyn).

Trump condemned this "pathetic attempt" to interfere with the election.[51] "It's not just my freedom on the line, but yours as well—and I will NEVER let them take it from you." The campaign assailed the indictment as

> nothing more than the latest corrupt chapter in the continued pathetic attempt by the Biden Crime Family and their weaponized Department of Justice to interfere with the 2024 presidential election. . . . Why was it announced the day after the big Crooked Joe Biden scandal broke out from the Halls of Congress? The answer is, election interference The lawlessness of these persecutions of President Trump and his supporters is reminiscent of Nazi Germany in the 1930s, the former Soviet Union, and other authoritarian, dictatorial regimes. President Trump has always followed the law and the Constitution, with advice from many highly accomplished attorneys.

Trump lawyer John Lauro said his client was "entitled" to "trust advice of counsel." Lauro planned to seek a change of venue to West Virginia, which was "close by" and "much more diverse than Washington D.C., which I think went 95 percent for Mr. Biden." (Actually, 92 percent, compared to

30 percent in West Virginia. Black people are 3 percent of the population in West Virginia, 45 percent in DC.) Lauro vowed to "relitigate every single issue in the 2020 election," using the "subpoena power."

Rep. McCarthy denounced this effort to "attack the frontrunner for the Republican nomination" and distract from the Bidens.[52] Republican hopefuls jumped on the bandwagon. DeSantis called for a law allowing defendants to remove a case from DC to their home districts. (That would almost certainly be unconstitutional, as this Harvard law graduate knew.) "A D.C. jury would indict a ham sandwich and convict a ham sandwich if it was a Republican ham sandwich. . . . I think the juries are stacked."

> Washington, D.C. is a "swamp" and it is unfair to have to stand trial before a jury that is reflective of the swamp mentality. One of the reasons our country is in decline is the politicization of the rule of law. No more excuses—I will end the weaponization of the federal government.

Scott said: "We're watching Biden's D.O.J. continue to hunt Republicans while protecting Democrats." Ramaswamy called the indictment "unAmerican." "The corrupt federal police just won't stop until they've achieved their mission: eliminate Trump." "Trump isn't responsible for what happened on Jan. 6. The real cause was systematic and pervasive censorship of citizens in the year leading up to it." But Pence, abruptly reversing course, saw a chance to separate himself from the pack: "Anyone who puts himself over the Constitution should never be President of the United States."

The case was randomly assigned to DDC Judge Chutkan (Obama), who had imposed some of the harshest sentences on January 6 defendants (an average of 103 percent of prosecutors' recommended prison time, compared to 70 percent for all Democratic appointees, see Abel 2025: Tables 4.1, 4.2).[53] Sen. Cruz called her "far left," falsely accusing her of being "the only federal judge in Washington, D.C. who has sentenced Jan 6 defendants to sentences longer than the government requested."[54] (Judges Jackson, Lamberth, and Cooper also had done so.)

Before leaving for arraignment in DC, Trump said on Truth Social: "I AM NOW GOING TO WASHINGTON, D.C. TO BE ARRESTED FOR HAVING CHALLENGED A CORRUPT, RIGGED, & STOLEN ELECTION. IT IS A GREAT HONOR, BECAUSE I AM BEING ARRESTED FOR YOU."[55] He said of the anticipated Georgia case: "I NEED ONE MORE INDICTMENT TO ENSURE MY ELECTION!" (See Chapter 3.2.) After pleading not guilty, Trump assailed the "political persecution."

> If these illegal persecutions succeed, if they're allowed to set fire to the law, then it will not stop with me. Their grip will close even tighter around YOU. It's not just my freedom on the line, but yours as well, and I will NEVER let them take it from you.

"It was also very sad driving through Washington, D.C., and seeing the filth and the decay and all of the broken buildings and walls and the graffiti. This is not the place that I left." (As president, he had seen the city only from his helicopter.) The campaign said Smith "has conducted a dirty, politically motivated investigation of President Trump to prevent him from winning back the presidency." Other Republican candidates hedged their bets. DeSantis suggested he would pardon Trump "just like Ford pardoned Nixon" (not a great precedent) but added that claims the election had been stolen were "unsubstantiated." Not to be upstaged (and waffling once again), Pence said he would "always give a thoughtful, prayerful consideration" to "whatever pardon request comes before me."

Responding to the indictment, *The New York Times* said: "of all the ways that Donald Trump desecrated his office as president, the gravest . . . was his attempt to undermine the Constitution and overturn the results of the 2020 election, hoping to stay in office."[56] *The Washington Post* urged that Trump "be drummed out of the GOP" and "never again be allowed anywhere near the oval office."

DDC Mag. Judge Moxila A. Upadhyaya ordered Trump not to communicate with any witnesses except through lawyers or in their presence.[57] "I want to remind you it is a crime to intimidate a witness or retaliate against anyone for providing information about your case to the prosecution, or otherwise obstruct justice. Do you understand these warnings, sir?" Trump nodded yes and swore he could comply. Within a day, however, he threatened on Truth Social: "IF YOU GO AFTER ME, I'M COMING AFTER YOU!" His campaign defended the post as the "definition of political speech." A spokesman explained it was "in response to the RINO, China-loving, dishonest special interest groups and Super PACs, like the ones funded by the Koch brothers and the Club for no Growth." Trump protested he was "not allowed to speak," but insisted defiantly: "I will talk about" the trial. "They're not taking away my First Amendment rights." "They want to take away my freedom because I will never let them take away your freedom. They want to silence me because I will never let them silence you." Lauro rationalized that "because of the campaign and I would say because of his personality, it's impossible for him not to speak out on issues." Judge Chutkan replied that "the fact that he is running a political campaign . . . must yield to the orderly administration of justice." "If that means he can't say exactly what he wants to say about witnesses in this case, then that's how it's going to be." She instructed Lauro: "to the extent your client wants to make statements on the internet, they have to always yield to witness security and witness safety." "I will take whatever measures are necessary to safeguard the integrity of these proceedings." She sought to protect "sensitive materials," like "personally identifying information" about witnesses and any testimony before the grand jury.

Seeking to distinguish himself, Pence doubled down on Trump's culpability.[58] "The American people deserve to know that President Trump and his advisers didn't just ask me to pause. They asked me to reject votes, return votes, essentially to overturn the election." A furious Trump retorted he never told "Pence to put me above the Constitution, or that Mike was too honest." "He's delusional, and now he wants to show he's a tough guy." "WOW, it's finally happened! Liddle' Mike Pence, a man who was about to be ousted as Governor Indiana [sic] until I came along made him V.P., has gone over to the Dark Side." (Pence had been elected governor in 2012 by 75,000 votes, a margin of 3 percent.) "I never told a newly emboldened (not based on his 2% poll numbers!) Pence to put me above the constitution, or that Mike was 'too honest.'" Trump also complained that the "deranged" Smith waited to bring the case until "RIGHT IN THE MIDDLE" of the election campaign.

Lauro asserted: "What President Trump didn't do is direct Vice-President Pence to do anything. He asked him in an aspirational way."[59] (Actually, Trump had told Pence that if he certified the vote he would be a "wimp" and a "pussy," adding: "I don't want to be your friend anymore." See Abel 2024b: Chapter 4.5.) The Georgia phone call to Raffensperger also "was an aspirational ask." (Actually, Trump had warned that Raffensperger was committing a "criminal offense" and taking a "big risk." See Abel 2024b: Chapter 4.4.) "When it comes to political speech, you can not only advocate for a position, but you can take action, you can petition, you can ask even your vice-president to pause the vote. Asking is aspirational. Asking is not action. It's core free speech." "Mr. Trump is not a lawyer . . . he's a political leader and a businessman. What Mr. Eastman was saying, as an attorney is that there is a constitutional pathway to making this ask." (A California State Bar Court judge has recommended that Eastman be disbarred for that advice, see Chapter 5.4.6.) "The Vice President will be our best witness."

> President Trump wanted to get to the truth. At the end he asked Mr. Pence to pause the voting for 10 days, allow the state legislatures to weigh in, and then they could make a determination to audit or re-audit or certify.

Pence pushed back:

> What I want the American people to know is that President Trump was wrong then and he's wrong now: that I had no right to overturn the election, I had no right to reject votes or return votes, and that, by God's grace, I did my duty under the Constitution of the United States, and I always will.

Trump boasted: "I am leading in all Polls, including against Crooked Joe, but this is not a level playing field. It is Election Interference, & the Supreme Court must intercede. MAGA!"[60] He said on Truth Social on August 5:

> THERE IS NO WAY I CAN GET A FAIR TRIAL WITH THE JUDGE "ASSIGNED" TO THE RIDICULOUS FREEDOM OF SPEECH/FAIR

> ELECTIONS CASE. EVERYBODY KNOWS THIS, AND SO DOES SHE! WE WILL BE IMMEDIATELY ASKING FOR RECUSAL OF THIS JUDGE ON VERY POWERFUL GROUNDS, AND LIKEWISE FOR VENUE CHANGE OUT IF [sic] D.C.

Chutkan was "the judge of [Smith's] 'dreams' (WHO MUST BE RECUSED!)." "She obviously wants me behind bars. VERY BIASED & UNFAIR." Among his "many reasons" for seeking a change of venue was "that I am calling for a federal takeover of this filthy and crime ridden embarrassment to our nation." He falsely asserted that homicides in D.C. "just shattered the all-time record," and "other violent crimes have never been worse." (Homicides increased from 2022–23 but dropped below the 2022 level in 2024. At least 12 Jan. 6 defendants had made similar change of venue motions, all of which were denied. Chutkan said in one case: "defendant's assumptions concerning party affiliation in the District are not an appropriate basis for changing venue.")

The day after Trump warned on Truth Social: "If you go after me I'm coming after you," Abigail Jo Shry left a voice mail at Chutkan's chambers, using a racial slur and threatening that "If Trump doesn't get elected in 2024, we are coming to kill you, so tread lightly, bitch."[61] Shry also threatened to kill Rep. Sheila Jackson Lee (D-Texas) and all Washington Democrats. Chutkan got other racist threats. (Shry was promptly charged and jailed.)

In a motion seeking a January 2, 2024, trial date, prosecutors revealed they had given the defense 11.6 million documents or pages plus a hard drive.[62] They wanted the trial "as soon as possible" because Trump was posting about it almost daily, which "potentially prejudices the jury pool." The defense proposed April 2026, saying it would have to review 99,762 pages a day to finish the initial government production by Dec. 11, when jury selection would begin. Trump declared "the trials should be after the election. Because this is just election interference." Lauro claimed he needed two years because there were 250 potential government witnesses. "For a federal prosecutor to suggest that we could go to trial in four months is not only absurd, it's a violation of the oath of justice." When he cited *Powell v. Alabama*, the 1932 Supreme Court decision reversing the notorious convictions of the Black Scottsboro boys, Judge Chutkan said the two cases were "profoundly different": Trump would face trial seven months after being indicted, whereas Powell did so in just a week. She scheduled the trial for March 4, 2024. The defense request for April 2026 was "far beyond what is necessary" to prepare. Prosecutors said there would be only "a limited amount" of classified information—about 5–10 sensitive documents of less than 100 pages and 125 pages of transcript interviews—and they would not introduce any classified documents at trial. Trump complained on Truth Social that Chutkan, "a biased, Trump Hating Judge gave me only a two months extension, just what our corrupt government wanted." "I will APPEAL!"

Trump asked Chutkan to recuse herself because of her statements when sentencing January 6 defendants: "people in the mob were there in fealty, in loyalty, to one man—not the constitution"; "it's a blind loyalty to one person who, by the way, remains free to this day"; "the people who may be the people who planned this and funded it haven't been charged"; "people who exhorted you and encouraged you and rallied you to go and take action and to fight have not been charged."[63] She denied the motion, saying Trump's lawyers had applied a "hypersensitive, cynical, and suspicious" reading of her language. The Court "was fulfilling its duty to expressly evaluate the defendants' arguments that their sentences should be reduced because other individuals whom they believed were associated with the events of Jan. 6 had not been prosecuted." "Motions for recusal could also be wrongfully deployed as a form of judge shopping" and "a procedural weapon to harass opponents and delay proceedings."

Prosecutors asked Chutkan to limit Trump's speech because

> the defendant's repeated, inflammatory public statements regarding the District of Columbia, the Court, prosecutors, and potential witnesses are substantially likely to materially prejudice the jury pool, create fear among potential jurors, and result in threats or harassment to individuals he singles out.[64]

The motion listed those threatened after Trump condemned their refusal to support his false election allegations. Trump claimed that Smith inappropriately met with White House officials before the Florida indictment. But Trump "well knows" from documents that prosecutors "conducted a routine investigative interview of a career military official at that official's duty station—the White House." The same day Trump said Smith "wants to take away my right to speaking [sic] freely and openly." A Trump spokesman accused the DoJ of "corruptly and cynically continuing to attempt to deprive President Trump of his First Amendment rights." Trump again called Smith "deranged." "They Leak, Lie, & Sue, & they won't allow me to SPEAK?" "These people are sick. They want to silence me because I will never let them silence you." "I'm campaigning for President against an incompetent person who has WEAPONIZED the DOJ & FBI to go after his Political Opponent, & I am not allowed to COMMENT?" "How else would I explain that Jack Smith is DERANGED, or Crooked Joe is INCOMPETENT?"

Three weeks later prosecutors renewed their gag motion.[65] Trump had continued to wage "a sustained campaign of prejudicial public statements" against witnesses, prosecutors and others, including Pence, Barr, and Milley. "No other criminal defendant would be permitted to issue public statements insinuating that a known witness in his case [i.e., Milley] should be executed." Furthermore, Trump had "either purchased a gun in violation of the law and his conditions of release or seeks to benefit from his supporters' mistaken belief that he did so."

Before issuing the order, Chutkan read aloud Trump's recent statements and asked both sides if these would violate it. She then prohibited all parties from "publicly targeting" Smith and his staff, her own staff, or "any other court personnel" and their families, or comment on witnesses.[66] "This is not about whether I like the language Mr. Trump uses. This is about language which presents a danger to the administration of justice." "Mr Trump can certainly claim he's being unfairly prosecuted, but I cannot imagine any other case where a defendant is allowed to call the prosecutor 'deranged,' a 'thug' or anything else." Trump could criticize Pence but not "about the events in this case. Without this restriction, there is a real risk that other witnesses may be intimidated, or other witnesses may be reluctant to come forward lest they be subject to the same harassment or intimidation." The First Amendment did not let Trump "launch a pretrial smear campaign" against those involved in the case. Lauro objected that none of those named "have suggested the criticism by Trump has led to any diminution of their ability to do their jobs. They give as good as they take." Chutkan was skeptical: "You're saying that Milley has suggested Mr. Trump should be executed?" "To write in all caps DEATH to a witness, doesn't that go too far?" The campaign denounced the order as "an absolute abomination and another partisan knife stuck in the heart of our Democracy. President Trump will continue to fight for our Constitution, the American people's right to support him and to keep our country free of the chains of weaponized and targeted law enforcement." Lauro proposed "one simple solution: Let's have this trial after the election and solve this problem." Trump complained: "they put a gag order on me, and I'm not supposed to be talking about things that bad people do. . . . I'll be the only politician in history where I won't be allowed to criticize people." He appealed the order, insisting he was "not saying anything wrong." Chutkan stayed it for eight days, pending the appeal.

Within 48 hours, Trump again railed against "Deranged Jack Smith" and threatened retaliation.[67] "These people are dirty players and they go after the political opponents. And it's a two-way street now. It can happen the other way too." "The judge doesn't like me too much. Her whole life is not liking me." After a news report that Meadows had testified in exchange for immunity, Trump said on social media: "Some people would make that deal, but they are weaklings and cowards, and so bad for the future of our Failing Nation." "I don't think that Mark Meadows is one of them, but who really knows?" Smith urged Chutkan to reissue her order because of the "immediate risk" that testimony "could be influenced or deterred by the defendant's documented pattern of targeting" witnesses. Prosecutors urged her to clarify that the ban on communications with witnesses included "indirect messages to witnesses made publicly on social media or in speeches." But the ACLU called Chutkan's order "impermissibly vague" and "broad."

Chutkan reinstated her order.[68] "The First Amendment rights of participants in criminal proceedings must yield, when necessary, to the orderly administration of justice." Trump "simply fails to acknowledge . . . evidence" that his public statements often were followed by harassment and threats against those he named. He violated her order 75 minutes after it was reinstated. "I called Bill Barr Dumb, Weak, Slow Moving, Lethargic, Gutless, and Lazy, a RINO WHO COULDN'T DO THE JOB." "So now this Moron says about me, to get even, 'his verbal skills are limited.' Well, that's one I haven't heard before. Tell that to the biggest political crowds in the history of politics, by far. Bill Barr is a LOSER!" Nineteen minutes later Trump complained: "The Corrupt Biden administration just took away my First Amendment Right To Free Speech." Within hours, Trump again called Chutkan a "very biased, Trump hating judge."

The DC Circuit (Millet and Pillard (both Obama) and Garcia (Biden)) stayed Chutkan's order while it decided the case.[69] Trump's lawyers told the court: "No court has ever imposed a gag order on the political speech of a candidate for public office, let alone a candidate for president of the United States—until now."[70] The court unanimously reinstated a narrowed order. Millet wrote: "the First Amendment unquestionably affords political speech robust protection. But . . . the existence of a political campaign or political speech does not alter the court's historical commitment or obligation to ensure the fair administration of justice in criminal cases."

> Many of former president Trump's public statements attacking witnesses, trial participants, and court staff pose a danger to the integrity of these criminal proceedings. That danger is magnified by the predictable torrent of threats of retribution and violence that the district court found when Mr. Trump speaks out forcefully against individuals in connection with this case and the 2020 election aftermath on which the indictment focuses.

Trump could talk about Smith but not other lawyers, witnesses, or court staff or the members of their families "if those statements are made with the intent to materially interfere with or to cause others to materially interfere with, counsel's or staff's work in this criminal case, or with the knowledge that such interference is highly likely to result." The en banc DC Circuit rejected a further appeal, saying no judge had requested a vote. Trump called for a government shutdown, "the last chance to defund these political prosecutions against me and other Patriots." "Republicans in Congress can and must defund all aspects of Crooked Joe Biden's weaponized Government."

Trump also moved to dismiss, asserting presidential and absolute immunity, political persecution, vagueness, double jeopardy (based on his second impeachment), and violations of the First Amendment.[71] Prosecutors replied that Trump "attempts to rewrite the indictment, claiming that it charges him with wholly innocuous, perhaps even admirable conduct." The allegation of "selective and vindictive prosecution" was "contrived from two newspaper articles citing anonymous sources." "The defendant has an established record of attempting to disrupt and delay the court's carefully considered trial date and pretrial schedule. Now the defendant has timed his motion to stay these proceedings for maximum disruptive effect."

Trump asked Chutkan to televise the trial because Smith "sought to proceed in secret."[72] Prosecutors said that was "clearly foreclosed" by federal law. Television would make the trial "a media event," with a "carnival atmosphere from which [Trump] hopes to profit by distracting, like many fraud defendants try to do, from the charges against him."[73] Prosecutors accused Trump and his lawyers of drafting court filings "with the goal of gathering media coverage rather than lawful relief."

Trump's lawyers filed 70 pages of legal motions asking Chutkan to compel prosecutors to disclose information about the FBI, DoJ national security and election integrity units, the Intelligence Community, and the DHS response to foreign interference and other threats to the election, claiming this related to Trump's belief in the fraud allegations "and related arguments regarding good faith and the absence of criminal intent."[74] They made 59 requests to identify "informants and other undercover operatives" in the January 6 riot security measures and for assessments of cyberattacks. They also sought communications between—or "coordination" by DoJ with—the Biden administration and family and DoJ interactions with Pence, who could have been motivated to align his story with prosecutors because of the investigation of his possession of classified papers (see 4.1). Chutkan denied an earlier Trump request to subpoena House members, the National Archivist, and attorneys for Biden and DHS. She wrote: "The broad scope of the records that Defendant seeks, and his vague description of their potential relevance, resemble less 'a good-faith effort to obtain identified evidence' than they do 'a general fishing expedition' that the law does not allow." Trump defended his lawyers' discovery requests.[75] "One of the great things about these trials, if the judge allows us . . . we want to show how we won the election." He claimed the government was withholding information about alleged January 6 rioters, antifa, pipe bombs found near the Capitol, and "informants, cooperators [and] undercover agents . . . involved in the assistance, planning or encouragement" of the riot. Prosecutors responded that they had produced everything they had. Defense lawyers wanted the government to "identify all Capitol Police Officers" present on January 6. Trump declared: "the cops should be charged and the protesters should be freed."

Chutkan rejected the claim of absolute immunity, citing the Federalist Papers and Washington's farewell address.[76] Trump had attempted to "usurp the reins of government." "Former presidents enjoy no special conditions on their federal criminal liability." "Defendant's four-year service as commander-in-chief did not bestow on him the divine right of kings to evade the criminal accountability that governs his fellow citizens." "While a former president's prosecution is unprecedented, so too are the allegations that a president committed the crimes with which defendant is charged." "Despite defendant's doom-saying, he points to no evidence that his criminal liability in this case will open the gates to a waiting flood of future federal prosecutions." The prospect of liability would not violate the principle that the president should operate without fear of future litigation or other "unacceptable risks." "Indeed, it is likely that a president who knows that their actions may one day be held to criminal account will be motivated to take greater care that the laws are faithfully executed" (i.e., Art. II, Section 3 of the Constitution). Chutkan also denied the claim of double jeopardy (based on the second impeachment) and invocation of the First Amendment, which "does not protect speech that is used as an instrument of a crime."

Prosecutors asked the Supreme Court for a quick review of Chutkan's decision and sought expedited DC Circuit review if the Supreme Court declined to act.[77] Within hours, the Court agreed to hear the request, telling Trump's lawyers to respond by December 20. The DC Circuit ordered them to respond by December 13. The Trump campaign objected: "There is absolutely no reason to rush this sham trial except to injure President Trump and tens of millions of his supporters." In a fundraiser, Trump said requiring him to stand trial amounted "to the DEATH of America." His lawyers asked the Court to eschew an expedited schedule: a "reckless rush to judgment" would "irreparably undermine public confidence in the judicial system." The case should be "resolved in a cautious, deliberative manner—not at breakneck speed" or "with reckless abandon." The Court declined to fast-track the appeal, leaving the issue to the DC Circuit.

Chutkan suspended pretrial hearings pending the appeal but retained the gag order.[78] The Trump campaign called her action "a big win for the rule of law." "The American people, not the courts, should decide who becomes president." Despite the suspension, prosecutors notified Chutkan they had sent Trump's legal team a draft list of exhibits they planned to use "to help ensure that trial proceeds promptly if and when" it resumes. Hours later Trump's team complained that prosecutors had "improperly and unlawfully attempted to advance this case," illicitly producing thousands of pages of discovery, which the defense refused to review "until and unless the court lifts the stay order." Lauro asked Chutkan to hold prosecutors in contempt for submitting papers during the stay. She declined to do so because prosecutors had not violated the "clear and unambiguous terms" of her order or "acted in bad faith" but directed both sides not to file "substantive" motions without permission.

After attending the DC Circuit hearing, Trump declared: "as a president you have to have immunity. If it's during the time [in office], you have absolute immunity."[79] "I think they [i.e., prosecutors] feel this is the way they're going to try and win, and that's not the way it goes." He threatened: "It'll be bedlam in the country. It's a very bad thing. It's a very bad precedent. As we said, it's the opening of a pandora's box." "I just hope we get fair treatment. Because if we don't our country's in big, big trouble. Does everybody understand what I'm saying? I think so." Biden was critical: "Trump won't do what an American president must do; he refuses to denounce political violence. So hear me clearly, I will say what Donald Trump won't: political violence is never acceptable in the United States—never, never, never." Trump repeated his threat: "Joe would be ripe for indictment. . . . He has to be careful because that can happen to him also."

Because the DC Circuit had not decided the immunity claim by February 2, Chutkan abandoned her March trial date.[80] On February 6, the Circuit (Henderson (GHWB), Pan (Biden) and Childs (Obama)) rejected immunity. The per curiam opinion began: "Former President Trump has become citizen Trump, with all of the defenses of any other criminal defendant. But any executive immunity that may have protected him as President no longer protects him against this prosecution." "Instead of inhibiting the President's lawful discretionary action, the prospect of federal criminal liability might serve as a structural benefit to deter possible abuses of power and criminal behavior." "[T]he risk that former Presidents will be unduly harassed by meritless federal criminal prosecutions appears slight." "It would be a striking paradox if the President, who alone is vested with the constitutional duty to 'take Care that the Laws be faithfully executed,' were the sole officer capable of defying those laws with impunity." "Former President Trump's alleged efforts to remain in power despite losing the 2020 election were, if proven, an unprecedented assault on the structure of government." "At bottom, former President Trump's stance would collapse our system of separated powers by placing the President beyond the reach of all three branches."

Trump took the six days the Circuit granted to seek review and then, on February 12, asked the Supreme Court for more time to seek en banc review. That Court gave prosecutors eight days to respond, but they did so in just two, stressing the "national interest in seeing" the issue resolved promptly. On February 16, the Circuit denied en banc review in a per curiam opinion by the seven Democratic appointees (Srinivasan (Obama), Millett (Obama), Pillard (Obama), Wilkins (Obama), Childs (Biden), Pan (Biden), and Garcia (Biden)). The four Republican appointees dissented (Rao, Katsas, and Walker (all Trump) and Henderson (GHWB), who had changed her mind in the intervening ten days). The presumptive executive privilege may "be defeated only by a strong showing of need," which had to be demonstrated through a process that allowed Trump to object.

On February 28, the Supreme Court scheduled argument for April 25 (the latest possible date) and issued its opinion on July 1, the last day of the term.[81] The conservative majority gave presidents "presumptive" immunity for all "official" actions unless the government could show that prosecution would pose no "dangers of intrusion on the authority and functions of the Executive Branch." The president's immunity extended to the "outer perimeter" of official acts so long as they were "not manifestly or palpably beyond his authority." Courts could not consider motive, and acts were not rendered unofficial because they violated the law. Even when prosecuting unofficial acts, the government could not introduce evidence concerning official acts. With unusual acerbity, Roberts rebuked the dissenters for their "tone of chilling doom," engaging in "fear mongering on the basis of extreme hypotheticals," "concocting" models and paradigms, using "cherry-picked sources," and being unable "to muster any meaningful textual or historical support." "We cannot afford to fixate exclusively, or even primarily, on present exigencies." Thomas concurred, gratuitously exploiting the case to address the appointment of special counsel, an issue not briefed by the parties, in order to instruct Cannon how to rule in the classified papers case (Chapter 4.1).

Sotomayor began her dissent for the three liberals by declaring that the decision "makes a mockery of the principle, foundational to our Constitution and system of Government, that no man is above the law." "A president's use of any official power for any purpose, even the most corrupt, is immune from prosecution. That is just as bad as it sounds, and it is baseless." It "narrows the conduct considered 'unofficial' almost to a nullity." The majority relied "on little more than its own misguided wisdom about the need for 'bold and unhesitating action' by the President." It "invents immunity through brute force." Its doctrine "is utterly indefensible." It ignored "settled understandings of the Constitution." Sotomayor concluded by expressing her "fear for our democracy." Jackson concurred: "the seeds of absolute power for presidents have been planted." "I worry that, after today's ruling, our Nation will reap what this Court has sown."

The New York Times later disclosed some unusual behind-the-scenes strategizing.[82] Just six days after the Circuit denied en banc review, Roberts urged the Justices to accept the case, criticizing lower court judges for having "failed to grapple with the most difficult questions altogether" and predicting that "we will view the separation of power analysis differently." He initially assigned the case to Alito but decided to write it himself after the *Times* reported the upside-down flag flying at Alito's home. During an early conference, some Justices wanted to postpone argument to the next term, but Roberts and Kavanaugh agreed with the liberals to hear it that spring. When Roberts circulated his draft, Kavanaugh praised the "extraordinary opinion," and Gorsuch joined "in thanking you for your remarkable work." Sotomayor considered concurring in part if Roberts modified the draft, but he refused.

Biden warned that the decision meant "there are virtually no limits on what the president can do."[83] Sen. Schumer said: "treason or incitement of an insurrection should not be considered a core constitutional power afforded to a president." Obama's Attorney General Eric Holder declared that "our democracy has been gravely wounded" by this "Court constructed monstrosity." Speaker Johnson condemned Biden's comments as "despicable and dangerous." "The president has been trying to undermine our legal system." Trump praised the "BRILLIANTLY WRITTEN AND WISE" decision and predicted the charges against him would "WITHER INTO OBSCURITY." Sen. Vance called it "a massive win, not just for Trump but the rule of law." Then, without seeing any contradiction, Trump called on Truth Social for jailing 15 political leaders, including Biden, Harris, Pence, McConnell, Schumer, Pelosi, Kinzinger, Schiff, Raskin, Aguilar, Lofgren, and Thompson and a televised military tribunal trial of Cheney for treason (which would clearly be illegal). Vance seconded Trump, calling the appointment of a special counsel "totally reasonable." Sen. Rubio said the Court had "clarified what the law is." (The novel unspecified distinction between official and unofficial acts did just the opposite.) Vance and Rubio were lawyers and vice-presidential hopefuls. Two former Supreme Court clerks were critical. William Baude (who clerked for Roberts) said "it's hard to tell what exactly it is trying to do." Stephen McAllister (who clerked for Thomas) said "it's certainly not really tied to the Constitution." A Ninth Circuit judge appointed by Reagan said the decision was "untenable in a democracy."[84]

The Washington Post said the "bad" decision "invites presidents to push the boundaries" but was not "the end of democracy."[85] *The New York Times* was more damning. The Court had set aside "the bedrock principle that no one is above the law" and given "a free pass to Trump." Its columnists agreed. Jamelle Bouie denounced Trump's "get-out-of jail-free card." Kate Shaw assailed the "radical decision" for "enormously increasing the power and enormously reducing the accountability of the president." Jesse Wegman called it a "monumentally awful" decision. David French said it would help Trump "dodge accountability." Harvard law professor Laurence Tribe criticized the Court for having "dispensed with the rule of law by effectively depriving the American people of crucial information."

Senate Majority Leader Schumer condemned the Court for placing "a crown on Donald Trump's head."[86] Schumer was working on legislation "classifying Trump's election subversion as unofficial acts not subject to immunity." Ignoring the fact that Trump had called for his prosecution, Minority Leader McConnell accused Democrats of wanting "to turn Washington into the Hague." Their problem was "that they won't be able to prosecute official actions that they don't like." Rep. Morelle (the top Democrat on the House Administration Committee) was drafting a constitutional amendment; Rep. Ocasio-Cortez was planning to file articles of impeachment against the six Justices in the majority. Schumer and three dozen Democrats introduced the No Kings Act to eliminate presidential immunity and bar the Court from reviewing that law. Biden proposed a "No One Is Above the Law" constitutional amendment. Justice Gorsuch warned him to "be careful." (None of the Democratic proposals had any chance of success.)

On August 2, the Court returned the case to the DDC. The next day Chutkan denied a motion to dismiss on the ground of selective prosecution because the defense had offered "no meaningful evidence," and she scheduled a status conference for August 16.[87] But on August 8, Smith asked for a three-week delay to analyze the immunity decision; defense lawyers naturally did not object. Chutkan gave both parties until August 30 and rescheduled her next hearing for September 5. On August 27, Smith filed a superseding indictment by a new grand jury, which "reflects the Government's efforts to respect and implement the Supreme Court's holdings and remand instructions." It no longer accused Trump of trying to use the DoJ to investigate election fraud or urge state legislators to choose fake electors, and it dropped Jeffrey Clark as an unindicted co-conspirator. Trump called this "an act of desperation" and the new indictment "ridiculous." On September 4 he pleaded not guilty. During a status conference on September 5, Chutkan rejected Lauro's proposal to postpone the immunity hearing until after the election, which was "not relevant" to this case. She directed prosecutors to submit an opening brief on immunity by September 26 and the defense to respond by October 17, finish their argument about the need for more discovery by September 19, and make a request by October 24 to move to dismiss on the ground of Smith's appointment, commenting that she did not find Cannon's ruling "particularly persuasive." When Lauro unwisely said Justice Thomas had "directed" the defense to make that motion, Chutkan interrupted: "He directed you to do that?" Lauro corrected himself. On September 19, defense lawyers used the discovery motion to ask Chutkan to dismiss the case or change her schedule. Chutkan allowed Smith to submit a brief of up to 180 pages (four times the usual limit), explaining: "the Supreme Court directed this court to conduct a 'close' and 'fact specific' analysis 'of the indictment's extensive and interrelated allegations.'" The brief's length "reflects the uniquely 'challenging' and factbound nature of those determinations" and serves "the efficient resolution of the immunity issues in this case 'at the earliest possible stage.'" Without seeing the brief, the defense denounced it as a "false hit piece."

On October 2, Chutkan released a redacted version of the brief.[88] After a colleague at the TCF Center in Detroit where votes were being counted on November 4, 2020 said the number favoring Biden was correct, Trump's Election Day operations chief Mike Roman emailed: "find a reason it isn't" and "give me options to file litigation even if itbis" (it is bullshit). When the colleague warned that could lead to the chaos following the South Florida count in 2000, Roman responded: "Make them riot" and "Do it!!!" On January 6, 2021, as Trump watched the riot on television, an aide reassured him that Pence had been removed to a safe location, prompting the brusque reply: "so what?" On Marine One after the election, Trump told the passengers: "It doesn't matter if you won or lost the election. You still have to fight like hell." RNC chair McDaniel refused Trump's request that she promote a report of election fraud in her home state, Michigan, because a top state official had called the report "fucking nuts." Trump now said: "The DOJ pushed out this latest 'hit job' today because JD Vance humiliated Tim Walz last night in the Debate." (It was Chutkan who had done so.) Trump ranted:

> FOR 60 DAYS PRIOR TO AN ELECTION, THE DEPARTMENT OF INJUSTICE IS SUPPOSED TO DO ABSOLUTELY NOTHING THAT WOULD TAINT OR INTERFERE WITH SAID ELECTION. THEY DISOBEYED THEIR OWN RULE IN FAVOR OF COMPLETE AND TOTAL ELECTION INTERFERENCE. I DID NOTHING WRONG, THEY DID!

Chutkan approved the release of some redacted portions, saying the defense's "blanket objections to further unsealing are without merit" and concern about the election "is not a cognizable legal prejudice."

Trump treated this prosecution—arguably the most momentous—just as he did the other three. He spewed vituperation at the principal legal actors: Garland was "corrupt" and "unethical"; Smith was a "deranged," "vicious," "biased," "obsessed Trump hater"; Chutkan was "very biased & unfair" and "Trump hating"; and the jury would be biased because it was drawn from DC. The entire prosecution was election interference and weaponization of law enforcement (inverting the reality that Trump was charged with election interference, and he was politicizing the case). It resembled the abuse of law in Nazi Germany, the former Soviet Union, and "other authoritarian, dictatorial regimes." Trump warned supporters they were equally at risk and could be gagged: "They want to take away my freedom because I will never let them take away your freedom." But those supporters were not on trial for seeking to overturn the 2020 election, and neither were they trying to undermine the courts. Trump boasted that the prosecution was improving his poll numbers and helping him raise money (both unfortunately true).

Trump used every available tactic to delay the case beyond the election, hoping that—as president—he could order a compliant Attorney General to fire Smith and end the prosecution. Trump vowed to relitigate the 2020 election and the January 6 insurrection, making massive, overbroad discovery requests (which also served to delay). He moved for a change of venue, recusal of Chutkan, and dismissal, knowing these motions would be denied but would open the door to appeals that could consume more time. He threatened to appeal Chutkan's trial schedule (a non-appealable decision). He invoked an "advice of counsel" defense, which seems to have seduced even Pence (who had relied on his own lawyers in refusing to delay certification of the Electoral College votes). Trump sought television coverage of the trial in order to turn it into a spectacle—knowing the Federal Rules of Criminal Procedure have prohibited this for more than 75 years. He attacked potential witnesses and urged others not to testify against him. This led Judge Chutkan (like Justices Engoron and Merchan, see Chapters 2.3 and 3.1) to issue a gag order, which Trump promptly exploited to claim he was being denied his First Amendment rights even as he openly defied it. (The DC Circuit limited but affirmed the order.) Trump called for a shutdown of the entire government to halt the prosecution (even though that would not have affected the judiciary). Finally, Trump uttered thinly veiled threats: "if you go after me, I'm coming after you"; "Joe would be ripe for indictment. . . . He has to be careful because that can happen to him also"; "I just hope we get fair treatment. Because if we don't our country's in big, big trouble. Does everybody understand what I'm saying? I think so." This was frightening rhetoric from a president who had summoned his supporters to a "wild" demonstration on January 6, urged them to march on the Capitol (promising to accompany them), and watched television for hours as they attacked police officers and trashed the building.

Whereas Judge Cannon used Trump's dilatory motions—and took sua sponte actions—to delay the trial, Judge Chutkan saw through that transparent defense strategy. The request for 30 months to prepare was "far beyond what is necessary." As a Black woman, she bristled at the invocation of the Scottsboro boys (nine Black teenagers sentenced to death for rape after less than three days of "trial" before an all-white Alabama jury in 1931). Most importantly, Chutkan denied Trump's claim of presidential immunity, declaring that he enjoyed no "divine right of kings to evade the criminal accountability that governs his fellow citizens." And the DC Circuit quickly and strongly affirmed, declining to review en banc. But the Supreme Court, which had taken just <u>two</u> months to dismiss the Fourteenth Amendment challenge to Trump's eligibility to run for office (see Chapter 5.2.4), postponed both oral argument and judgment to the last possible moments, taking <u>six</u> months to decide and thereby ensuring there would be no trial before the election. And then the conservative majority did just what Trump earlier had hoped "his" Supreme Court would do (overturn the election, see Abel 2024b: Chapter 4), concocting a novel (and opaque) doctrine of presidential immunity that made it difficult, perhaps impossible, for the DDC to hold him accountable for his efforts to do just that. (Trump had said in September 2018: "The Supreme Court was one of the main reasons I got elected President.")[89]

4.3 Did the Federal Courts Successfully Resist Politicization?

These two cases present many illuminating differences. Both the facts and the laws involved in the classified papers case are simpler and more straightforward than those in the 2020 election case. Immunity is not an issue in the former because all of Trump's actions occurred after he left office, nor is the First Amendment relevant. Trump's efforts to cover up his unlawful retention of the papers arguably aggravate and help to prove his crimes (as Nixon's did after Watergate). Trump claimed victimization in both cases, sought to exploit them (especially the FBI search) for political gain, and repeatedly threatened violence. He attacked the DoJ and Jack Smith in both cases while directing his venom at Judge Chutkan and the potentially hostile DC jury and lauding Judge Cannon. Two weeks before the election he said: "I would fire [Smith] within two seconds." "It's so easy."[90]

The real difference, of course, was the judges themselves. (There was a similar difference between the judges who tried Paul Manafort, briefly Trump's 2016 campaign manager: DDC Judge Jackson (Obama) and ED VA Judge Ellis (Reagan), see Abel 2024a: Chapter 3.1.c.) Judge Cannon, a Federalist Society member whom Trump had appointed, was rated only "qualified" by the ABA because she had little legal experience and even less in the few criminal cases she prosecuted and tried. She had been on the bench less than two years when she was assigned the classified papers case. Judge Chutkan—a Black woman nominated by Obama—had worked for 11 years at Public Defender Services in DC and was a partner handling complex cases at a leading litigation firm when she became a judge in 2014, eight years before being assigned the 2020 election case. Judge Cannon delayed her case for three months at the outset by inappropriately appointing a special master, favored defense efforts to delay the trial further, ensuring it could not occur before the election, and defied precedent by finding the special counsel unlawfully appointed and funded. Judge Chutkan resisted the defense's similar dilatory strategies and scheduled the trial to begin more than six months before the election, only to be thwarted by the conservative Supreme Court Justices, who took six months to decide the immunity issue and then invented a new doctrine making it difficult, perhaps impossible, to hold Trump accountable. The other federal judges involved in these cases present a familiar picture (see Tables 4.1, 4.2). All 14 Democratic appointees and five Republican appointees

TABLES 4.1 Other Judges' Decisions in Trump's Federal Criminal Prosecutions

Case	*Judge*	*Appointing president*	*For/against prosecution*
Classified papers	EDNY Dearie	Reagan	For
Same	Eleventh Circuit Pryor, Grant, Brasher	GWB, Trump, Trump	For
Same	DDC Howell	Obama	For
Same	DC Circuit Pillard, Childs, Pan	Obama, Biden, Biden	For
Same	Eleventh Circuit Rosenbaum, Grant, Brasher	Obama, Trump, Trump	For
2020 Election	DC Circuit Millet, Pillard, Garcia	Obama, Obama, Biden	For
Same	DC Circuit Henderson, Pan, Childs	GHWB, Biden, Obama	For
Same	DC Circuit en banc Srinivasan, Millet, Pillard, Wilkins, Childs, Pan, Garcia	Obama, Obama, Obama, Obama, Biden, Biden, Biden	For
Same	DC Circuit en banc dissent: Rao, Henderson, Katsas, Walker	Trump, GHWB, Trump, Trump	Against
Same	Supreme Court Roberts, Thomas, Alito, Gorsuch, Kavanaugh, Barrett	GWB, GHWB, GWB, Trump, Trump, Trump	Against
Same	Supreme Court Sotomayor, Kagan, Jackson	Obama, Obama, Biden	For

TABLE 4.2 Decisions by Party of Appointing President

Party of appointing president	*Decision for prosecution*	*Decision against prosecution*
Democratic	14	1
Republican	5	10

Chi-square = 11.6268 $p = 0.00065$ (actually stronger because my chi-square calculator did not allow 0 as the number of Democratic-appointed judges who voted against prosecution)

(including two appointed by Trump) voted for the prosecutions; all ten votes against them were by Republican appointees (including six by Trump appointees); the statistical correlation with party was strongly significant ($p = 0.00065$). Politics trumped law in both cases, preventing federal courts from holding Trump accountable before the election.

A week after Trump won the election, Jack Smith said he and his lawyers would resign before Trump took office.[91] Two weeks later Smith withdrew both cases against Trump without prejudice. Chutkan dismissed hers; Cannon had already done so. The case against Nauta and de Oliveira remained on appeal before the Eleventh Circuit. Shortly after Smith announced he was preparing to release his final report, Trump's lawyer Todd Blanche asked Garland to stop this and Judge Cannon to block it. She immediately (and predictably) did so, but the Eleventh Circuit allowed the DoJ to release the 137-page report on Chutkan's case, which it did on January 14. Smith concluded that "but for Mr. Trump's election and imminent return to the presidency, the office assessed that the admissible evidence was sufficient to obtain and sustain a conviction at trial." It accused Trump of an "unprecedented criminal effort to overturn the legitimate results of the election in order to retain power," consistently encouraging "violence against his perceived opponents" and demonstrating an "ability and willingness to use his influence and following on social media to target witnesses, courts and department employees, which required the office to engage in time-consuming litigation to protect witnesses from threats and harassment." DoJ had interviewed more than 250 witnesses and obtained grand jury testimony from more than 55; the Special Committee's evidence was only "a small part of the office's investigative record." Trump promptly lashed back. The report was "based on information that the Unselect Committee of Political Hacks and Thugs ILLEGALLY DESTROYED AND DELETED because it showed how totally innocent I was, and how completely guilty Nancy Pelosi, and others, were." "Jack is a lamebrain prosecutor who was unable to get his case tried before the Election, which I won in a landslide. THE VOTERS HAVE SPOKEN!!!" On January 17, Cannon delayed deciding whether to allow Congress to see Smith's report on her case, ensuring this would not happen before Trump took office—and probably never.

Notes

1 Alemany, Dawsey, Hamburger & Parker, "National Archives had to retrieve Trump White House records from Mar-a-Lago," *WP* (2.7.22); Zapotosky, Alemany, Parker & Dawsey, "National Archives asks Justice Dept. to investigate Trump's handling of White House records," *WP* (2.9.22); Alemany, Barrett, Zapotosky & Dawsey, "Some Trump records taken to Mar-a-Lago clearly marked as classified, including documents at 'top secret' level," *WP* (2.11.22); Zapotosky, "National Archives confirms classified material was in boxes at Trump's Mar-a-Lago residence," *WP* (2.18.22); Alemany, Dawsey, Gardner & Hamburger, "Some records sent to Jan. 6 committee were torn up, taped back together—mirroring a Trump habit," *WP* (2.1.22); Parker, Dawsey, Hamburger & Alemany, "'He never stopped ripping things up': Inside Trump's relentless document destruction habits," *WP* (2.6.22); Allen, "Haberman book: flushed papers found clogging Trump White House toilet," *Axios* (2.11.22); Barrett, Alfaro, Dawsey & Alemany, "FBI searches Trump safe at Mar-a-Largo for possible

classified documents," *WP* (8.9.22); Wagner, "Trump claims political persecution after FBI search of Mar-a-Lago residence," *WP* (8.9.22); Wagner, "Republicans call for Garland, Wray to hold news conferences, testify to Congress," *WP* (8.9.22); Wagner, "McDaniel urges outraged Republicans to donate to GOP Senate candidates," *WP* (8.9.22); Feuer, "Republican officials reacted with fury to news of the search," *NYT* (8.8.22); Fawcett, "Republican Governors criticize the Mar-a-Lago search as 'unprecedented' and 'un-American,'" *NYT* (8.8.22); Feuer, "F.B.I. search ignited violent rhetoric on the far right," *NYT* (8.10.22); Barrett & Stein, "Justice Dept. seeks to unseal motion for search warrant at Trump's Mar-a-Lago," *WP* (8.11.22); Kornfield, Hsu & Bikales, "Gunman killed after trying to breach FBI office in Ohio, authorities say," *WP* (8.11.22); Barrett & Stein, "Justice Dept. seeks to unseal motion for search warrant at Trump's Mar-a-Lago," *WP* (8.11.22); Stein, "Justice Department opposes release of Mar-a-Lago affidavit," *WP* (8.16.22); Thompson, "A timeline of Trump's false and misleading statements on the Mar-a-Lago search," *NYT* (8.16.22); Alemany, Dawsey & Helderman, "Trump team claimed boxes at Mar-a-Lago were only news clippings," *WP* (9.17.22); Haberman & Schmidt, "Lawyer told Archives last year that Trump had no classified material," *NYT* (9.17.22); Haberman, "Trump was warned late last year of potential legal peril over documents," *NYT* (9.20.22).

2 Alemany, "Archives told Trump in April that FBI would examine more than 100 classified documents returned from Mar-a-Lago," *WP* (8.23.22); Dawsey, Leonnig, Alemany and Helderman, "FBI's Mar-a-Lago search followed months of resistance, delay by Trump," *WP* (8.24.22); Dawsey & Alemany, "Archives asked for records in 2021, after Trump lawyer agreed they should be returned, email says," *WP* (8.24.22); Broadwater, Benner & Haberman, "Inside the 20-month drive to get Trump to return presidential material," *NYT* (8.27.22); Alemany, Arnsdorf & Dawsey, "Inside Trump's war on the National Archives," *WP* (8.28.22); Barrett, Alemany, Stein, Dawsey, Marimow & Leonnig, "Skepticism before a search: inside the Trump Mar-a-Lago documents investigation," *WP* (12.21.22); see Rohde (2024: xviii, 191–98).

3 Thrush, Haberman & Protess, "Trump search said to be part of effort to find highly classified material," *NYT* (8.12.22); Haberman, Thrush & Savage, "The seized documents were part of an inquiry into violation of the Espionage Act and two other laws," *NYT* (8.12.22); Barrett & Dawsey, "Agents at Trump's Mar-a-Lago seized 11 sets of classified documents, court filing shows," *WP* (8.12.22); Haberman, Thrush & Savage, "Files seized from Trump are part of Espionage Act inquiry," *NYT* (8.12.22); Alemany, "Top lawmakers seek intelligence assessment of documents from Mar-a-Lago," *WP* (8.13.22); Haberman & Thrush, "Trump lawyer told Justice Dept. that classified material had been returned," *NYT* (8.14.22); Savage, "Presidential power to declassify information, explained," *NYT* (8.14.22); Stein, "Justice Department opposes release of Mar-a-Lago affidavit," *WP* (8.16.22); Shear, "It's rare for a president to flout the tightly restricted records procedures," *NYT* (8.23.22); Broadwater, "Intelligence officials will assess security risks from Mar-a-Lago documents," *NYT* (8.28.22); Wagner, "Pence pushes back against GOP calls to 'defund the FBI,'" *WP* (8.17.22); Thompson, "A timeline of Trump's false and misleading statements on the Mar-a-Lago search," *NYT* (8.16.22); Dawsey & Arnsdorf, "Trump rakes in millions off FBI search at Mar-a-Lago," *WP* (8.17.22).

4 Bensinger & Frenkel, "Talk of 'civil war,' ignited by Mar-a-Lago search, is flaring online," *NYT* (10.5.22).

5 Feuer, "Judge in Trump search case issues written order seeking redactions," *NYT* (8.22.22); Haberman, Thrush & Feuer, "Trump, without the presidency's protections, struggles for a new strategy," *NYT* (8.24.22); Feuer, "Judge in Trump search

case issues written order seeking redactions," *NYT* (8.22.22); https://ballotpedia.org/ABA_ratings_during_the_Trump_administration; Feuer & Haberman, "Judge signals intent to appoint special master in Mar-a-Lago search," *NYT* (8.28.22); Barrett, "Trump's Mar-a-Lago documents already examined by FBI, Justice Dept. tells judge," *WP* (8.29.22); Stein, "Judge grants Trump request for special master to review Mar-a-Lago documents," *WP* (9.5.22); Savage, "'Deeply problematic': experts question judge's intervention in Trump inquiry," *NYT* (9.6.22); Mazzei, Haberman & Feuer, "Trump ruling lifts profile of judge and raises legal eyebrows," *NYT* (9.6.22); Musgrave, "Palm Beach County man gets 18 month sentence for death threats to Nancy Pelosi, other top women," *Palm Beach Post* (4.4.22); Paybarah, "Trump's lawsuit against Clinton was filed in court with judge he appointed," *WP* (9.9.22); Gregorian, "Judge dismisses Trump's lawsuit against Clinton and others as 'political manifesto,'" *NBC News* (9.9.22); Savage, "Judge fines Trump lawyers in Clinton conspiracy suit tossed in September," *NYT* (11.11.22).

6 Barrett & Stein, "Affidavit to search Trump's Mar-a-Lago says 184 classified files found in January," *WP* (8.26.22); Savage, "Possibility of obstruction looms over Trump after thwarted efforts to recover documents," *NYT* (8.27.22); Barnes & Mazzetti, "Classified materials on human intelligence sources helped trigger alarm," *NYT* (8.27.22); "The Trump affidavit shows the Mar-a-Lago search was hardly capricious," *WP* (8.26.22).

7 Stein & Barrett, "Justice Dept. seeks to regain access to classified Mar-a-Lago documents," *WP* (9.8.22); Thrush, Haberman & Schmidt, "She went out on a limb for Trump. Now she's under Justice Dept. scrutiny," *NYT* (10.12.22); "National Archives rejects Trump claim on former presidents' records," *Reuters* (10.11.22); Barrett & Stein, "Justice Dept. says it would accept Trump's candidate for special master," *WP* (9.12.22); Barrett & Stein, "Dearie named special master to review Trump's Mar-a-Lago documents," *WP* (9.16.22); Savage, Feuer & Thrush, "Judge keeps block on inquiry into Mar-a-Lago files and names special master," *NYT* (9.16.22); Barrett, "Justice Dept. appeals judge's rulings on classified material in Mar-a-Lago case," *WP* (9.17.22); Thrush, Feuer & Savage, "U.S. asks appeals court to restore access to sensitive records seized from Trump," *NYT* (9.17.22); Stein, Barrett & Jacobs, "Special master prods Trump lawyers: 'You can't have your cake and eat it,'" *WP* (9.21.22); Feuer & Savage, "Special master expresses skepticism of declassification claims by Trump's lawyers," *NYT* (9.21.22).

8 Barrett, "Appeals court: Justice Dept. can use Mar-a-Lago documents in criminal probe," *WP* (9.21.22); Trump v. U.S., 11th Circuit (9.21.22); Savage, Thrush & Feuer, "Appeals court frees Justice Dept. to use sensitive files seized from Trump," *NYT* (9.22.22); Thrush, Feuer & Savage, "Trump claims he declassified documents. Why don't his lawyers say so in court?" *NYT* (9.23.22); Barnes & Barrett, "Trump asks Supreme Court to intervene in Mar-a-Lago search case," *WP* (10.4.22); Stein & Barnes, "Justice Dept. asks Supreme Court to deny Trump request in Mar-a-Lago case," *WP* (10.12.22); Liptak, "Supreme Court rejects Trump request to intervene in documents case," *NYT* (10.14.22); Stein, "Justice Dept. asks appeals court to end Mar-a-Lago special master," *WP* (10.14.22); "The latest Mar-a-Lago ruling underscores the frivolity of Trump's complaints," *WP* (10.15.22).

9 Stein, "Dearie asks Trump lawyers whether they believe FBI lied about seized documents," *WP* (9.22.22); Thomsen & Lynch, "Trump objects to verifying list of property seized from Florida estate—court filing," *Reuters* (9.28.22); Stein, "Judge rules Trump lawyers don't have to clarify Mar-a-Lago document claims," *WP* (9.29.22); Savage & Feuer, "Judge overrules special master's demands to Trump in document review," *NYT* (9.29.22); Savage & Thrush, "Jan. 6 and Mar-a-Lago inquiries converge in fights over executive privilege," *NYT* (10.1.22);

Savage & Feuer, "In documents review, special master tells Trump team to back up privilege claims," *NYT* (10.19.22).

10 Mark, "Trump says presidents can declassify docs 'even by thinking about it,'" *WP* (9.22.22); Dawsey & Alemany, "Trump's lawyer refused his request in February to say all documents returned," *WP* (10.3.22); Folmar, "National Archives alerted Trump of missing Kim Jong Un letter in May 2021," *The Hill* (10.3.22); Barrett & Dawsey, "Trump worker told FBI about moving Mar-a-Lago boxes on ex-president's orders," *WP* (10.12.22); Raju, "Top GOP senators reject Trump's declassification comments and call for proper storage of secret records," *CNN* (9.22.22).

11 Paybarah, "Barr says no 'legitimate reason' for Trump to have classified documents," *WP* (9.3.22); Thrush, "Barr dismisses Trump's request for a special master," *NYT* (9.3.22); Gans, "Barr says DOJ 'getting very close' to having enough evidence to indict Trump," *The Hill* (9.7.22); Schmidt, Haberman & Benner, "Justice Dept. is said to believe Trump has more documents," *NYT* (10.7.22).

12 Savage & Feuer, "F.B.I. found 48 empty folders that had contained classified documents at Trump's home," *NYT* (9.3.22).

13 Stein & Devlin, "Trump Mar-a-Lago special master struck down by appeals court," *WP* (12.1.22); Feuer & Savage, "Appeals court scraps special master review in Trump documents case," *NYT* (12.2.22); Stein, "Mar-a-Lago special master formally dismissed; Trump not expected to appeal," *WP* (12.9.22); Savage & Feuer, "Two Trump-appointed judges rebuke a third for bending the law in his favor," *NYT* (12.3.22); Quinn, "Judge formally dismisses Trump's case over Mar-a-Lago search after special master review ends," *CBS News* (12.12.22).

14 "Donald Trump is not above the law," *NYT* (8.26.22); Bellware, "There will be 'riots in the street' if Trump is prosecuted, Graham says," *WP* (8.30.22); "Lindsey Graham's prediction of riots reads more like a threat," *WP* (8.30.22); Marcus, "Trump again summons the mob," *WP* (8.30.22); Edmonson, "McCarthy embraces Trump's assault on the Justice Department over the Mar-a-Lago search," *NYT* (9.2.22); Tankersley, "Biden calls Trump 'irresponsible' over Mar-a-Lago documents," *NYT* (9.19.22).

15 Stein & Barrett, "Garland to name special counsel for Trump Mar-a-Lago, 2020 election probes," *WP* (11.18.22); Thrush, Savage, Haberman & Feuer, "Garland names special counsel for Trump inquiries," *NYT* (11.19.22); "The new Trump probe special counsel should move quickly," *WP* (11.19.22).

16 Dawsey, Alemany & Hsu, "Judge rules Trump lawyer Corcoran must testify, people familiar say," *WP* (3.17.23); Barber, "Trump attorney ordered to testify again," *WSJ* (3.18.23); Feuer & Haberman, "Judge rules Trump lawyer must testify in documents inquiry," *NYT* (3.18.23); Feuer, "Trump documents inquiry prompts clash in appeals court," *NYT* (3.22.23); Dawsey, Barrett, Alemany & Weiner, "Trump lawyer must turn over evidence on classified documents, court rules," *WP* (3.22.23); Feuer, "Trump documents inquiry prompts clash in appeals court," *NYT* (3.22.23); Haberman, Feuer, Protess & Rashbaum, "Court action underscores peril for Trump in documents investigation," *NYT* (3.24.23).

17 Pager, Barrett, Alemany & Stein, "Justice Dept. reviewing classified documents found in Biden's post-Vice Presidential office," *WP* (1.10.23); Linskey, "Biden think tank had classified files," *WSJ* (1.10.23); Stein, Barrett & Viser, "Garland appoints special counsel to probe Biden classified documents," *WP* (1.12.23); Shpigel, "Biden papers: how events have unfolded," *NYT* (1.13.23); Thrush, Baker & Savage, "Special counsel to review handling of Biden records," *NYT* (1.13.23); Pager, Leonnig & Barrett, "More classified documents found at Biden's Wilmington home, White House says," *WP* (1.14.23); Palmer, "Donald Trump calls special counsel investigating him a 'terrorist,'" *Newsweek* (1.17.23); Shear &

Rogers, "Investigators seize more classified documents from Biden's home," *NYT* (1.22.23); Viser & Pager, "Justice Dept. search of Biden home in Wilmington turns up more documents," *WP* (1.21.23); Thrush & Broadwater, "Washington adjusts to altered landscape after Justice Dept. installs special counsel," *NYT* (1.24.23); Paybarah & Knowles, "Classified documents discovered at home of former Vice President Mike Pence," *WP* (1.24.23); Haberman, "Classified documents found at Pence's home in Indiana," *NYT* (1.25.23); Schmidt, "How the hasty packing of Biden papers led to a special counsel inquiry," *NYT* (2.10.23); Stein, "Justice Dept. search Pence's office; no classified items found, aide says," *WP* (2.18.23); Abutaleb, "No visitors logs exist for Biden's Wilmington home, White House says," *WP* (1.17.23); Stein & Dawsey, "FBI finds one additional document with classified markings at Pence home," *WP* (2.11.23); Stein, "Justice Dept. search Pence's office; no classified items found, aide says," *WP* (2.18.23); Haberman & Thrush, "Pence won't face charges in documents investigation," *NYT* (6.3.23); Alemany, Dawsey, Hsu, Barrett & Helderman, "Items with classified markings found at Trump storage unit in Florida," *WP* (12.8.22); Feuer, "Judge rules for Justice Dept. in dispute with Trump over documents search," *NYT* (1.6.23); Dawsey, "Trump legal team hands over additional classified folder to Justice Department," *WP* (2.10.23); "Special counsel Robert Hur's report on Biden's handling of classified documents," *CNN* (2.8.24).

18 Palmer, "Donald Trump calls special counsel investigating him a 'terrorist,'" *Newsweek* (1.17.23).

19 Barrett, Dawsey & Stein, "Justice Dept. said to have more evidence of possible Trump obstruction at Mar-a-Lago," *WP* (4.3.23); Paybarah, Harwell & Marimow, "Trump claims judge overseeing New York case 'hates' him. His lawyer says it isn't true," *WP* (4.3.23).

20 Alemany, Hsu, Barrett & Dawsey, "Trump lawyers ask Justice Dept. not to charge Trump in classified documents case," *WP* (6.5.23); Barrett, Stein & Dawsey, "Trump charged in classified documents case, second indictment in months," *WP* (6.8.23); Knowles, "Trump, defiant, some 2024 GOP rivals supportive as he faces Department of Justice charges," *WP* (6.9.23); Kessler, "Trump's indictment video features a litany of favorite falsehoods," *WP* (6.9.23); Broadwater, "House Republicans rally behind Trump, adopting his false narrative about the indictment," *NYT* (6.9.23); Weisman, "Chris Christie says he found the case laid out in the indictment 'devastating,'" *NYT* (6.9.23); Nehemas & Weisman, "Carefully, backhandedly, DeSantis comes to Trump's defense," *NYT* (6.9.23); "Donald Trump should never again be trusted with the nation's secrets," *NYT* (6.12.23); Blake, "2024 GOPers start hitting Trump (gently) on classified documents," *WP* (6.13.23); Sargent, "Jim Jordan's tortured defense of Trump points to a coming GOP split," *WP* (6.13.23); Feuer, Haberman & Protess, "Trump has options for fighting charges, but they might face challenges," *NYT* (6.13.23); Glueck & Astor, "Christie attacks Trump, calling conduct detailed in indictment 'awful,'" *NYT* (6.13.23); "The Justice Department had no choice," *NYT* (6.11.23); "A shower full of secret documents leads to a solid Trump indictment," *WP* (6.9.23).

21 Savage & Feuer, "Judge in Trump documents case rejected suggestions to step aside," *NYT* (6.21.24).

22 Barrett, Dawsey, Stein & Alemany, "Indictment says Trump lied, schemed to keep highly classified secrets," *WP* (6.9.23); Savage, "Case lands in hands of judge who earlier ruled for Trump," *NYT* (6.9.23); Savage, "Trump appointee will remain judge in documents case, clerk says," *NYT* (6.10.23); Haberman, Feuer & Protess, "Trump indictment shows critical evidence came from one of his own lawyers," *NYT* (6.12.23); Schmidt & Savage, "Judge in Trump documents case has scant criminal trial experience," *NYT* (6.15.23); Alemany, "In audio recording,

Trump heard discussing sensitive Iran document," *WP* (6.27.23); Bump, "The Trump classified-document audio may be worse than we thought," *WP* (6.29.23); Feuer & Haberman, "Trump's lawyers unable to find file he mentioned in an interview," *NYT* (6.3.23); Barrett, Dawsey & Leonnig, "Prosecutors have recording of Trump discussing sensitive Iran document," *WP* (5.31.23); Haberman, Feuer & Swan, "Trump says 'secret' document he described on tape referred to news clippings," *NYT* (6.20.23); Bump, "Trump's evolving efforts to wave away the classified-documents recording," *WP* (6.29.23); Feuer & Haberman, "Investigation of Trump documents case continues after his indictment," *NYT* (7.1.23).

23 Barrett, "New details of Trump's Mar-a-Lago search warrant request unsealed," *WP* (7.5.23).

24 Arnsdorf & Knowles, "In Georgia speech, Trump stares down criminal jeopardy with bluffs and bluster," *WP* (6.11.23); Schmidt, Feuer, Haberman & Goldman, "Trump supporters' violent rhetoric in his defense disturbs experts," *NYT* (6.11.23); Jacobs, Nakamura, Allam & Arnsdorf, "Trump's Miami court date brings fear of violence, rally plans," *WP* (6.11.23); Weisman & Bensinger, "The 2024 G.O.P. field faces a choice: law and order or loyalty," *NYT* (6.12.23).

25 Jacobs, Ovalle, Barrett & Stein, "Trump arraigned, pleads not guilty to 37 classified documents charges," *WP* (6.13.23); Arnsdorf & Dawsey, "Trump greets arraignment with showmanship in bid to upstage charges," *WP* (6.14.23); Ives, "Fox News chyron calls Biden a 'wannabe dictator,'" *NYT* (6.24.23); Stein, "Judge Cannon sets pretrial conference in Trump documents case for July 14," *WP* (6.27.23); Barrett, "Judge appears to reject Trump bid to talk classified information at Mar-a-Lago," *WP* (9.14.23).

26 Qiu, "Trump's misleading defenses in the classified documents case," *NYT* (6.14.23).

27 Arnsdorf, Dawsey, Wells & Knowles, "Trump centers campaign on his prosecution, vilifying legal system," *WP* (6.15.23).

28 Swan, Savage & Haberman, "The radical strategy behind Trump's promise to 'go after' Biden," *NYT* (6.15.23).

29 Barrett, "Trump seeks trial delay, citing legal and political factors," *WP* (7.11.23); Feuer, "Prosecutors push back on Trump's request to delay documents trial," *NYT* (7.14.23); Feuer, "Prosecutors and Trump lawyers clash over timing in classified documents case," *NYT* (7.19.23); Stein & Berman, "Judge Cannon schedules Trump's classified documents trial for May 2024," *WP* (7.21.23); Stein, "Judge asks prosecutors to justify use of 2 grand juries in Trump documents case," *WP* (8.7.23); Feuer, "Trump asks again to delay documents trial until after election," *NYT* (10.6.23); Gregorian & Barnes, "Prosecutors push back on Trump bid to delay documents case until after the election," *NBC News* (10.10.23); Feuer, "Justice Dept. accuses Trump lawyers of dragging their feet in documents case," *NYT* (9.28.23); Stein & Barrett, "Trump's Florida case timeline may need to be pushed back, Judge Cannon says," *WP* (11.1.23); Feuer, "Judge hints at a delay in Trump documents trial," *NYT* (11.1.23); Barrett & Stein, "Judge Cannon keeps Trump trial date in documents case, with a caveat," *WP* (11.10.23); Polantz, "Judge Cannon keeps Trump classified documents trial scheduled for May," *CNN* (11.10.23); Feuer, "Judge puts off decision on whether to delay Trump documents trial," *NYT* (11.11.23).

30 Grayer, "House Judiciary chair proposes budget cuts to FBI and Justice Department," *CNN* (7.11.23); Barrett, "FBI director Chris Wray: 'insane' to say I'm biased against conservatives," *WP* (7.13.23).

31 Barrett, Stein, Hsu & Dawsey, "Trump charged with seeking to delete security footage in documents case," *WP* (7.28.23); Barrett, Hsu & Dawsey, "Trump aide Carlos de Oliveira's journey from failed witness to defendant," *WP* (7.28.23);

Dawsey, Barrett & Hsu, "Trump PAC has spent more than $40 million on legal costs this year for himself, others," *WP* (7.30.23); Barrett, "Special counsel says D.C. grand jury on Trump documents case has ended," *WP* (8.22.23); Protess, Goldman, Feuer & Haberman, "He was just the I.T. guy. Then he got caught in the Trump documents case," *NYT* (9.9.23).

32 Baker, "Pence undercuts Trump's defense in classified documents case," *NYT* (8.21.23).

33 Beitsch, "Canon indefinitely postpones Trump's Mar-a-Lago documents trial," *The Hill* (5.7.24).

34 Stein, "Unsealed motions in Trump's Fla. case suggest new evidence of possible obstruction," *WP* (5.21.24); Knowles, "Trump email falsely says Biden was 'locked & loaded' to 'take me out' in Mar-a-Lago search," *WP* (5.21.24); Cheney, "Lawyers found classified docs in Trump's bedroom 4 months after Mar-a-Lago search," *Politico* (5.21.24); Faulders & Mallin, "Special counsel suspected additional obstruction effort by Trump in classified docs case," *ABC News* (5.21.24).

35 Bump, "How Trumpworld convinced itself that the feds aimed to take out Trump," *WP* (5.22.24); Feuer, "It was legal boilerplate. Trump made it sound like a threat to his life," *NYT* (6.5.24); Kessler, "How Trump used his own court filing to claim an 'assassination' attempt," *WP* (5.23.24).

36 Barrett, "Special counsel seeks court order limiting Trump's false claims about FBI," *WP* (5.24.24); Feuer, "Prosecutors seek to bar Trump from attacking F.B.I. agents in documents case," *NYT* (5.24.24); Feuer, "Trump lawyers assail limited gag order request in documents case," *NYT* (5.28.24); Stein, "Judge rejects request to restrict Trump's speech on FBI, says motion was faulty," *WP* (5.28.24); Feuer, "Prosecutors try again to limit Trump's statements in documents case," *NYT* (6.1.24); Lebowitz & Barnes, "Special counsel again asks for modified release conditions for Trump in classified documents case," *NBC News* (5.31.24); Feuer, "Trump lawyers argue barring attacks on F.B.I. would censor 'political speech,'" *NYT* (6.14.24).

37 Feuer, "Judge reshuffles hearings in Trump documents case," *NYT* (6.6.24); Feuer & Haberman, "How one move illustrates Trump's tactics," *NYT* (6.14.24).

38 Stein & Barrett, "Judge Cannon strikes paragraph in Trump classified document indictment," *WP* (6.10.24); Feuer, "Judge strikes one element from Trump indictment in documents case," *NYT* (6.11.24).

39 Stein, "Judge holds hearing on Trump request to dismiss classified documents case," *WP* (6.21.24); Feuer & Sullivan, "For judge in Trump documents case, unusual rulings are business as usual," *NYT* (6.21.24); Cheney & Gerstein, "Judge rejects Trump's claims that FBI misled court in Mar-a-Lago search warrant," *Politico* (6.27.24).

40 Faulders & Charalambous, "Trump asks judge to delay his classified documents case following Supreme Court immunity ruling," *ABC News* (7.5.24); Feuer, "Judge delays some deadlines in Trump classified documents case," *NYT* (7.6.24); Feuer, "Judge denies effort by Trump co-defendant to have charges dismissed," *NYT* (7.6.24); Richards, "Jack Smith urges Trump classified docs judge to set aside Clarence Thomas opinion on special counsels," *NBC News* (7.12.24).

41 Barrett & Stein, "Trump's classified documents case dismissed by Judge Aileen Cannon," *WP* (7.15.24); Jouvenal, "Dismissal draws new scrutiny to Judge Cannon's handling of Trump case," *WP* (7.15.24); "Judge Cannon goes another step too far," *WP* (7.15.24); Katyal, "The dismissal of the Trump classified documents case is deeply dangerous," *NYT* (7.16.24); Mallin, "Special counsel files notice of appeal in Trump's classified documents case," *ABC News* (7.17.24); Stein & Barrett, "Jack Smith appeals Judge Cannon decision to throw out Trump case," *WP* (8.26.24); Allen, "Legal experts want Judge Cannon removed from Trump's

Mar-a-Lago documents case," *NPR* (9.4.24); Haberman, "Trump, trailing among women, lashes out at his female accusers," *NYT* (9.7.24); Stein, "Trump requests more time to reply to appeal of Florida case dismissal," *WP* (9.17.24); Barrett & Stein, "The Trump trials," *WP* (9.23.24).

42 Pengelly, Canales & Hurst, "Trump allegedly shared potentially sensitive information about US nuclear subs with Australian billionaire," *G* (10.6.23).

43 Rubin, "Aileen Cannon should not preside over the Trump trial," *WP* (6.13.23); Palmer, "Aileen Cannon move in Trump case leaves legal experts stunned: 'baffling,'" *Newsweek* (6.6.24).

44 Greer, "It is inexcusable how Judge Cannon is delaying the Trump documents case," *NYT* (5.18.24).

45 Blanchet, "Former judge puts Aileen Cannon on blast for 'sheer incompetence' in Trump docs case," *HuffPost* (6.6.24).

46 Paybarah, "Barr says no 'legitimate reason' for Trump to have classified documents," *WP* (9.3.22); Thrush, "Barr dismisses Trump's request for a special master," *NYT* (9.3.22); Gans, "Barr says DOJ 'getting very close' to having enough evidence to indict Trump," *The Hill* (9.7.22).

47 Stein & Barrett, "Garland to name special counsel for Trump Mar-a-Lago, 2020 election probes," *WP* (11.18.22); Thrush, Savage, Haberman & Feuer, "Garland names special counsel for Trump inquiries," *NYT* (11.19.22); "The new Trump probe special counsel should move quickly," *WP* (11.19.22); Palmer, "Donald Trump calls special counsel investigating him a 'terrorist,'" *Newsweek* (1.17.23); Dawsey & Stein, "Pence receives subpoena from prosecutors examining Trump's Jan. 6 role," *WP* (2.10.23); Luttig, "Mike Pence's dangerous gambit," *NYT* (2.24.23); Haberman, "Trump asks judge to block Pence's testimony to grand jury," *NYT* (3.5.23); Haberman & Feuer, "Former Trump officials must testify in 2020 election inquiry, judge says," *NYT* (3.25.23); Dawsey & Barrett, "U.S. judge says Pence must give some testimony in Trump Jan. 6 probe," *WP* (3.28.23); Cheney, "Appeals court rejects Trump's bid to block aides from testifying in Jan. 6 probe," *Politico* (4.4.23); Dawsey, "Pence won't appeal ruling that compels his grand jury testimony on Jan. 6," *WP* (4.5.23); Feuer, "Trump appeals decision forcing Pence to testify to Jan. 6 grand jury," *NYT* (4.11.23); Weiner, "Trump can't stop Pence from testifying to Jan. 6 grand jury, court rules," *WP* (4.27.23); Feuer, "Trump can't stop Pence from testifying to Jan. 6 grand jury, court rules," *NYT* (4.27.23); Cheney, "Appeals court rejects Trump's bid to block aides from testifying in Jan. 6 probe," *Politico* (4.4.23).

48 Stein, "Trump says he received a target letter in federal Jan. 6 investigation," *WP* (7.18.23); Haberman, "Trump says he's a target in special counsel's Capitol attack investigation," *NYT* (7.18.23); Bump, "Dissecting Trump's Truth Social post on his Jan. 6 probe-target letter," *WP* (7.19.23).

49 Wagner, Knowles & Alfaro, "DeSantis knocks Trump for Jan. 6 but says he didn't act with criminal intent," *WP* (7.19.23); Goldmacher & Haberman, "Republicans shrug at latest possible Trump indictment," *NYT* (7.19.23).

50 Barrett, Hsu, Stein, Dawsey & Alemany, "Trump charged in probe of Jan. 6 efforts to overturn 2020 election," *WP* (8.1.23); Savage & Goldman, "The Trump Jan. 6 indictment, annotated," *NYT* (8.1.23); Haberman, Swan & Broadwater, "Messages point to identity of co-conspirator 6 in Trump indictment," *NYT* (8.3.23).

51 Gurman & Viswanatha, "Trump is indicted in federal probe of his efforts to reverse 2020 election," *WSJ* (8.1.23); Trump Campaign Statement (8.1.23); Sargent, "Trump's lawyer drops an unsettling hint about his defense strategy," *WP* (8.2.23); Bump, "Hoping to undermine the Trump indictment, his allies are targeting D.C.," *WP* (8.3.23); Hulse, "Trump indictment presents new obstacle in spending fight as shutdown looms," *NYT* (8.5.23); Arnsdorf, Dawsey & Scherer,

"Trump plans to use charges to revisit 2020 election, a fraught topic for GOP," *WP* (8.4.23).

52 Huynh, "DeSantis suggests Trump can't get a fair trial in D.C. 'swamp,'" *NYT* (8.1.23).

53 Hsu & Jackman, "Judge Tanya Chutkan is a tough Trump critic, toughest Jan. 6 sentencer," *WP* (8.2.23).

54 Qiu, "Fact-checking the defense of Trump after his latest indictment," *NYT* (8.4.23).

55 Jackman, Hsu, Rizzo, Weiner & Barrett, "Trump pleads not guilty to charges that he plotted to overturn election," *WP* (8.4.23); Arnsdorf, Dawsey & Scherer, "Trump plans to use charges to revisit 2020 election, a fraught topic for GOP," *WP* (8.4.23); Lerer & Nehamas, "On the campaign trail, an impossible task ignoring Trump's latest challenges," *NYT* (8.5.23); Lerer & Epstein, "Campaign seeks to use politics as veto over the justice system," *NYT* (8.4.23).

56 "A president accused of betraying his country," *NYT* (8.2.23); "The Trump indictment's main finding: do you want this person as your president?" *WP* (8.2.23).

57 Thrush & Savage, "Trump, arraigned on election charges, pleads not guilty," *NYT* (8.4.23); Blake, "Trump's habitual line-stepping on witness tampering," *WP* (8.8.23); Stein & Hsu, "Prosecutors cite Trump's social media posts as they seek limits on handling of evidence," *WP* (8.6.23); Feuer & Haberman, "Jan. 6 prosecutors ask for protective order, citing threatening Trump post," *NYT* (8.6.23); Hsu, "Trump asks to extend deadline for Jan. 6 election interference trial," *WP* (8.9.23); Corasaniti & Gabriel, "Trump tells supporters his criminal indictments are about 'you,'" *NYT* (8.9.23); Hsu & Jackman, "Trump's speech will be limited to protect trial, witnesses, judge says," *WP* (8.11.23); Thrush & Feuer, "Judge limits Trump's ability to share Jan. 6 evidence," *NYT* (8.11.23).

58 Haberman, "Pence says Trump pressured him 'essentially to overturn election,'" *NYT* (8.4.23); Stein & Hsu, "Prosecutors cite Trump's social media posts as they seek limits on handling of evidence," *WP* (8.6.23).

59 Bogage & Slater, "Trump's moves to overturn 2020 election were 'aspirational,' not criminal, his lawyer argues," *WP* (8.6.23); Dowd, "Coup coup-ca-choo, Trump style," *NYT* (8.6.23); Broadwater & Astor, "Trump calls for judge's recusal as his lawyer deems effort to overturn election 'aspirational,'" *NYT* (8.6.23).

60 Gans, "Trump calls on Supreme Court to 'intercede' in legal fights," *The Hill* (8.4.23); Jackman & Hermann, "Trump insults D.C. to get his trial moved. The city rolls its eyes," *WP* (8.9.23); Hsu, "Judge Chutkan holds first hearing in election subversion case," *WP* (8.11.23); Hsu & Maese, "U.S. seeks Jan. 2 trial date for Trump election subversion case," *WP* (8.11.23); Haberman, Swan & Feuer, "'Biased.' 'Corrupt.' 'Deranged.' Trump's taunts test limits of release," *NYT* (8.16.23); https://www.crimedatadc.com/.

61 Cho, "Texas woman charged with threatening to kill judge on election case," *WP* (8.17.23); Robinson, "Trump's most racist supporters are coming to his defense," *WP* (8.18.23); Schmidt, Goldman, Feuer, Haberman & Thrush, "As Trump prosecutions move forward, threats and concerns increase," *NYT* (9.24.23); "Texas woman accused of threatening to kill judge overseeing Trump election case and a congresswoman," *AP* (8.16.23).

62 Hsu, "Trump asks to push Jan. 6 trial beyond 2024 election—to April 2026," *WP* (8.18.23); Weiner, Barrett & Vazquez, "Trump's D.C. election-obstruction trial set for March 4, 2024," *WP* (8.28.23); Feuer & Thrush, "Judge sets trial date in March for Trump's federal election case," *NYT* (8.29.23); Barrett, "Why Trump's vow to appeal his D.C. trial date probably won't work," *WP* (9.4.23).

63 Hsu & Weiner, "Trump demands recusal by Judge Chutkan in D.C. Jan. 6 trial," *WP* (9.12.23); Feuer, "Trump seeks recusal of judge in federal elections case,"

NYT (9.12.23); Weiner, Alexander & Hsu, "How Jamaica-born Judge Tanya S. Chutkan became Trump's latest target," *WP* (9.28.23); Hsu & Weiner, "Chutkan rejects Trump request to step aside as judge in his D.C. trial," *WP* (9.28.23); Beitsch, "Judge Chutkan denies Trump bid for her recusal in Jan. 6 case," *The Hill* (9.27.23); Faulders, "Trump asks judge in federal election interference case for 2-month extension to file pretrial motions," *ABC News* (9.28.23).

64 Weiner, "Justice Dept. asks court for 'limited' restrictions on Trump's words," *WP* (9.15.23); Feuer, "Special counsel seeking gag order on Trump in election case," *NYT* (9.16.23); Haberman & Swan, "Trump says he hopes Meadows will remain 'loyal' to him in election case," *NYT* (9.18.23).

65 Feuer, "Prosecutors reassert need for gag order on Trump in elections case," *NYT* (9.30.23); Hsu & Barrett, "Prosecutors cite Trump's supposed gun purchase as possible crime," *WP* (9.30.23).

66 "Judge Chutkan issues limited gag order for Trump in D.C. Jan. 6 case," *WP* (10.16.23); Feuer & Savage, "Judge imposes limited gag order on Trump in election case," *NYT* (10.16.23); Arnsdorf, "Trump campaign attacks gag order decision," *WP* (10.16.23); Jackman, "Chutkan explains limited gag order on Trump," *WP* (10.16.23); Weiner, "Trump lawyer again pushes for trial after 2024 election," *WP* (10.16.23); Jackman, "Judge concerned by Trump's seeming threat against Gen. Milley," *WP* (10.16.23); Gold, "Trump vows to reject Gazan refugees after Israel attack," *NYT* (10.17.23); "Trump is appealing a partial gag order imposed on him in his 2020 election interference case," *PBS* (10.17.23); Dolan, "Trump appeals gag order in federal 2020 election subversion case," *CNN* (10.17.23); Feuer, "Trump seeks freeze of gag order in election case during appeal," *NYT* (10.21.23); Bromwich, Protess & Feuer, "How judges restrain Trump: gag orders, fines and possible jail time," *NYT* (10.27.23); Kinstler, "Diary," *London Review of Books* (9.26.24).

67 Arnsdorf, Dasey & Hsu, "Trump seethes at gag order in federal case while his campaign relishes it," *WP* (10.24.23); Barrett, "Special counsel urges judge to crack down further on Trump's comments," *WP* (10.26.23); Tyler & Thrush, "Federal prosecutors push to reinstate gag order on Trump," *NYT* (10.26.23).

68 Barber, "Judge reinstates Donald Trump gag order," *WSJ* (10.29.23); Weiner & Hsu, "Judge imposes restrictions on Trump's speech in Jan. 6 case," *WP* (10.30.23).

69 Feuer, "Trump asks federal appeals court to lift gag order in election case," *NYT* (11.3.23); Feuer, "Appeals court temporarily frees Trump from gag order in election case," *NYT* (11.4.23).

70 Feuer, "Trump asks appeals court to throw out election case gag order," *NYT* (11.9.23); Weiner, "Trump gag order reinstated but narrowed in Jan. 6 case," *WP* (12.8.23); Feuer & Savage, "Appeals court upholds, but narrows, gag order on Trump in election case," *NYT* (12.9.23); Savage, "Full appeals court spurns request by Trump to end gag order in election case," *NYT* (1.24.24); "Trump urges government shutdown in unlikely bid to 'defund' his criminal prosecution," *Reuters* (9.21.23).

71 Wendling, "Trump seeks to dismiss election interference charges, saying he had presidential immunity," *BBC* (10.6.23); Hsu & Stein, "Trump files new challenges to federal election obstruction case in D.C.," *WP* (10.24.23); Feuer, "Trump files more motions to derail federal Jan. 6 case," *NYT* (10.24.23); Feuer, "Prosecutors assail Trump's bid to have federal election case dismissed," *NYT* (11.6.23).

72 Feuer & Haberman, "Trump asks judge to televise federal election trial," *NYT* (11.12.23); Feuer, "Federal prosecutors object to Trump request for broadcast of election trial," *NYT* (11.14.23).

73 Feuer, "Federal prosecutors object to Trump request for broadcast of election trial," *NYT* (11.14.23).

74 Hsu & Weiner, "Trump lawyers seek to probe U.S. handling of 2020 election fraud claims," *WP* (11.28.23).
75 Weiner & Arnsdorf, "Defending his 2020 fraud claims, Trump turns to fringe Jan. 6 theories," *WP* (12.4.23).
76 Feuer, "Federal judge rejects Trump's immunity claims in election case," *NYT* (12.1.23); "Trump is not immune from election-subversion prosecution, judge rules," *Politico* (12.1.23).
77 Barrett, Stein, Barnes & Weiner, "U.S. prosecutors ask Supreme Court to quickly take up Trump immunity claims," *WP* (12.11.23); Bravin & Barber, "Supreme Court agrees to consider special counsel's request to rule quickly on Trump's immunity," *WSJ* (12.11.23); Liptak & Feuer, "Special counsel asks Supreme Court to decide if Trump is immune from prosecution," *NYT* (12.11.23); Barrett, Stein, Barnes & Weiner, "Supreme Court will consider fast-tracking Trump appeal in D.C. trial," *WP* (12.12.23); Feuer, "Judge pauses Trump election case amid appeal of immunity issue," *NYT* (12.14.23); Liptak, "Trump asks Supreme Court to put off hearing case on immunity claim," *NYT* (12.21.23); Barnes & Stein, "Supreme Court won't fast-track ruling on Trump's claim of immunity," *WP* (12.22.23).
78 Barnes, Weiner & Barrett, "Supreme Court accepts Jan. 6 case that could affect or delay Trump trial," *WP* (12.13.23); Feuer, "Prosecutors try to nudge Trump election case ahead despite freeze on case," *NYT* (12.20.23); Feuer, "Trump wants prosecutors held in contempt in federal election case," *NYT* (1.5.24); Feuer, "Judge declines to hold prosecutors in contempt in Trump election case," *NYT* (1.18.24).
79 Arnsdorf, Dawsey & LeVine, "Trump's promotion of debunked election report reveals divisions in his circle," *WP* (1.7.24); Arnsdorf, "Trump warns of 'bedlam,' declines to rule out violence after court hearing," *WP* (1.10.24); Rosenberg, "Trump has suggested violence could erupt if court cases do not go his way," *NYT* (1.10.24).
80 Hsu & Weiner, "Trump D.C. trial drops off court's March calendar, clearing way for N.Y. case," *WP* (2.2.24); U.S. v. Trump (D.C. Circuit 2.6.24); Knappenberger, "DC Circuit denies Trump's claim of presidential immunity in election subversion case," *Courthouse News Service* (2.6.24); Howe, "Supreme Court takes up Trump immunity appeal," *Scotusblog* (2.28.24); In re: the Search of Information Stored at Premises Controlled by Twitter, Inc. (D.C. Circuit en banc 1.16.24).
81 Trump v. U.S.
82 Kantor & Liptak, "How Roberts shaped Trump's Supreme Court winning streak," *NYT* (9.15.24).
83 Viser, "Biden denounces Supreme Court decision on presidential immunity," *WP* (7.2.24); Marley, "Supreme Court's Trump immunity ruling poses risks for democracy, experts say," *WP* (7.2.24); Astor, "Republicans respond to Supreme Court immunity ruling with triumph, and Democrats with dismay," *NYT* (7.2.24); Cameron, "Trump amplifies calls to jail 15 top officials, invokes military tribunals," *NYT* (7.2.24); Astor, "J.D. Vance endorses Trump's call for a special prosecutor against Biden," *NYT* (7.7.24); Astor, "Marco Rubio, contender to be Trump's running mate, defends Supreme Court's immunity ruling," *NYT* (7.7.24); Kantor & Liptak, "How Roberts shaped Trump's Supreme Court winning streak," *NYT* (9.15.24).
84 Trott, "Why the Supreme Court's immunity ruling is untenable in a democracy," *WP* (10.7.24).
85 "The Trump immunity decision isn't the end of democracy—but it is bad," *WP* (7.2.24); "The Supreme Court gives a free pass to Trump and future presidents," *NYT* (7.2.24); Bouie, "Mr. President, your get-out-of-jail-free card is ready," *NYT*

(7.2.24); Shaw, "The Supreme Court creates a lawless presidency," *NYT* (7.2.24); Wegman & Arthur, "The Supreme Court made a 'monumentally awful' decision," *NYT* (7.2.24); Tribe, "The Trump decision reveals deep rot in the system," *NYT* (7.2.24); French, "The Supreme Court helps Trump—and future presidents—dodge accountability," *NYT* (7.2.24).

86 Kapur & Thorp, "Sen. Chuck Schumer eyes new bill hitting back at the Supreme Court's immunity ruling on Trump," *NBC News* (7.8.24); Adragna, "Schumer: Democrats will try to remove immunity from Trump Jan. 6 acts," *Politico* (7.8.24); Mascaro, "House Democrat is proposing a constitutional amendment to reverse Supreme Court's immunity decision," *ABC News* (7.3.24); Hulse, "Schumer promises year-end push as courts gain new political importance," *NYT* (8.2.24); Biden, "My plan to reform the Supreme Court and ensure no president is above the law," *WP* (7.29.24); Gerstein, "Gorsuch on Biden Supreme Court proposals: 'Be careful,'" *Politico* (8.4.24).

87 Preza, "Judge in election interference case hands Trump legal blow after SCOTUS immunity ruling," *MSN.com* (8.3.24); Irwin, "Chutkan sets Aug. 16 hearing in Trump election interference case," *The Hill* (8.3.24); Gerstein & Cheney, "Judge rejects Trump's claim of 'vindictive' prosecution by Biden allies," *Politico* (8.3.24); Hsu, "Special counsel seeks delay in Trump election subversion case in D.C.," *WP* (8.8.24); Feuer, "Judge gives Trump and prosecutors more time to assess presidential immunity," *NYT* (8.9.24); Barrett & Stein, "New Trump indictment tries to salvage case after Supreme Court ruling," *WP* (8.27.24); Feuer & Savage, "Special Counsel revises Trump election indictment to address immunity ruling," *NYT* (8.28.24); Barnes & Gregorian, "Trump to plead not guilty to revised federal election interference indictment," *NBC News* (9.4.24); Feuer, Savage & Sullivan, "Judge sets deadlines in Trump election case, saying campaign is 'not relevant,'" *NYT* (9.6.24); Feuer, "In Jan. 6 case filing, Trump lawyers again demand dismissal," *NYT* (9.20.24); Hsu, "Judge allows lengthy brief in Trump case, rejecting claim of election impact," *WP* (9.24.24).

88 Blake, "5 takeaways from the big new filing on Trump's 2020 election plot," *WP* (10.3.24); Hsu, Dawsey, Jackman & Gardner, "As rioters stormed Capitol with Pence inside, Trump allegedly said 'so what?'" *WP* (10.3.24); Cheney & Gerstein, "11 damning details in Jack Smith's new brief in the Trump lection case," *Politico* (10.3.24); Feuer & Savage, "Filing in Trump election case fleshes out roles of a sprawling cast," *NYT* (10.4.24); Stein & Hsu, "Trump says Department of Justice violated its own election rules. Lawyers disagree," *WP* (10.4.24); Hsu, "Judge approves releasing source documents with more Trump-January 6 evidence," *WP* (10.11.24).

89 Biskupic (2023: 15).

90 Wang & Kornfield, "Trump says he'd 'fire' special counsel Jack Smith in 'two seconds' if elected again," *WP* (10.24.24).

91 Jarrett, Shabad & Reilly, "Special counsel Jack Smith and his team to resign before Trump takes office," *NBC News* (11.13.24); Reid, Sneed & Cole, "Special counsel Jack Smith drops election subversion and classified documents cases against Donald Trump," *CNN* (11.25.24); Tucker, "Jack Smith finalizing Trump investigation report that could be released as early as Friday," *AP* (1.7.25); Stein, "Cannon temporarily blocks report on Trump classified-documents probe," *WP* (1.7.25); Sneed & Polantz, "Federal appeals court allows Garland to release special counsel's final Trump report, but more legal fights expected," *CNN* (1.9.25); Feuer & Savage, "Special counsel's report says Trump would have been convicted in election case," *NYT* (1.14.25); Brancolini, "Trump loses it over Jack Smith report finding only election saved him," *Daily Beast* (1.14.25); Feuer & Adams, "Judge mulls release to Congress of Trump classified documents report," *NYT* (1.18.25).

5

THE 2022 AND 2024 ELECTIONS

Elections are the ultimate mechanism by which presidents are held accountable. This chapter analyzes the 2022 and 2024 elections to understand how Trump and his supporters sought to undermine the essential elements of liberal democracy and to assess the efficacy of resistance.

5.1 The 2022 Midterm Election

At a March 2022 rally, Trump spoke in support of Herschel Walker, running for Senator from Georgia. Walker had lied about graduating in the top one percent at the University of Georgia (he failed to graduate), boasted about his business enterprises (many of which failed), and claimed to have worked in law enforcement (he was an honorary deputy sheriff) and been an FBI agent (he never was).[1] (He lost the race to the incumbent Raphael Warnock.) Trump used the occasion to reiterate his praise of dictators: Xi Jinping "runs 1.5 billion people with an iron fist"; Kim Jong-un was "tough" and Vladimir Putin "smart"; all this showed that "the smartest one gets to the top." Trump earlier had expressed "respect" for Kim and said Tayyip Erdoğan was "doing a very good job," Xi was "a strong guy, tough guy," Putin had "been a leader," and Rodrigo Duterte had done "an unbelievable job on the drug problem." (That last campaign caused an estimated 6,000–30,000 deaths.) Just before the 2024 election, Bob Woodward disclosed that, as president, Trump had secretly spoken to Putin at least seven times and sent him COVID-19 testing machines when they were in scarce supply in the US. Refusing to say whether that was true, Trump asserted it would have been a "smart thing."[2]

DOI: 10.4324/9781032629186-5

At the July 26, 2022, "America First Agenda Summit" in DC, Trump fired what sounded like the opening salvo in his campaign for the 2024 nomination.[3]

> Millions of illegal aliens are stampeding across our wide open borders, pouring into our country. . . . I believe we'll take in 15 million people. . . . It's an invasion. . . . We're poisoning our country . . . we can get rid of all of the bad ones. The police know almost immediately who the bad ones are. . . . The National Guard can be used to help find and remove criminal illegal aliens from our country. . . . We've also seen too many instances of illegal aliens who cross our borders with a history of sex crimes and sexual offenses at numbers that nobody's ever seen before. . . . Democrat run cities are setting all time murder records. . . . Our streets are riddled with needles and soaked with the blood of innocent victims. . . . I want to save our cities because you're going to have a time when nobody will be here anymore. . . . Homeless encampments are taken over every public park and every patch of green space. . . . Right now they're putting homeless in super luxury hotels . . . open up large parcels of inexpensive land in the outer reaches of the cities [for the homeless]. . . . We need to return to stop and frisk policies. . . . Let the people that have to have guns . . . have them. . . . Rare mistakes are made [by police], but we cannot allow every isolated policing mistake to be turned into a national crisis and all power taken away from our police. . . . [W]e need a no holds barred national campaign to dismantle gangs . . . ideally send them out [of the country]. . . . If you look at countries throughout the world, the ones that don't have a drug problem are those that institute a very quick trial, death penalty sentence for drug dealers. . . . [When] state [and] local levels refuse to protect public safety . . . the federal government will have no choice but to step in . . . weak mayors and cowardly governors . . . hate our country. It's the only reason they'd allow things like this to happen. . . . . Where there are radical and racist prosecutors denying citizens the full protection of the law, those offices need to be investigated by the federal government. . . . The sickos who are pushing sexual content in kindergartens or providing puberty blockers to young children who have no idea what a puberty blocker is—neither do I by the way. . . . We have to rescue our schools from the Marxist teachers unions. We need to completely demolish the corrupt education bureaucracy and liberate our children. . . . I used to listen to Fauci and whatever he said, I did the opposite. I came out very good. . . . I won a second time. Very corrupt. . . . We may just have to do it again . . . the unsecured drop boxes are a disaster . . . we want to ensure universal voter ID, but our goal should be same day voting with only paper ballots. . . . We need to get political correctness and left wing race and gender theories out of our military so that America can once again, fight

> and win wars. . . . To drain the swamp and root out the deep state, we need to make it much easier to fire rogue bureaucrats who are deliberately undermining democracy, or at a minimum just want to keep their job. . . . We need to break the choke hold of Silicon Valley censors and restore free speech in America . . . these next few years, our country will decide whether we are going to allow a corrupt and radical ruling class to snuff out the torch of Liberty, or whether we will resist the forces of decay. . . . Now, we have the January 6th unselect committee of political hacks and thugs. . . . Adam Shifty Schiff . . . an evil person, a sick person . . . you see what they're doing to people that in some cases didn't even enter the building, and you see the way they're being tortured and handled so horribly. . . . I have to save our country . . . because if I don't our nation is doomed to become another Venezuela or become another Soviet Union . . . a very large scale version of Cuba . . . we are a nation in decline. We are a failing nation . . . everyone knows that the Green New Deal will lead to the destruction of our country. . . . We're a nation that has weaponized its law enforcement . . . against the opposing political party. . . . We're a nation that no longer has a free and fair press . . . the true enemy of the people.

In September Trump posted an image of himself on Truth Social wearing a QAnon pin with its slogan "The Storm is Coming."[4] At a rally he denounced the civil and criminal actions against him (see Chapters 2–4). "Our cruel and vindictive political class is not just coming after me. They're coming after you, through me." A week later he said: "our biggest threat remains the sick, sinister and evil people from within our own country." In a speech in Sioux City, Iowa, on November 3, Trump uttered at least 58 false or misleading statements; in Latrobe, Pennsylvania, he made another 24. Fueling supporters' fears, he said: "large packs of sadistic criminals and thieves . . . [are] allowed to go into stores and openly rob them, beat up their workers, kill their customer, and leave with armloads of goods but not retribution." "You can't walk down a sidewalk in Chicago. Get hit over the head with a baseball bat from behind."

Trump's Congressional supporters echoed his lies.[5] Rep. Stefanik warned: "Radical Democrats are planning their most aggressive move yet: a PERMANENT ELECTION INSURRECTION. Their plan to grant amnesty to 11 MILLION illegal immigrants will overthrow our current electorate and create a permanent liberal majority in Washington." Rep. Biggs said in March: "The Leftists who are authoritarians with a DNA that leans toward tyranny, believe that loading up the nation with unskilled workers from underdeveloped nations will provide Democrats with voters. Democrats are so enamored of power that they want to legalize cheating in elections." Sen. Vance and Blake Masters (who lost the 2022 race for Arizona senator by 5 percent) also referred to replacement theory. Rep. Jackson had tweeted in April 2021: "Make no mistake about it, the most radical, anti-American leftists in Congress are in control! If you have a Democrat representing you, you MUST demand they stand up to the America Last Marxists that are radically and systematically DESTROYING our country." Rep. Brooks said in May: "America-hating Socialists seek to upend the American way of life based on freedom and liberty and replace it with dictatorial government that controls every aspect of our lives." Rep. Mary Miller called Democrats "evil" communists loyal to China, who want to "destroy" America and its culture. Sen. Tuberville accused Democrats of being "pro-crime": "They want crime because they want to take over what you got." Rep. Carter warned: "The liberal woke mob are attacking everything. Our National Anthem. Our Christian faith. Our Gun Rights. These people are SICK." Rep. Falon said in June: "Joe Biden needs to take a cognitive test. Now." Rep. Loudermilk declared: "Speaker Pelosi has turned the people's House into a dictatorship, and is apparently using her power to try to destroy her political enemies." Two members used the official House GOP Twitter account to retweet: "Pelosi loves Communist China" (particularly ironic given China's fury at her visit to Taiwan). Political rhetoric was sharply asymmetrical. Republicans who opposed certification of the Electoral College vote called their opponents socialist in more than 1,800 tweets; by comparison, Democrats called their opponents fascist in just 80.

In October 2022, Paul Pelosi, the 82-year-old House Speaker's husband, was attacked in his San Francisco home by David DePape, a 42-year-old Canadian, who fractured Pelosi's skull with a hammer, yelling "Where is Nancy?"[6] DePape, who had a list of other potential targets, told police he was on a "suicide mission" and intended to break Nancy Pelosi's kneecaps. A week earlier Rep. Emmer, chair of the National Republican Congressional Committee, had posted a tweet of himself firing a gun at a shooting range with the hashtag #FirePelosi. The right wing immediately concocted lies about the assault. Roger Stone called it an "alleged attack" and condemned the "stench" of mainstream reporting. Elon Musk hinted at "a tiny possibility there might be more to this story than meets the eye." Dinesh D'Souza said: "The Left is going crazy because we are not BUYING the wacky, implausible Paul Pelosi story but we are even LAUGHING over how ridiculous it is." Other fabrications, some disseminated by Donald Trump Jr., Sebastian Gorka, Raheem Kassam, and Reps. Greene and Higgins, claimed Pelosi had been in his underwear, drunk, and fighting with a male prostitute. Trump agreed the criminal complaint was not telling the entire story. Kari Lake provoked laughs at a campaign event by commenting snidely: "apparently [Pelosi's] house doesn't have a lot of protection." Rep. Tenney posted a photo on Twitter showing young white men holding hammers near a gay pride flag and "LOL."

A year later, a federal jury convicted DePape of attempted kidnapping and assault.[7] The following May, despite an apology, ND CA Judge Corley

(Biden) sentenced him to 30 years (prosecutors had sought 40): "the message has to be out there that it's absolutely unacceptable to our democracy." In June 2024, a California state court convicted DePape of five charges, including aggravated kidnapping, which carries a mandatory sentence of life imprisonment without the possibility of parole, after San Francisco Superior Court Judge Harry M. Dorfman dismissed the murder charge as double jeopardy. DePape did not contest the evidence in either trial.

Republican election campaigns aggressively exploited racism.[8] A National Republican Senatorial Committee ad juxtaposed the face of Lt. Gov. Mandela Barnes (who was Black and running for the Senate from Wisconsin) with three Democratic Representatives (all women of color) and the words "different" and "dangerous." (He lost by one percent.) An ad against Cheri Beasley, a Black Democrat running for the Senate from North Carolina, pictured the brother of a white state trooper killed 25 years earlier and quoted Beasley, when she was a public defender, saying the Black accused she represented "was actually a good person." (She lost by three percent.) Sen. Tuberville declared Democrats wanted reparations "for the people that do the crime." (He won by more than 20 percent.) Rep. Greene warned: "Joe Biden's five million illegal aliens are on the verge of replacing you." (She won by more than 30 percent.) America First Legal, founded by Stephen Miller, ran a radio ad accusing the Biden administration of "anti-white bigotry" and asking: "When did racism against white people become ok?"

Of the 291 Republicans who had denied Biden's 2020 victory and ran for Congress or statewide office in 2022, 170 won.[9] Republicans gained nine House seats to take control (222–213), but Democrats added one Senator for a two-seat majority. Murdoch's two US newspapers responded to the disappointing results by attacking Trump. The *Wall Street Journal* called him the Party's "biggest loser," having "flopped in 2018, 2020, 2021 and 2022." The *New York Post* caricatured him as "Trumpty Dumpty," exaggerating his obesity into an egg-like shape and asking: "Don (who couldn't build a wall) had a great fall—can all the G.O.P.'s men put the party back together again?" It dubbed DeSantis, Trump's closest Republican rival, "DeFuture." (Trump had ridiculed him as DeSanctimonious for drawing attention to the president's hush money payment to Stormy Daniels, see Chapter 3.1.) In a *New York Post* op ed, John Podhoretz called Trump "the most profound vote repellent in modern American history." Fox News's Laura Ingraham warned: "if the voters conclude that you're putting your own ego or your own grudges ahead of what's good for the country, they're going to look elsewhere." Trump lashed back: "For me, Fox News was always gone, even in 2015–16 when I began 'my journey.'" (You would not know that from his symbiotic relationship with the network up to the moment Fox called the race for Biden, see Abel 2024b.) "But now they're really gone." (In 2024, Fox News had 3.9 million primetime viewers, more than CNN and MSNBC combined.) Republicans agreed with these Murdoch outlets. Outgoing Maryland Gov. Hogan (who later ran for the Senate) claimed: "I've been saying since 2020 that we have to get back to a party that appeals to more people." New Hampshire Gov. Sununu (a possible presidential contender) said: "we've got to fix extremism right now." Sen. Cassidy declared: "We're not like, ok, there's one person who leads our party." Sen. Cotton concurred: "we don't have a single leader." Pence repeated that "the president's words were reckless" on January 6. "It was clear he decided to be part of the problem." Trump's tweets had "endangered" Pence's family. A month earlier Pence had said coyly about Trump running in 2024: "there might be somebody else I'd prefer more," i.e., himself.

5.2 Diversions

Both parties sought to influence or circumvent the 2024 election through tactics other than conventional campaigning. Congressional Republicans did so by seeking to impeach Biden (5.2.1) and his Homeland Security Secretary Mayorkas (5.2.2); a special prosecutor brought two cases against Hunter Biden (5.2.3). Democrats in several states sought to disqualify Trump as an insurrectionist under Article 3 of the Fourteenth Amendment (5.2.4).

5.2.1 Impeaching Joe Biden

In May 2023, SJC member Grassley released copies of "very significant allegations from a trusted F.B.I. informant implicating then-Vice President Biden in a criminal bribery scheme," asking: "did they sweep it under the rug to protect the candidate Biden?"[10] Alexander Smirnov, the source, declared Joe Biden was "going to jail" because the Ukrainian energy company Burisma had hired Hunter "to protect us, through his dad, from all kinds of problems." Republicans claimed Smirnov had 17 recordings to support his allegations that Burisma had paid each Biden $5 million. HJC chair Jordan said the FBI Form 1023 (which contained raw, unverified information) was "the most corroborating evidence we have"; House Oversight and Accountability Committee chair Comer called Smirnov "highly credible." Rep. Stefanik pronounced this "the biggest corruption scandal, not only in my lifetime, but I would say the past 100 years." She had said earlier: "You have multiple members of the Biden family profiting illegally from foreign governments. You also have the bombshell reporting, including potential tapes that exist, of while Joe Biden was Vice President taking a bribe from Burisma." Rep. Luna gloated: now "we have proof." Rep. Greene called it "damning information" that "not only did Joe Biden take a $5 million bribe, so did Hunter Biden." But on May 10, FBI Acting Assistant Director Christopher Dunham cautioned that "the mere existence of such a document would establish little beyond the fact that a confidential human source provided information and the F.B.I. recorded it."

In February 2024, Smirnov was arrested after flying into Las Vegas from overseas. Special Counsel David Weiss (handling the Hunter investigation) had charged Smirnov in CD CA with lying to the FBI. As early as 2020, the Bureau had told the DoJ that Smirnov's claims did not merit further investigation. Smirnov had contact with Burisma only after Joe Biden left office. Smirnov told the FBI he had seen a video of Hunter entering a Kyiv hotel, which Russia might have wired (the origin of the alleged audiotapes). But Hunter had never been to Ukraine. After Smirnov was released from custody on personal bond, Weiss asked that he be detained pending trial because he claimed connections to Russian intelligence. He was rearrested in Nevada and transferred to CD CA, where Judge Wright (GWB) ordered his detention, saying: "there is nothing garden variety about this case."

The Washington Post commented that this "ill-founded GOP crusade . . . seems finally to be reaching an embarrassing denouement." But Rep. Comer maintained that the president's impeachment "is not reliant" on Form 1023, and Rep. Jordan (a lawyer) bizarrely claimed that Smirnov's indictment "doesn't change the fundamental facts." Fox News journalists called the indictment "a smear job" (Jesse Watters) and "an intimidation tactic" (Maria Bartiromo). The right-wing media dismissed Smirnov as a "straw man" (*New York Post*) and "not a key witness" (*Washington Examiner*); a *Wall Street Journal* columnist said the probe "doesn't sink or swim on the bribery claims." Comer had cited Gal Luft as another "very credible witness on Biden family corruption, and Sen. Johnson claimed Luft had a "wealth of information" about the Bidens. But Luft inconveniently jumped bail and fled the country after his indictment for arms trafficking and lobbying violations was unsealed. In January 2025, after Smirnov admitted the falsity of his allegations about the Bidens, pleaded to multiple tax charges, and agreed to pay about $675,000 to the IRS, he was sentenced to six years.

Republicans in Congress tried to implicate Joe in his relatives' activities.[11] But his brother James testified the president "never had any involvement or any direct or indirect financial interest" in James's business activities. And Hunter asserted: "I did not involve my father in my business. Not while I was a practicing lawyer, not in my investments or transactions domestic or international, not as a board member, and not as an artist." Despite all this, Jordan insisted to Fox News: "There's a pattern with the Biden family: Hunter Biden goes out and tries to get business but the agreements and the deals never get done until [Joe] Biden shows up either on a phone call or by dropping by a lunch, dropping by a dinner." And the unsubstantiated allegations had done their work. A January 2024 Pew Research Center survey found that nine out of ten Republicans thought Biden's activities were grounds for impeachment, and more than half said that definitely was true. A Marquette

Law School poll found that three-quarters of Republicans believed Biden "has behaved corruptly."

White House Counsel Ed Siskel urged House Speaker Johnson to close the Biden impeachment inquiry.[12] Rep. Armstrong, who had written the authorizing resolution, acknowledged on March 13, 2024 that Republicans were not "anywhere close" to having the votes and suggested a referral to the DoJ under FARA. Rep. Comer agreed that accountability "looks like criminal referrals," assuring prospective donors he had "presented mountains of evidence." "When President Trump returns to the White House, it's critical the new leadership at the DOJ have everything they need to prosecute the Biden Crime Family and deliver swift justice." The three House committee chairs (Comer, Jordan and Smith) made criminal referrals of Hunter (for denying he was "corporate secretary" of Rosemont Seneca Bohai) and James (for saying Joe did not meet Tony Bubulinski in 2017). On the first day of the Democratic National Convention in August, the three committees produced a 291-page report, offering no evidence Biden had done anything for Hunter but asserting that "an abuse of power may also be present even if, as some claim, the Biden family was only selling the 'illusion' of influence and access."

5.2.2 Impeaching Alejandro Mayorkas

Republicans also attacked Homeland Security Secretary Mayorkas.[13] In January 2023, House Homeland Security Committee chair Mark Green filed an impeachment resolution. Two months later he bragged to a "V.I.P. Reception and Conversation with Conservative Heroes" he would impeach Mayorkas for his "dereliction of duty and his intentional destruction of our country through the open southern boundary." His committee would "put together a packet, and we will hand it to Jim Jordan and let Jim do what Jim does best." Mayorkas would testify on April 19, "and it's going to be fun." Sens. Johnson and Hawley had already demanded Mayorkas's resignation. In a closed-door committee meeting, Green called Mayorkas a "reptile with no balls" for not resigning.

The Washington Post cautioned that "impeaching Mayorkas would debase the House, not secure the border."[14] Biden denounced the threat as "baseless" and "unconstitutional." The House impeachment report characterized its action as "deporting Secretary Mayorkas from his position" for "willful and systematic refusal to comply with the law" and "breach of public trust." Republicans failed in their first effort by one vote (three Republicans voting against.) A few days later they succeeded by a single vote. (One Republican dissenter, Mike Gallagher, said he would not seek re-election, as did Green, the sponsor.)

Sen. Blumenthal said: "These charges are a total sham—really shameful—and they deserve absolutely no dignity. They're purely a political stunt by the far-right fringe of the MAGA movement and, I think, should be dismissed summarily."[15] Rep. Scalise warned Democrats: "If they ignore this and just throw it in the trash can without taking it as seriously as the American people do, then there will be accountability and consequences." But even Republican Sen. Lankford admitted: "it'll be dead on arrival when it comes over." Sen. Manchin complained that Republicans

> want to play with it like it's still hanging out there. They'll use all the leverage they can get out of it, and get all the mileage they can get out of it, because once it gets here, we'll bring it up and shoot it down and it's gone.

Republican Sen. Cramer conceded the impeachment was "a little peculiar." "We're ready to sit as a jury as quickly as possible and get it over with, but if it never comes over, I guess that's fine by me too."

Transmitting the 11 Republican impeachment managers' letter, Speaker Johnson told Senate Majority Leader Schumer that the Democrats' plan to dismiss summarily was "a violation of our constitutional order and an affront to the American people."[16] Schumer retorted that impeachment "should never be used to settle a policy disagreement." Minority Leader McConnell countered that "it would be beneath the Senate's dignity to shrug off our clear responsibility and fail to give the charges we'll hear today the thorough consideration they deserve." (But he had voted to dismiss Trump's second impeachment, see Abel 2025: Chapter 2.1.) Johnson accused Schumer of being "the only impediment to delivering accountability for the American people." Sen. Lummis shamelessly boasted he wanted "to make this as painful as possible if the Democrats are going to either move to dismiss or move to table."

Republicans rejected Schumer's offer to allow debate or create an impeachment committee and then tried to drag out the process by making repeated procedural objections, which they abused by injecting substantive remarks, calling for a closed session and moving to adjourn until April 30 (knowing they lacked the numbers to pass the motions).[17] The Senate then quickly voted along party lines to dismiss both charges as unconstitutional.

5.2.3 Prosecuting Hunter Biden

Unlike these blatantly political shenanigans by Republicans legislators, the criminal investigation and prosecution of Hunter respected the legal process.[18] In June 2023, Hunter entered an agreement with D DE US Attorney David C. Weiss (appointed by Trump) by pleading to two misdemeanor tax charges—for which he received two years' probation—and entering a pretrial diversion program for felony unlawful possession of a firearm. A month later, however, D DE Judge Maryellen Norieka (Trump) took the highly unusual step of rejecting the agreement for apparently conferring immunity from potential charges under FARA. Attorney General Garland made Weiss special counsel at the latter's request. In December, Hunter also was indicted in CD CA on nine tax charges (including three felonies). Judge Mark Scarsi (Trump) rejected six motions to dismiss, saying defense lawyers presented no evidence of selective and malicious prosecution. In April 2024, Judge Norieka denied a similar motion. "Defendant's claim is effectively that his own father targeted him for being his son, a claim that is nonsensical under the facts here." The Third Circuit held that Norieka's interlocutory decision was not appealable before a final judgment. After eight days of trial and three hours of deliberation, the jury found Hunter guilty of three felony charges. He sought a new trial on the ground of lack of jurisdiction and in view of the Supreme Court's recent decision about guns and domestic violence (*US v. Rahimi*). President Biden promised to accept the verdict and neither pardon Hunter nor commute his sentence. The Trump campaign dismissed the case as "nothing more than a distraction from the real crimes of the Biden Crime Family." The DC Court of Appeals suspended Hunter's law license (automatic following a felony conviction). After Judge Cannon dismissed the classified papers case, finding the appointment and funding of special counsel illegal (Chapter 4.1), Hunter's lawyers made a motion to dismiss on that ground, but Judge Scarsi denied it as "untimely," accusing Hunter's lawyers of issuing "false statements" in bringing it. At the start of his tax trial on September 5, Hunter offered an Alford plea (maintaining his innocence but acknowledging the likelihood of conviction). Scarsi said he could face up to 17 years and a fine of $1.3 million and set sentencing for Dec. 16. Judge Norieka scheduled sentencing for Nov. 13 but postponed it to Dec. 4. More than two years after *The New York Times* sought government records concerning Hunter, and just days after Joe withdrew from the election, the DoS released papers revealing Hunter's efforts to have the Department help his representation of Burisma when his father was Vice President. But on December 2, despite his earlier pledge, Biden gave his son a full pardon, blaming the prosecutions on "political opponents in Congress," who "sought to attack me and oppose my election." "[R]aw politics has infected this process and it led to a miscarriage of justice." Just before Trump took office, Special Counsel Weiss said Biden's "baseless accusations" threatened "the integrity of the justice system as a whole" and "undermine[d] the public's confidence in our criminal justice system."

5.2.4 Disqualifying Trump Under the Fourteenth Amendment

Democrats sought to declare Trump ineligible to serve as president because his efforts to overturn the 2020 election, including the January 6 riot (see Abel 2024b: Chapter 4), constituted engagement in an insurrection under Section 3.[19] As early as December 2022, 41 House Democrats introduced a bill to do this, but unsurprisingly it did not advance. Two conservative legal scholars made the argument for disqualification in August 2023 and were seconded by a conservative former judge, J. Michael Luttig, and a liberal Harvard law professor, Laurence Tribe.[20]

Challenges were filed in several states, three making significant progress. The Illinois State Board of Elections (4 Republicans, 4 Democrats) obtained a nonbinding opinion from a former Republican-appointed state judge, who said Trump had engaged in an insurrection, but the Board lacked authority to disqualify him. Two Republican members appointed by the Board to hear the matter also found Trump had engaged in an insurrection; but the Board unanimously agreed with the judge that it lacked the authority to decide. Democratic Cook County Circuit Court Judge Tracie R. Porter held the Board was wrong and Trump was disqualified but stayed her decision to allow an appeal. Maine's Democratic Secretary of State Sheena Bellows disqualified Trump from the primary ballot. "The weight of the evidence makes clear that Mr. Trump was aware of the tinder laid by his multi-month effort to delegitimize a democratic election, and then chose to light a match." The Trump campaign said she should have recused herself because she had been ACLU of Maine executive director and had criticized the vote to acquit in Trump's second impeachment. Bellows said the recusal was filed too late, but she would have denied it. A Trump spokesman accused her of "a hostile assault on American democracy."

Both actions were mooted by the Colorado case. Denver District Court Judge Sarah B. Wallace (appointed by a Democratic governor) held on September 6, 2023 that Trump "acted with the specific intent to disrupt the Electoral College certification of President Biden's electoral victory through unlawful means; specifically, by using unlawful force and violence" and "incited an insurrection on Jan. 6, 2021 and therefore 'engaged' in insurrection."[21] Although Trump was not an "officer of the United States," the section applied to those, like him, who swore an oath to "support the Constitution." Nevertheless, Wallace declined to disqualify him "without a clear, unmistakable indication" that the Amendment's authors intended it to apply. On December 18, the all-Democratic Colorado Supreme Court (4–3) disqualified Trump but stayed its ruling for two weeks to let him appeal. On January 4, 2024, the US Supreme Court agreed to hear the case, scheduling oral argument for February 8. Trump said: "All I want is fair. I fought really hard to get three, very, very good people in there, great people, very smart people, and I just hope that they're going to be fair. Because you know the other side plays the ref." On February 5, dozens of House Republicans declared that Trump's actions had not been an insurrection. On March 3, the Supreme Court reversed per curiam (with separate opinions by Barrett alone and jointly by Sotomayor, Kagan, and Jackson). Allowing individual states to disqualify candidates would create massive confusion. "Nothing in the

Constitution requires that we endure such chaos—arriving at any time or different times, up to and perhaps beyond inauguration." Michael Luttig called the decision "stunning in its overreach," whereas *The Washington Post* said it "ought always to have been clear."

5.2.5 Analysis

The two parties chose very different strategies to influence or avoid the election, none of which succeeded. House Republicans failed to implicate President Biden in the activities of his son Hunter (and brother James) or impeach the president, and Republicans impeached but failed to convict Homeland Security Secretary Mayorkas (voting along party lines). Although Judge Norieka's rejection of Hunter's plea bargain was highly unusual, the legal system handled the allegations against him appropriately—and many other presidents had embarrassing relatives: LBJ's brother Sam Houston, Richard Nixon's brother Donald, Jimmy Carter's brother Billy, Bill Clinton's brother Roger, and GHWB's son and GWB's brother Neil. Trump denounced Biden's pardon of his son as "an abuse and miscarriage of justice," which would give Trump cover for his promised pardon of January 6 defendants. Although state authorities in Illinois, Colorado, and Maine found Trump had engaged in insurrection, the Supreme Court unanimously decided that eligibility under the Fourteenth Amendment could not be decided piecemeal by the 50 states.

5.3 The 2024 Election

Announcing his candidacy a week after the midterms, Trump repeated calls to execute drug dealers and threatened that if cities failed to suppress civil unrest "we're going to insist that they take our help."[22] (No federal law authorized the first, and the Constitution barred the second.) He claimed to have completed the border wall and maintained: "it's 10 million people coming in, not three or four million. . . . We have no idea who they are and where they come from . . . we are being poisoned." (Trump built 452 miles of wall along the 1,954-mile border, but only 80 were new. 2.76 million people crossed the border in fiscal 2022, a majority of whom were returned.) Although the *New York Post* had endorsed him in 2020 with a front-page banner headline: "Make America Great Again Again," now it trivialized his candidacy on page 24 with a small snide heading: "Florida Man Makes Announcement" and "Been There, Don That." *The New York Times* wrote: "As president, he showed himself to be incompetent and self-dealing. He should have been convicted by the Senate in 2019 for abusing his power and in 2021 for inciting an insurrection."

Two weeks later Trump had dinner at Mar-a-Lago with the openly anti-Semitic rapper Ye, who brought along the white racist Nicholas

Fuentes.[23] Ye had said on Alex Jones's Infowars show: "I like Hitler. Hitler has a lot of redeeming qualities." "We got to stop dissing Nazis all the time." When Fuentes declared he was "very pro-Putin," Ye echoed: "I am also." (Trump later protested: "I'm not a Nazi," sounding disconcertingly like Nixon: "I'm not a crook.") Pence said: "President Trump was wrong to give a white nationalist, an antisemite and a Holocaust denier a seat at the table. I think he should apologize for it, and he should denounce those individuals and their hateful rhetoric without qualification." Chris Christie agreed: "This is just awful, unacceptable conduct from anyone but most particularly from a former President and current candidate." Mike Pompeo called anti-Semitism "a cancer." (All three were contemplating presidential runs.) Morton Klein, head of the right-wing Zionist Organization of America, said: "Donald Trump is not an antisemite . . . but he mainstreams, he legitimizes Jew hatred and Jew haters." Sen. Schumer termed Trump's actions "pure evil." Sen. McConnell predicted that anyone meeting with anti-Semites is "unlikely to ever be elected president." Trump retorted that McConnell was "a loser for our nation and for the Republican Party." Rep. McCarthy said: "I don't think anybody should have a meeting with Nick Fuentes." Trump claimed: "I never heard of [Fuentes]. I had no idea what his views were and they weren't expressed at the table in our very quick dinner, or it should not have been accepted." But Fuentes eagerly capitalized on the connection: "I love Donald Trump." Despite all this, 75 percent of Republicans still viewed Trump very or somewhat favorably—perhaps because only about half of them thought anti-Semitism and racism were problems.

After Twitter explained why it blocked links to an unconfirmed *New York Post* story about the alleged contents of Hunter Biden's laptop, Trump escalated his rhetoric on Truth Social.[24]

> So, with the revelation of MASSIVE & WIDESPREAD FRAUD & DECEPTION in working closely with Big Tech Companies, the DNC & the Democrat [sic] Party, do you throw the Presidential election results of 2020 OUT and declare the Rightful Winner, or do you have a new election. *A massive Fraud of this type and magnitude allows for the termination of all rules, regulations, and articles, even those found in the Constitution* [italics added]. Our great Founders did not want, and would not condone, False & Fraudulent Elections! . . . UNPRECEDENTED FRAUD REQUIRES UNPRECEDENTED CURE! . . . I wonder what Mitch McConnell, the RINOS, and all of the weak Republicans who couldn't get the Presidential Election of 2020 approved and out of the way fast enough, are thinking now?

Days later Trump repeated: "The biggest thing to come out of the Twitter targeting Hoax is that the Presidential Election was RIGGED—And that's as big as it can get!!!"[25] A spokesman added: "the latest revelations about how woke liberals at Twitter meddled in an election and suppressed important information is further proof that Big Tech put their thumb on the scale to benefit Democrats." Tucker Carlson was even more emphatic: "The last election was influenced by the FBI. If this were happening in another country, a third-world country, the State Department would declare the election illegitimate. . . . That's absolutely election interference." Trump vowed to ban federal agencies from "colluding" with business to censor Americans or label domestic speech misinformation or disinformation and promised to root out "every federal bureaucrat who has engaged in domestic censorship—directly or indirectly." Two weeks after that he added:

> The Government of the United States changed our Election Result and it just doesn't get any worse than that. Just look at the damage that's been done to our Country, and the World, in the last two years—it's incalculable. TRUMP WON!!!

In January 2023, Trump issued his "Plan to Protect Children from Left-Wing Gender Insanity," which called for ending all gender-affirming care, punishing doctors who provided it, and enacting a law that "the only genders recognized by the United States government are male and female and they are assigned at birth."[26] His education agenda would "keep men out of women's sports," eliminate tenure for teachers, and cut federal aid to schools that teach "critical race theory, gender ideology, or other inappropriate racial, sexual or political content onto our children." "As the saying goes, personnel is policy and at the end of the day if we have pink-haired communists teaching our kids we have a major problem."

Before the March 2023 CPAC meeting, Trump declared defiantly: "I wouldn't even think about leaving" the race if indicted, because that would just boost his poll numbers.[27] He told CPAC: "I am your warrior. I am your justice. And for those who have been wronged and betrayed, I am your retribution . . . if they win, we no longer have a country." "This is the final battle. They know it, I know it, you know it, everybody knows it." "We will use all necessary state, local, federal and military resources to carry out the largest domestic deportation operation in American history." He would require police departments to use stop-and-frisk and order the DoJ to investigate local prosecutors' charging decisions. (The last three would be illegal.) "Killings are taking place at a number like nobody's ever seen, right in Manhattan." (They declined in 2022 and 2023.) "We lost $85 billion worth of the greatest military equipment in the world" during the Afghanistan withdrawal. (Actually $7 billion.) "They want windmills all over the place that ruin our fields, kill our birds and are very unreliable and are the most expensive energy ever developed." (An estimated 328,000 birds were killed by windmills annually, compared with 4 billion by cats, 14.5 million by fossil fuel plants and 988 million by buildings. By 2027, wind-generated electricity would be cheaper than that from coal, nuclear, biomass, or hydroelectric.) He also claimed that offshore windmills made whales beach themselves by "driving them a little batty."

Sounding like a potential candidate, Pence told the Gridiron Dinner in March:[28]

> [W]hat happened [on January 6th] was a disgrace, and it mocks decency to portray it any other way. . . . President Trump was wrong. I had no right to overturn the election. And his reckless words endangered my family and everyone at the Capitol that day. And I know that history will hold Donald Trump accountable.

In a rare attempt at humor, he added: "I will wholeheartedly, unreservedly support the Republican nominee for president in 2024. If it's me." Trump promptly retorted:

> Had [Pence] sent the votes back to the legislatures, they wouldn't have had a problem with Jan. 6, so in many ways you can blame him for Jan. 6. . . . He had the right to send them back, otherwise they wouldn't have changed the Voting Act [he meant the Electoral Count Act]. . . . I guess he figured that being nice is not working. But, you know, he's out there campaigning.

Trump held his first campaign rally at a regional airport in Waco, Texas, 30 years after the notorious federal raid.[29] Charles Pace, pastor of Mount Carmel (the former Branch Davidian compound), introduced him: "Donald Trump is the anointed of God. He is the battering ram that God is using to bring down the Deep State of Babylon." It was "a statement—that he was sieged [sic] by the F.B.I. at Mar-a-Lago and that they were accusing him of different things that aren't really true, just like [Branch Davidian leader] David Koresh was accused by the F.B.I. when they sieged him." (Pace was referencing the classified papers search, see Chapter 4.1.) Trump assured supporters: "You will be vindicated and proud. The thugs and criminals who are corrupting our justice system will be defeated, discredited and totally disgraced." "Our opponents have done everything they can to crush our spirit and to break our will. But they failed. They've only made us stronger. And 2024 is the final battle, it's going to be the big one."

> With you at my side, we will totally obliterate the deep state, we will banish the warmongers from our government, we will drive out the globalists, and we will cast out the communists and Marxists, we will throw off the corrupt political class, we will beat the Democrats, we will rout the fake news media, we will stand up to the RINOs.

His administration would erect monuments to "true American heroes" and rename schools and streets "not after communists but patriots." Trump would reestablish a presidential commission to promote a "patriotic" school curriculum. Parents would hire and fire principals. Trump would launch a "truth and reconciliation commission" to expose abuses by spy agencies and require all federal employees to pass a new civil service test including questions about due process rights, free speech, religious liberties, and the Fourth Amendment. He would relocate the homeless to tents outside cities: "Violators of these bans will be arrested." (He saw no contradictions in these promises.) After the rally, Trump asserted: "We won in 2016. We won by much more in 2020 but it was rigged." "For seven years, you and I have been taking on the corrupt, rotten and sinister forces trying to destroy America. They're not going to do it. But they do get closer and closer with rigged elections."

In April, Biden announced his re-election bid.[30] "When I ran for president 4 years ago, I said we were in a battle for the soul of America. And we still are." "Around the country, MAGA extremists are lining up to take on those bedrock freedoms": banning abortion and books, restricting voting. "Every generation of Americans has faced a moment when they've had to defend democracy, stand up for our personal freedoms, and stand up for our right to vote and our civil rights. This is ours." At the Howard University commencement, Biden denounced white supremacy as "the most dangerous terrorist threat," explaining that he decided to run in 2020 after Trump asserted there were "fine people on both sides" in the Charlottesville white racist march. At a September fundraiser, Biden said: "Donald Trump and his MAGA Republicans are determined to destroy American democracy. And I will always defend, protect and fight for our democracy. That's why I'm running." He elaborated that at the McCain Institute and Library:

> We should all remember: democracies don't have to die at the end of a rifle. They can die when people are silent—when they fail to stand up or condemn threats to democracy. . . . There is something dangerous happening in America. There is an extremist movement that does not share the basic beliefs of our democracy. The MAGA movement. . . . Trump says the Constitution gave him the right to do whatever he wants as president. I've never even heard a president say that in jest. Not guided by the Constitution or by common service and decency toward our fellow Americans, but by vengeance and vindictiveness.

The Trump campaign responded that "the Radical Left Democrats, now led by Joe Biden, are the greatest threat to democracy the United States of America has ever faced. Biden's claims that conservatives are a 'threat to democracy' are nothing but projection."

At a May "town hall" filled with Trump supporters, CNN let him rant for over an hour, declaring "our country is dying" and predicting a "day of infamy" (a reference to Roosevelt's characterization of the attack on Pearl Harbor) when the Biden administration's termination of the COVID-19 emergency, and therefore the Title 42 limits on asylum applications, would let "millions and millions" of migrants "released from prisons" and "mental institutions" swarm into the country.[31] Trump again advocated separating children from parents to discourage immigration: "If a family hears they're going to be separated, they love their family, they don't come." He repeated a host of lies: "I didn't ask [Georgia officials] to find anything"; Pelosi was "in charge" of security on January 6th; demonstrators "were there with love in their heart"; because only "a couple" of rioters "probably got out of control," he would pardon a "large portion" of them, who were "living in hell" in prison; Pence was never "in any danger"; the police officer who shot Ashli Babbitt was a "thug" who "went on television to brag about the fact that he killed her." Trump had an "absolute right" to keep his presidential records, which were "automatically declassified" when he took them to Mar-a-Lago. True the Vote "found millions of votes . . . on government camera, where they were stuffing ballot boxes." Later that month Trump promised an executive order on his first day in office ending birthright citizenship and requiring that one parent be a US citizen or lawful permanent resident. (He could not legally do this.) In June he repeated: "this is the final battle." "Either the communists win and destroy America, or we destroy the communists." He attacked the "Deep State," "globalists," "warmongers," and the "sick political class that hates our country." Two weeks later he told the Faith & Freedom Coalition meeting in DC: "You have power for the first time. Together we're warriors in a righteous crusade to stop the arsonists, the atheists, the globalists and the Marxists." Each indictment was a "great badge of courage." "I'm being indicted for you."

Launching his own campaign, Pence said:[32]

> I believe that anyone who puts themselves over the Constitution should never be president of the United States and anyone who asks someone else to put them over the Constitution should never be president of the United States again.

January 6 was "a tragic day in the life of our nation." "Trump's words were reckless and endangered my family and everyone at the Capitol. President Trump also demanded that I choose between him and the Constitution. Now voters will be faced with the same choice. I chose the Constitution and I always will." "I have no interest or no intention of pardoning those that assaulted police officers or vandalized our Capitol. They need to be answerable to the law."

Two months later Pence doubled down on Trump's responsibility. "The American people deserve to know that President Trump and his advisers didn't just ask me to pause. They asked me to reject votes, return votes, essentially to overturn the election." Trump retorted that he never told "Pence to put me above the Constitution, or that Mike was too honest." "He's delusional, and now he wants to show he's a tough guy."

Other Republican aspirants competed to outdo Trump's immigration demagoguery.[33] DeSantis urged using deadly force at the border, appropriating tough-guy slang. "If you drop a couple of these cartel operatives" showing hostile intent, "you're not going to have to worry about that anymore." He compared it to a home invasion: "I say use force to repel them. If you do that one time they will never do that again." "If the cartels are cutting through the border wall, trying to run product into this country, they're going to end up stone-cold dead." He, too, would end birthright citizenship, deploy the military along the border, finish the wall, exclude undocumented people from the Census, "close the Flores loophole" (limiting detention of children) and cut off "hundreds of millions of dollars in grants" to places that "try to thwart federal immigration law" by declaring themselves "sanctuaries." (Most of those proposals would be unconstitutional.) January 6 "was not an insurrection." "The idea that this was a plan to somehow overthrow the government of the United States is not true, and it's something that the media has spun up just to try to basically get as much mileage out of it and use it for partisan and for political aims." (The defendants' words at sentencing hearings disprove this, see Abel 2025: Chapter 4.1–4.3.) "I know a lot of people that were there who were just there. They didn't have any designs on doing anything . . . to say that they were seditionists is just wrong." "We're going to have all these deep state people, you know we're going to start slitting throats on Day One and be ready to go." He would eliminate the IRS and the Departments of Education, Commerce, and Energy, shrink the DoJ, and fire FBI Director Wray. Upping the ante, Vivek Ramaswamy would deport all undocumented people and said of the Departments of Education and Commerce, FBI, DoJ Bureau of Alcohol, Tobacco, Firearms and Explosives, IRS and Nuclear Regulatory Commission: "many of these should not exist." He would consider pardoning the January 6 defendants and said the next president should pardon Trump.

In September, DeSantis vowed to "put on the full armor of God" and attack the left's "woke mind virus."[34] "The battle lines are we must win the fight to restore religious freedom as the founding fathers intended it." At the Family Research Council's Pray Vote Stand Summit he promised to create new "divisions of conscience and religious freedom" in the Departments of Education and Labor, fund religious schools, and repeal the Johnson Amendment (prohibiting political activity by tax exempt churches). He would "appoint a special task force to rapidly review the cases of every political prisoner who has been unjustly persecuted by the Biden administration." "I'm sick and tired of being sick and tired of watching the weaponization of the Department of Justice against their political opponents, against pro-life activists." "You're going to have housecleaning at the Department of Justice." His rivals followed suit. Rick Scott said: "we should actually eliminate every single political appointee in all of the Department of Justice." Nikki Haley pronounced: "there's a lot of crazy woke things happening in schools." "I am very aware of a deep state. It's not just in D.C.; it's in every one of our states."

In July, Trump deployed his favorite rhetorical tactic—insinuation—to advance a patent lie about a bag of cocaine found in the White House: "Does anybody really believe that the COCAINE found in the West Wing of the White House, very close to the Oval Office, is for the use of anyone other than Hunter & Joe Biden."[35] (It probably was dropped by a tourist.) Trump also promoted an image of the flag with the slogan: "FUCK BIDEN." Just before that he reposted a Three Percenter claim of "41 MILLION INVALID VOTES in 2020 election," commenting: "A lot has been made of this lately. What do you think?"

In September, Trump declared at a rally that immigrants were "just destroying our country. And if we don't take it back . . . in '24, I really believe we're not going to have a country left."[36] He told the *National Post* that undocumented immigrants were "poisoning the blood of our country," repeating this on X:

> Nobody has any idea where these people are coming from, and we know they come from prisons. We know they come from mental institutions and insane asylums. We know they're terrorists. Nobody has ever seen anything like we're witnessing right now. It is a very sad thing for our country. It's poisoning the blood of our country. It's so bad, and people are coming in with disease. People are coming in with every possible thing that you could have.

Border crossings were an "invasion." "Upon my inauguration I will immediately terminate every open borders policy of the Biden administration. I'll make clear that we must use any and all resources needed to stop the invasion, including moving thousands of troops currently stationed overseas." He had told campaign rallies that South American countries sent mentally ill patients to the US. His spokesman responded to criticism of the words "poisoning the blood of our country" by claiming it was "a normal phrase that is used in everyday life. For anyone to think that is racist or xenophobic is living in an alternate reality consumed with nonsensical outrage." But Hitler had written in *Mein Kampf*: "all the great civilizations of the past became decadent because the originally creative race died out, as a result of contamination of the blood." Elsewhere Hitler linked "the poison which has invaded the national body" to an "influx of foreign blood."

Trump answered critics by turning up the volume.[37] "These people are very aggressive: They drink, they have drugs, a lot of things happening. It's the blood of our country: what they're doing is destroying our country." "People [are] pouring into our country, and we have no idea from where they come." He vowed that "we're going to have the largest deportation operation in history." After being criticized for calling Hezbollah militants "very smart" for the October 7 massacre (committed by Hamas), Trump said "we will implement strong ideological screening for all immigrants to the United States. In addition, we will aggressively deport resident aliens with jihadist sympathies," including Hamas supporters and critics of Israel. He would block "dangerous lunatics, haters, bigots and maniacs to get residence in our country," revoke student visas, deport anti-Israel demonstrators, expand the ban on people from Muslim majority countries (Syria, Somalia, Yemen, and Libya), and deny entry to refugees. "If you support Hamas or any ideas, ideologies that have to do with that or any of the other really sick thoughts that go through people's minds—very dangerous—you're disqualified." "If you empathize with radical Islamic terrorists and extremists, you're disqualified. If you want to abolish the state of Israel, you're disqualified," and so would any "communist, Marxist or fascist." Not to be outdone, DeSantis said the US should not accept Gaza refugees because "they are all antisemitic." "The Arab countries should take them." He, too, would deport student demonstrators. "You don't have a right to be here on a visa. You don't have a right to be studying in the United States." Scott also favored deporting foreign students who supported Hamas. Haley said the undocumented should be divided into those working and paying taxes and "those that are feeding off the system." "If they're feeding off the system, you send them back." At the fourth Republican debate, Ramaswamy promoted the conspiracy theories that January 6 was staged and the election stolen. He threatened to "smoke the terrorists" on the southern border and embraced the racist "great replacement theory." Haley and DeSantis supported Trump's proposed ban on migration from Muslim countries (which the Supreme Court had struck down, see Abel 2024a: Chapter 2). DeSantis ridiculed Arab clothing as "man dresses."

Trump returned to these tropes in December.[38]

> They let—I think the real number is 15, 16 million people into our country. When they do that, we've got a lot of work to do. They're poisoning the blood of our country. That's what they've done. They poison mental institutions and prisons all over the world, not just in South America, not just to three or four countries we think about, but all over the world. They're coming into our country from Africa, from Asia, all over the world.

He repeated this on Truth Social: "ILLEGAL IMMIGRATION IS POISONING THE BLOOD OF OUR NATION. THEY'RE COMING FROM

PRISONS, FROM MENTAL INSTITUTIONS—FROM ALL OVER THE WORLD." Criticized by the Biden campaign for having "parroted Adolf Hitler," Trump just reiterated that immigrants from Africa, Asia and South America were "destroying the blood of our country." He protested: "I never read 'mein [sic] Kampf'"; anyhow, Hitler said it "in a much different way." Undocumented immigrants "could be healthy. They could be very unhealthy. They could bring in disease that's going to catch on in our country." (This reprised his blaming China for COVID-19, see Abel 2024c.)

Trump said in New Hampshire in October 2023 that the criminal charges against him were "third-world stuff, 'arrest your opponent.' And that means I can do that, too."[39] Democrats had

> released the genie out of the box. . . . They have done something that allows the next party . . . if I happen to be president and I see somebody who's doing well and beating me very badly, I say "go down and indict them." They'd be out of business. They'd be out of the election.

He said on Truth Social:

> I'm 12 Points up on Crooked Joe Biden—But he's got the Justice Department and others suing me wherever and whenever possible—WEAPONIZATION, it's called, and maybe that can make a difference. This has never been done on this scale before, not in our Country, but it opens up a very big and dangerous Pandora's Box. Joe Biden should stop his Election Interfering Thugs before it is too late for him and the rest of the Country. As the leader of the Opposition Party, I should not be forced to campaign from inside a courthouse. . . . This is where they want me to spend my time and money, but it is not the way our system is supposed to work. . . . To ALL Democrats, be careful what you wish for.

Stephen Miller (who had been President Trump's senior adviser and expected an important position in a second term) said: "Trump will unleash the vast arsenal of federal powers to implement the most spectacular migration crackdown."[40] (This nonlawyer had been the source of many of President Trump's illegal immigration initiatives, see Abel 2024a: Chapter 2.) The "blitz" would overwhelm "the immigration legal activists," who "won't know what's happening." The government would conduct raids at work and other public places and build "vast holding facilities that would function as staging centers." In Florida on November 8, Trump compared immigrants to the fictional cannibal Hannibal Lecter. "That's what's coming into our country right now." He would reinvoke Title 42, citing "severe strains of the flu, tuberculosis, scabies, other respiratory illnesses like R.S.V. and so on, or just a general issue of mass migration being a public health threat and conveying a variety of communicable diseases." He would jettison due process to expel drug cartels and gang members under the Alien Enemies Act of 1798, which authorized deportation of people from countries that were at war with the US or had invaded it or engaged in "predatory incursion." Tom Homan (who had advocated family separation as Trump's ICE director) agreed to return to government and "help to organize and run the largest deportation operation this country's ever seen." In the first ten days of 2024, the "border" was mentioned 1,319 times in Republican political ads, more than any other word.

In a Veterans' Day speech, Trump promised to "root out" the "radical left thugs that live like vermin within the confines of our country."[41] ("Vermin" was another favorite Nazi trope.) "The threat from outside forces is far less sinister, dangerous and grave than the threat from within." Democrats "treat the illegal aliens pouring into our country better than they treat our vets." He praised China for executing drug dealers, asking the audience: "Let's have a vote. Who would be in favor of the death penalty . . . knowing that it will solve the problem?" He fawned over Xi: "He's like Central Casting. There's nobody in Hollywood that can play the role of President Xi—the look, the strength, the voice."

Trump campaign rhetoric descended to new levels of vulgarity and viciousness.[42] At an Iowa rally children wore hats with the slogan FJB (Fuck Joe Biden); other merchandise bluntly said: "Fuck Biden." T-shirts proclaimed: "Biden loves minors" (reprising the QAnon lies) and "Joe and the Ho Gotta Go!" (Black slang for whore). One shirt featured Biden and Harris having sex; another showed Trump giving the middle finger. At a Kansas GOP event in March, attendees were invited to kick and beat a mannequin wearing a rubber Biden mask and a "Let's Go Brandon" t-shirt (a euphemism for "Fuck Joe Biden"). On Truth Social, Trump posted an image of a truck sporting a giant Trump flag, with Biden bound hand and foot on its tailgate; vendors were selling bumper stickers of that image. Trump called one Republican opponent a "son of a bitch" and Haley a "birdbrain" and insulted Adam Schiff as "pencil neck," asking: "How does he hold up that fat, ugly face?" Trump said Biden was taking drugs and could not walk offstage. The rally speaker introducing Trump called anyone who took a knee a "disrespectful little shit." Trump declared: "Our country is going to hell. We have some people that either they don't care, they're not very smart or they hate our country, and nobody really knows the answer." A PRRI poll in October found that 38 percent of Americans and 48 percent of Republicans wanted a president "willing to break some rules" to "set things right."

Trump coupled his attacks on the criminal justice system and elections with appeals to racism.[43] He would "investigate every Marxist prosecutor in America for their illegal, racist-in-reverse enforcement of the law." He advised a white suburban Des Moines audience to scrutinize elections in Detroit, Philadelphia, and Atlanta (all cities with large minority populations). "You should go into some of these places, and we've got to watch those votes when they come in. When they're being, you know, shoved around in wheelbarrows and dumped on the floor and everyone's saying, 'what's going on?' We're like a third-world nation." "You look at any Democrat-run state, and it's just not the same—it doesn't work." New York, Chicago, Los Angeles, and San Francisco were crime dens (again cities with large minority populations). He also claimed: "Under Crooked Joe Biden, Christians and Americans of faith are being persecuted like nothing this nation has ever seen before. Catholics in particular are being targeted and evangelicals are surely on the watchlist as well." "Over the past three years, the Biden administration has sent SWAT teams to arrest pro-life activists." "The F.B.I. has been caught profiling devout Catholics as possible domestic terrorists and planning to send undercover spies into Catholic churches, just like in the old days of the Soviet Union." (The DoJ Inspector General found no evidence that "anyone ordered or directed" FBI agents to investigate Catholics because of their religion.)

Asked by Sean Hannity if he had "any plans whatsoever, if re-elected president, to abuse power? To break the law? To use the government to go after people?" Trump retorted: "You mean like they're using right now?"[44] When Hannity sought a promise not to "abuse this power as retribution against anybody," Trump replied: "Except for Day 1," when "we're closing the border. And were drilling, drilling, drilling. After that, I'm not a dictator." Polls showed high levels of Republican support for these threats: 52 percent thought the country needed "a strong president who should be allowed to rule without too much interference from courts and Congress" (Reuters-Ipsos, March); 74 percent supported Trump being "dictator for a day" (U. Mass. Amherst, February); 56 percent said things were so bad "we need a leader who is willing to break some rules to set things right" (NPR-PBS-Marist College, April); 40 percent of Trump voters wanted a president who will break "rules and laws" (Fox News, December 2022).

Kash Patel (who held senior national security positions under Trump and was expected to join a second administration) told Steve Bannon: "We will go out and find the conspirators, not just in government but in the media. . . . This is why we're dictators."[45] Patel added:

> The one thing we learned in the Trump administration the first go-around, is we got to put in all American patriots, top to bottom, and we got them for law enforcement. We got them for intelligence collection. We got them for offensive operations. We got them for [DoD], CIA, everywhere.

Bannon seconded this:

> The deep state—the administrative state, the fourth branch of government, never mentioned in the Constitution—is going to be taken apart, brick by brick, and the people that did these evil deeds will be held accountable and prosecuted, criminal prosecutions.

Trump had declared on Truth Social in September:

> I say up front, openly, and proudly, that when I win the Presidency of the United States they and others of the LameStream Media will be thoroughly scrutinized for their knowingly dishonest and corrupt coverage of people, things, and events. Why should NBC, or any other of the corrupt & dishonest media companies be entitled to use the very valuable Airwaves of the USA, FREE?

"Comcast, with its one-side [sic] and vicious coverage by NBC News, and in particular MSNBC," should be "investigated for its 'Country Threatening Treason.'" Trump would bring the FCC "back under presidential authority as the Constitution demands." The media "are a true threat to Democracy and are, in fact, THE ENEMY OF THE PEOPLE! The Fake News Media should pay a big price for what they have done to our once great country." After CBS interviewed his rival, Kamala Harris, Trump bellowed:

> Her REAL ANSWER WAS CRAZY, OR DUMB, so they actually REPLACED it with another answer in order to save her or, at least, make her look better. A FAKE NEWS SCAM, which is totally illegal. TAKE AWAY THE CBS LICENSE.

He claimed Democrats made CBS "do this," calling it "the single biggest scandal in broadcast history," "Election Interference," and "a major Campaign Finance Violation," and declaring Democrats should be forced to concede. He earlier had said ABC should lose its license because of the way it moderated his debate with Harris. At one of his last election rallies, Trump provoked audience laughter by referring to his two assassination attempts and saying: "to get to me, somebody would have to shoot through the fake news. And I don't mind that so much."

Trump made other promises for day one.[46]

> [T]he momentum of our great victory will immediately begin stopping the hordes of illegal-alien migrants who are charging across our border by the hundreds of thousands. . . . Safety will again be restored so that children can go outside with their parents—mother and father—and play in the

> park without being beat up, molested or shot. . . . I will sign a new EO to cut federal funding for any school pushing critical race theory, transgender insanity and other inappropriate racial, sexual or political content on our children. . . . I will not give one penny to any school that has a vaccine mandate or mask mandate. . . . I will keep men out of women's sports.

He later commented: "I talk about transgender, everyone goes crazy. . . . Five years ago, you didn't know what the hell it was."

The campaign energetically fostered idolatry of their candidate.[47] NFT INT, an official licensee of Trump's name and image, began selling a "Mugshot Edition" NFT set, featuring his scowling face when booked in Atlanta and including swatches of the blue suit and red tie he had worn: "the most historically significant artifact in American history" (a sacrilegious parody of the holy relics of a saint). The full set of 47 cards (the number of his anticipated second term) cost $4,653 and bought a dinner at Mar-a-Lago. Trump posted on Truth Social a video by the Dilley Meme Team (who styled themselves "Trump's Online War Machine"), declaring "God gave us Trump" and lauding his alleged achievements, ending each stanza with: "So God made Trump." Truth Social also displayed an image of Trump seated next to Christ (an unholy duality displacing the Holy Trinity). Followers wore t-shirts avowing: "Jesus Is My Savior. Trump Is My President" and depicting Christ laying hands on Trump (blessing or consecrating him) and sweatshirts proclaiming: "Jesus Has Chosen Him." The campaign marketed $399 gold Trump sneakers and a $99 Victory47 cologne in a gold bottle with a gold Trump head stopper. He followed that up with a $50 pin featuring his name on the flag in large gold letters (violating PL 94–344). In March 2024, Trump proclaimed: "Happy Holy Week!" "As we lead into Good Friday and Easter, I encourage you [to] go get a copy of the God Bless The USA Bible" his campaign was selling for $60 (1,000 copies with Trump's "hand-signed signature" for $1,000). Trump declared: "it's my favorite book," although he had been unable to cite any passage in the past and rarely attended church. (His enthusiasm for this Bible may be related to the fact that he reported a $300,000 royalty payment from its sales. Oklahoma ordered schools to buy 55,000 Bibles, whose specifications just happened to match Trump's version.) "Religion and Christianity are the biggest things missing from this country." "We must make America pray again." (The catchy phrase rhymed with MAGA, but the Supreme Court had held that government coercion violated the First Amendment.) Trump posted on Truth Social a *Washington Times* article headlined: "The Crucifixion of Donald Trump. As Easter Sunday approaches, much of the world will commemorate the arrest, death and resurrection of Jesus Christ—the holiest days of the Christian calendar." He also posted: "HAPPY EASTER TO ALL, INCLUDING CROOKED AND CORRUPT PROSECUTORS AND JUDGES THAT ARE DOING EVERYTHING

POSSIBLE TO INTERFERE WITH THE PRESIDENTIAL ELECTION OF 2024, AND PUT ME IN PRISON." In June, Trump again likened himself to Jesus (and saints bearing His stigmata):

> Together, we stood up to the communists, Marxists and fascists to defend religious liberty like no other president has ever done. And I have the wounds all over my body. . . . I take a lot of wounds, I can tell you, more than, I suspect, any president ever.

Just before the election he promised Christian leaders access "directly into the Oval Office—and me. We have to save religion in this country."

Despite the initial reluctance of many Republican politicians to ally themselves with Trump, the number of endorsements kept increasing, reaching 130 Representatives, 31 Senators, and 11 Governors by February 2024.[48] After abandoning her campaign, Nikki Haley signed on to Trump's, earning the promise of a place in the next administration. Sen. McConnell, who had called the president an "ill-tempered" "narcissist" and "despicable human being" in late 2020 and declared after January 6 he was "done with" Trump and "will never speak to him again," now joined the crowd because "we worked together to accomplish great things for the American people . . . a generational change of our federal judiciary—most importantly, the Supreme Court." Three months later he publicly shook Trump's hand.

Garland had named Robert Hur (Trump's US Attorney for D MD) as special counsel to investigate Biden's handling of classified papers (Chapter 4.1). In February 2024, Hur issued a 345-page report reprimanding the president but recommending against prosecution because it would be difficult to establish guilt "beyond a reasonable doubt," in part since a jury probably would find Biden "a well-meaning, elderly man with poor memory," negating the requisite "willfulness."[49] MAGA Inc. misrepresented this, declaring: "if you're too senile to stand trial, then you're too senile to be president." Sen. Rubio said Hur found that Biden had "age related dementia" (which Hur immediately denied). Trump said Hur's declination exposed his own classified papers case as "selective persecution." But promptly confirming Haley's observation that he had "his own mental deficiencies" and was "prone to temper tantrums and wild rants," Trump told a rally that a president "of a big country" had asked whether the US would protect it if Russia attacked, prompting a harsh rebuff: "You didn't pay [NATO obligations]. You're delinquent." "I would not protect you. In fact, I would encourage them to do whatever the hell they want." He also vowed to replace all foreign aid with loans, which would be due immediately if the recipient "turns against us, or strikes it rich." Biden denounced Trump's "un-American" sentiments. "No other president in our history has ever bowed down to a Russian dictator." At a Fox Town Hall,

Trump praised Russia as "a war machine," declaring: "They defeated Hitler" (ignoring the fact they had done so in alliance with the US and other nations).

Trump began his February 2024 talk to the National Religious Broadcasters with the national anthem sung by the J6 Prison Choir, calling them "hostages" and praising their "tremendous spirit."[50] Unlike the situation in World War II, "the greatest threat is not from outside of our country. . . . It's from the people within our country. . . . They're very sick people." Pro-Palestinian demonstrators were "foreign jihadists." Anyone voting for a Democrat was "crazy."

At CPAC that month, Trump warned that immigration would cause the "collapse" of Medicare and private health care, Social Security, and public education; millions of manufacturing jobs would be "choked off into extinction"; Hamas would "terrorize our streets." America would face "obliteration."[51] (At the same meeting, far-right conspiracy theorist Jack Posobiec boasted: "Welcome to the end of democracy. We are here to overthrow it completely. We didn't get all the way there on Jan. 6, but we will endeavor to get rid of it.") Trump exploited the death of Laken Riley, a nursing student, calling the undocumented murder suspect an "illegal alien animal." A poll found that immigration had become the most important political issue for the first time since 2019, most of the increase occurring among Republicans (from 37 to 57 percent). On a visit to the Texas border that month, Trump said: "We have languages coming into our country. We have nobody that even speaks those languages." The migrants "look like warriors to me." At March rallies in North Carolina and Virginia, he said Biden had "smuggled" violent anti-American forces across the border in a "conspiracy to overthrow the United States of America," "giving aid and comfort" to foreign enemies. Republicans needed to turn out voters so the election would be "too big to rig." Elsewhere Trump said: "last night they had four from the Congo" intercepted at the border and concocted an imaginary conversation: "I wonder what beautiful place do you live in the Congo? 'We are from prison.' What did you do? 'Murder.' They're in the United States right now." "[V]ery big population coming in from the jails of the Congo." He reaffirmed his 2018 "fine" comment about immigrants from "shithole countries." "Thousands" of Hannibal Lecters were "now in our country." "[B]y the time we get the worst president in our history out of office . . . it's going to be close to 20 million" more undocumented immigrants. "[T]hey're coming in from rough places and dangerous places." "In February alone, nearly 1 million jobs held by native-born Americans disappeared . . . black people, that's who lost the jobs. Hispanic people, that's who lost the jobs." After winning the Super Tuesday primaries on March 6 (effectively securing the Republican nomination), Trump said: "325,000 people were flown in from parts unknown." "THIS IS BOTH ILLEGAL AND CRAZY." (This was the number CBP approved after extensive vetting; those actually entering paid their own way.) Trump said: "It's the fascists and the communists that surround [Biden]—they're making the calls." He again denounced the "border blood bath"; the RNC had created a new website, BidenBloodbath.com, highlighting alleged crimes by undocumented people. In April, Trump said in Michigan: "every town is now a border town because Joe Biden has brought the carnage and chaos and killing from all over world [sic] and dumped it straight into our backyards."

In his State of the Union message, Biden drew a stark contrast with his opponent: "Instead of celebrating the contribution of immigrants to our country, to our economy and our communities, Donald Trump calls them vermin, poisoning the blood of America." "I will not separate families. I will not ban people because of their faith."[52] Trump retorted: "we are going to have to deport a lot of bad people, because our countries [sic] can't live like this, our cities are choking to death, our states are dying and frankly our country is dying." "Everything Joe Biden touches turns to shit." Trump railed against migrants: "some of these people are monsters," whom Biden's border policies left "free to kill." "Joe Biden has no remorse, he's got no regret, he's got no empathy, no compassion and worst of all he has no intention of stopping the deadly invasion that stole precious Laken [Riley]'s beautiful American life." (This echoed George H.W. Bush blaming Michael Dukakis for the murder committed by paroled criminal Willie Horton in 1988 and Trump's own exploitation of the 2015 shooting death of Kate Steinle in San Francisco by an undocumented Mexican immigrant, which a court found accidental, see Abel 2024a: 34–35.)

> I will stop the killing. I will stop the bloodshed. I will end the agony of our people, the plunder of our cities, the sacking of our towns, the violations of our citizens and the conquest of our country. These people are conquering our country.

If he lost the election, there would be "the largest stock market crash we've ever had." The economy was "collapsing in a cesspool of ruin." "We'll end up in World War III." (He predicted the US would lose that war, devastated by "weapons, the likes of which nobody has ever seen before. And the only thing standing between you and its obliteration is me.") His indictments were "all bullshit." He said on Truth Social a few days later: "My first acts as your next President will be to Close the Border, DRILL, BABY DRILL, and Free the January 6 Hostages being wrongfully imprisoned," whom he earlier described as "policemen . . . firemen . . . accountants . . . lawyers," as though that made their crimes less heinous rather than more.

Later in March Trump warned: "if I don't get elected . . . it's going to be a blood bath for the country."[53] (He subsequently claimed he had been referring to the effect of imports on the automobile industry.) He added more ominously: "I don't think you're going to have another election, or certainly not an election that's meaningful." He again praised the January 6 "hostages" and "political prisoners" as "unbelievable patriots." He said of immigrants: "I don't know if you call them 'people,' in some cases. They're not people in my opinion" but "animals." Biden was "a stupid president" and a "dumb son of a bitch." "Any Jewish person that votes for Democrats hates their religion." (He later added they "should be ashamed of themselves" and "should have their head examined," extending the latter insult to African Americans and Hispanics). "OUR ONCE GREAT COUNTRY IS GOING DOWN THE DRAIN. WE ARE A NATION IN DECLINE! VOTE FOR TRUMP, WHAT THE HELL DO YOU HAVE TO LOSE?" Asked why he parroted "the kind of language that Hitler and Mussolini used," Trump answered defiantly: "because our country is being poisoned." "These are people at the highest level of crime," coming from "a mental institution on steroids." At an April fundraiser, he said he wanted immigrants from "nice countries, you know like Denmark, Switzerland . . . Norway." (The Nazis viewed Norwegians as phenotypically Aryan, genetically superior even to Germans.) Instead, immigrants were coming from "disaster countries" like Yemen, "where they're blowing each other up all over the place."

After the White House issued its annual proclamation of Transgender Day of Visibility on March 31 (the date it had been celebrated since 2009), the Trump campaign falsely accused Biden of having "chosen" to do so on Easter, denounced this as "blasphemous," and demanded he "issue an apology to the millions of Catholics and Christians across America."[54] Trump also falsely accused Biden of prohibiting children from submitting religious egg decorations to the White House Easter Art Contest, although that ban had been instituted by the American Egg Board 45 years earlier.

Trump was a pathological and shameless liar.[55] Biden was "pushing the largest tax hike in American history," which would "quadruple your taxes." There would be "an all-electric mandate" for cars "in a very short period of time." Even military tanks would have to be electric. Under Trump "we had the best economy. We had no inflation." Gas cost $1.87. "Thousands of people were not allowed to vote" in Arizona. "We are a nation that screens its citizens viciously at all ports. But if you are an illegal alien, you're allowed to flow through our country with no check whatsoever." Trump said on Truth Social on April 11: "Biden and [Michigan Gov.] Whitmer are selecting and stealing your money to give free housing to illegal alien migrants and then asking you to quarter these foreign armies."

In an April 30 *Time* magazine interview, Trump repeated his promise to order the largest deportation ever "because we have no choice."[56] He would use local police and "give them immunity from prosecution if they're doing their job." (He could do neither.) He also would deploy the National Guard and "have no problem using the military." The Posse Comitatus Act barring this did not apply because "this is an invasion of our country." "Over the last three weeks, 29,000 people came in from China, and they're all fighting age, and they're mostly males." It was "possible" he would intern the undocumented in detention camps. He refused to believe violent crime was declining, because "the FBI fudged the numbers." On January 6 "nobody died other than Ashli [Babbitt]." If Democrats won in November, the next day "there won't be any more oil." A few weeks later he said: "we have millions of people here that are criminals." "Jail populations all over the world are way down . . . because they're sending people in their jails into the United States." (Penal Reform International reported that the global prison population had grown 500,000 since 2020, reaching a record high in 2023.) Trump posted on Truth Social (but quickly deleted) an image of a hypothetical newspaper article celebrating his November victory as "the creation of a unified Reich." (Hitler's ambition had been a Thousand Year Reich.) Trump declared again that Putin, Kim, Xi, and Erdoğan were "at the top of their game, whether you like it or not." He told a Bronx audience (mostly people of color): "The biggest negative impact" of the undocumented is "against our Black population and our Hispanic population who are losing their jobs, losing their housing, losing everything they can lose." He again promised the "largest deportation operation" in US history because immigrants "want to get us from within. I think they're building an army." Trump claimed the DHHS Office of Refugee Resettlement had "88,000 missing children now. . . . That's a holocaust." Three months later he nearly quadrupled that figure to 325,000, "many of whom have undoubtedly been raped, trafficked, killed, or horribly abused." "[T]ake your biggest stadium in California and you could fill it up five or six times." (He was misrepresenting an ORR report that it had not received an initial response to phone calls concerning 85,000 migrant children; but none was required, and 81 percent of follow-up calls were successful.) He said in Las Vegas that the immigrant "invasion" was "changing the fabric of our country," turning it into a "dumping ground." "We're not going to let them destroy our country." By May, Trump had questioned the integrity of the forthcoming election more than 500 times, more than once a day on average and more often than he had in 2020 or 2016.

In a fund-raising message (anticipating his sentencing by Justice Merchan, see Chapter 2.1) Trump threatened: "1 MONTH UNTIL ALL HELL BREAKS LOOSE! THEY WANT TO SENTENCE ME TO DEATH."[57] "GUILLOTINE." (This echoed his all-too-effective call to "be wild" on January 6.) He denounced his conviction: "it's a terrible, terrible path that they're leading us to, and it's very possible that it's going to happen to them." "Based on what they've done I would have every right to go after them . . . and it's easy, because it's Joe Biden and you see all the criminality, all of the money that's going into the family and him." "Sometimes revenge can be justified."

Stephen Miller further incited revenge, asking rhetorically on Fox News:

> Is every House committee controlled by Republicans using its subpoena power in every way it needs right now? Is every Republican D.A. starting every investigation they need to right now? Every facet of Republican Party politics and power has to be used right now to go toe-to-toe with Marxism and beat these communists.

Stephen Bannon agreed: "There are dozens of ambitious backbench state attorneys general and DAs who need to 'seize the day' and own this moment in history." Sen. Rubio declared it was time to "fight fire with fire." UC Berkeley law professor John Yoo advised in the *National Review*:

> In order to prevent the case of Trump from assuming a permanent place in the American political system, Republicans will have to bring charges against Democratic officers, even presidents. Only retaliation in kind can produce the deterrence necessary to enforce a political version of mutual assured destruction.

Rep. Jackson said: "I am going to encourage all of my colleagues and everybody that I have influence over as a member of Congress to aggressively go after the President and his . . . entire crime family." Rep. Jordan said there would be no money for Jack Smith. (The Republican House proposed to cut the DoJ budget 20 percent.) Jeffrey Clark urged "brave" DAs to file federal lawsuits seeking money damages.

Shortly before the first presidential debate on June 27, Trump declared: "crooked Joe" was going to get "a shot in the ass" and "come out all jacked up," reviving the rumor about "all that cocaine that was missing a month ago from the White House."[58] (A small package had been found in a public area the year before, probably dropped by a tourist.) On Truth Social Trump demanded: "DRUG TEST FOR CROOKED JOE BIDEN." This smear campaign was picked up by Republican Representatives and right-wing media. After the debate, watched by 51 million, there was widespread agreement that Trump just repeated his many lies, while Biden, in a voice weakened by a cold, often stumbled: mistaking names, garbling sentences, and failing to complete his thoughts. Excerpts of his poor performance circulated widely on social media. Trump looked younger than his 78 years, Biden older than his 81. Trump introduced new lies: he had been the first to cap the cost of insulin; there had been no terrorist attacks during his term; the only jobs Biden created went to illegal immigrants or were generated by the post-COVID "bounce back"; the Select Committee "destroyed and deleted" all the information Trump sought. He reprised his apocalyptic assertions: "the whole world is blowing up under" Biden. "We are living right now in a rat's nest.

They're killing our people . . . in every state of the union because we don't have borders anymore." He devised new insults: Biden was "like a Palestinian," a "Manchurian candidate" paid by China. Trump again threatened revenge: Biden was "a criminal" and "could be a convicted felon."

Most ominously, Trump agreed to accept the outcome only "if it is a fair and legal and good election." He had said in his *Time* interview: "if we don't win, you know it depends. It always depends on the fairness of an election." He told a Michigan rally on May 1: "Democrats rigged the presidential election in 2020, but we're not going to allow them to rig the presidential election . . . in 2024." He told the *Milwaukee Journal* on May 2: "if everything's honest, I'll gladly accept the results. . . . If it's not, you have to fight for the right of the country." Roger Stone had said: "this will be our last election unless we elect Donald Trump." Two vice-presidential aspirants, Tim Scott and Doug Burgum, and two prominent Republican Representatives, Elise Stefanik and Byron Donalds, would not commit to accepting the results. Sen. Rubio, another aspirant, said: "If it's an unfair election I think it's going to be contested by each side." Before being chosen by Trump, Vance said: "if we have a free and fair election, I will accept the results."

Many prominent Democrats were appalled by Biden's debate performance, though few would speak for the record.[59] Former Sen. McCaskill worried Biden had "failed" to "reassure Americans that he was up to the job at his age." Former HUD Secretary Julian Castro agreed the President "failed to clear" the "very low bar" and should step aside. Mark Buell, a prominent donor, wondered: "do we have time to put somebody else in there?" Former Speaker Pelosi thought it "legitimate" to ask whether Biden's debate performance was "an episode" or "a condition." Two vulnerable House Democrats, Jared Golden and Marie Gluesenkamp Perez, predicted Biden would lose. Reps. Grijalva, Doggett, Quigley, Moulton, and Craig urged withdrawal. On a conference call with House leaders, Reps. Nadler, Morelle, Takano, and Adam Smith joined them. On July 9, Rep. Sherrill became the tenth House member to call for withdrawal; the next day there were 13. But Nadler still maintained Biden was "going to be our nominee, and we all have to support him." Sen. Warner was organizing colleagues to urge withdrawal. Sen. Murray said Biden "must seriously consider the best way to preserve his incredible legacy." Sen. Bennet warned Trump might win "by a landslide and take with him the Senate and the House," but said no senator had called for withdrawal. The next day Welch became the first.

Journalists like Joe Scarborough, who had strongly supported Biden, turned critical.[60] Van Jones said he "failed" to meet the test "to restore the confidence of the country and of the base." *The New York Times* headlined its editorial: "To serve his country, President Biden should leave the race." That call "reflects the scale and seriousness of Mr. Trump's challenge to the values and institutions of this country and the inadequacy of Mr. Biden to confront him." *Times* columnists agreed. Thomas Friedman said Biden "must bow out of the race." Calling Biden "the best president of my adult life," Paul Krugman "join[ed] the chorus asking Biden to voluntarily step aside." Nicholas Kristof hoped Biden would withdraw. Maureen Dowd accused Biden of having "succumbed to behavior redolent of Trump" by still running. Michelle Goldberg and Bret Stephens (on opposite sides of the political spectrum) agreed Biden should withdraw. *The Washington Post* said the decision was up to the President; but five days later it urged him to say on July 4: "my season of service is nearing its close" and emulate George Washington in not running again.

In a rally the day after the debate, Biden stood firm: "I would not be running again if I didn't believe with all my heart and soul I can do this job."[61] The campaign received $14 million in the 36 hours after the debate and asserted Biden would remain the candidate. But in a meeting of PAC American Bridge that day, nearly all the four dozen major donors agreed he should step down. And Netflix co-founder Reid Hanson (who with his wife had recently given Democrats more than $20 million) urged withdrawal. The Leadership Now Project, 400 politically active current and former executives, said Biden should "pass the torch." Fundraisers for Next Generation PAC were seeking $100 million to support a replacement. Major donors Abigail Disney, Gideon Stein, and Damon Lindelof were withholding contributions. Former PayPal and Intuit CEO Bill Harris and others pledged $2 million for a "mini-primary" if Biden left the race. A group of 168 business executives and donors urged him to quit. A new group, Pass the Torch, planned to persuade convention delegates to vote against Biden. Major donors told the Future Forward super PAC that about $90 million in pledges would be withheld unless Biden stepped down. Major donors gave only half as much in July as they had in June. On July 19, Michael Moritz (a billionaire Silicon Valley venture capitalist who had given $7.8 million) called on Biden to withdraw; Zynga co-founder Mark Pincus had done so earlier.

Post-debate polls suggested Trump had slightly widened his lead: 49/43 percent with likely voters, 49/41 with registered voters; 74 percent said Biden was too old, including 59 percent of Democrats (up 8 percent).[62] A post-debate Wisconsin poll showed Trump ahead 50–45 percent; Biden trailed by 7 percent among voters over 49, although just 1 percent among those under 50. Other polls showed Trump leading by an average of 3.5 percent, compared with 1 percent before the debate. Real Clear Politics found Trump 3.3 percent ahead in an average of post-debate polls. A Washington Post-ABC News-Ipsos poll two weeks after the debate found that 67 percent of adults, including 56 percent of Democrats and over 70 percent of independents, thought Biden should step down. But 46 percent of registered voters still preferred each candidate, as they had in April.

Biden was adamant. On July 2, the White House declared he was "absolutely not" dropping out.[63] Three days later he sounded like Trump: "If the Lord Almighty said get out of the race, I'd get out of the race. The Lord Almighty's not coming down." However, his efforts to regain credibility were faltering. On radio shows with two Black hosts, he said he was proud to have been "the first Black woman to serve with a Black president," referred to Trump as "one of our colleagues," could not complete sentences, and flubbed his attack on the Supreme Court's immunity decision. After it emerged that Biden aides had provided the softball questions, one radio host resigned, and another radio station disclosed it had edited a Biden interview at the campaign's request. But when interviewed by former White House communications director George Stephanopoulos, Biden maintained: "I'm the most qualified person to beat [Trump], and I know how to get things done." "I get a cognitive test every day . . . not only am I campaigning, but I'm running the world." Yet he answered only four easy questions and insisted that "all the pollsters I talk to tell me it's a toss-up." Press Secretary Karine Jean-Pierre refused to explain the eight White House visits by neurologist and Parkinson's specialist Dr. Kevin Cannard, although Biden's own physician maintained there had been "no findings" of Parkinson's or other neurological disorders during the president's three annual physicals. Biden pushed back defiantly, inviting "any of these guys that don't think I should run [to] run against me. Announce for president, challenge me at the convention." "The voters of the Democratic Party have voted. They have chosen me to be the nominee of the party." He complained on MSNBC he was "getting so frustrated" by "the elites in the party who, they know so much more": "I don't care what the millionaires think."

All this bluster failed to persuade *The New York Times*.[64] During the Stephanopoulos interview Biden "continued to appear as a man in decline." He "has to pay attention to the will of the broader electorate that will determine the outcome in November." Former Democratic political adviser James Carville confidently predicted: "Joe Biden is going to be out of the 2024 presidential race." Paul Krugman was equally blunt: Biden had "utterly failed the test" in the debate. Thomas Friedman declared: "both men running for president right now are unfit for the job." The conservative columnist Bret Stephens said critically: "the man elected to banish his self-deluded, deceptive, disrespectful and destructive predecessor increasingly embodies those vices himself." George Clooney, who had been a strong Biden supporter, wrote in the *Times* that the President "is not the same man he was, and he won't win this fall." Making its sentiments clear, however, the *Times* also editorialized on July 11: "Donald Trump is unfit to lead." "He has demonstrated an utter lack of respect for the Constitution, the rule of law and the American people."

Republicans used Biden's poor debate performance to escalate their frightening rhetoric.[65] Kevin Roberts, president of the Heritage Foundation (which had coordinated Project 2025), warned on Bannon's "War Room" that conservatives' "second American revolution" would "remain bloodless" only "if the left allows it to be." "It's the left that has a long history of violence, so it's up to them to allow a peaceful transfer of power." The Project website proclaimed: "Our goal is to assemble an army of aligned, vetted, trained and prepared conservatives to go to work on Day One to deconstruct the Administrative State." Cheering the Supreme Court's *Loper* decision overruling *Chevron* deference to regulatory agencies, Sen. McConnell said: "dismantling the administrative state and empowering people who are actually elected to make decisions has been the motiving force" and "unifying issue" for nearly every "Federalist Society-type lawyer." At the same time, Trump claimed (unconvincingly) he knew "nothing about Project 2025" and had "no idea who is behind it" (although the authors included his former and likely future senior adviser Stephen Miller, and there were many other linkages with his administration and campaign). Some of the things they were saying "are absolutely ridiculous and abysmal."

Two vice-presidential aspirants curried favor with Trump. Sen. Vance (a Yale law graduate) said Trump's call for a special prosecutor to investigate Biden was a "totally reasonable thing" (see 5.2.1). Sen. Rubio (a University of Miami law graduate) said the Supreme Court's immunity decision had "clarified what the law is" because "we have reached an era where there are people in American politics who believe that our courts are now a weapon that can be used against their political opponents." (The one thing the Court did not do was clarify the law, see Chapter 4.2.) Seeing a political opportunity, House Oversight Committee Chairman Comer demanded that Biden's doctor testify about the president's health and subpoenaed Jill Biden's top aide Anthony Bernal and Biden's deputy chief of staff Annie Tomasini and senior adviser Ashley Williams. (Trump refused to release his own health records.)

Biden sought to undo the damage by holding a press conference following the July 11 NATO summit.[66] Although he performed far better, giving detailed answers to a wide range of foreign policy questions without notes for nearly an hour, almost as much attention was focused on his mistake during the summit of calling Zelensky Putin. Soon after the press conference, Rep. Hines became the fourteenth Democrat to urge Biden to withdraw. Rep. Schneider said Biden "did a fine job," but "we can't have a situation where every day we're holding our breath." He was joined by Reps. Sorensen and Peters, bringing the total to 20. Hours after Biden praised NATO, Trump repeated that the US would not protect its members from Russia if they did not increase military spending.

The next day Biden attacked Trump at a Michigan rally.[67] He asserted (correctly) that Judge Kaplan found that Trump had "raped" E. Jean Carroll (see Chapter 2.1) and that Trump did not object to chants about Biden to "Lock him up" (which echoed the "lock 'er up" chants Trump had led about Hillary Clinton in 2016). Biden insisted he would stay in the race and win because "Donald Trump is a loser." In his first 100 days he would propose a law enacting *Roe v. Wade*, sign the John Lewis Voting Rights Act (see Abel 2025: Chapter 5.2.11), and ban assault weapons. He included two proposals Sen. Sanders privately had urged on him two days earlier—expanding Social Security benefits and eliminating medical debts—leading Sanders to strongly endorse him in a *New York Times* op ed. Nevertheless, two more House members (Petterson and Levin) called for his withdrawal. And *The Washington Post* expressed concern that the press conference had not produced "the clarity many were looking for" and "veered toward the same kind of embarrassing mistakes" Biden had made in the debate. It urged "those with influence and access" to tell him "forcefully and candidly" what "the good of the country" "calls for now."

At a rally in Butler, Pennsylvania on July 13, Trump was shot in the ear by Thomas Matthew Crooks, who killed one man and critically wounded two others before being shot to death by the Secret Service.[68] (Crooks, 21, was a registered Republican who had researched the RNC and DNC and the whereabouts of Biden, Trump, Garland, Wray, and the Princess of Wales. The FBI found he had "no definitive ideology . . . either left-leaning or right-leaning.") Trump said on Truth Social: "it was God alone who prevented the unthinkable from happening." He later claimed he was "spared" because "God loves our country. And he thinks we're going to bring our country back." "God's hand was in this that day." Sen. Rubio (still hoping for the vice-presidential nomination) agreed: "God protected President Trump." House Speaker Johnson called it a "miraculous" sign of God's work. Billionaires Elon Musk and Bill Ackman promptly endorsed Trump.

Republicans immediately disseminated baseless conspiracy theories (emulating Trump's deliberately vague rhetoric).[69] Rep. Higgins said hours after the shooting: "The left will not stop MAGA Nation." Rep. Crane insinuated: "I don't want to . . . rule anything out because I don't put it past some of the people in our government to do anything necessary to hold on to power." Rep. Zinke asked: "did they willingly atrophy the security to put our president at risk?" Rep. Mills had "a very difficult time not leaning myself toward this was intentional as opposed to fecklessness." Rep. Van Orden was "not surprised that they tried to assassinate President Trump." Tim Sheehy (challenging Montana Sen. Tester in the 2024 election) said opaquely: "it culminated in them trying to kill him." Rep. Collins wrote (in a post on X seen by 4 million): "Joe Biden sent the orders" and should be charged with "inciting an assassination." Rep. Greene declared: "the Democrats and the media are to blame for every drop of blood spilled today." "Democrats wanted this to happen." Sen. Scott agreed the attempt was "aided and abetted by the radical Left and corporate media." "For years, Democrats and their allies in the media have recklessly stoked fears, calling President Trump and other conservatives threats to democracy. Their inflammatory rhetoric puts lives at risk." (The last two may have harbored unrealistic vice-presidential hopes.) RFK Jr.'s running mate Nicole Shanahan blamed the "DNC and legacy media" for inciting hysteria. Sen. Vance declared the shooting was "not just some isolated incident." "The central premise of the Biden campaign is that President Donald Trump is an authoritarian fascist who must be stopped at all costs. That rhetoric led directly to President Trump's attempted assassination." Rep. Scalise concurred: "for weeks Democrat leaders have been fueling ludicrous hysteria that Donald Trump winning re-election would be the end of democracy in America. Clearly, we've seen far-left lunatics act on violent rhetoric in the past. This incendiary rhetoric must stop." Don Jr. said: "Dems and their friends in the media knew exactly what they were doing" in comparing his father to Hitler. Rep. John James said: "They tried to silence him. They tried to jail him. Now they've tried to kill him." Chris LaCivita, a top campaign adviser, said: "they tried to keep him off the ballot, they tried to put him in jail and now you see this." Vivek Ramaswamy said virtually the same thing.

Right-wing posts on X, Truth Social, and Patriots win accused the Secret Service of deliberately failing to prevent the attack. Others said: "I guess because the court cases weren't going so well, they decided to try a different avenue"; "the Deep State tried to assassinate Donald Trump"; this was "the price you pay when you take down elite satanic pedophiles." 45Footwear promoted $299 sneakers with Trump's blood-streaked face and raised fist, ten of them autographed, under a licensing agreement with CIC Ventures, of which Trump was president, manager, secretary and treasurer.[70] The left advanced its own outlandish conspiracy theories: that Trump's blood was fake and his raised fist staged, the shooting was a "false flag," and the Secret Service had collaborated with the Trump campaign.

On July 23, following harsh Republican attacks and a disastrous performance at a House committee hearing, Director Kimberle Cheatle resigned after nearly 30 years in the Secret Service.[71] The same day Trump said on Truth Social: "The Biden/Harris Administration did not properly protect me, and I was forced to take a bullet for Democracy." Reps. Johnson and Jeffries agreed to a bipartisan task force to investigate the shooting, which the House approved 416–0. But when Republicans invited testimony from Reps. Crane and Mills, who had been excluded from the task force and claimed there was a second gunman and "criminal gross negligence" and "criminal intent" by the Secret Service, Democrats walked out of the hearing. (Crane also claimed the man charged in the second assassination attempt, discussed later, was an "asset" being "handled" by a foreign adversary, adding: "I don't believe [the F.B.I.] would give us the truth.") A month later Trump complained that Democrats had been calling him "a threat to democracy" for seven years. "I think I got shot because of that." "I think to a certain extent it's Biden's fault and Harris's fault . . . they were weaponizing government against me." Vance (now Trump's running mate) said Democrats failed to "beat him politically," "bankrupt him," and "impeach him," so "they tried to put him in prison" and "even tried to kill him."

On the day after the shooting, *The New York Times* published a four-page editorial (clearly written earlier) detailing "the failures of Donald Trump," which showed he "is unfit to lead."[72] "He has demonstrated an utter lack of respect for the Constitution, the rule of law and the American people." "He lies blatantly and maliciously, embraces racists, abuses women and has a schoolyard bully's instinct to target society's most vulnerable. He has delighted in coarsening and polarizing the town square with ever more divisive and incendiary language." The next day, however, the *Times* prudently editorialized that "the attack on Donald Trump is antithetical to America."

On July 15, two days after the assassination attempt and the first day of the RNC, Judge Cannon dismissed the classified papers case (see Chapter 4.2), and Trump picked Vance as his running mate.[73] In September 2021 (shortly after launching his senatorial campaign), Vance had said that when Trump won in 2024 he should

> fire every single midlevel bureaucrat, every civil servant in the administrative state, replace them with our people. Then when the courts stop you, stand before the country like Andrew Jackson did and say: "The chief justice has made his ruling. Now let him enforce it."

(That was a bizarre citation for a Yale law graduate; President Jackson was defying Chief Justice Marshall's ruling on tribal sovereignty.) Republicans should pack the DoJ with people who "actually take a side in the culture war." "[W]e have to get pretty wild, pretty far out there" (echoing Trump's invitation to the January 6 rioters to "be wild"). Conservatives should "seize the endowments" of left-leaning universities. "A transnational financial elite controls things in our country . . . they hate our society and . . . a lot of them are probably sex perverts, too" (the QAnon lie). In February 2024, Vance had boasted that had he been in the Senate on January 6 he would have refused to certify the Electoral College results. *The Washington Post* reported that he had delayed dozens of DoS appointments for more than a year by demanding that nominees answer questions about "gender dysphoria and gender transition care" for employees and dependents, "gender-neutral restrooms and locker rooms" at DoS facilities, support for LGBTQI+ children at overseas schools, and displays of the Progress flag during Pride Month.

The RNC adopted a platform that began: "we are a Nation in SERIOUS DECLINE. Our future, our identity, and our very way of life are under threat like never before."[74] It accused Democrats of doing "everything in their power to destroy our Country": "allowing our Borders to be overrun, our cities to be overtaken by crime, our System of Justice to be weaponized." It promised to "seal the border," "restore every Border Policy of the Trump administration" (all but one of which had been invalidated by courts), and "carry out the largest deportation operation in American history." It would require "same day voting, voter identification, paper ballots, and proof of citizenship." It would "cut federal funding for any school pushing critical race theory, radical gender ideology, and other inappropriate racial, sexual or political content on our children," "ban Taxpayer funding for sex change surgeries, and stop Taxpayer-funded Schools from promoting gender transition." It would "deport pro-Hamas radicals and make our college campuses safe and patriotic again." It would "keep foreign Christian-hating Communists, Marxists, and Socialists out of America," "champion the First Amendment Right to Pray and Read the Bible in school," "stand up to Marxist Prosecutors," and "fire Radical Left [college] accreditors."

Sen. Johnson said: "Today's Democrat agenda, their policies, are a clear and present threat to America, to our institutions, our values and our people."[75] (He then claimed he had been given the wrong speech "rather than the revision made in light of Saturday," when Trump was shot.) Rep. Greene called Democrats "the party of pedophiles." Thomas Homan (Trump's ICE director) accused Biden and Harris of "national suicide." "Because this administration has unsecured the border . . . deaths are skyrocketing. Rapes are skyrocketing." (In the first quarter of 2024, homicides decreased 26.4 percent, and all violent crimes, including rape, fell more than 15 percent.) On the second day of the RNC, West Virginia Gov. Jim Justice, running for the Senate, predicted the country would "become totally unhinged if Donald Trump is not elected in November." Bernie Moreno (running for Senate in Ohio), Sen. Rick Scott, and Trump accused Democrats of destroying the country. Scott said: "it was easy for Democrats to rig elections; they simply allowed all the noncitizens to vote." Trump warned: "Keep your eyes open because these people want to cheat and they do cheat. And frankly, it's the only thing they do well." Sen. Cruz said: "Americans are dying, murdered, assaulted, raped by illegal immigrants that the Democrats have released. Teenage girls and boys wearing colored wristbands are being sold into a life of sex slavery." Immigrant crime "happened because Democrats cynically decided they wanted votes from illegals more than they wanted to protect our children." "11.5 million people have crossed our border illegally under Joe Biden." Rep. Scalise said: "Biden and Harris want illegals to vote now that they've opened up the border." Eric Hovde, running for the Senate in Wisconsin, said Democrats had "emboldened drug cartels to flood our streets with fentanyl, killing over 100,000 Americans every year." Peter Navarro, recently released from prison for contempt of Congress (see Abel 2025: Chapter 2.2.2), said: "if they can come for me, and if they can come for Donald Trump, be careful. They will come for you." Rep. Gaetz sneered: "they can run Biden from the nursing home. We are on a mission to rescue and save this country." Kimberly Guilfoyle referred to immigrants as "violent criminal aliens." Attendees waved signs "MASS DEPORTATION NOW," chanting "Send them back!"

On July 17, Biden tested positive for coronavirus and canceled a Las Vegas rally to isolate in Delaware.[76] House Minority Leader Jeffries and Senate Leader Schumer had warned Biden the previous week he could hurt Democratic Congressional prospects, but he insisted he was the nominee and planned to win. Obama privately told Democratic leaders Biden should reconsider, as did Pelosi. Rep. Schiff (running for Senate in California) became the latest prominent Democrat to call publicly for Biden to withdraw. Sen. Tester (seeking re-election) became the second senator to do so. Rev. Al Sharpton said he had told Biden to "take a serious calculation of where we're at." The multiple uncertainties apparently convinced the co-chairs of the rules committee for the Democratic Convention (beginning August 19) to postpone a virtual roll call of delegates to at least August 1. Sens. Brown, Heinrich and Manchin and Reps. Lofgren, Vasquez, MacCollum, and McGarvey publicly called for withdrawal, raising the number of Congressional Democrats to 37. But on July 19, campaign chair Jen O'Malley Dillon said Biden "absolutely" was staying in the race.

Although Trump had slightly tempered his angry rhetoric at the RNC, in his next rally on July 20 he repeatedly called Biden "stupid" and Harris "nuts" and "crazy."[77] In response to critics who accused Trump of being "a threat to democracy," he retorted: "Last week, I took a bullet for democracy." He again said of Project 2025, which he insisted on calling "Project 25": "They're seriously extreme, but I don't know anything about it."

On July 21, Biden withdrew and endorsed Harris, declaring: "The defense of democracy, which is at stake, is more important than any title."[78] "Whether we keep our republic is now in your hands." "The great thing about America is here, kings and dictators do not rule. The people do." Democratic donors praised his decision. House Speaker Johnson pronounced: "if Joe Biden is not fit to run for President, he is not fit to serve as President. He must resign the office immediately." Rep. Stefanik echoed him. Trump outdid them: "Crooked Joe Biden was not fit to run for President, and is certainly not fit to serve—And never was!" Other Republicans called for invoking the Twenty-fifth Amendment (no more likely to happen now than it was in 2021). Within hours, 185 Democratic members of Congress and governors (out of 263) endorsed Harris; by early the next day 210 had done so, including Schumer, Jeffries, and Pelosi. So did Bill and Hillary Clinton.

Harris raised more than $100 million from 1.1 million donors by the end of July 22, while Future Forward (FF) PAC, the largest outside group, said it had received $150 million in commitments in the 24 hours following Biden's announcement. In the first week after Biden withdrew, the Harris campaign raised $200 million. *The Washington Post* editorialized: "With Biden stepping aside, Democrats must now embrace an open process." But by the end of July 22, Harris had been endorsed by 2,764 delegates (more than 70 percent of the 3,949) from more than three dozen states; she needed only 1,976. Trade unions also endorsed her: the AFL-CIO, United Steelworkers, UFW, AFT, IBEW, SEIU, and UAW. More than 58,000 new volunteers signed up, 232 times the usual daily total.

At an Ohio rally, Vance threatened "civil war" if Trump lost.[79] Trump himself said: "They stole the race from Biden after he won it in the primaries—A First! These people are the real THREAT TO DEMOCRACY!" He again reasserted: "I have nothing to do with, and know nothing about, Project 25." He deliberately mispronounced "Kamala." Just before the Obamas endorsed Harris, Trump's spokesman referred to "Barack Hussein Obama" and called Harris "a Marxist fraud." Immediately after Biden's withdrawal, Rep. Burchett labeled Harris a "DEI vice president," Rep. Hageman said she was "a DEI hire," and Rep. Grothman accused Democrats of choosing her "because of her ethnic background."

In 2021, Vance had complained the US was being run by "childless cat ladies" like Harris, "who are miserable at their own lives and the choices that they've made" and have no "direct stake" in the future of the nation.[80] Now Kerstin Emhoff (Douglas Emhoff's former wife) said: "For over 10 years, since Cole and Ella were teenagers, Kamala has been a co-parent with Doug and I. She is loving, nurturing, fiercely protective and always present. I love our blended family and am grateful to have her in it." Ella added: "How can you be 'childless' when you have cutie pie kids like Cole and I."

Republicans condemned the replacement.[81] House Speaker Johnson asserted: "it's not possible to simply just switch out a candidate who has been chosen through the democratic—small d—democratic process over such a long period of time." "Democrats have been complicit in the largest political cover-up in history." Rep. Massie called it "a coup of a puppet regime." Rep. Alford accused "progressive democrats" of "taking a wood chipper to democracy by shredding the will of 14 million primary voters." Sen Hawley declared: "Now the Democrats are rigging their *own* elections."

After urging supporters to vote in November, Trump made a bizarre and frightening promise: "In four years, you don't have to vote again. We'll have it fixed so good you're not going to have to vote."[82] (He had said something similar at a Faith and Freedom Coalition event in June: "all you have to do is [vote] this time.") Three days later he repeated to Laura Ingraham: "You have to vote on Nov. 5. After that, you don't have to worry about voting anymore . . . because . . . the country will be fixed and we won't even need your vote anymore." Trump said Harris "was a bum three weeks ago. She was a bum, a failed vice president." In dealing with foreign leaders, she would "be like a play toy. They look at her and they say, 'We can't believe we got so lucky.' They're going to walk all over her. And I don't want to say as to why. But a lot of people understand it." The next day he told the National Association of Black Journalists that Harris "happened to turn Black . . . I don't know, is she Indian or is she Black?" She "was Indian all the way" but then "became a Black person." He also reiterated that "nobody died" on January 6th, and he "absolutely" would pardon rioters who attacked police "if they're innocent" because they were convicted under a "tough system." Vance loyally seconded Trump, saying Harris "pretends to be somebody different, depending on the audience she's talking to" and used "a fake Southern accent" speaking to a largely Black Atlanta audience. Then Trump doubled down: "Crazy Kamala is saying she's Indian, not Black. This is a big deal. Stone cold phony." The right-wing media echoed him. Laura Loomer said Harris "pretends to be black" to meet a "delusional, Democrat DEI quota." Lil Pump, a Trump supporter and rapper with 20 million followers, said: "Kamala Harris isn't even black . . . she's Indian."

The Heritage Foundation's Project 2025 shut down and postponed publication of its manifesto until after the election.[83] Susie Wiles and Chris LaCivita said: "President Trump's campaign has been very clear for over a year that Project 2025 has nothing to do with the campaign, did not speak for the campaign, and should not be associated with the campaign or the President in any way." Trump had claimed in July he had "no idea who is in charge of it." But *The Washington Post* reported that Trump had flown on a private plane with Heritage Foundation President Kevin Roberts to attend an April 2022 Foundation conference, where Trump lauded the Project in a keynote speech: "They're going to lay the groundwork and detail plans for exactly what our movement will do." As recently as April 2024, Roberts told the *Post*: "I personally have talked to President Trump about Project 2025." Over half of Project 2025's 307 authors had served in the Trump administration, campaign, or transition team. Vance had called Heritage "the most influential engine of ideas for Republicans from Ronald Reagan to Donald Trump" and had written in a foreword to Roberts's book "Dawn's Early Light": "in the fights that lay ahead, these ideas are an essential weapon." Vance also promoted "Unhumans," by right-wing conspiracy theorist Jack Posobiec and ghostwriter Joshua Lisec, which declared: "As [leftists] are opposed to humanity itself, they place themselves outside of the category completely, in an entirely new misery-driven subdivision, the unhuman." "Our study of history has brought us to this conclusion: Democracy has never worked to protect innocents from the unhumans."

> The great American counterrevolution to depose the Cultural Marxists must occur on all terrains of society they currently possess and on those they aim to seize. It is achievable but only with the resolve of Franco and the thoroughness of [Joseph] McCarthy.

Vance wrote the lead blurb:

> In the past, communists marched in the streets waving red flags. Today, they march through H.R. [human relations], college campuses and courtrooms to wage lawfare against good, honest people. Jack Posobiec and Joshua Lisec reveal their plans and show us what to do to fight back.

In a Fox News interview, Vance asserted that the reason "housing costs so much" was "20 million illegal aliens who shouldn't be here and who are competing with Americans for scarce homes." In June he had said: "Not having 20 million illegal aliens who need to be housed (often at public expense) will absolutely make housing more affordable for American citizens."

On August 2, Harris formally obtained more than enough votes to secure the nomination.[84] Four days later she chose Minnesota Gov. Tim Walz as her running mate. Trump initially refused to debate Harris at the scheduled ABC event on September 10, saying he would do so only on Fox on September 5 with a "full arena audience." But after Harris reaffirmed she would be on ABC on September 10, Trump capitulated. On August 8 LULAC broke with tradition and endorsed the Harris-Walz ticket. (Three months earlier Voto Latino, UnidosUS Action Fund, Mi Familia Vota, America's Voice, and Latino Victory Project had committed $50 million to oppose Trump, calling his deportation plans a threat to democracy.) Troubled by news reports about the size of Harris's audiences, Trump declared on social media that the crowd at her Detroit airport rally "DIDN'T EXIST," "nobody was there." She had " 'A.I.'d' it" and should be "disqualified because the creation of a fake image is ELECTION INTERFERENCE." "Anyone who does that will cheat at ANYTHING!" The local news outlet MLive estimated 15,000 people inside the airport hanger and more on the tarmac. But Trump insisted: "we have the biggest crowds ever in the history of politics" (just as he had lied about the size of his 2017 inauguration audience).

He called Harris "crazy," "stupid," "lunatic"; "she's not smart, she's not intelligent." Asserting that "I'm entitled to personal attacks," he pronounced: "I am much better looking than her." She was "a radical California liberal who broke the economy, broke the border and broke the world." "All we have to do is define our opponent as being a communist or a socialist or somebody that's going to destroy our country." He falsely claimed that "government numbers" demonstrated that "Kamala's inflation price hikes . . . cost a typical family $28,000." He said in Michigan that in big cities, "almost all run by Democrats, you can't walk across the street to get a loaf of bread, you get shot, you get mugged, you get raped." Replacing Biden was a "vicious violent" "overthrow of a president," "the first coup of the history of our country, and it was very successful."

On Truth Social, Trump posted images of Biden, Harris, Hillary Clinton, Pelosi, Fauci, and others in prison uniforms and made a vulgar joke about Harris (and Willie Brown) and Clinton (and Monica Lewinsky): "funny how blowjobs impacted both their careers differently." He called for jailing the January 6 Select Committee members, sentencing Mark Zuckerberg to life imprisonment for donating to election officials, and trying Obama in a military tribunal; and he promised to "get the resignations of every single senior official who touched the Afghanistan calamity." He reposted the QAnon slogan. He exhorted the Fraternal Order of Police to "watch for voter fraud . . . you can keep it down by watching because . . . they're afraid of you people . . . more than anything else." He accused six Democratic states of allowing executions of babies after birth. He would make reporters disclose the source of the leaked *Dobbs* opinion by threatening them with prison rape. He would "rapidly review the cases of every political prisoner unjustly victimized" and "sign their pardons." If he lost the election, Colorado, Illinois, and Maine "will be taken over by migrants."

Trump said Robert F. Kennedy Jr., who had ended his independent campaign, would be "very much involved" in a government panel on "chronic health problems and childhood diseases."[85] As a campaigner, Kennedy had boosted ivermectin and hydroxychloroquine as "devastatingly effective" against COVID (emulating Trump's disastrous response to the pandemic, see Abel 2024c). Now he planned to tell NIH: "we're going to give infectious disease a break for about eight years." Trump agreed with Kennedy's opposition to childhood vaccines: "I want to do small doses." The present dose "looks like it's meant for a horse, not uh, you now, a 10-pound or 20-pound baby." "And then you see the baby all of sudden starting to change radically, I've seen it too many times. And then you hear that it doesn't have an impact, right? But you and I talked about that a long time ago." Kennedy's Children's Health Defense planned to release the film "Vaxxed 3: Authorized to Kill," which asserted that COVID vaccines caused "tragic outcomes of either death or serious injury." Kennedy also claimed: "On January 20, the Trump White House will advise all U.S. water systems to remove fluoride from public water." Trump agreed: "it sounds ok to me." After Trump said he was going to let Kennedy "go wild" on health, food, and medicines, Kennedy announced that Trump had "promised" him "control of the public health agencies" "to clean up corruption and conflicts at the agencies," listing CDCP, FDA, and NIH. Trump called Kennedy "a very talented guy" with "strong views." "He can do anything he wants." Although the campaign warned this was "premature," Howard Lutnick, head of the transition team, said that after speaking to Kennedy for 2.5 hours he had been converted to vaccine skepticism, repeating the false claim that they caused autism.

In response to critics of his speeches, Trump protested: "I don't ramble. I'm a really smart guy." His speaking style was "the weave . . . I'll take about like nine different things and they all come back brilliantly together."[86] But his words told a different story. He said in response to a question about childcare:

> Well, I would do that, and we're sitting down, I was somebody, we had Senator Marco Rubio, and my daughter Ivanka was so impactful on that issue. It's a very important issue, but I think when you talk about the kind of numbers that I'm talking about that because the childcare is childcare, it's, couldn't, you know, there's something, you have to have it. In this country you have to have it. But when you talk about those numbers compared to the kind of numbers that I'm talking about, by taxing foreign nations at levels that they're not used to. . . . Those numbers are so much bigger than any numbers that we're talking about, including child care, that it's going to take care.

He was equally confused about the dollar's role as a reserve currency:

> Trump is always right. I hate to be right. . . . Many countries are leaving the dollar. You're not going to leave the dollar with me. I'll say, "You leave the dollar, you're not doing business with the United States, because we're going to put 100 percent tariff on your goods." [That country would reply] "Sir, we would like very much to get back to the dollar immediately. Thank you very much." It's so easy.

Vance warned that Harris would let undocumented people vote and "destroy" Americans.[87] "When she let in millions of illegal aliens, it made our communities less safe—but it did give the Democrats a lot of voters." "What happens when you have massive amounts of illegal immigration? It actually starts to create ethnic conflict. It creates higher crime rates." His authority for this was "Gangs of New York," a fictional film about mid-19th-century violence. Vance said Gov. Walz "signed legislation . . . that would take children away from their parents if their parents don't want to do sex changes." Trump told Moms for Liberty: "Your kid goes to school and comes home a few days later with an operation." (He later claimed that if a prisoner just says: "I'm thinking about" transitioning, "they throw you on an operating table.")

Large numbers of Republicans quickly voiced support for Harris. Two hundred thirty-eight former George W. Bush, John McCain, and Mitt

Romney staffers endorsed her in an open letter to *USA Today*, warning that a second Trump presidency "will hurt real, everyday people and weaken our sacred institutions."[88] McCain's son James added his support, as did Liz and Dick Cheney and 17 former Reagan staffers. (Trump lashed back, calling Liz Cheney "dumb," "stupid," a "moron" and suggesting she be put in front of a firing squad.) Barbara Bush (George W. Bush's daughter) campaigned for Harris. Susan Molinari and Bill Paxon, former Republican members of Congress, voted for Harris. Arnold Schwarzenegger endorsed her because "rejecting the results of an election is as un-American as it gets." One hundred eleven former GOP officials said Trump's "dangerous qualities," including an "unusual affinity" for dictators, made him "unfit to serve." A dozen former Republican White House lawyers wrote in Fox News: "Trump's attempt to prevent the peaceful transfer of power after losing the election proved beyond any reasonable doubt his willingness to place his personal interests above the law and values of our constitutional democracy."

For only the second time in its 180-year history, *Scientific American* made a presidential endorsement, again against Trump, who "endangers public health and safety and rejects evidence, preferring instead nonsensical conspiracy theories." A bipartisan assemblage of more than 700 current and former national security officials, including former Secretaries of State and Defense, ambassadors, and retired generals, called the election a "choice between democracy and authoritarianism . . . effective leadership requires in-depth knowledge, careful deliberation, understanding of your adversaries and empathy for those you lead . . . listening to those with expertise and not firing them when they disagree with you." *The New York Times* published quotes critical of Trump from 91 of his former associates: he "undermined American democracy unnecessarily" (Homeland Security Adviser Thomas Bossert); "equality and freedom can never be equated with white supremacists" (National Economic Council Director Gary Cohn); "the F.B.I. is under attack by the President of the United States" (FBI Deputy Director Andrew McCabe); Trump "admires autocrats and murderous dictators" (White House Chief of Staff John Kelly); he was "a threat to democracy" (Defense Secretary Mark Esper). JCS Chair Mark Milley told Bob Woodward that Trump was "a total fascist, "the most dangerous person to this country."

Trump warned that his debate with Harris would be "dishonest" because she was "going to get the questions in advance."[89] (Afterwards he said ABC should lose its license because Harris had seemed "awfully familiar with the questions." "I hear she got the questions, and I also heard she had something in the ear." The first was false; what she wore was pearl earrings.) At the debate Trump repeated his old lies: "nobody on the other side was killed" as a result of the January 6 riot. (He later said: "it was love and peace"; "no one had a gun." "January 6 will go down in history as the day the government staged a riot to cover up the fact that they certified a fraudulent election.")

"There's so much proof" of fraud in the 2020 election, but "no judge looked at it." Harris was "a Marxist" because "her father's a Marxist professor." She was "mentally disabled." "21 million people" had poured into the country. Democrats were "trying to get [illegal immigrants] to vote." Both the previous governor of West Virginia and Walz said "execution after birth" was "okay." "Crime in countries all over the world is way down" because they sent criminals to the US. FBI statistics were "defrauding statements." Biden "was found essentially guilty on the documents case." He got "$3.5 million from the mayor of Moscow's wife." Polling shortly after the debate found that higher percentages of the audience felt Harris had won than that Trump had: 63–37 (CNN), 54–31 (YouGov). But they still preferred Trump on the economy (55–35) and immigration (56–33).

Most insidiously, Trump repeated to the 67 million television viewers the lies concocted by Vance, Cruz, the House Republican campaign arm, and the HJC that Haitian immigrants were eating people's pets in Springfield, Ohio. When the debate moderator said the city manager denied this, Trump insisted: "I've seen people on television . . . say 'my dog was taken and used for food.'" Vance obsequiously agreed: "I know that geese are certainly . . . being consumed." Two days after Trump said: "you have to get them the hell out," Rep. Higgins repeated the falsehood about Haitians eating pets, calling them "thugs" and Haiti the "nastiest country in the western hemisphere."

The lie took off.[90] End Wokeness (with 2.9 million followers) reposted a Facebook post on X, where it was viewed 4.8 million times. Charlie Kirk's post on X was viewed by 3.9 million. Don Jr. repeated the lie in even more explicit language: "You look at Haiti, you look at the demographic makeup, you look at the average I.Q.—if you import the third world into your country, you're going to become third world. . . . It's not racist. It's just fact." Elon Musk posted a video of a social media influencer at a Springfield City Commission meeting maintaining ducks were being decapitated in a city park; although the influencer retracted his claim, it got 20 million views. After Vance's statement got more than 10 million views he gloated: "keep the cat memes flowing." Seeming to admit he had lied, he shamelessly declared: "If I have to create stories so that the American media actually pays attention to the suffering of the American people, then that's what I'm going to do." An AI fake image of Trump hugging a duck and a kitten got 71 million views. In the three days after the debate there were 1.1 million posts on X about pets being eaten. YouTube ads by major brands were accompanied by similar lies.

The Springfield Police Division said it had received "no credible reports or specific claims." City manager Bryan Heck deplored that the "disappointing" narrative had been "skewed by misinformation circulating on social media and further amplified by political rhetoric in the current highly charged presidential election cycle." Mayor Rob Rue said: "a national politician that has a national platform and takes mics needs to understand how their words can hurt a city like ours." (Both were Republicans.) Ohio's Republican Gov. DeWine called the story "a piece of garbage that was simply not true." He was born in Springfield and had spent his entire life ten miles away. The city had "a rich history of providing refuge for the oppressed and being a place of opportunity." DeWine was "saddened by how [Trump, Vance] and others continue to repeat claims that lack evidence and disparage the legal migrants living in Springfield." Thirty-six bomb threats forced the evacuation of City Hall and local schools and the lockdown of two hospitals. Two local colleges held classes remotely. Springfield canceled a two-day CultureFest celebrating diversity. Haitians throughout the country were threatened, as was a local businessman who praised his Haitian workers. The KKK and a neo-Nazi group demonstrated, and strangers insulted Haitians in public.

Trump was unmoved: "I don't know what happened with the bomb threats. I know that [Springfield's] been taken over by illegal migrants, and that's a terrible thing that happened." "[T]hey are illegal immigrants as far as I'm concerned." "They're destroying the town . . . they'll end up destroying the state." He promised "large deportations in Springfield. We're going to get these people out." He "absolutely" would revoke Temporary Protected Status. Trump made equally false claims about "Venezuelan gangs taking over Aurora, Colorado." "Getting them out will be a bloody story . . . but we'll do it" under the Alien Enemies Act of 1798 (last used to intern German, Italian, and Japanese Americans during World War II—actions that President Reagan and the Supreme Court later repudiated). Aurora's mayor and a city council member (both Republican) denied that buildings had been "taken over"; the problem was lack of maintenance by "out-of-state slumlords." Nevertheless, Trump bragged: "I'm going to Springfield, and I'm going to Aurora." Channeling John Wayne, he added: "You may never see me again, but that's ok. Gotta do what I gotta do." Vance persisted in calling Haitians in Springfield "illegal" even though many had TPS. He claimed that "murders are up by 81 percent because of what Kamala Harris has allowed to happen to this small community." (The small annual numbers fluctuated without any trend and had increased from 5 to 13 under Trump.) Vance said: "25 million illegal aliens competing with Americans for scarce homes is one of the most significant drivers of home prices in the country." (Economists disagreed; and there were fewer than 12 million undocumented workers.) He told "illegal aliens": "pack your bags. Because in four months you're going home."

In North Carolina, Trump warned that "this invasion is destroying the fabric of our country. Every job in this country produced over the last two and a half years has gone to illegal aliens." (False.) In Pennsylvania, Vance denounced "people who shouldn't be here, people who are competing against you and your children to buy the homes that ought to be going to American citizens." Trump called the administration's border policy a "crime."

"There's no greater act of disloyalty than to extinguish the sovereignty of your own nation." Other nations were "dumping" "killers" in "our country and I never had proof. You know why? It's common sense." He falsely told residents of Charleroi, Pennsylvania: "the town is virtually bankrupt. This flood of illegal aliens is also bringing massive crime." Visiting Aurora, he said "thugs" took over hundreds of towns and cities "including the big ones. Look at New York." "If Kamala is reelected [sic] your town, and every town . . . the heartland, the coast . . . will be transformed into a third-world hellhole." He vowed to "liberate Wisconsin and our entire nation from this mass migration invasion of murderers, child predators, drug dealers, gang members and thugs" who "are destroying our country." "Many of them murdered far more than one person, and they're now happily living in the United States . . . it's in their genes. And we got a lot of bad genes in our country right now." Calling violent immigrants "animals," "barbaric thugs," and "sadistic monsters," he demanded the death penalty "for any migrant that kills an America citizen." He warned that Maine's "radical-left governor" (Janet Mills, whom he misrepresented as male) "wants to resettle 75,000 migrants . . . turning your state into a dumping ground . . . Maine's unique character will be lost forever." He declared in Nevada that the US was an "occupied country" but promised that Election Day "will be liberation day in America." Trump's final ads screamed "innocent victims" of the "border crisis" were "bludgeoned, raped, strangled, stabbed, shot and murdered." "A little girl" was "raped and buried alive," yet "Kamala allowed convicted sex offenders to live near schools and parks."

At a Madison Square Garden rally less than two weeks before the election, Trump's warm-up speakers insulted everyone. Tony Hinchcliffe said: "These Latinos, they love making babies too. There's no pulling out, they don't do that, they come inside, just like they did to our country . . . there's literally a floating island of garbage in the middle of the ocean right now. I think it's called Puerto Rico." (A campaign spokeswoman said the joke was "in poor taste" but the crowd did not mind—precisely the problem. Vance responded: "we have to stop getting so offended at every little thing in the United States of America.") Hinchcliffe joked about Blacks carving watermelons for Halloween. Palestinians were "going to throw a rock every time," while Jews "have a hard time throwing that paper" money. Grant Cardone, a businessman and prominent Scientologist, warned that Harris's "pimp handlers will destroy our country." (Vendors did a land-office business in t-shirts declaring: "Say No to the Ho.") Cardone added: "we need to slaughter" Trump's opponents. Sid Rosenberg, a radio host, called Hillary Clinton "some sick bastard . . . a sick son-of-a-bitch"; "the whole fucking party" of Democrats were "a bunch of degenerates, lowlives, Jew-haters." "You got homeless and veterans, Americans, Americans, sleeping in their own feces on a bench in Central Park. But the fucking illegals, they get whatever they want." Scot

LoBaido flipped the bird at Democrats while praising Trump as "the greatest fucking president in the world." Rudy Giuliani said Palestinians were "taught to kill Americans at [age] 2." David Rem, Trump's childhood friend, called Harris "the devil" and "the Antichrist." Don Jr. said Democrats decided "it would just be easier to replace" Americans "with people who would be reliable voters." (A week earlier Tucker Carlson had accused Democrats of "trying to replace" Americans.) Stephen Miller said Trump would declare "America is for Americans and Americans only" (a slogan popularized by the Ku Klux Klan). The audience was entertained with "Dixie," a song closely associated with the Confederacy.

Hinchcliffe's insult of Puerto Ricans provoked a backlash, even among Republicans (especially from Florida, with more than a million from the island).[91] Sen. Scott said the joke was "not funny and it's not true." Sen. Rubio said: "Puerto Rico isn't garbage." Rep. Salazar was "disgusted." Reggaeton star Nicky Jam withdrew his endorsement of Trump. But Biden undercut the impact by putting his foot in his mouth: "The only garbage I see floating out there is supporters—his, his demonization of Latinos is unconscionable and it's unAmerican." After being criticized he said he was referring only to Hinchcliffe. (The White House later inserted an apostrophe to make it "supporter's," which the stenography office denounced as a violation of protocol.) Harris said: "I strongly disagree with any criticism of people based on who they vote for." But Sen. Rubio maintained at a rally that Biden "stated that our supporters are garbage." Trump linked the word to Hillary Clinton's use of "deplorables." "You can't be president if you hate the American people, and there's a lot of hatred there." Vance accused Kamala of "attacking half of the country." But then he paraphrased Hinchcliffe's insult: "In two short days, we're going to take out the trash, and the trash's name is Kamala Harris," earning a standing ovation.

On October 28, Harris held a large rally at the Ellipse because Trump had "stood at this very spot nearly four years ago and sent an armed mob to the United States Capitol to overturn the will of the people in a free and fair election—an election he knew he lost."[92] He was an "unstable" "petty tyrant," "consumed with grievance" and "out for unchecked power." "I pledge to listen to experts, to those who will be impacted by the decisions I make—and to people who disagree with me," whereas Trump called them "the enemy" and "wants to put them in jail."

In posts on Truth Social and X, Trump also engaged in anticipatory delegitimation of this election (as he had those in 2016 and 2020, see Abel 2024b: Chapter 2) and threatened vengeance.[93]

> CEASE & DESIST. I, together with many Attorneys and Legal Scholars, am watching the Sanctity of the 2024 Presidential Election very closely because I know, better than most, the rampant Cheating and Skullduggery

> that has taken place by the Democrats in the 2020 Presidential Election. It was a Disgrace to our Nation! Therefore, the 2024 Election, where Votes have just started being cast, will be under the closest professional scrutiny and, WHEN I WIN, those people that CHEATED will be prosecuted to the fullest extent of the LAW, which will include long term prison sentences so that this Depravity of Justice does not happen again. We cannot let our Country further devolve into a Third World Nation, AND WE WON'T! Please beware that this legal exposure extends to Lawyers, Political Operatives, Donors, Illegal Voters, & Corrupt Election Officials. Those involved in unscrupulous behavior will be sought out, caught, and prosecuted at levels, unfortunately, never seen before in our Country.

A week later, the 65 Project (named after Trump's 65 lawsuits failing to overturn the 2020 election) placed ads in swing-state legal journals warning: "Don't risk your law license by joining an effort to subvert democracy. We—and the public—are watching." (For discipline of such lawyers, see Chapter 2.4.) Trump may have learned of this and sought to pre-empt it by declaring: the "only way we're going to lose, [is] because they cheat." More than two dozen advocacy groups urged Congress to commit to certifying the Electoral College vote. But House Speaker Johnson said he would allow this "only if we have a free, fair and safe election." Vance again refused to acknowledge Trump had lost in 2020, which had "serious problems . . . big tech rigged the election." Two hundred thirty-six Republican candidates for Congress or senior state offices, nearly half of those running, expressed doubt about the integrity of the forthcoming election. An October poll found that six in ten respondents were concerned or very concerned about fraud: 88 percent of Trump voters compared with 29 percent of Harris voters. Less than two weeks before the election Trump said: "We want proof of citizenship. Democrats are registering Illegal Voters by the TENS OF THOUSANDS." He urged House Republicans to shut down the government and again condemned mail ballots: "you have the rest of your life to vote anytime you want." Days before the election he accused Democrats of "fighting so hard to steal this damn thing." "Pennsylvania is cheating, and getting caught at large scale levels rarely seen before." (That was false.)

Trump continued to monetize himself and his campaign (in which he had invested none of his own wealth).[94] He was hawking "fifty all new stunning digital trading cards" showing him "dancing and even holding some bitcoins." Each cost $99; buying 15 got purchasers a physical card and "an authentic piece of my suit that I wore for the presidential debate"; buying all 75 for $7,425 included a gala dinner at Mar-a-Lago. Trump also was selling a new book of photos of himself for $99, or $499 with an autograph. "Never Surrender Gold Low Tops" and "Crypto President" bitcoin orange sneakers cost $499; "Fight Fight Fight" shoes featuring his bloody face and raised fist were a bargain at $299. He flogged "The Official Trump Watch Collection: a "Fight Fight Fight" model ($499), a gold tone version of it ($799), and the Tourbillion watch ($100,000). He also hawked "The President Donald J. Trump First Edition Silver Medallion" for $100.

On September 15, Secret Service spotted a suspected assassin with a gun in the bushes surrounding Trump International Golf Club, where the candidate was playing.[95] Ryan Wesley Routh was chased, arrested, and charged with firearms offenses. He had a long history of prior charges. He had contributed to Democratic causes, spent time in Ukraine, and written in his LinkedIn profile: "I would tremendously enjoy the invitation to join any monumental worthy cause to bring about real change in our world." He had left a note declaring: "Dear World. This was an assassination attempt on Donald Trump but I failed you" and offering a six-figure reward to "finish the job."

Trump proclaimed afterwards: "I WILL NEVER SURRENDER," asserting that Routh "believed the rhetoric of Biden and Harris, and he acted on it. Their rhetoric is causing me to be shot at, when I am the one who is going to save the country, and they are the ones that are destroying the country—both from the inside and out." They were the "enemy from within," "the real threat." "Because of this Communist Left Rhetoric, the bullets are flying, and it will only get worse!" He had said at the debate: "I probably took a bullet to the head because of the things that they say about me." He denied using "highly inflammatory language" while boasting he could do so "far better than they can." Vance observed: "no one has tried to kill Kamala Harris in the last couple of months, and two people now have tried to kill Donald Trump in the last couple of months. I'd say that's pretty strong evidence that the left needs to tone down the rhetoric." "Don't lecture Donald Trump about softening his rhetoric after two people try to kill him." In a 1,200-word post on Truth Social, Vance accused Democrats of "moral blackmail." "The logic of censorship leads directly to one place, for there is only one way to permanently silence a human being: put a bullet in his brain."

Trump declared that "OUR JUSTICE SYSTEM IS CORRUPT AND DISCREDITED, especially as it pertains to the 45th President of the United States, Donald J. Trump. LET FLORIDA HANDLE THE CASE!" He dismissed the initial weapons charges as "a slap on the wrist," accusing the DoJ and FBI of "DOWNPLAYING" the threat to him because they "HAVE BEEN COMING AFTER ME NONSTOP with Weaponized Lawfare." "The DOJ and FBI have a Conflict of Interest since they have been obsessed with 'Getting Trump' for so long." (Trump later predicted the cases against him would "go away" if he were elected. "I don't think they'll impeach me if I fire Jack Smith," who was "mentally deranged" and "should be thrown out of the country.") Prosecutors subsequently added charges of assault on a federal officer and attempted assassination of a major presidential candidate. The case was randomly assigned to Judge Cannon. Asserting without evidence that both assassination attempts "possibly do [involve] Iran," Trump threatened: "we're going to blow your largest cities and the country itself to smithereens." Cannon denied a motion to recuse based on reports that Trump might nominate her to a higher court or the DoJ.

On October 4, Trump returned to Butler (scene of the first assassination attempt), declaring with calculated ambiguity: "those who want to stop us . . . have slandered me, impeached me, indicted me, tried to throw me off the ballot, and who knows, maybe even tried to kill me."[96] He praised "the hand of providence and the grace of God" for saving his life, eliciting chants of "God bless Trump." Eric echoed his father: "They tried to kill him. And it's because the Democratic Party, they can't do anything right." Eric's wife Lara said: "If you had any question whether God exists and he performs miracles, we got our answer right here on July 13th. . . . He spared Donald Trump's life because he was not finished with Donald Trump." A local radio host agreed: "A lot of us believe that it was God's will that [Trump] turned his head." A billboard displayed Jesus standing behind Trump, saying: "It's okay. They called me guilty too." A country song described Trump's survival as the will of God. A video bizarrely compared the shooting to George Washington crossing the Delaware (because both occurred in Pennsylvania?). Vance said: "Donald Trump took a bullet for democracy." Elon Musk warned that if people did not vote for Trump "this will be the last election."

Three weeks before the election Trump declared: "the bigger problem is the enemy from within . . . very bad people . . . sick people, radical left lunatics" like Adam Schiff, who were "more dangerous than China, Russia and all these countries."[97] (A day after reports that North Korea had sent troops to Russia to support its war on Ukraine, Trump added "We had no problem with Kim Jong Un." "Putin and the whole group, Kim Jong Un, they're tough guys . . . and they're smart and they're streetwise, and they're at the top of their game.") Democrats "are so bad and frankly, they're evil . . . they've weaponized our elections. They've done things that nobody thought was even possible." He warned of violence surrounding the election but offered the assurance that "it should be very easily handled by, if necessary, by National Guard, or if really necessary, by the military" (apparently forgetting he was not commander-in-chief). (Vance claimed Trump supported using the military against "far-left people who commit acts of violence." Speaker Johnson said Trump meant "marauding gangs of dangerous, violent people who are destroying public property," words that best described the January 6 rioters Trump extolled. The Posse Comitatus Act prohibited using the military.) Two former generals who had served under Trump responded critically. JCS Chair Mark Milley called him "fascist to the core," "the most dangerous person to [sic] this country." Former White House chief of staff John Kelly agreed Trump was "fascist": "using the military on—to go after—American citizens is . . . a very, very bad thing." Trump had told Kelly: "I need the kind of generals that Hitler had. People who were totally loyal to him that follow orders" and had "commented more than once that, 'you know, Hitler did some good things, too.'" Trump lashed back: Kelly was a "total whack job," "a total degenerate," "a nutjob to start off with," "dumb as a rock." More than a dozen former Trump officials agreed with Kelly that "this is who Donald Trump is." "The American people deserve a leader who won't threaten to turn armed troops against them, won't put his quest for power above their needs, and doesn't idealize the likes of Adolf Hitler." Trump's Defense Secretary Mark Esper said Trump was a fascist. Harris concurred, warning that he "wants unchecked power." "He's going to sit there, unstable, unhinged, plotting his revenge, plotting his retribution, creating an enemies list."

Trump renewed his threats against the media:[98]

> It has been determined that Google has illegally used a system of only revealing and displaying bad stories about Donald J. Trump, some made up for this purpose while, at the same time, only revealing good stories about Comrade Kamala Harris. That is an ILLEGAL ACTIVITY, and hopefully the Justice Department will criminally prosecute them for this blatant interference of [sic] Elections. If not, and subject to the Laws of our Country, I will request their prosecution at maximum levels, when I win the Election, and become President of the United States.

He threatened to sue CBS for allegedly editing the transcript of a Harris interview, calling this "a major Campaign Finance Violation" and "Election Interference and Fraud." (He later filed such a suit, see Chapter 2.2.3.) "60 Minutes should be immediately taken off the air," and "CBS should lose its license." Trump also said: "people should be put in jail the way they talk about our judges and our justices" because such criticism was "totally illegal" and denied "the legality of these people taking a brilliant judge and demeaning her." He meant Cannon, who had dismissed the classified papers prosecution (see Chapter 4.1).

Trump intensified his attack on transgender people.[99] He would simply exclude them from girls' sports: "The president bans it." (He could not.) At a Reno rally he screened a video, which showed Rachel Levine (the Biden administration's most senior transgender official) wishing people a happy Pride Month and then cut to a TikTok video of a drag queen. Vance said that because of intense competition to enter elite universities, "the one way that [upper-middle class white applicants] can participate in the D.E.I. bureaucracy in this country is to be trans." Trump repeatedly called Anderson Cooper "Allison," mocking him for being openly gay. Republicans spent more than $65 million on anti-trans ads between August and November 2024.

The New York Times called Harris "the only patriotic choice for president."[100] Trump was "unworthy," "morally unfit," and would "degrade the values, defy the norms and dismantle the institutions that have made our country strong." "Mr. Trump denies the legitimacy of elections, defies constitutional limits on presidential power and boasts of plans to punish his enemies. And in these attacks on America's democracy, he is also attacking the foundations of American prosperity." The newspaper devoted two full pages to enumerating his many misdeeds. A month later it warned: "Trump is telling us what he would do. Believe him." The next day it spent four pages detailing its front-page headline: "If Donald J. Trump wins, he is ready to radically reshape American government from the moment he regains the White House." A day later it printed two pages about "what a second term would bring": "Donald Trump says he will prosecute his enemies, order mass deportations, use soldiers against citizens, abandon allies, play politics with disasters. Believe him." Nine columnists wrote about why each was voting for Harris. The *Times* gave two more pages to a narrative of Harris's "distinctly American rise" and another two to claims that Trump was authoritarian. Three days before the election its lead editorial "Vote to end the Trump era" repeated all the reasons, with links to 27 editorials, columns, and stories. Two days before the election it published seven columns warning against a Trump administration. The day before the election the *Times* emphasized the importance of Congress. On Election Day it said: "setting aside differences over policy is necessary to preserve the laws and institutions that will allow Americans to work through those differences." It even published a lead op ed critical of Trump the day after the election. But the *Times* may have focused on the wrong issue: only seven percent of Americans said democracy was the most important issue in the election.

By contrast, the billionaire owners of *The Washington Post* (Jeff Bezos) and the *Los Angeles Times* (Patrick Soon-Shiong) vetoed presidential endorsements, the first abstention in 36 years for the *Post* and 20 for the *Times*. The *Post* editor said it would never make another. Marty Baron, a predecessor, condemned the paper's "cowardice, with democracy as its casualty." Bob Woodward and Carl Bernstein (arguably the paper's most famous journalists) said the decision "ignores The Post's own overwhelming reportorial evidence on the threat Donald Trump poses to democracy." Twenty-one columnists called it "a terrible mistake . . . an abandonment of the fundamental editorial convictions of the newspaper." Three editorial board members resigned from that position, two leaving the *Post* for *The Atlantic*. The board sought to circumvent the ban. An editorial anticipating Harris's speech at the Ellipse said: "Mr. Trump's unprecedented efforts to overturn his defeat in the 2020 election, combined with promises to pardon supporters convicted of crimes committed that day, represent Ms. Harris's strongest argument for why voters shouldn't return him to the White House." A second editorial praised her speech and harshly criticized Trump. A third warned: "Donald Trump's retro economic plan could be a disaster." The Washington Post Guild was "deeply concerned." 250,000 readers canceled their subscriptions.

Bezos responded that presidential endorsements "create a perception of bias . . . of non-independence." But he acknowledged his own political dependence: "every day, somewhere, some Amazon executive or Blue Origin executive or someone from the other philanthropies and companies I own or invest in is meeting with government officials." Indeed, Amazon's CEO phoned Trump the day after he was nominated and was asked for a big campaign contribution. And Blue Origin executives had spoken to Trump the day before the *Post* declined to publish the Harris endorsement its board had drafted. The *Los Angeles Times* editorial page editor also resigned, explaining: "in dangerous times, honest people need to stand up." Two editorial board members joined her. Elon Musk retorted that the decision by the publisher (his fellow South African émigré billionaire) "makes sense." Murdoch's *New York Post* endorsed Trump, uncritically parroting his campaign rhetoric.

On October 20, Greek Americans took a full-page *New York Times* ad declaring that Harris and Walz were "committed to our shared values of democracy, freedom and opportunity"; and The Over Holland Foundation took a two-page ad offering David Hammon's "Puzzling Times" painting to a major US museum if Trump lost.[101] Survivors for Kamala took a full-page ad "to remind you that Donald J. Trump was found liable for sexual abuse in a court of law." (Soon thereafter Stacey Williams, a former model, said that in 1993 Trump had groped her in Trump Tower while chatting to Jeffrey Epstein; at least 15 women had made similar accusations.) The Business Roundtable called voting "the bedrock of our democracy"; a group of business associations, including the Main Street Alliance and the Black Economic Alliance, declared that "a vibrant and stable economy relies on a strong democracy." Microsoft founder Bill Gates privately gave the Harris campaign $50 million, although he systematically avoided party politics. That apparently shamed Michael Bloomberg into donating the same amount. Eighty-two US Nobel Prize winners wrote an open letter calling this "the most consequential presidential election . . . perhaps ever, for the future of science and the United States" and warning that Trump would "jeopardize any advancements in our standards of living, slow the progress of science and technology and impede our response to climate change." J. Michael Luttig, a retired Court of Appeals judge, told his "fellow Republicans, it's time to say enough with Trump." "There could be no higher duty of American citizenship than to decisively repudiate a man who betrayed the nation."

While (again) refusing to disclose his own medical records, Trump claimed that Harris's revealed "deeply serious conditions that clearly impact her functioning."[102] (They showed only hives, experienced by a fifth of the population, and seasonal allergies.) He called her "lazy as hell," saying she spent a day "sleeping" and used a rhetorical question to insinuate: "Does she drink? Is she on drugs?" Two hundred fifty-eight "Doctors for Harris" replied: "Trump is falling concerningly short of any standard of fitness for office and displaying alarming characteristics of declining acuity" and "displaying irrationality and irritability." On October 24, 225 mental health professionals took a full-page ad in *The New York Times* declaring Trump "an existential threat to democracy. His symptoms of severe, untreatable personality disorder—malignant narcissism—makes [sic] him deceitful, destructive, deluded and dangerous. He is grossly unfit for leadership." Harris called him "increasingly unstable and unhinged." Walz said Trump had "been forgetting things" and was "confused" and "ranting and rambling." During a three-hour podcast, Trump told Joe Rogan: "there's no reason to think that Mars and all those planets don't have life." "Maybe it's life that we don't know about." He had interviewed "solid" jet pilots who claimed to have seen "very strange things."

Donald Trump won the November 5 election by a popular vote margin of less than 1.5 percent and an Electoral College vote of 312 to 226. In his victory speech he declared MAGA "the greatest political movement of all time" and claimed he had been given an "unprecedented and powerful mandate."[103] (No: barely a quarter of eligible voters supported him, almost the same proportion were opposed, and more than half sat it out.) "Many people have told me that God spared my life for a reason . . . to save our country and restore America to greatness." But the process was in many ways a travesty of democracy. The Electoral College is a profoundly undemocratic institution. A voter in Wyoming wields more than three times the power of one in California because an Electoral College vote represents fewer than 200,000 people in the former but more than 700,000 in the latter; other states display similar, if less extreme, inequalities. Red states and cities sought to suppress voting, especially by mail. Gerrymandering is pervasive, tolerated by the Supreme Court, and deeply entrenched. In the same election, Ohio voters rejected a referendum that would have regulated partisan gerrymandering, which polls showed they favored, misled by ballot language written by the Republican legislature and approved by the Ohio Supreme Court's Republican majority (some of them elected after huge campaign expenditures).[104] Trump had spent eight years aggressively undermining trust in elections: in 2023, just 22 percent of Republicans had high confidence votes would be counted accurately (compared to 71 percent of Democrats).[105] All this may have contributed to the fact that less than 70 percent of Americans eligible to vote are registered and only 65 percent of registrants voted in 2024—less than half of all eligibles. Social media disseminated massive numbers of falsehoods. Elon Musk, who became Trump's fervent supporter, made more than 3,000 posts in October to his 202 million followers on X (the former Twitter platform he bought for $44 billion), falsely alleging voter fraud and warning: "If Trump is not elected, this will be the last election." The world's richest man also spent more than $120 million on the campaign.[106] In his victory speech, Trump praised Musk as "a new star." Russia and Iran exploited AI to distribute fake news and photos.[107] Trump lied without restraint or consequence, indulged in blatant racism and sexism, and debased political discourse to the vulgar level of a schoolyard or barroom brawl. Most disturbingly, he inflamed anti-immigrant sentiment to new, frightening extremes: an October 2024 poll found that 58 percent favored deporting all illegal immigrants.[108]

Trump embodied and legitimated Americans' inchoate anger.[109] He said defiantly: "Of course I'm angry. . . . I'm angry about Venezuelan gangs taking over Aurora, Colorado. And I'm angry about illegal Haitian migrants taking over Springfield, Ohio."

> I am angry about young American girls being raped and murdered by savage criminal aliens that come into our country very easily but very illegally, I'm angry about rampant inflation destroying our middle class. And the American people are damn, damn angry too. We are all angry. Country's being wrecked.

Trump won the Senate 53–47 and had a bare majority of 220–215 in the House, with five seats undecided.[110] The composition of both chambers may change as Trump appoints members to his Cabinet and other positions. The electorate got the candidate it sought, lured by promises he will not or cannot keep, policies that will hurt most of them, and most of all by the deep visceral anger he directed against immigrants.

5.4 Analysis

Readers will have noted the repetition in my sampling of Trump's campaign speeches. That was deliberate. I wanted to illustrate the demagogue's rhetorical strategy: (1) Pick a few issues and hammer them so hard the audience knows what to expect and will internalize the message (even joining call and response). (2) The effect of that message depends on the emotions evoked; it is not a set of programmatic proposals to be evaluated for desirability and practicality.[111] Here I reorganize the tropes thematically to emphasize both features.[112]

Trump's overriding issue was immigration (as it had been in his 2016 and 2020 campaigns and four years in office, see Abel 2024b). "That beats out the economy. . . . It's not even close." "[T]here's nothing more important than the fabric of our country being destroyed." A chronological review of his falsehoods reveals the increasingly inflammatory language, intended to inspire and intensify outrage in his audience. Biden was "giving aid and comfort" to America's enemies. He had "flown in" 325,000 immigrants, opened the border to 15 million, then 20 million, an "invasion" that was "destroying our country." Foreign countries had deliberately emptied prisons and mental hospitals of criminals, murderers, rapists, cannibals, animals, monsters, drug users and traffickers, people infected with disease—"every possible thing that you could have." These included terrorists, 29,000 "fighting age" Chinese men, "warriors," who were "building an army." Trump claimed that "13,099 convicted illegal alien murderers are now on the loose . . . many of them murdering many more than one person." But the number represented the 40-year total of those not in ICE jails, including many who were in other prisons or had served their terms.[113] He showed videos: a girl swinging in a park, captioned "A little girl was raped and murdered by 2 illegals THAT KAMALA SET FREE"; a man with a knife stalking a woman: "No one is safe with Kamala's open border"; dark haired children in an overcrowded classroom; brown men with tattoos and tank tops. Immigrants came from the Congo and other "shithole countries," "rough and dangerous places," "disaster countries" like Yemen, not "nice" (overwhelmingly white) countries like Norway, Denmark, and Switzerland. Immigrants introduced "carnage and chaos and killing" "into our backyards," producing a "border blood bath." They were "poisoning the blood of our country" (a Nazi trope), "conquering our country," "changing the fabric of our country," turning it into a "dumping ground." Black and Hispanic people were "losing their jobs, losing their housing, losing everything they can lose." He warned Black people that because "their cities are being used as illegal alien dumping grounds. . . . the Black community loses its political power forever." "Kamala is killing Black and Hispanic heritage; she is killing their legacy and their rights." "You cannot get into a hospital . . . because the migrants have all the beds."

Trump vowed to eliminate the imaginary dangers by launching the "largest deportation operation in American history," which might require the military and detention camps. (This was neither feasible nor legal.) "The United States is now an occupied country. But on Nov. 5, 2024, that will be liberation day in America." "Nothing can be as serious as this—because this gets down to the very fabric of our society. Your way of life." He claimed that "as president, you have tremendous power—it's called extreme power." (There is no such legal concept.) "You can, just by the fact, you say, 'close the border,' and the border's closed . . . very, very simple." Two weeks before the election he said: "We're a dumping ground. We're like the garbage can for the world." (That may have inspired Hinchliffe's insult.) Republican and conservative spending on television ads about immigration jumped from $37 million in July 2024 to $106 million in August, compared with Democrats' $6.1 and $24.6 million.

Trump complemented this scapegoating of immigrants by stoking wider fears of crime, which he insisted was increasing, dismissing evidence to the contrary: "The FBI fudged the numbers." Emulating Duterte (one of his heroes), Trump proposed to let the police get "extraordinarily rough" and have "one real rough, nasty day . . . I mean real rough—the word will get out, and it will end immediately."[114] He planned to relocate the homeless to tent camps outside cities (as the US did Japanese-Americans in World War II), immunize police from liability, and remove state prosecutors who were insufficiently harsh on crime. If all else failed, he would take over cities and even states. (He lacked authority to do any of this.) He would regulate the mainstream media while preventing the government and private IT companies from blocking or even responding to lies (like his) on social media (disregarding the First Amendment). He would revive Schedule F to pack the civil service with MAGA supporters and "clean house" at the FBI and DoJ: "We're going to fire the people responsible" for his first impeachment. In October 2024, Don Jr. vowed the new administration would "cut out so many people" in the civil service that "people's heads are going to spin." Vance called this "keeping the snakes out of the administration."[115]

Trump condemned efforts to limit climate change, cheering on the fossil fuel industry: "drill, baby, drill," while predicting "the ocean will rise one-eighth of an inch in the next 500 years."[116] He warned that the "green new bullshit" was "going to get rid of all the cows. People will be next" and declared: "we don't have electricity. In California you have brownouts or blackouts every week . . . the place is stone cold broke, no electricity." Solar farms in the desert "looks [sic] like hell" and presented a "terrible" threat to rabbits. Electric car charging stations would cost $9 trillion. (His criticism paralleled and undoubtedly promoted changes in public opinion. From 2020 to 2024, the percentage of Republicans favoring measures to combat global warming fell dramatically: more solar farms (from 84 to 64), more wind farms (75 to 56), making renewable energy a national priority (65 to 38)—while Democrats' views were unchanged.)[117] He called for voter ID and opposed mail ballots but then urged Republicans to make their turnout "too big to rig," anticipatorily delegitimating a Democratic victory, which he claimed could occur only if massive numbers of undocumented people voted. He sought to appropriate the culture wars reignited by DeSantis, attacking transgender people, sex education, critical race theory, even school mandated vaccines (despite the pride he took in the COVID-19 vaccine).[118]

Trump lionized the January 6 defendants whom he had summoned to the Capitol to "be wild," calling them "hostages," "political prisoners," "unbelievable patriots," "policemen . . . firemen . . . accountants . . . lawyers" (identities that federal judges of both parties treated as aggravating factors in sentencing, see Abel 2025: Chapter 4.1), and he "absolutely" promised to pardon them. By contrast (emulating Sen. Joe McCarthy), he attacked the "socialists," "communists," "Marxists" and "fascists" (making no distinctions), "vermin" (a favorite fascist slur), and "very sick people," who constituted "the threat from within." He claimed the criminal cases against him really were directed at his followers. He accused Garland of politicizing criminal justice (even though the Attorney General had chosen Trump-appointed prosecutors to investigate Joe Biden's handing of classified papers and Hunter Biden's alleged crimes). And he used that accusation to promise retribution because "revenge can be justified." He warned Democrats to "be careful what you wish for," declaring he had "every right" to go after them and order indictments of his enemies.[119]

Whereas politicians used to be embarrassed when caught uttering falsehoods, Trump lied shamelessly and without apparent consequences (as he had during his two previous campaigns and four years in office): miles of wall built, crime rates, bird deaths from windmills, range of electric cars, military gear lost in Afghanistan, what he asked Raffensperger to do, videos of ballot stuffing, who was responsible for security on January 6, how many died in the riot, whether Pence had been in danger, prison conditions of January 6 defendants, the attack on Paul Pelosi.[120] He falsely accused Biden of imposing the "largest tax hike" ever and mandating electric vehicles. He made the absurd claim that all the documents he took to Mar-a-Lago were automatically declassified. He vowed to repeat the illegal acts he had committed or threatened during his first term: ending birthright citizenship, executing drug dealers, taking control of cities and states, deploying the military along the border.

He memorably declared about his 2020 loss: "A massive Fraud of this type and magnitude allows for the termination of all rules, regulations, and articles, even those found in the Constitution." As dictator for a day, he promised to close the border illegally and drill for oil. He praised dictators like Putin, Xi, Kim, Erdoğan, and Duterte and dined with Ye and Fuentes, proud fans of Hitler. Trump's followers shared his frightening vision: 74 percent wanted him to be dictator for a day; about half of Republicans preferred a president "willing to break some rules" and "rule without too much interference from courts and Congress." Vance and House Speaker Johnson joined Trump in refusing to acknowledge he had lost in 2020.[121]

Trump encouraged idolatry by his followers. At his first campaign rally, the Mount Carmel pastor introduced him as "anointed of God." Trump told supporters he was being "indicted for you" and even claimed to suffer numerous wounds—inviting comparisons to both the crucifixion of Christ and saintly stigmata. He reposted a video with the repetitive refrain: "And God gave us Trump." His followers wore t-shirts depicting him with Jesus. He sold his personalized Bibles. He falsely accused Democrats of being anti-Christian and especially anti-Catholic (particularly implausible in an observant Catholic like Biden). He promised to end the separation of church and state. After the first assassination attempt, Trump said: "it was God alone who prevented the unthinkable from happening." After the second, he said: "God has now spared my life—it must have been God . . . not once, but twice."[122] At the same time, he presented himself as a false idol: announcing his 2016 candidacy while descending a golden escalator, displaying a life-size golden statue of himself at the CPAC conference, marketing a cologne bottle with his golden head as the stopper, selling golden sneakers, emblazoning his name in gold on the flag—another Midas who turned everything he touched to gold (disregarding the myth's tragic denouement). At a Pennsylvania rally for Vance, evangelist Lance Wallnau said Trump was chosen by God, while Harris engaged in "the seduction of what I would say is witchcraft," embodying an "occult spirit . . . similar to with Obama," working "on her and through her" (an anathema that combined racism and sexism).[123] In one of his final rallies, Trump told Christian leaders they would have access "directly into the Oval Office-and me. We have to save religion in this country."

Trump's language, and his followers' words and actions, grew increasingly incendiary, threatening and vulgar: the euphemism "Let's Go Brandon" became the explicit "Fuck Joe Biden," "Joe and the Ho gotta go," Biden loves minors (invoking the QAnon slander of pedophilia). There were depictions of Biden hog-tied on the back of a truck and of Trump hitting him with a golf ball (just as Trump had fantasized knocking Biden down in 2020, see Abel 2024b: Chapter 1). Trump called Biden "stupid," a "dumb son of a bitch," declaring: "everything Joe Biden touches turns to shit." Harris had been "a shit vice president." Anyone voting for Biden was "crazy"; Jews who did so must "hate their religion" and should "have their heads examined" and "be ashamed of themselves." A rural rally invited the audience (children as well as adults) to beat and kick a Biden mannequin, like a Mexican piñata. Once Harris became the presidential candidate, Trump called her "nuts," "crazy," "mentally disabled," born "mentally impaired," "a bum," and a "play toy for foreign leaders," challenging her to say: "is she Indian or is she Black?" A Halloween parade float featured a woman dressed as Harris in shackles being pulled behind a truck driven by a man dressed as Trump and armed with a rifle, all escorted by men resembling Secret Service agents.[124] Elon Musk became Trump's most vociferous and lavish supporter in the campaign's final weeks. His PAC placed an ad saying: "Kamala Harris is a C Word. You heard that right, A big ole C Word." Musk later said he meant communist, but he clearly wanted listeners to think "cunt." When a supporter called out at a rally that Harris "worked on the corner," i.e., was a prostitute, Trump just chuckled, saying "this place is amazing" and "remember, it's other people saying it." Trump said Whoopi Goldberg (who had endorsed Harris) was "demented," "filthy, dirty, disgusting" (the historic white racist stereotype). Trump used swear words 69 percent more often in his 2024 campaign than he had in 2016: serious profanity at least 140 times in 2024–1,787 times including "damn" and "hell."[125] Trump's repetitions of the lies about Haitians eating pets (and other immigrant myths) and the litany of racist abuse in the warm-up acts of his Madison Square Garden rally infantilized political discourse, distracting attention from his multiple betrayals of liberal democracy and the policy differences between the two parties.

Trump's peroration was eschatological. "Our country is dying," "going to hell," "going down the drain," "a nation in decline." Our economy was "collapsing in a cesspool of ruin." "Our cities are choking to death, our states are dying and frankly our country is dying." We "aren't going to have a country anymore." Medicare, Social Security, health care, public education, and manufacturing jobs would collapse. There would be a "blood bath for the country." "There won't be any more oil." Harris would raise energy costs so high farmers "won't have a farm very long." Harris "wants to get rid of your cows" and wanted "no windows in buildings." There would be "the largest stock market crash we've ever had." "America will be condemned to a fate of decline, desperation and despair." "If I don't win I believe Israel will be eradicated." "The whole world is blowing up" under Biden. "We'll end up in World War III," devastated by "weapons, the likes of which nobody has ever seen before."[126]

The GOP platform echoed this apocalyptic scenario, beginning: "we are a Nation in SERIOUS DECLINE. Our future, our identity, and our very way of life are under threat like never before." Republicans auditioning to be Trump's running mate echoed his hyperbole. Doug Burgum said: "Under Joe Biden, we're actually living under dictatorship today." JD Vance (who won the prize) explicitly warned of "civil war": "the United States is on the verge of going up in smoke . . . electing Trump represents the only hope that Americans have for getting off the path to literal civilization collapse."

Trump called the election the "final battle," the Biblical Armageddon. His loss would be a "day of infamy" (like Pearl Harbor). "I don't think you're going to have another election, or certainly not an election that's meaningful." But if he won, "in four years . . . we'll have it fixed so good you're not going to have to vote." Anticipating his sentencing by Justice Merchan, Trump threatened: "1 MONTH UNTIL ALL HELL BREAKS LOOSE! THEY WANT TO SENTENCE ME TO DEATH." "GUILLOTINE." (This repeated his call to supporters to join the "wild" demonstration on January 6 and his absurd claim the FBI planned to assassinate him during the Mar-a-Lago search.) He concluded: "The only thing standing between you and . . . obliteration is me." In one of his last speeches before the election Trump said:[127]

> For the past nine years we have been fighting against the most sinister and corrupt forces on earth. With your vote in this election, you can show them once and for all that this nation does not belong to them—this nation belongs to you. . . . We will not be invaded, we will not be occupied, we will not be overrun, we will not be conquered.

He won that battle. Let's hope it is not final.

Notes

1 Helmore, "'Smartest one gets to the top': Trump again praises Putin at Georgia rally," *G* (3.27.22); Fisher, "Leaders of democracies increasingly pro-Putin in authoritarian tilt," *WP* (10.17.22); Sides et al. (2022: 56); "How many people have been killed in Rodrigo Duterte's war on drugs?" *The Economist* (11.22.21).
2 Baker, "Trump secretly stayed in touch with Putin after leaving office, book says," *NYT* (10.8.24); Woodward (2024); Gold & Cameron, "Trump says it would be 'smart thing' if he had talked to Putin," *NYT* (10.15.24).
3 https://www.rev.com/blog/transcripts/donald-trump-speaks-at-america-first-agenda-summit-in-washington-dc-transcript; Colvin, "Trump, Pence speeches put stark GOP divide on display," *AP* (7.27.22); Edsall, "Trump has big plan for 2024, and he doesn't care whether you think he'll win," *NYT* (8.3.22).
4 Feuer & Haberman, "Trump rally plays music resembling QAnon song, and crowds react," *NYT* (9.19.22); Goldberg, "A heartless QAnon embrace," *NYT* (9.27.22); Edwards (2021: 295); Sherer, Dawsey, Barrett & Stein, "Trump faces growing legal peril as he seeks to raise profile ahead of 2024," *WP* (9.22.22); Arnsdorf, "How a QAnon splinter group became a feature of Trump rallies," *WP* (9.26.22); Arnsdorf, "Trump speeches use dozens of lies, exaggerations to draw contrast with Biden," *WP* (11.7.22).
5 Valentino-DeVriews & Eder, "For Trump backers in Congress, 'Devil Terms' help rally voters," *NYT* (10.23.22); Goodwin, "Racist GOP appeals heat up in final weeks before midterms," *WP* (10.15.22).
6 Scott, Stein, Kane, Bonos & Davis, "Assailant shouted 'Where is Nancy?' in break-in at speaker's home, attack on Paul Pelosi," *WP* (10.28.22); Tolan, Devine, Bronstein & Medina, "'Absolutely no evidence': police, FBI affidavit debunks salacious conspiracy about Pelosi attack pushed by conservatives," *CNN* (10.31.22); Bailey, "Pelosi's attacker told police he was on a 'suicide mission,' court filings allege," *WP* (11.1.2); "Paul Pelosi's attack is not grounds for jokes and unfounded rumors," *WP* (11.2.22); Karni, "Making jokes and false claims to score political points," *NYT* (11.2.22); Wang & Hennessy-Fiske, "Republicans blame 'both sides' for political violence after Paul Pelosi attack," *WP* (10.31.22); Karni, Khurana & Thompson, "How Republicans fed a misinformation loop about the Pelosi attack," *NYT* (11.5.22).
7 Levin, "David DePape found guilty in hammer attack on Nancy Pelosi's husband," *G* (11.16.23); Arango & Wolfe, "Intruder who bludgeoned Pelosi's husband gets 30-year sentence," *NYT* (5.18.24); Stern & Arango, "Man who invaded Nancy Pelosi's home apologizes for attacking her husband," *NYT* (5.29.24); Vinall, "Man who attacked Paul Pelosi convicted in California on further charges," *WP* (6.22.24); Rodriguez, Knight & Arango, "Man who attacked Nancy Pelosi's husband is convicted in California trial," *NYT* (6.23.24); Karlamangla, "Judge dismisses attempted murder charge over attack at Pelosi home," *NYT* (6.6.24).
8 Weisman, "With ads, imagery and words, Republicans inject race into campaigns," *NYT* (10.27.22); Bender, "Inflammatory radio ads from 2 Trump-aligned groups are airing in battleground states," *NYT* (11.2.22).
9 Blanco, Wolfe & Gardner, "Tracking which 2020 election deniers are winning, losing in the midterms," *WP* (12.18.22); Peters, "Murdoch's news outlets extend their criticism of Trump," *NYT* (11.11.22); Podhoretz, "Here's how Donald Trump sabotaged the Republican midterms," *New York Post* (11.9.22); Bender & Haberman, "Trump, ignoring midterms' verdict on him, announces a 2024 run," *NYT* (11.16.22); Stephens, "Donald Trump is finally finished," *NYT* (11.16.22); Astor, "Republicans seek distance from Trump, and other news from the Sunday shows," *NYT* (11.14.22); Hassan, "Pence escalates criticism of Trump's Jan. 6 actions, calling him 'reckless,'" *WP* (11.14.22); "Fox News Channel tops all of

television in primetime viewership during the week of July 8–14 as network delivers highest-rated weekend ever," *Fox News Media* (7.16.24).

10 Barrett, "Former FBI informant charged with lying about Biden business," *WP* (2.15.24); Thrush, "Ex-F.B.I. informant is charged with lying over Biden's role in Ukraine business," *NYT* (2.16.24); Broadwater, "Indictment of informant undercuts G.O.P.'s impeachment drive," *NYT* (2.17.24); Barrett, "Informant charged with lies about Bidens also claimed Russian contacts, feds say," *WP* (2.21.24); Thrush & Feuer, "Ex-informant accused of lying about Bidens said he had Russian contacts," *NYT* (2.21.24); Barrett, "Informant who allegedly lied about the Bidens is rearrested," *WP* (2.23.24); "The Biden impeachment inquiry has utterly collapsed," *WP* (2.22.24); Broadwater & Thrush, "Ignoring warnings, G.O.P. trumpeted now-discredited allegations against Biden," *NYT* (2.24.24); Grynbaum & Bensinger, "A Biden accuser was discredited. Right-wing media is undeterred," *NYT* (2.23.24); Stanley-Becker & Barrett, "Judge orders Biden informant Alexander Smirnov to remain in jail," *WP* (2.26.24); Forrest, Ballhaus & Viswanatha, "FBI informant in Hunter Biden case left trail of broken promises," *WSJ* (2.29.24); Bump, "Hunter Biden gives House Republicans the rebuttal they didn't want," *WP* (2.29.24); Broadwater, "Six takeaways from Hunter Biden's testimony," *NYT* (3.2.24); Stanley-Becker, "FBI informant accused of smearing Bidens had past credibility issues," *WP* (3.9.24); Rodriguez, Knowles & Kornfield, " 'Not going to be nice': Trump, Harris trade sharp attacks as 2024 race resets," *WP* (7.24.24); Alfaro & Sotomayor, "House GOP leaders ask members to stop making racial attacks against Harris," *WP* (7.24.24); Olorunnipa, "Biden seeks to define his legacy in address explaining his campaign exit," *WP* (7.24.24); Blake, "Another GOP 'informant.' Another indictment and link to Russia," *WP* (2.22.24); Stein, "Informant accused of lying about Biden's family reaches plea deal," *WP* (12.13.24); Cohen, "Ex-FBI informant behind fake Biden-Ukraine bribery allegations sentenced to 6 years in prison," *CNN* (1.8.25).

11 Viser, "James Biden says President Biden had no involvement in his business deals," *WP* (2.22.24); Schnell, "Hunter Biden opens impeachment testimony: 'I did not involve my father in my business,'" *The Hill* (2.28.24); Bump, "Republicans struggle to escape their Biden impeachment quagmire," *WP* (2.23.24).

12 Broadwater, "As Biden impeachment flails, House Republicans explore criminal referrals," *NYT* (3.14.24); Viser, "White House counsel urges House speaker to end GOP impeachment inquiry," *WP* (3.15.24); Bump, "James Comer makes his final anti-Biden push . . . to prospective donors," *WP* (3.26.24); Broadwater, "House Republicans issue criminal referrals of Hunter and James Biden," *NYT* (6.6.24); Broadwater, "House G.O.P. makes impeachment case against Biden without proof of crime," *NYT* (8.19.24).

13 Hesson, "U.S. House Republicans pursue impeachment of Biden border official," *Reuters* (2.1.23); Demirjian, "Key Republican tells donors he will pursue impeachment of Mayorkas," *NYT* (4.19.23).

14 "Impeaching Mayorkas would debase the House, not secure the border," *WP* (2.3.24); Doyle, "Biden denounces Mayorkas impeachment effort as 'baseless' and 'unconstitutional,'" *NBC News* (2.5.24); Alemany, Wang, Sotomayor & Kane, "In a stunning vote, House fails to impeach Mayorkas over border issues," *WP* (2.6.24); Demirjian, "Congressman who broke with G.O.P. on Mayorkas vote will not seek re-election," *NYT* (2.11.24); Alemany, "House Republicans impeach Alejandro Mayorkas by a single vote," *WP* (2.14.24); Karni, "On Capitol Hill, Republicans use bigoted attacks against political foes," *NYT* (2.14.24); Edmondson, "Republican who oversaw Mayorkas impeachment will not seek re-election," *NYT* (2.15.24).

15 Demirjian, "Senate looks to quickly reject Mayorkas impeachment charges in speedy trial," *NYT* (2.15.24); Broadwater, "Republicans' dilemma on Mayorkas impeachment: when to take the loss," *NYT* (3.7.24).
16 Broadwater, "House Republicans demand full impeachment trial for Mayorkas," *NYT* (3.29.24); Alemany & Goodwin, "Mayorkas impeachment moves to Senate, where trial could end fast," *WP* (4.17.24); Broadwater, "House delivers impeachment articles against Mayorkas, calling for a trial," *NYT* (4.17.24).
17 Alemany & Goodwin, "Senate votes to dismiss impeachment charges against Mayorkas," *WP* (4.17.24).
18 Schmidt & Entous, "Hunter Biden to plead guilty on misdemeanor tax charges," *NYT* (6.20.23); Gurman, Linskey & Byron, "Hunter Biden's courtroom reversal extends his legal limbo, political exposure," *WSJ* (7.27.23); Savage, "U.S. Attorney investigating Hunter Biden is made a special counsel," *NYT* (8.11.23); Whitehurst, "Hunter Biden is indicted on 9 tax charges, adding to gun charges in a special counsel investigation," *AP* (12.8.23); Stein, "Judge says Hunter Biden lawyers presented no evidence tax charges are political," *WP* (3.27.24); Thrush, "Judge rejects Hunter Biden claim of selective prosecution in gun case," *NYT* (4.13.24); Habesian, "Hunter Biden's federal gun charges to go to trial after appeal dismissed," *Axios* (5.10.24); Stein, Barrett & Viser, "Hunter Biden found guilty in gun trial. What it means and what's next," *WP* (6.11.24); "Hunter Biden's conviction shows there's not a two-tier system of justice," *WP* (6.12.24); Viser & Pager, "Biden says he will not pardon Hunter or commute his sentence," *WP* (6.14.24); Saric, "Hunter Biden seeks new trial on federal gun charges," *Axios* (6.24.24); Thrush, "Hunter Biden, citing Trump's classified documents ruling, seeks dismissal of cases," *NYT* (7.18.24); Barrett, "Hunter Biden to be sentenced Nov. 13—a week after Election Day," *WP* (8.2.24); Vogel, "Hunter Biden sought State Department help for Ukrainian company," *NYT* (8.14.24); Richer, "Judge knocks down Hunter Biden's bid to use Trump ruling to get his federal tax case dismissed," *AP* (8.19.24); U.S. v. Rahimi (6.21.24); Oglivie, Viser & Stein, "Hunter Biden offers plea in tax case, in an effort to avoid second trial," *WP* (9.5.24); Mordock, "Hunter Biden's gun sentencing pushed to December," *Washington Times* (9.19.24); Sher & Kanno-Youngs, "Biden issues a 'full and unconditional' pardon of his son Hunter Biden," *NYT* (12.2.24); Stein & Viser, "Hunter Biden special counsel defends probe, denounces Biden's DOJ criticism," *WP* (1.13.25); Barrett & Thrush, "Special counsel report on Hunter Biden denounces president's criticism of case," *NYT* (1.14.25).
19 Papenfuss, "41 House Democrats introduce bill to bar 'insurrectionist' Trump from presidency," *HuffPost* (12.16.22); Wilentz, "The case for disqualification," *New York Review of Books* 6 (2.22.24).
20 Baude & Paulsen (2024); Liptak, "Conservative case emerges to disqualify Trump for role on Jan. 6," *NYT* (8.10.23); Luttig & Tribe, "The Constitution prohibits Trump from ever being president again," *The Atlantic* (8.19.23); Smith, "Illinois hearing officer, ex-G.O.P. judge, says Trump engaged in insurrection," *NYT* (1.29.24); Smith, "Trump stays on ballot in Illinois, state board rules," *NYT* (1.30.24); Smith, "Judge orders Trump removed from Illinois primary ballot," *NYT* (2.28.24); Gershan, "Maine becomes second state to bar Trump from 2024 primary ballot," *WSJ* (12.29.23); Marley, "Donald Trump removed from Maine primary ballot by secretary of state," *WP* (12.29.23).
21 Trump v. Anderson, 601 U.S. 100 (2024); Karlik, "Trump cleared for 2024 Colorado ballot, Denver judge rules after eligibility challenge," *Colorado Politics* (11.17.23); Timms, "Trump disqualified from 2024 presidential primary ballot Colorado Supreme Court rules," *WSJ* (12.19.23); Marley & Paybarah, "Trump

disqualified from Colorado's 2024 primary ballot by state supreme court," *WP* (12.20.23); Marimow & Marley, "Supreme Court says it will decide if Trump qualifies for Colorado ballot," *WP* (1.5.24); Broadwater, "Dozens of House Republicans declare Trump's Jan. 6 actions were not insurrection," *NYT* (2.6.24); Marimow, "Supreme Court keeps Trump on ballot, rejects Colorado voter challenge," *WP* (3.4.24); Blake, "4 takeaways from the Supreme Court's ruling on Trump and 14th amendment," *WP* (3.3.24); "The Supreme Court makes the right call keeping Trump on the ballot," *WP* (3.5.24); Kantor & Liptak, "How Roberts shaped Trump's Supreme Court winning streak," *NYT* (9.15.24).

22 Arnsdorf & Scherer, "Trump, who as president fomented an insurrection, says he is running again," *WP* (11.15.22); Qiu, "We fact-checked Trump's speech," *NYT* (11.16.22); Robertson, "New York Post takes aim at Trump, and hits a nerve," *NYT* (11.19.22); "America deserves better than Donald Trump," *NYT* (11.20.22); Giles, "Trump's wall: how much has been built during his term?" *BBC News* (1.12.21); Ainsley, "Migrant border crossings in fiscal year 2022 topped 2.76 million, breaking previous record," *NBC News* (10.22.22); Cillizza, "The New York Post just brutally trolled Donald Trump," *CNN* (11.16.22).

23 Scott & Dawsey, "Trump criticized for dining with far-right activist Nick Fuentes and rapper Ye," *WP* (11.26.22); Wang, Alfaro & Goodwin, "Pence, other Republicans issue rare rebuke of Trump over dinner with Fuentes and Ye," *WP* (11.29.22); Weisman, "Jewish allies call Trump's dinner with antisemites a breaking point," *NYT* (11.29.22); Scott, "McConnell: anyone meeting with antisemites is 'unlikely to ever be elected president,'" *WP* (11.29.22); Arnsdorf, Dawsey & Sotomayor, "Trump's dinner with antisemites provides test of GOP response to extremism," *WP* (11.30.22); Baker, "Trump embraces extremism as he seeks to reclaim office," *NYT* (12.2.22); Wagner, "Trump expresses solidarity with Jan. 6 rioters who stormed the Capitol," *WP* (12.2.22); Bump, "Donald Trump's grip on the GOP, in four charts," *WP* (12.8.22); Abutaleb & Arnsdorf, "Harris vows unity in closing message while Trump lashes out," *WP* (11.3.24).

24 Marcus, "Trump's call for suspending the Constitution is too dangerous to ignore," *WP* (12.4.22); Demirjian & Olorunnipa, "White House rebukes Trump's suggestion to suspend Constitution over 2020 election," *WP* (12.3.22); Astor, "Trump's call for 'termination' of Constitution draws rebukes," *NYT* (12.4.22); Wang, "GOP lawmakers largely silent after Trump suggests 'termination' of Constitution," *WP* (12.5.22).

25 Arnsdorf, "Trump reinvents 'rigged' election myth around Twitter allegations," *WP* (12.16.22); Stanley-Becker, "The latest: Trump continues to incorrectly insist he won the election," *WP* (12.23.22); Rubin, Steakin & Faulders, "Trump hosts event featuring QAnon, 'Pizzagate' conspiracy theories at Mar-a-Lago," *ABC News* (12.7.22); Scott, "White House condemns Greene over claim she would have 'won' Jan. 6 insurrection," *WP* (12.12.22); Weisman, "A New York gala draws incoming G.O.P. lawmakers, and extremists," *NYT* (12.15.22); Sides et al. (2022: 263).

26 Edsall, "This is Trump's 'magic' trick," *NYT* (3.1.23).

27 Bender, Haberman & Goldmacher, "Trump says he would stay in 2024 race if indicted," *NYT* (3.5.23); Goldmacher, Bender & Haberman, "Eyeing DeSantis, Trump readies for a long primary battle," *NYT* (3.5.23); Qiu, "Fact-checking Trump's speech at CPAC," *NYT* (3.5.23); Haberman & Goldmacher, "Trump, vowing 'retribution,' foretells a second term of spite," *NYT* (3.8.23); Arnsdorf & Stein, "Trump touts authoritarian vision for second term: 'I am your justice,'" *WP* (4.21.23); Breanne & Vu, "Fact-checking Trump's claims on whale deaths, 'windmills,' and more," *Washington Examiner* (9.26.23).

28 Terris, "Pence says 'history will hold Donald Trump accountable' for Jan. 6th," *WP* (3.11.23); Arnsdorf & Reston, "Trump claims violence he inspired on Jan. 6 was Pence's fault," *WP* (3.13.23).
29 Homans, "A Trump rally, a right-wing cause and the enduring legacy of Waco," *NYT* (3.24.23); Colvin & Price, "Trump, facing potential indictment, holds defiant Waco rally," *AP* (3.26.23); Arnsdorf & Stein, "Trump touts authoritarian vision for second term: 'I am your justice,'" *WP* (4.21.23); Arnsdorf & Knowles, "Trump extends election-rigging myth to his potential criminal charges," *WP* (3.28.23).
30 Olorunnipa, Pager & Scherer, "Biden announces he is running for reelection in 2024," *WP* (4.25.23); "Biden is right. We're still fighting a battle for the soul of America," *WP* (4.26.23); Olorunnipa, "Biden calls white supremacy greatest terrorism threat as 2024 race heats up," *WP* (5.15.23); Goldmacher & Epstein, "Biden, warning Trump could 'destroy' democracy, moves past G.O.P. primary," *NYT* (9.23.23); Pager & Sanchez, "Biden delivers unusually sharp rebuke of Trump on democracy," *WP* (9.29.23); Shivaram & Khalid, "Biden warns against threats to democracy and says Americans must speak out," *NPR* (9.28.23).
31 Wemple, "Donald Trump steamrolls CNN's Town Hall," *WP* (5.11.23); Arnsdorf & Reston, "Trump's CNN town hall: defending rioters, mocking sexual assault, threatening default," *WP* (5.11.23); Kessler, "Trump fills his CNN town hall with a fire hose of old and new false claims," *WP* (5.11.23); Qiu, "Trump revives election lies and false boasts in CNN Town Hall," *NYT* (5.11.23); "Fact-checking Trump's CNN town hall in New Hampshire," *CNN* (5.11.23); Goldmacher, Swan, Haberman & Lai, "Trump's second-term goal: shattering the norms he didn't already break," *NYT* (5.12.23); Gabriel & Epstein, "Immigration politics returns to the forefront as the 2024 race picks up pace," *NYT* (5.13.23); Hesson, "Trump vows to end birthright citizenship for children of immigrants in U.S. illegally," *Reuters* (5.30.23); Swan, Haberman & Nehamas, " 'This is the final battle': Trump casts his campaign as an existential fight against his critics," *NYT* (6.11.23); Vigdor, "In pitch to evangelists, Trump casts himself as Christian crusader who helped to end Roe v. Wade," *NYT* (6.25.23).
32 LeVine & Parker, "Pence unleashes sharp attacks on Trump as he launches White House bid," *WP* (6.7.23); Glueck, "5 takeaways from Mike Pence's CNN town hall," *NYT* (6.7.23); Swan, "Pence delivers strong rebuke to Trump in campaign announcement," *NYT* (6.8.23); Haberman, "Pence says Trump pressured him 'essentially to overturn election,'" *NYT* (8.4.23); Stein & Hsu, "Prosecutors cite Trump's social media posts as they seek limits on handling of evidence," *WP* (8.6.23).
33 Wells & Knowles, "DeSantis proposed 'deadly force' to combat drug smugglers breaching border," *WP* (6.27.23); Vigdor, "Ron DeSantis tells Russell Brand that Jan. 6 'was not an insurrection,'" *NYT* (7.22.23); Astor, "Where the Republican candidates stand on border security and immigration," *NYT* (7.26.23); Knowles & Rein, "DeSantis calls for 'slitting throats' in government, escalating rhetoric," *WP* (8.4.23); Medina, "G.O.P. contenders feed voter distrust in courts, schools and military," *NYT* (8.8.23); Wells, Rieger, Paybarah, Mourtoupalas & Hays, "Where the 2024 candidates stand on elections, democracy and Jan. 6," *WP* (8.23.23); Dawsey, Scherer & LeVine, "Republicans clash sharply in combative debate with no Trump," *WP* (8.24.23); Knox, "Invade Mexico and six other takeaways from the GOP debate," *WP* (8.24.23); Astor, "DeSantis and Ramaswamy call Proud Boys' sentences 'excessive' and 'wrong,'" *NYT* (9.8.23); Cameron & Savage, "Ramaswamy says he would fire most of the federal work force if elected," *NYT* (9.13.23).
34 Goldmacher & Cameron, "Facing off in Washington, DeSantis tries to shake Trump's hold on the Christian right," *NYT* (9.16.23); Miller, "Why does every Republican candidate sound the same," *NYT* (9.17.23).

35 Blake, "Yes, Trump is getting more reckless on social media," *WP* (7.6.23).
36 Gold, "'I'm being indicted for you' Trump tells South Dakota rally," *NYT* (9.9.23); Gabriel, "Trump escalates anti-immigrant rhetoric with 'poisoning the blood' comment," *NYT* (10.6.23); Layne, "Trump says if elected he will send troops to U.S.-Mexico border," *Reuters* (9.20.23); Nehamas & Sullivan, "With unrealistic immigration proposals, DeSantis and Trump try to outdo each other," *NYT* (10.2.23).
37 Leine & Kornfield, "Trump's immigrant onslaught sparks fresh alarm heading into 2024," *WP* (10.12.23); Arnsdorf, "Trump faults Netanyahu, calls Hezbollah 'very smart' amid Israel war," *WP* (10.12.23); Arnsdorf, "Trump, under fire for Israel comments, proposes fresh crackdown on Muslim immigrants," *WP* (10.17.23); Gold, "Trump vows to reject Gazan refugees after Israel attack," *NYT* (10.17.23); Sullivan, "Trump, citing Hamas attacks, vows sweeping immigration crackdown if elected," *CNN* (10.17.23); Ulloa, "Haley, pledging to 'close' the border, is asked: what about migrants who are already here?" *NYT* (11.4.23); Arnsdorf, Wells & Itkowitz, "Key takeaways from the fourth Republican debate," *WP* (12.7.23); Corasaniti, "Defending Trump, Ramaswamy rattles off right-wing conspiracy theories," *NYT* (12.7.23); Philbrick & Bentahar, "Donald Trump's 2024 campaign, in his own menacing words," *NYT* (12.5.23).
38 Gold, "Trump defends 6 Republicans charged in scheme to overturn his 2020 loss," *NYT* (12.18.23); Gibson, "Trump says immigrants are 'poisoning the blood of our country.' Biden campaign likens comments to Hitler," *NBC News* (12.17.23); Gold, "Trump, attacked for echoing Hitler, says he never read 'Mein Kampf,'" *NYT* (12.20.23); Arnsdorf & Iati, "Trump makes demonizing immigrants a core message with 'blood' refrain," *WP* (12.22.23).
39 Arnsdorf, Dawsey & Barrett, "Trump and allies plot revenge, Justice Dept. control in a second term," *WP* (11.5.23); Vazquez, "Trump says on Univision he could weaponize FBI, DOJ against enemies," *WP* (11.10.23); Basu, "Trump unleashes grievances, warnings in wild 24 hours on Truth Social," *Axios* (11.29.23).
40 Savage, Haberman & Swan, "Sweeping raids, giant camps and mass deportations: inside Trump's 2025 immigration plans," *NYT* (11.11.23); Paquette & Rodriguez, "Trump rhetoric, Republican candidates' ads frighten immigrants in Iowa," *WP* (1.10.24).
41 Gold, "In Veterans Day speech, Trump promises to 'root out' the left," *NYT* (11.12.23); Bender & Gold, "Trump's dire words raise new fears about his authoritarian bent," *NYT* (11.21.23); Evans (2024: 469), citing Welzer (2005: 246–68).
42 Knowles, "Vulgarities, insults, baseless attacks: Trump backers follow his lead," *WP* (11.20.23); Astor & Gold, "Texas governor endorses Trump, lauding his border policies," *NYT* (11.20.23); Bender & Gold, "Trump's dire words raise new fears about his authoritarian bent," *NYT* (11.21.23); Gowen, "Biden effigy beaten, kicked at Kansas county GOP event, drawing outrage," *WP* (3.11.24); Huynh, "Attendees at Kansas G.O.P. punch and kick mannequin wearing a Biden mask," *NYT* (3.12.24); Paybarah, "Donald Trump shares an image of Joe Biden with hands and feet tied," *WP* (3.29.24); Cameron, "Trump shares video featuring image of a hog-tied Biden," *NYT* (3.29.24).
43 Gold, "Trump's defense to charge that he's anti-democracy? Accuse Biden of it," *NYT* (12.3.23); Savage, Swan & Haberman, "Why a second Trump presidency may be more radical than his first," *NYT* (12.4.23); Fichera, "Biden's Christian 'persecution'? We assess Trump's recent claims," *NYT* (12.30.23); Thrush & Goldman, "No bias found in F.B.I. report on Catholic extremists," *NYT* (4.19.24).
44 Gold, "Trump says he wouldn't be a dictator, 'except for day 1,'" *NYT* (12.6.23); LeVine, Arnsdorf & Dawsey, "Trump 'dictator' comment reignites criticism his camp has tried to curb," *WP* (12.7.23); Blake, "The increasingly authoritarian-curious Republican Party," *WP* (4.8.24).

45 Swan, Haberman & Savage, "A new Trump administration will 'come after' the media, says Kash Patel," *NYT* (12.6.23); Fortinsky, "Bannon, Patel say Trump 'dead serious' about revenge on media: 'we're going to come after you,'" *The Hill* (12.5.23); Svitek & Wang, "Trump calls for CBS to lose broadcasting rights over Harris interview," *WP* (10.9.24); Taheri, "Donald Trump's lawsuit threat 'entirely unnecessary'—legal analyst," *Newsweek* (10.20.24); Knowles & Kornfield, "Trump says he doesn't mind someone shooting at journalists at rally," *WP* (11.3.24).

46 Gold, "Trump mixes grievance politics with bread-and-butter G.O.P. issues," *NYT* (12.19.23); Grossman & Hopkins (2024: 99); Palmer, "Trump says supporters more concerned about transgender issues than taxes," *Newsweek* (6.11.23).

47 Friedman, "Trump is selling pieces of his mug shot suit," *NYT* (12.15.23); Friedman, "More than gum with Trump cards," *NYT* (12.17.23); Friedman, "Those $399 gold sneakers are about a lot more than shoes," *NYT* (2.22.24); Buettner, "Martyr Inc.: How Trump monetized a persecution narrative," *NYT* (7.11.24); Vigdor, "Trump hawks American flag pins with his name in gold splashed across them," *NYT* (6.23.24); Gold & Haberman, "Trump's newest venture? A $60 bible," *NYT* (3.26.24); Willingham, "The Christian reaction to Trump's bible endorsement goes deeper than you think," *CNN* (3.28.24); https://godblesstheusabible.com/; LeVine, Vazquez & Arnsdorf, "Trump spreads violent rhetoric by suggesting migrants should fight for sport," *WP* (6.23.24); Goldmacher, Buettner & Haberman, "Trump made $300,000 for endorsing Bible, financial disclosure shows," *NYT* (8.15.24); Meckler, "Okla. Is buying schools 55,000 Bibles. Specs match the $60 Trump Bible," *WP* (10.5.24); Danner, "Getting out the fear vote," *New York Review of Books* (11.7.24); Dias, "Trump promises to bring about a new era of Christian power," *NYT* (11.3.24).

48 Jain & Thomas, "Trump has devoured the Republican establishment," *NYT* (2.4.24); Wells & Svitek, "Nikki Haley says she will vote for Trump in 2024 election," *WP* (5.23.24); Vigdor, "Trump warms up to bring Haley 'on our team in some form,'" *NYT* (5.24.24); Bolton, "McConnell exposes deep anti-Trump sentiment within Senate GOP," *The Hill* (10.18.24).

49 Stein & Barrett, "Special counsel: no charges for Biden in classified documents probe," *WP* (2.8.24); Thomas & Lucey, "Biden's age back in spotlight after special counsel report, verbal flubs," *WSJ* (2.8.24); Viswanathan & Gurman, "Biden knowingly kept and shared classified material, special counsel concludes," *WSJ* (2.8.24); Viser & Pager, "Biden responds angrily to special counsel report questioning his memory," *WP* (2.8.24); Shear, "Special counsel's report puts Biden's age and memory in the spotlight," *NYT* (2.9.24); Goldmacher, Epstein & Glueck, "Eight words and a verbal slip put Biden's age back at the center of 2024," *NYT* (2.9.24); Gold & Thrush, "Trump calls his classified documents case 'selective persecution,'" *NYT* (2.10.24); Ulloa, "Attacking Biden, Nikki Haley says Trump has 'his own mental deficiencies,'" *NYT* (2.10.24); LeVine, "Trump suggests he'd disregard NATO treaty, urge Russian attacks on allies," *WP* (2.11.24); Warrick, Birnbaum & Rauhala, "Trump's NATO-bashing comments rile allies, rekindle Euro fears," *WP* (2.12.24); Wang, "Biden forcefully condemns Trump's NATO comments as 'un-American,'" *WP* (2.13.24); Parker, "Russia looms over yet another Trump presidential campaign," *WP* (2.26.24).

50 Arnsdorf, "Trump equates his domestic political opponents to World War II enemies abroad," *WP* (2.23.24); Gold, "Trump frames election as battle against 'wicked' system bent on attacking Christians," *NYT* (2.23.24).

51 Swan & Bender, "At CPAC, Trump invokes clashing visions of America's future," *NYT* (2.25.24); Goggin, "Calls to 'fight' and echoes of Jan. 6 embraced by CPAC attendees," *NBC News* (2.23.24); Frazier, "Republicans call for immigration

crackdown after college student's death," *Politico* (2.26.24); Fausset & Sassoon, "Arrest of migrant in Georgia killing turns city into latest battleground on immigration," *NYT* (2.28.24); Knowles, "Trump said he spoke to murder victim's family. The victim's sister said it never happened," *WP* (4.2.24); Garrity, "Americans say immigration most important national issue for first time since 2019 in Gallup poll," *Politico* (2.27.24); Paybarah & Cadenhead, "Watch Biden, Trump take on immigration, each other in border speeches," *WP* (3.1.24); Abutaleb & LeVine, "Biden and Trump trade accusations at southern border," *WP* (3.1.24); Gold, "Trump makes baseless claims about immigration and voter fraud," *NYT* (3.3.24); Kessler, "Trump has a bunch of new false claims. Here's a guide," *WP* (3.14.24); Timms, "Trump claims 2024 will be rigged, putting Republican turnout at risk," *WSJ* (3.20.24); Milbank, "This is why Trump supporters will believe absolutely anything," *WP* (4.12.24); Miroff, LeVine & Alfaro, "Trump repeats questionable accusation on migrants during victory speech," *WP* (3.6.24); Alvarez, "Fact Check: Trump claims 325,000 migrants 'were flown in from parts unknown,'" *CNN* (3.7.24); Fichera, "Trump's super Tuesday speech: assessing 10 false and misleading claims," *NYT* (3.7.24); Goldmacher, "With Haley's departure, the rematch between Biden and Trump is now set," *NYT* (3.7.24); Kessler, "Taxpayer dollars being used to fly 'illegal aliens' into U.S.? Nope," *WP* (4.5.24); Gold & Huynh, "Trump again invokes 'blood bath' and dehumanizes migrants in border remarks," *NYT* (4.3.24); Parti & Hackman, "Why immigration is now the No. 1 issue for voters," *WSJ* (4.5.24).

52 Weisman, "In two speeches, Trump and Biden offer starkly different views of the country," *NYT* (3.9.24); Pager and LeVine, "Biden and Trump, in dueling rallies, go on attack in Georgia," *WP* (3.9.24); Parker, LeVine & Godwin, "Trump's freewheeling speeches offer a dark vision of a second term," *WP* (3.10.24); Gold, "Trump vilifies migrants and mocks Biden's stutter in Georgia speech," *NYT* (3.10.24); Rosen, Brito & Rinaldi, "Trump says he'll free Jan. 6 defendants as one of 'first acts' if he's elected again," *CBS News* (3.12.24); Dowd, "Donald Trump's insatiable bloodlust," *NYT* (4.6.24).

53 Huynh & Gold, "Trump says some migrants are 'not people' and predicts a 'blood bath' if he loses," *NYT* (3.16.24); Iati, "Trump says some undocumented immigrants are 'not people,'" *WP* (3.16.24); Blake, "3 takeaways from primaries in Illinois, Ohio and elsewhere," *WP* (3.20.24); Alfaro, "Trump says Jewish Democrats 'hate' their religion and Israel," *WP* (3.18.24); Astor, "Trump defends his warning of a 'blood bath for the country,'" *NYT* (3.18.24); Astor, "Trump doubles down on migrants 'poisoning' the country," *NYT* (3.17.24); Barber & Leary, "Trump kicks off general election with dark rhetoric, vows to help Jan. 6 'hostages,'" *WSJ* (3.23.24); Gold, "Trump again insults Jews who support Biden," *NYT* (4.11.24); Gold, "Trump again, and repeatedly, denounces Jews who support Biden," *NYT* (5.10.24); Rodriguez, "Trump tries softer tone but reprises false migrant claims at Univision town hall," *WP* (10.16.24).

54 Wang, "Trump attacks Biden over Easter coinciding with transgender day of visibility," *WP* (3.31.24).

55 Fichera, "The method behind Trump's mistruths," *NYT* (4.8.24); Kessler, "Trump and allies say Biden pays rent for 'illegals' in Michigan. Not true," *WP* (4.29.24).

56 https://time.com/6972022/donald-trump-transcript-2024-election/; Bump, "Why Donald Trump ended up praising Hollywood's most famous cannibal," *WP* (5.13.24); Qiu, "Assessing Trump's and Biden's claims about immigration and border security," *NYT* (6.20.24); Astor, "Trump shares, then deletes, a video with headlines about a 'unified Reich' if he wins," *NYT* (5.21.24); Somasundaram & Vinall, "Trump again praises authoritarian leaders at Bronx rally," *WP* (5.24.24); LeVine, "Trump holds South Bronx campaign rally to court Black,

Latino voters," *WP* (5.24.24); Arnsdorf, "Trump compares misleading claim about migrant children with 'holocaust' that murdered millions," *WP* (6.7.24); Knowles, "At scorching Vegas rally, Trump bashes migrants—and courts Latinos," *WP* (6.10.24); Gold, "In Las Vegas, Trump appeals to local workers and avoids talk of conviction," *NYT* (6.11.24); Yourish & Smart, "Trump's pattern of sowing election doubt intensifies in 2024," *NYT* (5.24.24); Gold, "At a Trump rally in the Bronx, chants of 'build the wall,'" *NYT* (5.24.24); Qiu, "How a Fox News host's misleading question about migrant children morphed into a Trump talking point," *NYT* (10.11.24).

57 Dawsey & Arnsdorf, "Trump cranks up false, inflammatory messages to rake in campaign cash," *WP* (6.23.24); Knowles, "Trump again suggests political opponents may face prosecution, too," *WP* (6.5.24); Swan, Haberman & Savage, "The G.O.P. push for post-verdict payback: 'fight fire with fire,'" *NYT* (6.5.24); Cameron, "Trump defends vow to prosecute rivals, saying sometimes revenge can be justified," *NYT* (6.6.24); Edmondson, "House G.O.P. pushed deep cuts to federal law enforcement," *NYT* (6.27.24).

58 Gold & Levin, "Trump suggests Biden may use supplements to get 'jacked up' for debate," *NYT* (6.23.24); Knowles, "Trump keeps baselessly claiming that Biden will be on drugs at debate," *WP* (6.26.24); Blake, "How Trump's baseless claim that Birden is 'jacked up' on drugs spread," *WP* (6.26.24); Blake, "5 takeaways from the first Trump-Biden 2024 debate," *WP* (6.28.24); Cameron, "Trump, asked about revenge, says Biden 'could be a convicted felon,'" *NYT* (6.28.24); Kessler, "Fact-checking the first Biden-Trump 2024 presidential debate," *WP* (6.28.24); Ulloa, "On immigration, Biden offers a muted, muddled message," *NYT* (6.29.24); Gold & Cameron, "Donald Trump, repeating his 2020 election lies, tells a Milwaukee newspaper that he will not commit to accepting the 2024 outcome," *NYT* (5.2.24); Homans, "Listen to Trump," *New York Times Magazine* (4.28.24); Svitek, "Top Republicans, led by Trump, refuse to commit to accept 2024 election results," *WP* (5.9.24); Vigdor, "JD Vance says he would accept the election results, with a caveat," *NYT* (5.13.24); Astor, "Rubio, a Trump vice presidential contender, won't commit to accepting 2024 results," *NYT* (5.20.24); Yourish & Smart, "Trump's pattern of sowing election doubt intensifies in 2024," *NYT* (5.24.24).

59 Parker, "Democrats panic over Biden's debate performance, doubt his future," *WP* (6.28.24); Baker, "A fumbling performance, and a panicking party," *NYT* (6.28.24); Cameron, "Julian Castro, a 2020 opponent of Biden, says he should step aside," *NYT* (7.2.24); Blake, "A shift in how Democrats talk about Biden's dropping out," *WP* (7.3.24); Balk, "Raul Grijalva is second House Democrat to call for Biden to drop out," *NYT* (7.4.24); Caldwell & Goodwin, "Sen. Mark Warner seeks to assemble group of Democratic Senators to ask Biden to exit race," *WP* (7.5.24); Scherer, Pager & Dawsey, "Biden thought he had it under control. Then it got worse," *WP* (7.6.24); "Two vulnerable House Democrats say Biden will lose against Trump," *NYT* (7.2.24); Cameron, Astor & Balk, "Two more House Democrats say Biden should drop out," *NYT* (7.6.24); Viser & Harris, "As Biden digs in, another elected Democrat calls on him to exit race," *WP* (7.6.24); Shearer & Pager, "House Democrat joins donor discussion about replacing Biden on ballot," *WP* (7.8.24); "Several senior House Democrats want Biden to step aside, according to three people on a leadership call," *WP* (7.7.24); Viser, Sotomayor & Reston, "Nine House Democrats call for Biden to step aside as he seeks to energize his campaign," *WP* (7.7.24); Edmondson, "Biden's appeal fails to quiet criticism from Democrats in Congress," *NYT* (7.8.24); Alfaro, Sotomayor & Alemany, "Hill Democrats remain divided on Biden, with one senator

fearing Trump 'landslide,'" *WP* (7.9.24); Welch, "Biden should withdraw for the good of the country," *WP* (710.24).

60 Grynbaum, "One by one, Biden's closest media allies defect after the debate," *NYT* (6.29.24); "To serve his country, President Biden should leave the race," *NYT* (6.29.24); Friedman, "Joe Biden is a good man and a good president. He must bow out of the race," *NYT* (6.29.24); Krugman, "The best president of my adult life needs to withdraw," *NYT* (6.29.24); Kristof, "President Biden, I've seen enough," *NYT* (6.27.24); Dowd, "The ghastly vs. the ghostly," *NYT* (6.29.24); Bouie, Goldberg, Healy & Stephens, " 'Is it too late?' Four writers on what Democrats should do about Biden," *NYT* (6.29.24); "How Biden and the Democrats should think through what to do now," *WP* (6.28.24); "What if Biden spoke these words?" *WP* (7.4.24).

61 Pager & Reston, "Biden rallies boisterous crowd as he tries to tamp down debate concerns," *WP* (6.28.24); Balz, "Biden tries to calm nervous Democrats. It won't happen instantly," *WP* (6.29.24); Schleifer, Vogel, Goldmacher & Kelly, "Big donors turn on Biden. Quietly," *NYT* (7.3.24); Schleifer, "Netflix co-founder becomes one of the biggest Democratic donors to call for Biden to step aside," *NYT* (7.4.24); Vogel, "A group of business leaders call on Biden to step aside," *NYT* (7.4.24); Vogel, Schleifer & Hirsch, "Major Democratic donors devise plans to pressure Biden to step aside," *NYT* (7.5.24); Meyer, "Donors pledge $2 million for 'mini-primary' if Biden drops out," *WP* (7.5.24); Nehamas & Shear, "Defiant Biden says people are trying to 'push' him out of the race," *NYT* (7.5.24); Glueck, Nehamas & Leer, "As Biden digs in, more supporters look to push him out," *NYT* (7.6.24); Goldmacher, "Donors tell pro-Biden Super PAC roughly $90 million in pledges is frozen," *NYT* (7.11.24); Epstein & Haberman, "Biden's support from big donors is said to plummet," *NYT* (7.18.24); Goldmacher & Schleifer, "Michael Moritz, Democratic megadonor, urges Biden exit: 'clock has run out,'" *NYT* (7.19.24).

62 "Goldmacher, "Trump widens lead after Biden's debate debacle, Times/Siena poll finds," *WP* (7.4.24); "Biden dismisses concerns, says in ABC interview he won't leave race," *WP* (7.5.24); Igielnik, "Trump leads Biden by 5 percentage points in post-debate Wisconsin poll," *NYT* (7.9.24); https://www.realclearpolling.com/polls/president/general/2024/trump-vs-biden; Balz, Clement & Guskin, "Most Democrats want Biden to drop out, but overall race is static, poll finds," *WP* (7.11.24).

63 "Biden 'absolutely not' dropping out, White House says," *WP* (7.3.24); Shear, "Biden stumbles over his words as he tries to steady re-election campaign," *NYT* (7.5.24); Ball, "Biden's ABC interview showed a president in denial," *WSJ* (7.5.24); Shear, "Biden aides provided questions in advance for his radio interviews," *NYT* (7.6.24); Paybarah, "Radio station parts ways with host who interviewed Biden with questions from his aides," *WP* (7.7.24); Markus, Wang, Svitek & Alfaro, "Biden dares Democrats to 'run against me,' change him at convention," *WP* (7.8.24); Shear, "White House briefing devolves into shouting over questions about Biden's health," *NYT* (7.8.24); Diamond & Abutaleb, "Parkinsons specialist evaluated Biden for physical, White House says," *WP* (7.8.24); Goldmacher, "How Biden is leveraging his defiance to try to stem Democratic defections," *NYT* (7.9.24); Schleifer, Epstein, Hirsch & Goldmacher, "Biden tries to soothe his top fund-raisers on a private call," *NYT* (7.8.24); Shear, "Biden says he is 'firmly committed' to staying in the race," *NYT* (7.9.24); Bensinger, "Wisconsin radio show says it edited Biden interview at campaign's request," *NYT* (7.11.24); Bensinger, "Biden campaign has long fed softball questions to friendly interviewers," *NYT* (7.11.24).

64 "The Democratic Party must speak the plain truth to the president," *NYT* (7.8.24); Carville, "Biden won't win. Democrats need a plan. Here's one," *NYT* (7.9.24); Krugman, "Please, Mr. President, do the right thing," *NYT* (7.9.24); Friedman, "The devil may be enjoying this election season, but I am not," *NYT* (7.10.24); Stephens, "The abyss stares back at Joe Biden," *NYT* (7.9.24); Clooney, "I love Joe Biden. But we need a new nominee," *NYT* (7.10.24); "Donald Trump is unfit to lead," *NYT* (7.11.24).

65 Astor, "Heritage Foundation head refers to 'second American revolution'" *NYT* (7.4.24); Hulse, "Architects of the Trump Supreme Court see culmination of conservative push," *NYT* (7.4.24); Loper Bright Enterprises v. Raimondo (2024); Chevron U.S.A. v. Natural Resources Defense Council, 467 U.S. 837 (1984); Svitek, "Trump tries to distance himself from Project 2025 plan," *WP* (7.5.24); Dawsey & Knowles, "Democrats focus attacks on right-wing Project 2025 pushed by Trump allies," *WP* (7.8.24); Astor, "JD Vance endorses Trump's call for a special prosecutor against Biden," *NYT* (7.7.24); Astor, "Marco Rubio, contender to be Trump's running mate, defends Supreme Court's immunity ruling," *NYT* (7.7.24); Diamond, "House GOP demands Biden's doctor testify on president's health," *WP* (7.7.24); Thompson, "House Oversight subpoenas top Biden aides over his mental fitness," *Axios* (7.10.24); Blitzer, "Inside the Trump plan for 2025," *New Yorker* (7.22.24); Shao & Wu, "The many links between Project 2025 and Trump's world," *NYT* (10.22.24).

66 Ball, "Biden's press conference won't stem tide of defections," *WSJ* (7.11.24); Alfaro, "A handful of Hill Democrats break with Biden after news conference," *WP* (7.11.24); Baker, "NATO on the edge: Biden praises and Trump denigrates a 75-year alliance," *NYT* (7.11.24).

67 Abutaleb & Wootson, "Biden delivers newly fiery speech declaring Trump unfit to be president," *WP* (7.12.24); Nehamas & Epstein, "A fiery Biden, ignoring critics, attacks Trump to chants of 'lock him up,'" *NYT* (7.12.24); Stein, "Why Sanders, AOC threw Biden a lifeline as his candidacy floundered," *NYT* (7.13.24); Sanders, "Joe Biden for President," *NYT* (7.15.24); "Biden remains in denial. He needs to come to grips with reality," *WP* (7.12.24).

68 Cho, Masih & Lee, "What we know about the Trump rally shooting in Pennsylvania," *WP* (7.14.24); Ellison, Zakrzewski & Morse, "Misinformation spreads swiftly in hours after Trump rally shooting," *WP* (7.14.24); Yaffe-Bellany, "After Trump attack, conspiracy theories spring up on Truth Social," *NYT* (7.14.24); "Turn down the heat, let in the light," *WP* (7.14.24); Homans, "Republicans place shooting in Trump's narrative of persecution," *NYT* (7.14.24); Baker, "An assassination attempt that seems likely to tear America further apart," *NYT* (7.14.24); Weisman, "An attempt to kill an ex-president, caught in real time, stuns the country," *NYT* (7.14.24); Lorenz, "'BlueAnon' conspiracy theories flood social media after Trump rally shooting," *WP* (7.14.24); Bender, Trunsky & Vigdor, "After Saturday, Trump's devotees see 'God's protection,'" *NYT* (7.16.24); Bump, "Trump's argument of electoral inevitability adds an ally: God," *WP* (8.28.24); Stein & Barrett, "FBI identifies no motive or foreign links in Trump assassination attempt," *WP* (8.28.24); Thrush, "Would-be assassin's interest in violence went back to 2019," *NYT* (8.28.24).

69 Karni, "Some Republicans embrace conspiracy theories on Trump assassination attempt," *NYT* (8.1.24).

70 LaFraniere, "A fist pump and a flag: Trump sneakers for sale," *NYT* (7.17.24).

71 Sacchetti & Leonnig, "Secret Service Director Cheatle resigns in connection with Trump rally shooting," *WP* (7.23.24); Haberman & Swan, "Trump accuses Biden-Harris administration of failing to 'properly protect me,'" *NYT* (7.23.24);

Foran, Grayer & Talbot, "House votes to set up bipartisan task force to investigate Trump assassination attempt," *CNN* (7.24.24); Broadwater, "Congress leaders agree to form task force on Trump assassination attempt," *NYT* (7.23.24); Arnsdorf, "Trump baselessly blames assassination attempt on Democratic messaging," *WP* (8.20.24); LeVine, "Trump, without evidence, in part faults Biden, Harris for assassination attempt," *WP* (8.28.24); Broadwater & Sullivan, "Task force on Trump assassination attempt sinks into partisanship," *NYT* (9.26.24); Karni, "As lawmaker claims Trump shooting was inside job, G.O.P. indulges him," *NYT* (10.5.24).

72 "The Failures of Donald Trump," *NYT* (7.14.24); "The attack on Donald Trump is antithetical to America," *NYT* (7.15.24).

73 Bump, "Trump chooses a vice president who would do what Mike Pence wouldn't," *WP* (7.15.24); Hudson, "Leaked memo shows JD Vance's anti-woke ideology on foreign affairs," *WP* (7.19.24); Flegenheimer, "How JD Vance thinks about power," *NYT* (8.5.24).

74 https://www.presidency.ucsb.edu/documents/2024-republican-party-platform.

75 Browning & Corasaniti, "Republican speakers wrestle with a 'unity' theme," *WP* (7.16.24); "FBI releases 2024 quarterly crime report and use-of-force update" (6.10.24); Blake, "4 takeaways from night 2 of the Republican National Convention," *WP* (7.16.24); Kessler, "Fact-checking day 2 of the 2024 Republican National Convention," *WP* (7.17.24); Parker, "Vance focuses on hardscrabble roots, military service in RNC address," *WP* (7.17.24); Andrews, "Joe Manchin calls on Biden to 'pass the torch,'" *WSJ* (7.21.24); Cohen, "Republicans could file challenges if Biden replaced, Speaker Johnson says," *Politico* (7.21.24); Qiu, "Trump keeps decrying rampant crime. Here's how his misleading claim has shifted," *NYT* (11.4.24).

76 Olorunnipa, "President Biden tests positive for covid, cancels Las Vegas events," *WP* (7.17.24); Pager & Scherer, "Jeffries, Schumer privately warned Biden he could imperil Democrats," *WP* (7.17.24); Epstein, "Dissent rising, a vote on Biden is pushed back," *NYT* (7.17.24); Pager & Scherer, "Obama tells allies Biden needs to seriously consider his viability," *WP* (7.18.24); Epstein, "Jamie Raskin, a key Democrat, urged Biden to reconsider campaign," *NYT* (7.18.24); Olorunnipa, Pager & Parker, "Biden faces fresh wave of Democratic doubt as party's fissures deepen," *WP* (7.18.24); Sotomayor, Alemany & Kane, "Pelosi has told House Democrats that Biden may soon be persuaded to exit race," *WP* (7.18.24); Browning, "Senator Jon Tester, facing tough re-election fight, urges Biden to drop out," *NYT* (7.18.24); Epstein, "Sharpton says he told Biden that staying in the race could imperil his legacy," *NYT* (7.18.24); "Biden is 'absolutely' staying in race, campaign chair says," *WP* (7.19.24); "12 more Democratic lawmakers call on Biden to step aside," *WP* (7.19.24); Scherer, Pager, Dawsey, Parker, Kane & Sotomayor, "Behind the scenes as Joe Biden lost control of the Democratic Party," *WP* (7.19.24); Olorunnipa, Caldwell & Sotomayor, "Twelve more Democrats, including two senators, call on Biden to drop out," *WP* (7.19.24).

77 Gold & Levien, "A week after shooting, Trump leaves unity behind and returns to insults and election denial," *NYT* (7.21.24).

78 Shear, "Biden drops out of presidential race, endorses Harris," *NYT* (7.21.24); Zemple, "House Speaker Mike Johnson reacts to President Biden dropping out of presidential race," *KTTC* (7.21.24); Godfrey, Blanco, Perry, Dormido & Lau, "The Democrats who have endorsed Kamala Harris to replace Biden as nominee," *WP* (7.21.24); Goodwin & Wang, "Manchin weighs options after Biden exits presidential race," *WP* (7.21.24); "With Biden stepping aside, Democrats must now embrace an open process," *WP* (7.22.24); "Democratic support for

Harris grows as she starts her bid for president," *NYT* (7.22.24); Goldmacher, "Democrats donate more than $50 million online after Biden's exit," *NYT* (7.22.24); Levien, "After Biden drops out, Trump says he was 'never' fit to be president," *NYT* (7.22.24); Kapur, "Some Republicans call on Biden to resign the presidency, too, after he ended his campaign," *NBC News* (7.21.24); "Harris gains enough pledged delegate support for a likely Democratic nomination," *WP* (7.22.24); Olorunnipa, "Democrats coalesce around Harris, as she kicks off bid with attacks on Trump," *WP* (7.22.24); Caldwell & Sotomayor, "Early Brief," *WP* (7.23.24); Shao & Gomez, "Here are the state delegations that have endorsed Kamala Harris," *NYT* (7.23.24); Goldmacher & Epstein, "Harris clinches majority of delegates as she closes in on nomination," *NYT* (7.23.24); Scherer, De Vynck & Reston, "Historic flood of cash pours into Harris campaign and allied groups," *WP* (7.23.24); Pager & Olorunnipa, "Barack and Michelle Obama endorse Kamala Harris for president," *WP* (7.25.24); Astor, "Harris campaign says it raised $200 million since Biden dropped out," *NYT* (7.29.24); Nehamas & Scheiber, "U.A.W. says Harris has endorsement for president," *NYT* (8.2.24).

79 Corasaniti & Rutenberg, "Trump tries to flip the script on democracy after Biden's withdrawal," *NYT* (7.23.24).

80 Rogers, "Vance denigrated Harris for being childless. Her blended family is defending her," *NYT* (7.25.24).

81 Quinn, "Some Republicans are threatening legal challenges to keep Biden on the ballot. But will they work?" *CBS News* (7.23.24); Yourish & Gamio, "Harris's rise elicits scorn from G.O.P.," *NYT* (7.25.24).

82 "Donald Trump address the Faith and Freedom Coalition in Washington—June 22, 2024," *Roll Call* (6.24.24); Knowles, Meckeler & Rozsa, "Trump calls Harris a 'bum,' complains about Biden's withdrawal," *WP* (7.26.24); Vazquez & Ellison, "Trump faces backlash for 'in four years, you don't have to vote again' remark," *WP* (7.27.24); Astor, "Trump again says that Christians 'won't have to vote anymore' if they vote for him," *NYT* (7.30.24); Arnsdorf, "Trump suggests Harris would struggle with world leaders based on her appearance," *WP* (7.31.24); Wootson & Rodriguez, "Trump's attack on Harris's racial identity moves contest into new phase, *WP* (8.1.24); Levien, "Trump says he would pardon Jan. 6 rioters who attacked police," *NYT* (8.1.24); Bensinger, "Trump elevates racial attacks to center stage," *NYT* (8.2.24); Bradner, & Maher, "Vance defends Trump over former president's false claims about Harris' racial identity," *CNN* (8.1.24).

83 Arnsdorf & Dawsey, "Project 2025 to end policy work after Democratic attacks angered Trump," *WP* (7.31.24); Arnsdorf, Dawsey & Knowles, "Trump took a private flight with Project 2025 leader in 2022," *WP* (8.7.24); Homans, "Vance's links to the Project 2025 leader complicate Trump's attempts at distance," *NYT* (8.1.24); Goldberg, "JD Vance just blurbed a book arguing that progressives are subhuman," *NYT* (8.6.24); Lloyd & Relman, "JD Vance said migrants are the reason it's so expensive to rent or buy homes. He's wrong," *Business Insider* (8.7.24); Shao & Wu, "The many links between Project 2025 and Trump's world," *WP* (10.22.24).

84 Scherer, "Kamala Harris officially secures Democratic nomination for president," *WP* (8.2.24); "Harris picks Tim Walz as VP ahead of multistate tour," *WP* (8.6.24); Arnsdorf, Scherer & Cheeseman, "Trump backs out of ABC debate, says he will only debate Harris on Fox," *WP* (8.3.24); Faulders & Santucci, "Trump agrees to ABC News debate with Harris," *ABC News* (8.8.24); Ulloa, "Latino rights group breaks with its history to endorse Harris-Walz ticket," *NYT* (8.9.24); Ulloa, "Latino advocacy groups call Trump's deportation plans a danger to democracy," *NYT* (5.4.24); Cha, "Trump falsely accuses Harris of campaign of fabricated AI crowd photos," *WP* (8.11.24); Blake, "Republicans practically beg Trump to change it up. He's not listening," *WP* (8.15.24); Gold, "At news

conference, Donald Trump says he's 'entitled to personal attacks' against Kamala Harris," *NYT* (8.16.24); LeVine & Arnsdorf, "Trump escalates gendered personal insults against Harris, defying GOP pressure," *WP* (8.17.24); Itkowitz & Allam, "With false 'coup' claims, Trump primes supporters to challenge a Harris win," *WP* (8.19.24); Kessler, "Trump's new absurdity: 'Kamala price hikes cost a typical family $28,000,'" *WP* (8.18.24); Grynbaum & Nerkar, "Trump's media blitz: talk radio, a video game celebrity and Elon Musk," *NYT* (8.19.24); Bender & Gold, "Trump's carefully scripted week kept veering off script," *NYT* (8.24.24); Krugman, "Trump's made-up 'Kamala crime wave,'" *NYT* (8.22.24); Knowles, "24 hours of Trump: QAnon tributes, crude attacks and hawking pieces of his suit," *WP* (8.28.24); Gold, "Trump reposts crude sexual remark about Harris on Truth Social," *NYT* (8.28.24); Bensinger, Yourish & Gold, "Trump keeps turning up the dial on vulgarity. Will he alienate the voters he needs?" *NYT* (8.30.24); Gold & Corasaniti, "Trump urges police officers to watch for voter fraud," *NYT* (9.7.24); Savage, Haberman, Swan and Gold, "Trump steps up threats to imprison those he sees as foes," *NYT* (9.9.24).

85 O'Brien & Weisman, "In leaked phone call, Trump tries to coax Kennedy into his camp," *NYT* (7.16.24); Gold, "Trump lays out vision for bending the federal government to his will," *NYT* (9.8.24); Adeosun, "Donald Trump warns getting migrants out will be a 'bloody story,'" *Newsweek* (9.7.24); Baumgartner, "What R.F.K. Jr.'s alliance with Trump could mean for public health," *NYT* (9.21.24); Diamond, Roubein & Weber, "Trump, RFK vow to 'make America healthy again,' raising hopes and doubts," *WP* (10.18.24); "Trump rally speakers invoke racist tropes in denouncing Harris," *WP* (10.27.24); O'Brien, "R.F.K. Jr. said Trump promised him control of public health agencies. The campaign called that premature," *NYT* (10.30.24); Astor, "Trump's transition team head says R.F.K. Jr. converted him to a vaccine skeptic, *NYT* (10.31.24); Diamond, Weber, Dawsey, Scherer & Roubein, "RFK Jr. set for major food, health role in potential Trump administration," *WP* (11.1.24); Diamond, "Trump will push to get fluoride out of drinking water, RFK Jr. says," *WP* (11.3.24); Burns & Marquez, "Trump doesn't rule out banning vaccines if he becomes president: 'I'll make a decision,'" *NBC News* (11.3.24).

86 Kilander, "Trump's psychologist niece says he's 'dementing' in wake of 'gibberish' answer on childcare question," *Yahoo! News* (9.8.24); Baker, "As debate looms, Trump is now the one facing questions about age and capacity," *NYT* (9.10.24); Krugman, "Donald Trump on the dollar, in his own words," *NYT* (9.10.24).

87 Ulloa & Garvey, "In JD Vance's backyard, conspiracy theories about migrants and voting abound," *NYT* (8.18.24); Ulloa & Cameron, "Vance defends unsubstantiated claims about immigration and crime," *NYT* (8.18.24); Qiu, "Assessing JD Vance's appeals to middle class on the campaign trail," *NYT* (9.2.24); Gold, Rappeport & Levien, "Trump calls for efficiency commission pitched by Elon Musk," *NYT* (9.5.24); Balk, "Trump's verbal deturs heighten down stretch," *NYT* (11.5.24).

88 Alfaro & Masih, "More than 200 former Bush, McCain and Romney staffers endorse Harris," *WP* (8.27.24); Vazquez & Alfaro, "John McCain's son says he will support Harris," *WP* (9.4.24); Vazquez, "Republican Liz Cheney says she will vote for Kamala Harris this election," *WP* (9.5.24); Svitek, Ferguson & Olorunnipa, "Former Vice President Dick Cheney says he will vote for Harris," *WP* (9.6.24); Baker, "111 former G.O.P. officials back Harris, calling Trump 'unfit to serve,'" *NYT* (9.17.24); Rubin, "For only the second time, a top science journal endorses for president," *WP* (9.19.24); Astor, "More than 700 current and former national security officials back Harris," *NYT* (9.22.24); "The dangers of Donald Trump, from those who know him," *NYT* (9.25.24); Masih, "These are the Republicans endorsing Harris over Trump," *WP* (10.12.24); Cramer, "Trump is

'fascist to the core,' Milley says in Woodward book," *WP* (10.12.24); Balk, "Barbara Bush, scion of Republican royalty, knocks on doors for Kamala Harris," *NYT* (10.29.24); Astor, "Arnold Schwarzenegger endorses Harris, rips Trump's effort to overturn the 2020 election," *NYT* (10.30.24); Bradner, "Trump says 'war hawk' Liz Cheney should be fired upon in escalation of violent rhetoric against his opponents," *CNN* (11.1.24); Edwards, "Former members of Congress, both Republicans, are voting for Harris," *WP* (10.31.24).

89 Gold, "Trump questions fairness of next week's debate at a town hall," *NYT* (9.5.24); Gardner, "Trump uses debate to spread election falsehoods, defend Jan. 6 role," *WP* (9.10.24); Cameron, "Trump campaign amplifies false claim about Haitian immigrants in Ohio," *NYT* (9.9.24); Knowles, "Vance leans into unsubstantiated claims of immigrants eating pets," *WP* (9.10.24); Kessler, "Fact-checking 55 suspect claims, mostly Trump's, in debate with Harris," *WP* (9.11.24); Grynbaum, "Trump assails ABC, but he's not thrilled with Fox News, either," *NYT* (9.11.24); Shear, Aleaziz & Ulloa, "How Trump uses vitriol for migrants to sideline other issues," *NYT* (9.12.24); Arnsdorf & Cheeseman, "Trump spreads baseless claims about Harris's debate performance," *WP* (9.13.24); McDaniel, "GOP Congressman posts, then deletes, racist comments about Haitians," *WP* (9.25.24); Gold, "Trump's answer to Harris's border trip: calling her 'mentally disabled,'" *NYT* (9.29.24); Blake, "How resounding was Kamala Harris's debate win? Let's look at the polls," *WP* (9.12.24); Kornfield, "Trump sidesteps question on committing to peaceful transfer of power," *WP* (10.16.24); Haberman, Gold & Igielnik, "Trump tries to rewrite the history of Jan. 6 in campaign's final stretch," *NYT* (10.19.24).

90 Ellison & Merrill, "How false claims of pet-eating immigrants caught on," *WP* (9.12.24); Balk, "Trump's false tale of immigrants' eating pets draws pushback and derision," *NYT* (9.12.24); Paybarah & Wang, "Springfield bomb threat used 'hateful' language toward migrants, Haitians, mayor says," *WP* (9.12.24); Viser, Paybarah, Cheeseman & Arnsdorf, "Biden lashes out at Trump over false claims about Haitian migrants," *WP* (9.13.24); Lupkat, "Springfield upended by bomb threats, school evacuations over false pet-eating claims," *WSJ* (9.13.24); Paquette & Brulliard, "As Trump demonizes immigrants, two targeted communities fear what's next," *WP* (9.14.24); Weisman & Ciaglo, "How the false story of a gang 'takeover' in Colorado reached Trump," *NYT* (9.14.24); Levien, "Donald Trump Jr. piles on with racist comments about Haitians," *NYT* (9.14.24); Astor, "JD Vance doubles down on debunked pet-eating claims roiling Ohio city," *NYT* (9.15.24); Gupta, "The fallout of Trump's false claims," *WP* (9.17.24); Baker, "Trump, outrage and the modern era of political violence," *NYT* (9.17.24); Jordan, "Ohio Governor sending state police to Springfield after rash of bomb scares," *NYT* (9.17.24); Maer, Bauerlein & Hobbs, "How the Trump campaign ran with rumors about pet-eating migrants—after being told they weren't true," *WSJ* (9.18.24); Jordan, "Far from Ohio, Haitian Americans feel the sting of threats in Springfield," *NYT* (9.18.24); Hackman, "In Colorado, a murder and a viral video stoke fears of migrant crime," *WSJ* (9.19.24); Gans, "Trump vows to travel to Springfield following false pet-eating claims," *The Hill* (9.18.24); Astor, "Vance says he will keep calling Haitians legally in Springfield 'illegal,'" *NYT* (9.18.24); DeWine, "I'm the Governor of Ohio. I don't recognize the Springfield that Trump and Vance describe," *NYT* (9.20.24); Mullin, "Threats against Haitians land at the doorstep of *The Haitian Times*," *NYT* (9.20.24); Hsu & Thompson, "On YouTube, major brands' ads appear alongside racist falsehoods about Haitian immigrants," *NYT* (9.20.24); Bender, "On the trail, Trump and Vance sharpen a nativist, anti-immigrant tone," *NYT* (9.22.24); Vigdor & Gold, "Trump criticizes Harris on the border and the economy in Michigan," *NYT* (9.27.24); Bogel-Burroughs, "'Quiet place' in Pennsylvania is thrust into loud immigration debate," *NYT* (9.28.24); Jordan, "An Ohio businessman faces death

threats for praising his Haitian workers," *NYT* (9.30.24); Qiu, "Fact-checking Vance and Walz on the campaign trail," *NYT* (10.1.24); Siegel, "Vance says immigrants caused a housing shortage. Economists disagree," *WP* (10.3.24); Smialek, DePillis & Rodriguez, "Trump blames immigrant surge for housing crisis. Most economists disagree," *NYT* (10.12.24); Astor, "Trump says he would try again to revoke Haitian immigrants' protections," *NYT* (10.3.24); Krugman, "Why Trump is lying about disaster relief," *NYT* (10.4.24); Wang, "Trump again insists Haitians who are in U.S. legally are 'illegal immigrants,'" *WP* (10.8.24); Knowles & Dawsey, "How Trump warped and weaponized a small Pennsylvania town's immigration story," *WP* (10.9.24); Wells, "In pivotal Arizona, Vance and Walz offer an immigration split screen," *WP* (10.10.24); Rodriguez, "Trump turns to immigration as closing appeal as edge on economy fades," *WP* (10.11.24); Gold, "Trump's remarks on migrants illustrate his obsession with genes," *NYT* (10.10.24); Astor, "Trump repeatedly referred to Maine's female governor as a man," *NYT* (10.11.24); Rodriguez, "Trump amplifies falsehoods about immigrants in closing appeal," *WP* (10.11.24); Gold & Weisman, "Trump rally in Aurora, Colorado, is marked by nativist attacks," *NYT* (10.11.24); Jordan, "Many Haitians prospered in Springfield, Ohio. Then came the hate," *NYT* (10.12.24); Knowles & Arnsdorf, "Trump rally speakers lob racist insults, call Puerto Rico 'island of garbage,'" *WP* (10.27.24); Goldberg, "At Madison Square Garden, MAGA prepares to reject another election," *NYT* (10.28.24); "Knowles, Kornfield & Rodriguez, "At Trump's events, vulgar t-shirts disparaging Harris are in demand," *WP* (10.27.24); Goldmacher, Haberman & Gold, "Trump at the Garden: a closing carnival of grievances, misogyny and racism," *NYT* (10.28.24); Astor, "The misogynistic, bigoted and crude rally remarks Trump hasn't addressed," *NYT* (10.28.24); Alfaro & Kornfield, "Vance seeks to distance Trump campaign from comedian's racist Puerto Rico remark," *WP* (10.28.24); Baker & Freedman, "Trump long ago cross the line from propriety to profanity. Then came the Garden," *NYT* (10.28.24); Astor, "The misogynistic, bigoted and crude rally remarks Trump hasn't disavowed," *NYT* (10.30.24); Weisman, "Harris's and Trump's closing messages, as seen through their ads," *NYT* (11.4.24).

91 Swan & Haberman, "Trump and his allies link Biden's 'garbage' comment to 2016 'deplorables' remark," *NYT* (10.29.24); Nehamas, "Harris tries to distance herself and move on from Biden's 'garbage' remark," *NYT* (10.30.24); Nehamas, Swan & Medina, "At dueling rallies, Harris stresses unity as Trump attacks Biden's 'garbage' remark," *NYT* (10.30.24); Haberman, Swan & Gold, "Trump team fears damage from racist rally remarks," *NYT* (10.28.24); Cameron & Ulloa, "Nicky Jam, a reggaeton star, withdraws his endorsement of Trump," *NYT* (10.30.24); Kanno-Youngs, "White House altered official transcript of Biden's remarks on Trump and 'garbage,'" *NYT* (11.2.24); Cameron & Levien, "Vance mocks Harris as 'trash' in one of his final rallies," *NYT* (11.5.24).

92 Abutaleb & Viser, "Harris holds rally at Ellipse, warning of Trump's threats to democracy," *WP* (10.29.24).

93 Haberman, "Trump threatens lawyers, donors and others with prosecution after election," *NYT* (9.7.24); Itkowitz, "Advocacy groups urge Congress to commit to certifying election results," *WP* (9.30.24); Feuer, "Legal watchdog group warns pro-Trump lawyers against subverting democracy in November," *NYT* (9.18.24); Young, "Defiant JD Vance says 'no,' Trump did not lose 2020 election," *Daily Beast* (10.16.24); Morse, Hawkins & TerBush, "More than 230 Republican candidates have cast doubt on the 2024 election," *WP* (10.22.24); Parks, "Driven by Republicans, most Americans are concerned about fraud in the 2024 election," *NPR* (10.23.24); Saad, "Partisan split on election integrity gets even wider," *Gallup* (9.25.24); Marley, "GOP focus on rare noncitizen

voting may continue long after election day," *WP* (10.26.24); LeVine, Marley & Sanchez, "Trump escalates false claims of fraud, setting stage to cry foul if he loses," *WP* (11.4.24); Alfaro, "Trump claims, without evidence, that Democrats will cheat during election," *WP* (11.5.24); Schwartz & Homans, "Despite Trump's claim, no ballots have been found fraudulent in Lancaster county," *NYT* (11.4.24).

94 Dawsey & Parker, "Trump cashes in during final weeks of his presidential campaign," *WP* (9.8.24); Bump, "Trump keeps creating avenues for people to quietly give him money," *WP* (9.27.24); Edsall, "Trump has something he's like to sell you," *NYT* (10.8.24); Yourish & Gamio, "The contests, clubs, merch and big promises of Trump's fundraising emails," *NYT* (10.15.24).

95 Gurman, "Trump safe after another apparent assassination attempt," *WSJ* (9.16.24); Forrest, "Suspected gunman in apparent Trump assassination attempt said he was willing to fight and die in Ukraine," *WSJ* (9.16.24); "Suspect in potential Trump assassination attempt charged with two gun-related crimes," *WP* (9.16.24); Lucey & Leary, "Campaigns carry on despite apparent assassination attempt of Trump," *WSJ* (9.17.24); Gold & Astor, "Trump, using harsh language, urges Democrats to tone down theirs," *NYT* (9.17.24); Kornfield, "Vance blames Democrats for threats against Trump, criticizes media's Springfield coverage," *WP* (9.17.24); Lerer, "Trump tries to close off a chief line of attack: that he's a danger to democracy," *NYT* (9.17.24); Rosza, Stein & Barrett, "Trump gunman said to have left note: 'This was an assassination attempt,'" *WP* (9.23.24); Arnsdorf & Dawsey, "Trump foments distrust of federal law enforcement over assassination attempt probe," *WP* (9.24.24); Stein & Berman, "Alleged Trump golf course gunman charged with assassination attempt," *WP* (9.24.24); LeVine & Birnbaum, "Trump, without evidence, suggests possible Iranian involvement in two assassination attempts," *WP* (9.25.24); Feuer & Haberman, "With criminal cases looming, Trump has a personal stake in the election," *NYT* (10.27.24); Stein, "Judge Cannon won't recuse from trial of accused Trump golf course gunman," *WP* (10.29.24).

96 Arnsdorf & McDaniel, "Trump stages dramatic return to site of Pa. assassination attempt," *WP* (10.5.24).

97 Vazquez, "Trump urges using military to handle 'radical left lunatics' on Election Day," *WP* (10.13.24); Lerer & Gold, "Trump escalates threats to political opponents he deems the 'enemy,'" *NYT* (10.16.24); King, "At town hall on women's issues, Trump renews 'enemy within' talk," *NYT* (10.16.24); Edwards, "Kelly becomes second former general who served under Trump to say GOP nominee is 'fascist,'" *WP* (10.22.24); Wells, "Walz on report Trup said he wanted general like Hitler had: he's descending into 'madness,'" *WP* (10.22.24); Schmidt, "As election nears, Kelly warns Trump would rule like a dictator," *NYT* (10.22.24); Svitek, Edwards & Pager, "Harris says she concurs with assessment that Trump is a fascist," *WP* (10.23.24); Hass & Ho, "6 key moments from the Kamala Harris town hall with CNN," *WP* (10.24.24); Rogers & Nehamas, "Harris calls Trump's reported remarks on Hitler and Nazis 'deeply troubling,'" *NYT* (10.23.24); Samuels, "Former Trump officials offer support for John Kelly after 'fascist' remark," *The Hill* (10.25.24); Kornfield & Knowles, "Trump slams John Kelly, who warned about ex-president's fitness for office," *WP* (10.26.24); Balk, "13 ex-Trump aides back Kelly's 'dictator' warning, saying Trump seeks 'absolute, unchecked power,'" *NYT* (10.25.24); Knowles, Paybarah & Ables, "Trump says domestic foes worse than Kim Jong Un during meandering Joe Rogan interview," *WP* (10.26.24); Kornfield & Knowles, "Trump slams John Kelly, who warned about ex-president's fitness for office," *WP* (10.26.24); Alfaro & Oremus, "Vance defends Trump on using U.S. military against Americans," *WP* (10.27.24).

98 Haberman, Grant & Gold, "Trump threatens to prosecute Google for showing 'bad stories' about him," *NYT* (9.27.24); Blake, "Trump keeps talking about criminalizing dissent," *WP* (9.24.24); Taheri, "Donald Trump's media lawsuit threat 'entirely unnecessary'—legal analyst," *Newsweek* (10.20.24); Grynbaum & McCabe, "Trump ratchets up threats on the media," *NYT* (10.21.24).

99 King, "At town hall on women's issues, Trump renews 'enemy within' talk," *NYT* (10.16.24); Caldwell, Goodwin & McDaniel, "Republicans lean into anti-transgender message in closing weeks," *WP* (10.22.24); Healy & Gessen, "The real reasons the G.O.P. is spending millions on anti-trans ads," *NYT* (10.28.24); Astor, "Trump repeatedly refers to CNN's Anderson Cooper as 'Allison,'" *NYT* (10.29.24); Cameron, Levien & Vigdor, "Vance tells Rogan: teens become trans to get into Ivy League," *NYT* (11.1.24).

100 "The only patriotic choice for president," *NYT* (9.30.24); "American business cannot afford to risk another Trump presidency," *NYT* (10.19.24); "Trump is telling us what he would do. Believe him," *NYT* (10.25.24); "If Donald J. Trump wins, he is ready to radically reshape American government from the moment he regains the White House," *NYT* (10.26.24); Lewis, "On political endorsement," *WP* (10.25.24); "Post columnists respond," *WP* (10.26.24); Chan, "Los Angeles Times editorials editor resigns after owner blocks presidential endorsement," *Columbia Journalism Review* (10.23.24); Mullin & Robertson, "Endorsing presidents ends at Post," *NYT* (10.26.24); "The Post endorses Donald Trump for president—the clear choice for a better future," NY Post (10.25.24); Sullivan, "The Washington Post and LA Times refused to endorse a candidate. Why?" G (10.25.24); "What a second term would bring," *NYT* (10.27.24); Mullin & Robertson, "How the Post put an end to endorsing," *NYT* (10.28.24); Roig-Franzia, Scribner & Wagner, "For The Post, more outrage from readers who say they've canceled," *WP* (10.27.24); "Why I'm voting," *NYT* (10.28.24); Karlamangla & Hubler, "War in Gaza cited for L.A. Times lack of endorsement," *NYT* (10.28.24); Roig-Franzia, "Post editorial board members step down in wake of endorsement decision," *WP* (10.28.24); Bezos, "The hard truth: Americans don't trust the news media," *WP* (10.28.24); "The right place to make the best case against Trump," *WP* (10.28.24); Izadi, "After non-endorsement, 250,000 subscribers cancel The Washington Post," *WP* (10.29.24); 21 Post opinion columnists, "Post columnists respond," *WP* (10.25.24); Stanley-Becker, Davis, Dawsey & Davenport, "For Jeff Bezos and his businesses, Washington has become more important," *WP* (10.29.24); "Kamala Harris's closing argument: 'It doesn't have to be this way,'" *WP* (10.30.24); Draper, "One final barrier in a distinctly American rise," *NYT* (10.31.24); Baker, "Trump clings to his image as strongman," *NYT* (11.1.24); Shear & Kim, "They now call him 'fascist' and 'unfit,'" *NYT* (11.1.24); Stetler, "Two Washington Post writers who resigned over Bezos' non-endorsement join The Atlantic," CNN (11.1.24); "Vote to end the Trump era," *NYT* (11.2.24); Lerer & Goldmacher, "Harris aims to disqualify Trump but reach out to his voters," *NYT* (10.31.24); Klein, "This election pits guardians against counterrevolutionaries," *NYT* (11.3.24); Dowd, "All the demons are here," *NYT* (11.3.24); Goldberg, "What I fear if Trump returns," *NYT* (11.3.24); Bouie, "Autocracy is on the ballot," *NYT* (11.3.24); Collins, "Let's not blow it again," *NYT* (11.3.24); Kristo, "How to end a democracy," *NYT* (11.3.24); Levitsky & Ziblatt, "There are ways to keep autocrats out of power. Why don't we use them?" *NYT* (11.3.24); "Donald Trump's retro economic plan could be a disaster," *WP* (11.3.24); "Every vote in every state matters," *NYT* (11.4.24); "There are no sidelines in this election," *NYT* (11.5.24); Meacham, "What historians like me got wrong about Trump," *NYT* (11.6.24); Hubler, "Harris asked voters to protect democracy. Here's why it didn't land," *NYT* (11.7.24).

101 https://www.businessroundtable.org/business-roundtable-voting-is-the-bedrock-of-our-democracy; https://www.businessanddemocracy.org/business-organizations-and-associations-support-safe-and-secure-elections; Miller, "82 American Nobel Prize winners endorse Kamala Harris," *NYT* (10.24.24); Baker, "A scandal-plagued career nears a decisive moment," *NYT* (10.23.24); Schleifer, "Bill Gates privately says he has backed Harris with a $50 million donation," *NYT* (10.24.24); Goldstein & Steel, "Former model accuses Donald Trump of groping her in 1993," *NYT* (10.26.24); Schleifer, "Bloomberg, after months of pressure, donates $50 million to help Harris," *NYT* (10.28.24); Luttig, "My fellow Republicans, it's time to say enough with Trump," *NYT* (10.29.24). "'A man who does not accept NO': Trump sexual assault accusers warn us on election results," The Reidout, MSNBC (10.23.24).

102 Neal, "Trump tears into Harris over her medical records—while refusing to release his own," *Daily Beast* (10.15.24); "Harris, Trump converge on battleground state of Pennsylvania," *WP* (10.14.24); Rodriguez & Arnsdorf, "Trump attacks Harris with racist stereotype, eye's 'extreme power' as president," *WP* (10.22.24); Gold, "Trump's attacks again turn nasty in campaign's waning days," *NYT* (10.22.24); Knowles, Paybarah & Ables, "Trump says domestic foes are worse than Kim Jong Un during meandering Joe Rogan interview," *WP* (10.26.24); Gold, Balk & Levien, "6 takeaways from Donald Trump's 3-hour podcast with Joe Rogan," *NYT* (10.25.24); Dowd, "How bad do you want it, ladies? *NYT* (10.27.24).

103 "Donald Trump's victory speech in full," *Newsweek* (11.6.24).

104 Wines, "Ohio voters reject ban on partisan gerrymanders," *NYT* (11.6.24); Henry & Tebben, "How partisan supreme court elections are shaping Ohio," *Ohio Capital Journal* (10.7.24).

105 Cassidy & Sanders, "GOP confidence in 2024 vote count low after years of false election claims, AP-NORC poll shows," *AP* (7.10.23); Baker, "U.S. vote was peaceful, but Trump's fraud claims hurt trust, international observers say," *WP* (11.6.24).

106 Conger, "What Elon Musk told his 203 million followers on Election Day," *NYT* (11.5.24); Conger, Krolik, Nerkar & Freedman, "How Elon Musk's own account dominates X," *NYT* (11.5.24); "Trump's victory speech was the worst thing you could imagine," *TNR* (11.6.24).

107 Barnes & Myers, "Russia escalates effort to subvert election and 'instill fear in voters,' U.S. says, *NYT* (11.5.24); Thompson, "5 reasons early voting is overwhelmed with falsehoods," *NYT* (11.5.24).

108 "New Marquette Law School poll national survey finds presidential race extremely tight, enthusiasm for voting high among both Democrats and Republicans but low among independents," *Marquette University News Center* (10.16.24); Jordan, "Voters were fed up over immigration. They voted for Trump," *NYT* (11.7.24).

109 Daner, "Getting out the fear vote," *New York Review of Books* (11.7.24).

110 Baker, "Trump swings wrecking ball at status quo," *NYT* (11.18.24).

111 McCreesh, "Some believe in Trump without believing him," *NYT* (10.15.24).

112 See also "The next Trump presidency will be worse," *The Atlantic* 4–63 (01–02.24).

113 Alfaro & Miroff, 'How Trump is distorting immigration and crime data in new attacks on Harris," *WP* (9.30.24); Kessler, "Trump's outrageously false claim of 13,000 migrant murderers 'on the loose,'" *WP* (10.3.24); Swan, Haberman & Igielnik, "Trump thinks the border got him elected in 2016. He's convinced it will do so again," *NYT* (10.19.24); Qiu, "Trump's claims that blame migrants: false or misleading," *NYT* (10.19.24); McCreesh, "A weary Trump whips up anger in Atlanta," *NYT* (10.16.24); Swan, Haberman & Igielnik, "Trump thinks the border got him elected in 2016. He's convinced it will do so again," *NYT* (10.19.24); Rodriguez & Arnsdorf, "Trump attacks Harris with racist stereotype,

eyes 'extreme power' as president," *WP* (10.22.24); Samuels, "Trump: America 'like a garbage can for the world,'" *The Hill* (10.24.24); Haberman & Swan, "Ahead of Harris's speech in Washington, Trump tries to focus on immigration," *NYT* (10.29.24); Medina, "Trump widens the us-v.-them target audience," *NYT* (10.31.24).

114 Svitek, "Trump floats 'one really violent day' for police to combat retail crime," *WP* (9.30.24).

115 Ball, How Donald Trump Jr. became the crown prince of MAGA world," *WSJ* (10.6.24); Cameron, "On the trail, Vance is dogged by questions about Trump's loss in 2020," *NYT* (10.12.24).

116 Quoted in Finchelstein (2024: 49); "Yes, this is what Donald Trump really sounds like. No, you cannot ignore it," *WP* (10.13.24); Krugman, "Trump has become unmoored in time," *NYT* (10.15.24); Rodriguez & Arnsdorf, "Trump attacks Harris with racist stereotypes, eyes 'extreme power' as president," *WP* (10.22.24).

117 "The Ezra Klein Show," *NYT* (6.28.24)

118 Confessore, "'America is under attack': inside the anti-D.E.I. crusade," *NYT* (1.20.24); Goldmacher, "Trump and Republicans bet big on anti-trans ads across country," *NYT* (10.8.24).

119 Schmidt, "What Omarosa, John Kerry and Michael Cohen have in common," *NYT* (10.8.24).

120 Qiu & Leventhal, "Trump's closing argument lies, distortions and inaccuracies," *NYT* (11.3.24); Baker, "Trump's wild claims, conspiracies and falsehoods redefine presidential bounds," *NYT* (11.3.24); Adair (2024).

121 Alfaro, "Johnson won't say Biden won in 2020, raising worries on 2024's process," *WP* (10.6.24); Bender, "Vance, given 5 chances to say Trump lost in 2020 takes none," *NYT* (10.11.24); Cameron, "On the trail, Vance is dogged by questions about Trump's loss in 2020," *NYT* (10.12.24); Bohannon, "Vance avoids saying Trump lost 2020 race—again—in latest interview," *Forbes* (10.13.24).

122 McCreesh, "Trump says he's in danger. So why did he seek out the embrace of 100,000 fans?" *NYT* (10.2.24).

123 Dias & Cameron, "Vance appears at event of evangelical leader who spoke of Harris's 'witchcraft,'" *NYT* (9.29.24); Kornfeld & Allam, "Vance appears at event hosted by hard-right Christian nationalist," *WP* (9.29.24); French, "JD Vance and the prophets of Trumpism," *NYT* (10.6.24); Dias, "Trump promises to bring about a new era of Christian power," *NYT* (11.3.24).

124 Levenson, "Halloween parade float in Pennsylvania denounced as racist," *NYT* (11.2.24).

125 Baker, Freedman, Clarke & Byrd, "Trump's speeches, increasingly angry and rambling, reignite the question of age," *NYT* (10.6.24); Philbrick & Wu, "The 9 elements of a Trump rally," *NYT* (10.8.24); "Yes, this is what Donald Trump really sounds like. No, you cannot ignore it," *WP* (10.13.24); LeVine & Arnsdorf, "Trump fixates on Arnold Palmer as 'all man' in showers during profane rally," *WP* (10.19.24); Baker & Freedman, "Trump long ago crossed the line from propriety to profanity, Then came the Garden," *NYT* (10.28.24); Fahrenthold, "Musk's PAC hints at vulgar taunt against Harris in ad," *NYT* (10.29.24); Gold, "Trump laughs as supporter yells that Harris 'worked on the corner,'" *NYT* (11.3.24).

126 Gold, "Trump's consistent message online and onstage: be afraid," *NYT* (10.2.24); Bidgood, "Trump's ugly closing argument," *NYT* (10.7.24); Main, "Trump picks a fight with Detroit," *CNN* (10.10.24); Milbank, "Donald Trumps hysterical closing argument: save the cows!" *WP* (10.18.24).

127 Ball, "America faces a third referendum on Trump' dark message," *WSJ* (11.4.24).

6

EVALUATING RESISTANCE TO AUTOCRACY

My three previous books described and analyzed how Trump sought to distort the electoral process to gain and retain power (Abel 2024b), abused that power in his assault on immigrants and interference in the prosecution of cronies and others (Abel 2024a), and attacked experts seeking to cope with the COVID-19 pandemic (Abel 2024c). The companion volume (Abel 2025) and the present volume examine the aftermath of his administration: political responses and criminal prosecutions following the January 6 insurrection, efforts to suppress or distort voting, civil and criminal actions seeking to hold Trump accountable, and his campaign to return to office in 2024. This conclusion draws on all five books to evaluate the efficacy of resistance to autocracy over those eight years and suggest lessons for addressing ongoing threats to liberal democracy.

Trump once candidly admitted: "I value loyalty more than anything else—more than brains, more than drive, more than energy."[1] As president he demanded unquestioning fealty from subordinates, replacing expert civil servants with inexperienced but compliant acolytes, firing anyone he felt had betrayed him (e.g., Attorney General Sessions for recusing himself from the Russia investigation, FBI Director Comey for reversing himself about Hillary Clinton), and railing against any institution that displayed insufficient obeisance: the CIA, FBI, DoJ, courts, Inspectors General, FDA, CDCP, NIH, Census Bureau, National Archives, and USPS. He took pleasure in wielding untrammeled power to fire subordinates, reliving his experience in business and on his television show *The Apprentice*. Furious at those who defied him, Trump sought to delegitimate refractory institutions, even threatening to defund them. Cabinet turnover was one of the highest among recent presidents. He expected similar fealty from Republicans in Congress and state governments, backing primary opponents against those he maligned

DOI: 10.4324/9781032629186-6

as RINOs. He even sought to use the military for political ends (as in his farcical parade across Lafayette Square). Most of the time Trump got his way. Almost all of the very few Republican politicians who initially balked at his efforts to overturn the 2020 election, including his involvement in the January 6 insurrection, returned to the fold—many quickly, others as soon as his nomination for the 2024 race became inevitable. The US, unlike some other countries, has no tradition of principled resignation. The rare senior officials who quit did so at the end of Trump's term, knowing they had no future under Biden. So did the few who belatedly defied him, such as Barr, Rosen, Donoghue, and some of the White House counsel. There was greater opposition from those who had retired or had no further political ambitions and from state and local officials less exposed to Trump's power (although the latter could suffer threats and violence from his followers).

Other forms of resistance had their own limitations. There was extraordinary mass action in the earliest days of the Trump administration. Between 3.3 and 4.6 million people joined the Women's March on the day after the inauguration—the largest mobilization in US history; demonstrators in Washington were three times the size of Trump's audience.[2] His first Muslim ban, issued a week later, sparked protests in major cities and airports and an outpouring of lawyers volunteering to represent stranded travelers.[3] There were large demonstrations in support of women's right to choose and against police killings of Black men. But there was nothing like the sustained and effective mass action that characterized the civil rights, anti-war, and environmental movements of the 1960s and 1970s. Undocumented immigrants were too exposed; and documented Latinos were divided (as Jews had been between earlier immigrants from Germany and later waves from Eastern Europe).[4] Indeed, it was the violent and armed extreme right that dominated the streets: battling "antifa" in Portland, celebrating white racism in Charlottesville, and trashing the Capitol to overturn the 2020 election. Although some religious leaders opposed Trump, he enjoyed virtually unanimous support from evangelical Christians. Some large corporations objected when Trump crossed red lines: immigration (high-tech industries needed skilled workers), voting (egregious restrictions in Georgia and Texas), and the January 6 insurrection. But business leaders quickly retreated to "neutrality" and passivity, anxious to preserve access to and influence with Republican officials and politicians. Most established media reported critically about and editorialized against Trump (briefly joined by Fox News and the Murdoch papers). Trump's defamation actions against them failed, partly because of *New York Times v. Sullivan*, which both he and Justice Thomas wanted overruled. But Trump supporters relied on right-wing outlets, especially social media, which was virtually unregulated and increasingly unfiltered after Musk transformed Twitter into X.

The COVID-19 pandemic, the greatest domestic challenge of Trump's presidency, displayed a different dynamic. He relied on "instinct" and "gut," sidelining experts and subordinating science to politics (especially his 2020 re-election campaign), just as he has proposed to tame the independent Federal Reserve in a second term, boasting: "I have a better instinct than in many cases people that would be on the Federal Reserve or the chairman."[5] He was openly contemptuous, and jealous, of Jerome Powell (as he had been of Anthony Fauci): "You show up to the office once a month and you say, 'Let's see—flip a coin,' and everybody talks about you like you're a god." Trump controlled what subordinates said about the pandemic. He used temporary and acting appointments to avoid the confirmation process. He elevated outsiders who echoed his views (Alexander, Atlas), just as he embraced anti-vaxxer Robert F. Kennedy Jr. during his 2024 campaign.[6] Other scientists exploited their elite credentials to join the chorus, quacks chimed in, and professional associations seemed unable to discipline those spreading misinformation. The right-wing media eagerly provided an echo-chamber. Trump's base resented government measures to control the pandemic (masks, social distancing, closures, vaccine mandates) and was skeptical about science (more than half of Republicans believe in creationism). Military and emergency workers—trained to follow orders and reliant on science to do their jobs—were paradoxically prominent among those defying pandemic precautions. Despite all this, resistance to Trump was effective. Experts in government (who enjoyed civil service protections), as well as those outside, insisted on following the science and telling the truth. Politics is no more able to negate scientific facts than to control the market. Big Pharma, which needed to preserve its credibility to sell products like the COVID vaccine, welcomed the objectivity of FDA protocols for testing drugs. Nevertheless, lay resentment of experts, which Trump manipulated and fueled, continues to play a prominent role in the right-wing playbook: stripping teachers of control over their curricula, librarians over the books they lend, and medical professionals over how they minister to women's reproductive needs and to gender dysphoria.[7]

After the Senate failed to convict in Trump's first impeachment, he boasted he was "the chief law enforcement officer of the country."[8] He sought to politicize the law throughout his term: pushing the DoJ to investigate Hillary Clinton, trying to derail the Mueller inquiry into Russian interference in the 2016 election, and urging the investigation of Peter Strzok and Lisa Page (who were exonerated, settling their cases against the government for $1.2 million and $800,000 respectively).[9] Some of Trump's most egregious perversion of justice occurred in the prosecutions of his cronies: Stone, Flynn, Manafort, and Gates. Attorney General Barr, an obsequious yes-man who worried aloud that he could do the President's bidding only if Trump made his orders less obvious, replaced and overruled AUSAs and US Attorneys (some of whom quit or changed positions) in order to drop charges or seek lesser penalties. Trump aggressively wielded his power to grant clemency or pardons (unlimited, like that to fire subordinates), not just for cronies and the undeserving (at least seven subsequently charged with other crimes) but also convicted war criminals.[10] He even considered pardoning himself after January 6.

In his landmark opinion in *Marbury v. Madison*, Chief Justice Marshall famously declared that in a liberal democracy defined by the separation of powers, "it is emphatically the province and duty of the judicial department to say what the law is."[11] Courts faithfully performed that essential role in cases concerning immigration, criminal justice, the pandemic, and the 2020 election (analyzed in Abel 2024a, 2024b, 2024c). Since Trump's departure from office, they have done so with respect to the January 6th Select Committee (Abel 2025: Chapter 2), prosecution of January 6 defendants (Abel 2025: Chapter 4), civil actions against Trump (Chapter 2), state and federal prosecutions of Trump (Chapters 3 and 4), and election cases (Abel 2025: Chapter 5). When Trump disparaged CD CA Judge Tiger as an "Obama judge," Chief Justice Roberts angrily countered with the essential myth of liberal legalism: "We do not have Obama judges or Trump judges, Bush judges or Clinton judges."[12] Trump, an instinctive legal realist, retorted: "you do indeed have 'Obama judges,' and they have a much different point of view than the people who are charged with the safety of our country." He boasted to Republicans before the 2018 mid-term election: "we're going to have great judges, conservative, all picked by Federalist Society."[13] In the last days of his presidency he exulted in appointing Barrett to the Supreme Court (the first nominee in a century and a half confirmed without a single vote from the opposition party), after Senate Majority Leader McConnell had blocked Garland's appointment in the last year of the Obama administration.[14] Former SJC chairman Graham urged Circuit Court judges to retire so Trump could appoint successors "to make sure the judiciary is right of center."[15] (Four years later, at the end of the Biden administration, McConnell warned that Democratic appointees who withdrew their retirements in anticipation of Trump's second term could face "significant ethics complaints.")[16] In the last year of Trump's presidency, McConnell acknowledged receiving a list of potential judicial nominees from the Federalist Society and bragged that if Democrats won, "there will not be a single circuit court vacancy," and "they won't be able to do much about this for a long time to come."[17] Trump threatened to break up the Ninth Circuit, denouncing it as "a dumping ground for certain lawyers looking for easy wins and delays." He was right: lawyers opposed to his actions preferred the Ninth and Second Circuits, just as those seeking to advance his policies preferred the Fifth Circuit and particular District Judges within it.[18] Republican judges have defied a recent US Judicial Conference rule limiting such judge shopping.[19]

In two earlier books about the fate of the rule of law during the US "war on terror," I analyzed the relationship between federal judges' political preferences (as indicated by the party of the appointing president) and decisions to favor or oppose the administration. I found very significant correlations ($p < 0.001$) in cases involving habeas corpus petitions by Guantánamo detainees (Abel 2018b: Table 5.1) and civil damages actions by "war on terror" victims (Abel 2018b: Table 6.2) and an even stronger correlation ($p < 0.00002$) for electronic surveillance cases (Abel 2018a: Table 5.1). By contrast, there were no statistically significant differences in damages claims by terrorism victims (Abel 2018b: Table 6.3), criminal prosecutions for terrorism (Abel 2018b: Table 2.1), and judicial review of military commissions (Abel 2018b: Table 4.1).

I reached similar conclusions about judges' votes in cases involving the Trump administration. (There is independent confirmation for my index of partisanship in data showing that Biden and Trump judicial appointees made campaign contributions almost exclusively to Democratic and Republican candidates, respectively.)[20] There were even stronger statistical differences in cases about immigration, the pandemic, the January 6th Select Committee, most of the election cases, and federal prosecutions of Trump (see Table 6.1).

There were no significant differences in sentences for January 6 defendants, state and federal civil actions involving Trump and state prosecutions of Trump, and federal election cases between the 2020 election and the 2021 Inauguration (because almost all were decided against Trump; see Table 6.2).

I see a pattern across all seven books and more than two decades, one that transcends the profound differences between judicial responses to the "war on terror"— an external terrorist threat—and to the Trump presidency—an internal autocratic threat. In both contexts, some confrontations were patently political: al Qaeda's 9/11 attacks and the subsequent US wars in Afghanistan and Iraq; Trump's three election campaigns and his first term

TABLE 6.1 Statistically Significant Differences in Judicial Decisions

Subject of cases	*Difference*	*Source*
Federal Election Cases before 11.3.20	$p = 0.000018$	Abel 2024b: Table 2.2
State Election Cases 11.3.20–1.20.21	$p = 0.00001$	Abel 2024b: Table 3.2
Immigration Cases (Circuit Courts)	$p < 0.000001$	Abel 2024a: Table 4.3
Immigration Cases (District Courts)	$p = 0.016$	Abel 2024a: Table 4.4
Pandemic Cases	$p < 0.00001$	Abel 2024c: Table 4.2
January 6th Select Committee	$p = 0.007$	This volume: Table 2.2
Post-January 6 Federal Election Cases	$p < 0.00001$	Abel 2025: Table 5.2
Judges' Decisions Related to Federal Prosecutions of Trump	$p = 0.00065$	This volume: Table 4.2

TABLE 6.2 No Statistically Significant Difference in Judicial Decisions

Subject of cases	*Difference*	*Source*
Federal Election Cases 11.3.20–1.20.21	$p = 0.609$	Abel 2024b: Table 3.1
Sentences for January 6 defendants	Percent of Prosecution request: Democratic Appointees 70; Republican Appointees 66	Abel 2025: Table 4.2
Federal and State Judges Deciding Civil Actions Against Trump and Supporters	All against	This Volume: Table 2.1
Judges' Decisions Related to State Prosecutions of Trump	All for (except Thomas, Alito, Vyskocil)	This Volume: Table 3.1

and program for his second. It is unsurprising that judges' votes in these cases tended to reflect their political preferences, especially since, for decades, Republicans have been packing the courts with Federalist Society members and using an anti-abortion litmus test in Supreme Court appointments. (During his first impeachment, Trump gloated that "Republicans are up to 191 Federal Judges & Two Great New Supreme Court Justices."[21] Trump and Biden appointees displayed very different demographic profiles: women were 24 and 63 percent, respectively, whites 84 and 39 percent.)[22] Political preferences were reflected in cases involving three facets of the "war on terror"—Guantánamo detainees, collateral civilian damage, and electronic surveillance—and those involving many facets of the Trump administration—immigration, the pandemic, the three elections (2020, 2022, 2024), the January 6th Select Committee, and federal prosecutions of Trump for withholding classified papers and seeking to overturn the 2020 election. More surprising are the cases that seem relatively unaffected by the deep political divide. In the "war on terror," these included damage claims by terrorism victims (who elicited sympathy from judges of both parties) and reviews of military commissions (whose glaring due process violations outraged judges from both parties). It is noteworthy that during both the "war on terror" and the Trump administration, routine, well-institutionalized legal proceedings seemed relatively insulated from political distortion: criminal prosecutions of both accused terrorists and January 6 rioters, and state and federal civil actions and state prosecutions involving Trump and his supporters. Such seemingly apolitical adjudication was more characteristic of trial judges, who (with or without juries) resolve factual controversies under relatively settled law, than it was of appellate judges and especially Supreme Court Justices, who often make new law (most egregiously by creating a novel doctrine of presidential immunity). In immigration cases, there was far less difference among judges by party in District Courts ($p = 0.016$) than in Courts of Appeal and the Supreme Court ($p < 0.00001$ in both) (see Abel 2024a: Tables 4.2, 4.3, 4.4). Yet there were pronounced political differences between some District Judges: Cannon (Trump) and Chutkan (Obama) in Jack Smith's two prosecutions of Trump (Chapter 4), McFadden (Trump) with his DDC colleagues in the January 6 prosecutions (Abel 2025: Chapter 4), and DDC Judge Jackson (Obama) and ED VA Judge Ellis (Reagan) in the prosecutions of Paul Manafort (Abel 2024a: Chapter 3.c).

The companion volume, "How Autocrats Subvert Elections" (Abel 2025), chronicled other efforts to hold Trump accountable. Chapter 2 documented the limitations of political processes. Mueller felt constrained by OLC opinions not to recommend prosecution of Trump for collaborating with Russian interference in the 2016 election (while declining to exonerate him in opaque language). After January 6, Republicans blocked efforts to invoke the Twenty-fifth Amendment (for incapacity) and the Fourteenth Amendment (to disqualify Trump as an insurrectionist). Republican Senators prevented his conviction in the second impeachment (as they had in the first). Republicans obstructed a bipartisan commission on the January 6 insurrection (modeled on the successful 9/11 commission) and forced House Speaker Pelosi to create a Select Committee by proposing House members implicated in the January 6 riot (who would be investigating themselves). Although Republicans tried to frustrate the Select Committee's work by refusing to testify and may have sought to influence witnesses (like Cassidy Hutchinson), it nevertheless produced riveting televised hearings and a comprehensive, damning report. But this lacked an enforcement mechanism; there is little evidence it changed public opinion; and Republican revisionism widened the partisan divide in reactions to January 6 (see Abel 2025: Chapter 3).

Criminal prosecutions of the January 6 rioters were far more effective (see Abel 2025: Chapter 4). All but two of the more than 1,500 accused were convicted. DDC judges appointed by presidents of both parties harshly chastised many defendants and displayed no partisan differences in sentencing (measured as a proportion of prosecution recommendations). But these proceedings had their own limitations. DC Circuit judges and Supreme Court Justices again displayed greater partisanship (including the latter's narrow interpretation of the Sarbanes-Oxley Act). Most convictions and sentences received little publicity (except in hometown media). Some defendants openly proclaimed defiance and lack of remorse (sometimes immediately after sentencing), while others undoubtedly harbored similar feelings, possibly aggravated by imprisonment. Many sentences were far less severe than those prosecutors sought. Although leaders of Oath Keepers and Proud Boys received substantial sentences, some judges expressed regret that the ultimate wrongdoers were beyond their reach (notably Trump). Republicans sought to sanctify the January 6 defendants, misrepresenting them as hostages and political prisoners; some accused raised large defense funds (far exceeding their legal needs). Trump played their recordings at campaign rallies and vowed to pardon them. And he did just that on Inauguration Day.

The two civil and four criminal cases against Trump share some common characteristics (see Chapters 2–4). Four deal with behavior that, though reprehensible, was marginal to his autocratic actions and ambitions: sexual abuse and defamation of E. Jean Carroll, fraud by the Trump Organization, failure to disclose the hush money payment to Stormy Daniels, even the retention of classified papers. Only the Georgia and DDC prosecutions directly address Trump's efforts to overturn the 2020 election. He aggressively sought to politicize all six, very different, cases, attacking prosecutors, the NY Attorney General, opposing counsel, judges (and their staff and families), parties, and witnesses, using racist, sexist, even anti-Semitic language. Judges had to anonymize jurors for their own safety, and judges, prosecutors, and witnesses received threats, requiring security.

Trump appeared less interested in winning these cases than in delegitimating the courts (just as he sought to discredit every institution that could limit his power: the media, Congress, the DoJ and FBI, civil servants, science, the Democratic Party, even RINOs in the GOP, and especially elections). He repeatedly indulged in behavior that could only serve to anger judges (without securing favorable procedural rulings) and alienate jurors who would decide his fate (e.g., by stalking out of the courtroom). Provoked by Trump's outrageous behavior, judges imposed gag orders acknowledging that the paltry penalties could not deter a billionaire but (wisely) refraining from imprisoning him for violations (which might confer the martyrdom he claimed). Trump welcomed, even invited, those orders, citing them as further proof of victimization, absurdly comparing himself to Nelson Mandela (jailed 27 years), Alexei Navalny (killed in prison), even Jesus Christ (crucified). Trump absurdly maintained that the judicially authorized FBI search of Mar-a-Lago while he was safely ensconced in his club in Bedminster, New Jersey, a thousand miles away, was an attempt to execute him and his family. He shamelessly exploited every case to raise money (while spending campaign contributions on litigation). He repeatedly called on supporters to protest, issuing veiled threats of violence. He filed pointless motions to dismiss, change venue, and recuse judges and equally frivolous collateral attacks and appeals (all of which he lost). Republicans in Congress backed him up by attacking prosecutors, over whom they had no authority. Despite all this, one federal jury, two New York juries and Justice Engoron decided against Trump. Defamation cases against Trump supporters were equally successful, leading to large judgments; and his numerous retaliatory actions failed.

Five of the trial judges (Democrats Kaplan, Engoron, Merchan, and Chutkan and Republican McAfee) presided judiciously and impartially. This contrasted sharply with Cannon, a recent Trump nominee whom the ABA (unusually) declined to rate well qualified. She appointed a special master to conduct a privilege review of the papers Trump had wrongly withheld (superfluous, since the FBI had already done this). But though she was slapped down by the Eleventh Circuit (including two Republican appointees), she succeeded in delaying the case for three months. In the aftermath of that debacle, she rebuffed the advice of her District's chief judge and another colleague to decline the case because of her inexperience and demonstrable bias. She ensured further delay by scheduling unnecessary hearings. And she heeded Justice Thomas's gratuitous suggestion (in the immunity case) to find the Special Counsel unauthorized and unfunded—jettisoning decades of established precedent. Trump vilified Jack Smith and made the ridiculous claim that, as president, he could declassify papers merely by thinking about them. The evidence against him is arguably stronger than in the other cases, further bolstered by the attempted cover-up, a key player in which has agreed to testify for prosecutors. If Cannon's decision is overturned (as many expect), the Supreme Court's 6–3 immunity decision still leaves Trump vulnerable to prosecution for unofficial conduct, which should include all his actions involving classified papers, since they occurred after he left office. But it is Cannon who will make that determination and, if he is convicted, pass sentence.

The ultimate effect of these six cases is not yet known. Trump may have to pay over a half billion dollars to Carroll and New York State, more than his cash reserves. After Merchan gives Trump a noncustodial sentence, he will appeal all three cases, further delaying execution of judgment. The Supreme Court took six months to decide the immunity case, thereby ensuring it could not go to trial before the election. Fani Willis's imprudence made it impossible for her to begin the Georgia case before the election, and an appellate court has removed her as prosecutor. If the Florida, Georgia and DDC cases resume after Trump's second term, Judges Cannon, McAfee, and Chutkan will have to distinguish between his official and unofficial acts—decisions ultimately subject to review by the Supreme Court, which constructed that novel and opaque categorization.

Given the demonstrated limitations of both political and legal institutions in resisting autocracy, the 2024 election became the ultimate defense. Republicans approached it by seeking to disenfranchise potential Democratic voters, pack state election offices with Republicans and election deniers, create obstacles to voting, and gerrymander Congressional districts, empowered by permissive Supreme Court decisions (see Abel 2025: Chapter 5). They sought (unsuccessfully) to impeach Joe Biden and Alejandro Mayorkas and to use Hunter Biden's prosecutions against his father.

Democrats invoked the Fourteenth Amendment to find Trump ineligible to hold office as an insurrectionist, but the Supreme Court restricted that power to Congress, rendering it just as ineffective as impeachment, given Republican intransigence.

Trump's 2024 campaign reprised his two previous contests and first term. He vilified immigrants in even more extreme language, calling them criminals, mentally and physically diseased, even cannibals. He borrowed Hitler's phraseology, accusing immigrants of "poisoning the blood of our country" and reviling Democrats as "vermin" who should be exterminated. The "bigger problem is the enemy from within . . . very bad people . . . sick people, radical left lunatics," who were "more dangerous than China, Russia." They "should be very easily handled . . . by National Guard, or . . . the military." He lied about the number of immigrants, planned to revive family separation, vowed to end birthright citizenship (which would be illegal), and promised the largest deportation ever. He claimed that the Biden administration persecuted Christians and declared that Jews who voted for Biden "should have their head examined." He exaggerated crime rates (calling for more death sentences and deportation without trial of gang members) as well as the threat of the homeless (whom he planned to relocate to detention camps outside cities). He swore to take over cities and states that defied him (which would be illegal). He embraced the culture wars, demonizing transgender people. He proposed to overturn all measures to limit climate change. He denigrated teachers and determined to rewrite history. He planned to revive Schedule F and replace tens of thousands of expert civil servants with GOP faithful. He vowed to pardon all the January 6 defendants. He declared the media the "true enemy of the people" (Stalin's favorite characterization) and strategized about how to control it while preventing government from responding to lies on social media. He claimed to have been chosen by God, who saved him from assassination, even comparing himself to Christ. He boasted he would be a dictator on Day 1, asserted that election fraud "allows for the termination of all rules, regulations, and articles, even those found in the Constitution," and told supporters: "I am your retribution," promising ominously that if he were victorious, "in four years, you don't have to vote again." He indulged in vulgar obscenities against Biden and racist and sexist language against Harris, whom he accused of a "coup." He concluded with eschatological warnings that the US now resembled Cuba, Venezuela, and the Soviet Union. Atheists, globalists, Marxists, and fascists were responsible for the "obliteration" of America," the "sacking of our towns," the "conquest of our country." If Trump lost, there would be a "blood bath," the economy would collapse "in a cesspool of ruin," causing the "largest stock market crash we've ever had," and we would enter World War III, attacked by weapons "nobody has ever seen before."

Taking Trump's threats of vengeance seriously, Biden issued preemptive pardons to former JCS Chair Milley, former NIAID director Fauci, the Select Committee members, and his three siblings and their spouses.[23] Trump, in turn, pardoned or commuted all the Jan. 6 rioters who had been sentenced and ordered the DoJ to terminate further prosecutions. After eight years of Trump's vile attacks on immigrants, nearly a third of Americans supported deporting all undocumented people who had arrived in the last four years, and more than half wanted to deport all undocumented. On his first day in office, Trump signed executive actions ending birthright citizenship, declaring a national emergency at the border, resuming construction of the wall, directing the military to seal the border, designating drug cartels as terrorist organizations, terminating Temporary Protected Status, reviving his Remain in Mexico policy, ending asylum, pausing refugee resettlement for four months, and removing four top Immigration Court officials. He ousted the top Coast Guard Admiral and revived Schedule F, preparing the way for mass firing of civil servants. He also ended federal recognition of expressed gender identity. NGOs immediately challenged these actions, as well as the new Department of Government Efficiency.

When I was in high school 70 years ago, I wondered what prevented a democratic polity like ours from choosing to turn autocratic. We now know the answer: very little. Just as Hitler took power with only 44 percent of the votes in the last democratic German election, Trump has done so 90 years later with support from just a quarter of eligible voters. We can only hope the result will not be as catastrophic.

Notes

1 Trump & Zanker (2007: 160).
2 Waddell, "The exhausting work of tallying America's largest protest," *The Atlantic* (1.23.17); Wallace & Parlapiano, "Crowd scientists say Women's March in Washington had 3 times as many people as Trump's Inauguration," *NYT* (1.22.17).
3 Doubek, "Thousands protest at airports nationwide against Trump's immigration order," *NPR* (1.29.17).
4 "From Haven to Home: 350 Years of Jewish Life in America," *Library of Congress*; https://www.loc.gov/exhibits/haventohome/haven-century.html.
5 "Trump signals interest in influencing Federal Reserve decisions if he regains White House," *Reuters* (8.8.24); Rappeport & Swanson, "Trump brags about his math skills and economic plans. Experts say both are shaky," *NYT* (10.16.24).
6 Svitek, "Trump adds Kennedy, Gabbar to transition team," *WP* (8.27.24); Stolberg, "Resistance to public health, no longer fringe, gains foothold in G.O.P. politics," *NYT* (10.9.24).
7 Selig, "Meteorologists face harassment and death threats amid hurricane disinformation," *NYT* (10.14.24).
8 Olorunnipa & Reinhard, "Post-impeachment, Trump declares himself the 'chief law enforcement officer' of America," *WP* (2.19.20).
9 "Two former FBI officials settle lawsuits with Justice Department over leaked text messages," *NBC News* (7.26.24).

10 Vogel & Lipton, "Another Trump clemency recipient faces domestic violence-related charges," *NT* (10.15.24).
11 5 U.S. 1 Cranch 137 (1803).
12 Williams, "In rare rebuke, Chief Justice Roberts slams Trump for comment about 'Obama judge,'" *NBC News* (11.21.18).
13 Zengerle, "How the Trump administration is remaking the courts," *NYT* (8.22.18).
14 Biskupic (2023: Chapter 4, 248–57).
15 Carney, "Graham urges senior judges to step aside so Trump, GOP can replace them," *The Hill* (5.28.20).
16 Raji, "Trump's election sparks fight over judicial retirements, new judgeships," *WP* (12.24.24).
17 Johnson, "Wave of young judges pushed by McConnell will be 'ruling for decades to come,'" *NPR* (7.2.20).
18 Hellman, "Liberalism Triumphant? Ideology and the En Banc Process in the Ninth Circuit Court of Appeals," 31 *William & Mary Bill of Rights Journal* 1 (2023); Schwartz, "How a federal court in New Orleans is driving the conservative agenda," *NYT* (8.26.24).
19 Raymond, "Conservative US judges criticize new rule curbing 'judge shopping,'" *Reuters* (3.13.24); Schwartz, "An effort to end 'judge-shopping' turns into a political firestorm," *NYT* (4.6.24); Raymond, "Alabama judge to weigh sanctioning LGBTQ lawyers for 'judge shopping,'" *Reuters* (6.24.24); but see Cowley, "Judge balks at shopping for a court," *NYT* (11.4.24). The Supreme Court will hear F.D.A. v. R. Reynolds Vapor in the 2024–25 Term.
20 Schwartz & Kim, "Voters will set the course for a federal court system at a crossroads," *NYT* (11.1.24).
21 Biskupic (2023: 172).
22 Schwartz & Kim, "This election is also a choice between two visions of the federal courts," *NYT* (10.24.24).
23 Peters & Igielnik, "Support for Trump's policies exceeds support for Trump," *NYT* (1.19.25); Parti, "Trump signs executive orders focused on the border and energy," *WSJ* (1.20.25); Alemany & Stein, "Trump administration quickly removes top immigration court officials, *WP* (1.20.25); Hsu, Jackman, Knowles & Morse, "Trump pardons almost all involved in Jan. 6 riot, commutes remaining 14 sentences," *WP* (1.20.25); Lamothe, "Trump administration ousts top Coast Guard admiral," *WP* (1.21.25); Rosen, "Federal worker union sues Trump over ending job protections," *Bloomberg* (1.21.25); Gerstein & Cheney, "First law suits against Trump administration target DOGE," *Politico* (1.20.25).

REFERENCES

Abel, Richard L. 2008. *Lawyers in the Dock: Learning from Attorney Disciplinary Proceedings*. New York: Oxford University Press.

Abel, Richard L. 2011. *Lawyers on Trial: Understanding Ethical Misconduct*. New York: Oxford University Press.

Abel, Richard L. 2018a. *Law's Wars: The Fate of the Rule of Law in the U.S. "War on Terror."* New York: Cambridge University Press.

Abel, Richard L. 2018b. *Law's Trials: The Performance of Legal Institutions in the U.S. "War on Terror"*. New York: Cambridge University Press.

Abel, Richard L. 2024a. *How Autocrats Abuse Power: Resistance to Trump and Trumpism*. Abingdon: Routledge.

Abel, Richard L. 2024b. *How Autocrats Seek Power: Resistance to Trump and Trumpism*. Abingdon: Routledge.

Abel, Richard L. 2024c. *How Autocrats Attack Expertise: Resistance to Trump and Trumpism*. Abingdon: Routledge.

Abel, Richard L. 2025. *How Autocrats Subvert Elections: Resistance to Trump and Trumpism*. Abingdon: Routledge.

Adair, Bill. 2024. *Beyond the Big Lie: The Epidemic of Political Lying, Why Republicans Do It More and How it Could Burn Down Our Democracy*. New York: Atria.

Baude, William and Paulsen, Michael Stokes. 2024. "The Sweep and Force of Section Three," 172 *University of Pennsylvania Law Review* 605.

Biskupic, Joan. 2023. *Nine Black Robes: Inside the Supreme Court's Drive to the Right and Its Historic Consequences*. New York: William Morrow.

Bowden, Mark and Teague, Matthew. 2022. *The Steal: The Attempt to Overturn the 2020 Election and the People Who Stopped It*. New York: Atlantic Monthly Press.

Edwards, George C., III. 2021. *Changing Their Minds? Donald Trump and Presidential Leadership*. Chicago: University of Chicago Press.

Evans, Richard J. 2024. *Hitler's People: The Faces of the Third Reich*. New York: Penguin.

Finchelstein, Federico. 2024. *The Wannabe Fascists: A Guide to Understanding the Greatest Threat to Democracy*. Berkeley: University of California Press.

Grossman, Matt and Hopkins, David A. 2024. *Polarized Degrees: How the Diploma Divide and the Culture War Transformed American Politics*. New York: Cambridge University Press.
Isikoff, Michael and Klaidman, Daniel. 2024. *Find Me the Votes: A Hard-Charging Georgia Prosecutor, a Rogue President, and the Plot to Steal an American Election*. New York: Twelve.
Raffensperger, Brad. 2021. *Integrity Counts*. Forefront Books.
Rohde, David. 2024. *Where Tyranny Begins: The Justice Department, the FBI and the War on Democracy*. New York: W. W. Norton.
Sides, John, Tausanovitch, Chris and Vavreck, Lynn. 2022. *The Bitter End: The 2020 Presidential Campaign and the Challenge to American Democracy*. Princeton, NJ: Princeton University Press.
Trump, Donald and Zanker, Bill. 2007. *Think BIG and Kick Ass in Business and Life*. New York: Harper Collins.
Welzer, Harald. 2005. *Täter: Wie aus ganz normalen Menschen Massenmörder warden*. Frankfurt am Main: Fischer S. Verlag GmbH.
Woodward, Bob. 2024. *War*. New York: Simon & Schuster.
Zirin, James D. 2019. *Plaintiff in Chief: A Portrait of Donald Trump in 3,500 Lawsuits*. New York: All Points Books.

INDEX

Kolibri 360 GmbH
Ferdinand-Jühlke-Straße 7
99095 Erfurt, Deutschland
produktsicherheit@kolibri360.de